WITCH(
IN ENG
1558–1618

Eliza Wheaton

20/12/04

WITCHCRAFT IN ENGLAND, 1558–1618

EDITED BY

Barbara Rosen

The University of Massachusetts Press

AMHERST

Copyright © 1969 by Barbara Rosen
Preface to the Paperback Edition © 1991 by Barbara Rosen
First paperback edition published in 1991 by
The University of Massachusetts Press
All rights reserved
LC 91-18279
ISBN 0-87023-753-5

Library of Congress Cataloging-in-Publication Data

Witchcraft.
    Witchcraft in England, 1558–1618 / edited by Barbara
Rosen.
        p. cm.
    Reprint with new introd. Originally published:
Witchcraft. New York : Taplinger, 1972, c1969. (The
Stratford-upon-Avon library ; 6)
    Includes bibliographical references.
    ISBN 0-87023-753-5 (pbk. : alk. paper)
        1. Witchcraft—England. I. Rosen, Barbara, 1929–   .
II. Title.
BF1581.W79   1991
133.4'3'094209031—dc20   91–18279
                                              CIP

British Library Cataloguing in Publication data are available.

Contents

Preface to the Paperback Edition

Much has happened in the world of scholarship since this book first appeared. I believe, however, that the introduction, originally designed as a general scholarly survey of English witchcraft, retains its usefulness and that the need for an edition of selected basic documents is greater than it was in 1969.

Serious study of English witchcraft began with research in surviving legal materials. The pioneering efforts of Kittredge and the monumental labors of Ewen, who looked at over a quarter of a million decaying parchments in the Public Records Office, have been supplemented by the concentrated work of Macfarlane in the records of Essex and by Thomas's wide-ranging assault on the files of ecclesiastical and regional courts. Younger researchers are mining the same lodes.

But unfortunately, a less kindly climate for academic publishing has meant that recent scholars have not been able to reproduce their basic data with the fullness and completeness possible for Ewen; abbreviated summaries and selective quotations leave us grateful but full of queries. Compression increases the possibility of misinterpretation in the use of historical records.

Scholars know that their documents must be studied with the awareness that complementary material has been lost or, perhaps, was never recorded; many a Dogberry existed and enforced the law, although he never succeeded in being written down an ass. It is the achievement of the last generation to have made us conscious of the quality of the silence that shapes surviving texts. At the same time, new developments in critical theory have pointed up the value of the written records that remain.

An astonishing variety of critical approaches has been turned upon the documents of witchcraft in the last twenty years. In America, demographic and sociological studies by Boyer and Nissenbaum, Demos and others have proposed practical and secular reasons for the persecutions at Salem; Karlsen's New England research found a pattern of vandalism followed by accusations of witchcraft against women who became the sole owners of property. Starting from Inquisitorial records, Ladurie and Ginzburg attempted to uncover the popular thinking behind certain forms of supposed heresy or witchcraft. New historicists like Greenblatt have focused on the social conditions surrounding those cases of possession attributed to witchcraft. Feminist studies initially treated all witch-persecutions alike, as attacks on independent women by a patriarchal society; current researchers have placed these outbreaks in context by studying women of many classes and occupations and the general treatment of other marginalized groups. Cohn and others at the one-time Columbus Centre correlated witch-hunts with the results of different forms of prejudice—anti-Semitism, racism, anti-Communism. As a result of all this, it has become increasingly clear that no one approach is adequate to the complex phenomenon of witchcraft because each leaves out of account important elements crucial to other approaches.

The work of Larner, therefore, has become a landmark because of its interdisciplinary nature. With this approach she produced an analysis of limited and specific examples of witch-persecution in Scotland, showing each to be the juncture of a number of apparently unrelated social, economic, religious, and political circumstances. This difficult and delicate work does not pretend to answer the large general questions that stand in the forefront of research—why most executed witches were women, for instance. Till we have more solid information on the changing status of women in particular areas and places, Larner indicates, such questions must remain unanswered in any but a limited and provisional way. "While witch-hunting involves woman-hunting the link is indirect," she warns, "and the two cannot be completely identified."

Sometimes, however, it is helpful to rephrase a question that cannot be answered. "Witch" still means to most scholars a woman with a legal record of her trial and death and a pamphlet account of her crimes. But a closer look into ecclesiastical records and into the background of pamphlet and instructional literature suggests that a much larger number of English witches were "good witches" never brought to trial by their neighbors, who regarded them as an asset to the community. If we wonder about the persecution accorded to the minority, we must also take into account the admiration offered to the majority whose existence we must infer from brief comments, suggestive legal records, and significant gaps in narration. Reginald Scot, for instance, regales his readers with stories of powerful and influential witches like Mother Bungie, who lived prosperously and died naturally. George Gifford in his *Dialogue* suggests that the superstition that keeps his parishioners running to good witches and cunning men (once to find a stolen communion cup) is far more pervasive and spiritually dangerous than the activities of the bad witches themselves.

Part of the problem was that although ministers and preachers insisted that both good and bad witches or cunning folk worked by the powers of evil, ordinary people refused to categorize the sources of the good operator's power. Some witches, when pressed, declared that they worked by the fairies; Gifford's countryman suggests hopefully, "Some of the cunning men say, they have Moses or Elias, or the Spirit of some holy man." Ordinary people were concerned by only two distinctions between practitioners: a (sometimes sex-linked) difference in charges between high-tech and low-tech operators, and the supposed wish of a good witch to help and a bad one to hurt.

Roughly speaking, higher technology meant a higher price for the customer and deeper suspicion of the art. The magician or the astrologer had many instruments and a library; the cunning man or woman might have a mirror or a perspective glass; the witch, good or bad, usually had nothing but a herbal remedy or two, several common-place spells, and an effective tongue for cursing or blessing. Therein lay her danger, because she could not be separated from her power except by her death. Yet therein also lay her safety, because most good witches worked for a pittance or for goodwill only, and her accessibility was seen as an advantage to the community in which she lived.

It is hard for modern scholars—focusing with determined skepticism upon the melodrama of witches pursued to death for imaginary crimes—to acknowledge that witchcraft, as one form of superstitious practice, is an accepted and prosaic part of life for large segments of the populace, even in "developed" countries. For example, in a three-week period in 1990, Connecticut's major newspaper reported on haunted houses; grave robbery and devil-worship; a weeping icon; a Gypsy and her daughter brought to court for extracting money from respectable citizens in return for diverting demonic attacks on their welfare; an academic survey that found that 49 percent of people polled believed in the possibility of possession by evil spirits and that 25 percent believed in ghosts. How many other similar events never reached court or newsprint?

When an Elizabethan witch was perceived as bad, the community's first impulse was to avoid the alien vagaries of the law and instead to contain the damage she could create by placating her or by using the resources of a local good witch against her. Among the Elizabethan poor and middle class, superstition was usually balanced by the skepticism that comes of low expectations. Nothing was expected to work well all the time, neither weather, marriage, prayers, nor spells; it took extraordinary exploitation to produce complaint, which is why most everyday magic and witchcraft never reached the Elizabethan pamphlet or secular court. This attitude in Elizabethan England worked against any quick or single-issue reaction to suspected witchcraft and made the development of witch-hunts, as Thomas and Macfarlane have shown, a slow and collaborative process.

Though more men than women were witnesses in court, the pamphlets indicate that the initial complainants were frequently women. Village economies, out of which most accusations grew, were built upon physical barter, but also upon a kind of emotional exchange. This emotional economy was largely controlled by relationships among women, whose society was physically closer— more intimately bound by household borrowing, childbirths, and gossip than that of their husbands. Everyone had ups and downs, but the village "favor bank" (to adopt Tom Wolfe's useful phrase) could not indefinitely carry anyone who drained its physical or emotional resources and gave neither cash nor comfort in return. However, it seems to have taken some time to become bankrupt. Women brought to ecclesiastical courts, according to Macfarlane, were sometimes described as "long suspected" or "suspected . . . for over twenty years." Yet an accused witch was frequently able to summon four or more respectable people to act as compurgators on her behalf. The decision to go to secular law was a last resort, when all local coping strategies failed, the favor bank ran dry, and the balance of suspicion tipped decisively.

The activities of good witches in creating or confirming hostility toward another woman (whether or not they were internalizing dominant male attitudes) were far more potent than the suggestions of the "preacher men" or a baffled doctor. Few poor people visited doctors and they were cynical about the clergy, but they did visit witches, wise women, or cunning men in circumstances where healer, client, and suspected bad witch were all part of the same society and equally aware of its hidden dynamics. After such consultations belief in the intrinsically evil nature of the bad witch's skill was signaled by the identification of an external conduit for it—a pet dog or cat or toad. The good witch's cat was just a cat; the bad witch's cat could be suddenly and ominously identified as a spirit-messenger of harm.

What is important about the witch pamphlets, as Macfarlane says, is that they show more than the abbreviated court records; in them we can track the accumulation of irritants from which accusations arose—refusal to return borrowed goods, constant begging, vicious gossip, and, above all, violent cursing (the single quality most often recorded of accused witches). Subjection to the words of others (landlords, lawyers, priests) is the very condition of illiterate poverty; hostile words produce real effects like eviction, distraint, imprisonment, or execution. Why should not a heartfelt curse produce real effects on the body or goods? Even today, words have auras more powerful than their simple meanings and can, in defiance of fact or proof, render people "guilty by suspicion." It is not then surprising that the law of Elizabethan times, while demanding legal proof of harm by witchcraft, could not escape from the popular conviction that threats and malicious words did themselves inflict damage upon the body physical and the body politic—harm that the good witch could identify but rarely prevent.

Scholarly recognition of the relationship between community situations and witch-belief has developed greatly over the last twenty years, but perhaps the most notable change is that a protective denial, which allowed us to distance witchcraft beliefs as obsolete patterns of thought and to distance the treatment accorded to witchcraft offenders as relics of a barbarous past, can no longer be maintained. The move from terror of magical attack or religious heresy to terror of corruption by political unorthodoxy, noticed twenty years ago, has intensified. Demonization of political or ethnic adversaries and the scale and brutality of consequent attacks on them continue to grow; it seems increasingly easy to mobilize irrational fear and irrational cruelty. As we ask of the witch-hunters, will historians one day ask of us "But what were they afraid of?" To look around us may be the best clue to the meaning of witchcraft in these written records. Sir George Mackenzie, writing the defense of a witch in 1678, might sum up our position just as briefly and sadly: "to kill one another because we cannot comprehend the reason of what each other do, is the effect of a terrible distraction."

Supplementary Bibliography

Anglo, S., ed. *The Damned Art.* London, 1977.

Boyer, Paul, and Stephen Nissenbaum. *Salem Possessed: The Social Origins of Witchcraft.* Cambridge, Mass., 1974.

Cohn, Norman. *Europe's Inner Demons.* London, 1975.

Demos, John. *Entertaining Satan: Witchcraft and the Culture of Early New England.* New York, 1982.

Douglas, Mary, ed. *Witchcraft Confessions and Accusations.* London, 1970.

Ehrenreich, B., and D. English. *Witches, Midwives and Nurses.* London, 1974.

Ginzburg, Carlo. *The Night Battles: Witchcraft and Agrarian Cults in the Sixteenth and Seventeenth Centuries.* Trans. John and Anne Tedeschi. New York, 1983.

———. *Ecstasies: Deciphering the Witches' Sabbath.* Trans. Raymond Rosenthal. New York, 1991.

Greenblatt, Stephen. *Shakespearean Negotiations.* Berkeley, 1988.

Harris, Anthony. *Night's Black Agents.* Totowa, N.J., 1980.

Karlsen, Carol F. *The Devil in the Shape of a Woman: Witchcraft in Colonial New England.* New York, c. 1987.

Kieckhefer, R. *European Witch Trials.* London, 1976.

Ladurie, Emmanuel Le Roy. *Montaillou.* Trans. Barbara Bray. New York, 1978.

Larner, C. *Enemies of God.* London, 1981.

———. *Witchcraft and Religion.* Oxford, 1984.

Macfarlane, A. *Witchcraft in Tudor and Stuart England.* London, 1970.

Marwick, M. G., ed. *Witchcraft and Sorcery.* Harmondsworth, 1970.

Midelfort, H. C. Erik. *Witchhunting in Southwestern Germany, 1562–1684.* Stanford, 1972.

Monter, E. W. *Witchcraft in France and Switzerland.* Ithaca, 1976.

Rowbotham, Sheila. *Hidden from History.* London, 1973.

Russell, Jeffrey. *Witchcraft in the Middle Ages.* Ithaca, 1972.

Thomas, Keith. *Religion and the Decline of Magic.* London, 1971.

Trevor-Roper, H. R. *The European Witch-Craze of the Sixteenth and Seventeenth Centuries.* Harmondsworth, 1969.

Walker, A. P. *Unclean Spirits.* Philadelphia, 1981.

Comprehensive bibliographies and references may be found in the works by Larner, Thomas, and others.

List of Illustrations

Acknowledgments

The pamphlets reprinted in this book are seldom attractive to a modern reader in their original state. Illiteracy and dialect speech in the informants, poor and hurried writing by the authors, and hasty blackletter printing often combine to make barbarous reading. In this edition, therefore, orthographic conventions, spelling, punctuation and capitalisation have been modernised to make the meaning as clear as possible; grammatical correctness could have been obtained only by extensive re-writing. A few misprints have been corrected without notice; omissions are detailed in the notes and any additions to the text have been placed in square brackets.

Obsolete words and grammar (these are marked with an asterisk in the text) have been retained and referred to the glossary, except in a few cases where retention of a very common archaic form would have seemed pedantic. These exceptions are listed at the end of the glossary. Names and places are listed as they appear in my text; variant spellings found in the original are noted in brackets in the same list.

I am grateful to the trustees and staff of many libraries—those at the Folger Library, the British Museum, Lambeth Palace, the London Library, the Bodleian Library, the Society of Antiquaries, the Shakespeare Institute and the University of Connecticut Library. The Henry Huntington Library gave permission to reprint part of a text from microfilm and illustrations appear by courtesy of the Archbishop of Canterbury and the trustees of the Lambeth Palace Library, the trustees of the Bodleian, the Henry Huntington Library and the British Museum.

The County Archivist of Essex provided valuable information in answer to a query; I owe thanks to Professor Mark Eccles for resolving several difficulties. Professor Gene Barbaret gave advice on French translation and Rex Warner on Latin (any mistakes that remain are my own responsibility). Dr. Macfarlane most generously allowed me to use material from a thesis soon to be published in book form (see bibliography).

This book could not have been undertaken without the consent and assistance of my family; it would certainly not have reached completion without my parents' gift of time and my husband's unfailing patience, encouragement and scholarship.

I Introduction

Witchcraft

It would be pleasant to be able to start this book with a neat definition of terms; unfortunately scholarly distinctions drawn between various kinds of magic, sorcery and witchcraft are simply not valid when applied to the superstitious beliefs of Elizabethan England. The balanced and sensible work of Miss Katherine Briggs[1] has shown how many different kinds of superstition go to make up the Elizabethan idea of fairies and the matter is even more complex with witches.

The very word 'witch' describes a state of mind on the part of the speaker rather than any generally accepted conception of a type and that state of mind is an exceedingly primitive and confused one. Witch, wizard, wise woman, magician, necromancer—any learned Elizabethan will define them and distinguish between them; unfortunately few of the lists agree with each other, or have much to do with what the non-reading public, the witches and the bewitched, thought and did about the subject.

People were tried and executed for all kinds of deeds—good, bad and (mainly) impossible. They were dreaded and accused by those amongst whom they lived for two reasons only—they had the power to do things 'above nature', and the will to do harm by this power. So a crucial question for the definition of a witch is one of defining what is 'beyond nature'.

The 'natural' world of the fifteenth and sixteenth centuries was an extremely restricted one; miraculous interventions of saints and devils accounted for the less usual phenomena of existence, and in popular tradition, any notable skill or achievement was regarded as 'beyond nature' and therefore probably the result of magic.

Magical powers were attributed to most early scientists (Roger Bacon for one), and to most men who achieved power by breaking class barriers (Cardinal Wolsey was credited with a magic ring and serviceable devil). Even the poet Virgil lived in folklore as a man of magical powers (combined with an intellectual's laughable lack of

[1] K. M. Briggs, *The Anatomy of Puck* (London, 1959); *Pale Hecate's Team* (London, 1962).

commonsense); the blackletter *Lyfe of Virgil* (1550?) is full of wonderful tales of magic gardens and invincible weapons, alternating with very funny and very vulgar misadventures in love.

Magic

It is hard to describe magic in any precise fashion, since its content is constantly shifting. Science takes over some ground, as its explanations filter into common knowledge; some scientific discoveries, before their operations are fully understood, are incorporated into magical belief and practice. This happened to wireless in its early days, when people grew terrified of their neighbours 'putting thoughts into their heads' by wireless waves.

Magic is the art of compelling destiny, by means neither religious nor explicable in 'natural' terms. It attempts to propitiate or constrain the random element in the universe with which organised religion will have no dealings, speaking only of the unknowable will of God. It seeks out Fortune, the lack of congruence between virtue and reward, vice and punishment, which is felt by all who question the argument of Job's comforters and resist Job's acceptance of enigma.

Prayer is petitionary, and the petitioner submits his request to the judgment of a god; a spell sets up man's will as arbiter, and tries to compel fulfilment of a request. In form there may be little to differentiate a spell from a prayer—but a spell is without humility and felt to be free of the limitations imposed by the religious system. For this reason, prayers of past religions often become spells and even the mass could have its power stolen for magic.

'*Natural*' magic at its most practical level was thought of as the working of secret correspondences in the nature of things to produce automatic results not understood by the science of the day, but accepted as scientific. As Reginald Scot pointed out in *The Discovery of Witchcraft* (1584), most medicine was of this kind; each disease had an appropriate remedy, to be found out by some particular similitude with the nature of the illness. Sometimes mere likeness in appearance was sufficient, and qualities could be transferred simply by propinquity. A famous Biblical example was provided by Jacob,[2] who half-peeled twigs from certain trees and let the sheep see them as they copulated. As a result, the lambs were born parti-coloured.

Thomas Hill, in a book of *Naturall and Artificiall Conclusions* (trans-

[2] *Genesis* 30: 25–42.

lated from the Italian in 1586) described many ways of astonishing one's friends with skills that range from preserving roses fresh through the winter, to finding a drowned person with a loaf of bread. Most of the acts described, however, are what we should call parlour-tricks, the application of simple scientific data to everyday objects. Unfortunately the boundaries of 'natural' and 'artificial' were none too clear and an expert juggler might easily find himself accused of being 'unnatural' rather than 'artful', or 'natural'.

Art Magic was regarded by some of its Neo-Platonic practitioners as an extension of natural magic into the spiritual realm, an attempt to draw down or compel spiritual beings by an accumulation of appropriate qualities drawn from natural things and welded together by the skill of the magician. Different spirits demanded different approaches — different names, different prayers, different instruments, different perfumes; some responded to polite address, some had to be threatened. The skill resided in knowing the right approach for the right spirit.

Less intellectual magicians were content to divide the spirits they sought to compel into two categories, good and bad. 'Elementals' and even fairies occur quite frequently, but mostly as a face-saving device. The conjurations of T.R. (reprinted by Reginald Scot)[3] which seek the appearance of the 'fairy' Sybilia must be carried out by binding the spirit of a suicide or executed felon; necromancy is the blackest of all conjuring rites, and not likely to be used save for the purpose of raising the most dangerous demons, whatever they may be called in print.

Although conjuration was technically forbidden by Church law, argument continued as to the possibility of procuring the appearance of evil spirits without concession or blasphemy, merely by the power of God's name and the natural qualities of things. This, of course, would be non-heretical. As a matter of fact, magicians were seldom troubled by the Inquisition unless they had engaged in sorcery by sacrificing to the spirits, or asking them to divine the future.

A great deal more art magic was practised in the fifteenth and sixteenth centuries than is generally supposed, since it could be applied to the purposes of divination and alchemy, which were both important to the ruling classes. (The great Lord Burghley wrote humble letters to the adventurer Edward Kelley, begging him to return to England and make gold for his country.)[4] The play *Doctor Faustus* produced

[3] Reginald Scot, *Discovery of Witchcraft* (London, 1584), Bk. 15, Ch. 1–20.
[4] John Strype, *Annals of the Reformation* (London, 1725). Vol. IV, Appendix, No. 3.

deep shock and horror because it dealt so luridly with something that was known to be going on in a multitude of ways at the time.

Art magic retained its lure and its credibility because it worked so strongly upon the minds of its adepts, sometimes producing hallucinations that were unexpected enough to seem like visitations from creatures of independent existence. Jean Bodin, the French jurist, rather matter-of-factly describes such an event in 1580:

> ... I knew a person (I will not name him, because he is still alive) who confessed to me that he was much troubled by a spirit which followed him and appeared to him in many shapes; and at night pulled him by the nose and wakened him up, and often beat him. And however he begged it to let him sleep, it would do nothing of the sort, and tormented him unceasingly, saying to him 'Give me something to do!' And, thinking that it might leave him, or that he might find a cure for his trouble, he had come to Paris under cover of a case that he had to plead.
>
> I could see plainly that he dared not tell me everything. I asked him what advantage he had gained from subjecting himself to such a master; he told me that he had expected to win worldly good and advancement, and to understand occult secrets, but the spirit had always cheated him, and for one truth he told three lies.
>
> And that the spirit had never been able to make him richer by a 'double', nor let him enjoy the woman he loved, which was the chief cause which had led him to invoke him. And that he had not taught him the properties of plants, or of animals, or of stones, or other secret skills as he had hoped, and that he talked to him of nothing but revenging himself on his enemies, or bringing about some swindle or malicious trick.
>
> I told him that it was easy to rid himself of such a master, and that whenever the spirit came, he should call the name of God to his aid, and zealously address himself to the service of God. As I have not seen the person since, I do not know whether he repented ...[5]

This poor would-be Faustus seems indeed to have been a conjuror or sorcerer rather than a true magician—one who had attempted a short-cut by using rites overtly blasphemous or evil, and had thus paid homage to the evil spirits. This ensured their appearance but risked the operator's soul, and often put him in their power.

Any dealings with evil spirits on these terms was indisputably sorcery or black magic, and of concern to the civil and ecclesiastical

[5] Jean Bodin, *De la Démonomanie des Sorciers* (Paris, 1580) V2–V2ᵛ. (Translation by B. Rosen.)

courts. But the public at large was much more concerned with results than means. London in the reigns of Elizabeth and James supported swarms of seedy, disreputable conjurors, who played up their black reputations as advertisement for their skills in palm-reading, fortune-telling, finding lost things, providing love-philtres and poisons. They risked more than the law; one unfortunate failure or success could change the climate of public opinion with startling suddenness and a man could be torn in pieces by an angry mob, as was Dr. Lambe.

Dr. Lambe, 'The Duke's Devil', was a wizard in the service of the Duke of Buckingham at the beginning of the seventeenth century. He not only cured diseases and found lost things by the aid of familiar spirits, but used magic to bring about death by poisoning. Sentenced to death for this, and then again for rape while in prison, he escaped both sentences by the influence of his master; but the London mob caught him in the streets and beat him to death.[6]

This illustrates dramatically the fact that the essence of sorcery or witchcraft was less what magic one did, than how one was regarded. Most of the physical adjuncts of magic were common to all. A spell worked automatically and anyone could use it; a white witch often employed spells and ceremonies known to her neighbours but was credited with some special undefined power to obtain results. There is some suggestion that the witch thought this power to consist simply in the belief of the client that the witch could do what was asked. The blasphemous analogy, seldom admitted to consciousness, was of course with the faith in Christ which enabled him to perform miraculous cures. What the Inquisition dimly recognised and fought against was the suggestion that faith, no matter in what, could produce results 'beyond nature'; if non-Catholic belief did so, it must at least implicitly be faith in the Devil.[7] Most 'white witches' simply did not explore the matter as far as this.

The 'white witch', wise woman or cunning man often believed in his powers as inborn and took pride in them. Cunning Murrell,[8] a cunning man of Essex who died in 1860, left behind a trunk full of books and

---

[6] *A brief description of the notorious life of John Lambe, otherwise called Doctor Lambe* (Amsterdam, 1628).

[7] The Epistle Dedicatorie to William Perkins' *Discourse of the Damned Art of Witchcraft* (Cambridge, 1608) shows the same attitude in full strength when it speaks of 'the Samaritans in the Old Testament and the superstitious Athenians in the New' worshipping '*an unknown God*, that is, the Devil'.

[8] *Folk Lore*, Vol. 71, March 1960, 'Cunning Murrell'.

papers, in which he had recorded and catalogued every smallest scrap of information about his neighbours and clients. Despite this impressive evidence of research, he believed in his magical ability. To be the seventh child of a seventh child; to have been born at a certain hour; to have met the fairies; to be unusually shrewd or even a little simple— all these things could make one a 'white witch'.

To be feared as a 'black witch', one had simply to be believed to possess powers 'beyond Nature' as the 'white witch' did, but one was also credited with ill-will towards others; this was *maleficium*, the desire and ability to do harm and it stems from social unacceptability. All legal and theological formulations in England come after this basic suspicion and rationalise it, and it is this which is the reality of witch-craft. Someone who maintains 'the old way' of religion, Catholic or pagan; someone who is outside the mores of the group or always in collision with them: to believe in such a person as she utters her spells is to believe in something very 'different' and therefore evil. For this reason, it is to the black witch that people go for unhallowed demands, and for help in their anti-social desires. She bears the burden of self-hatred left by the client when he returns to the group.

Jews, heretics and witches are all groups on to which society successively projected its fears and guilts; for no human satisfaction is greater than that of seeing the Devil in one's unloved neighbour. To be odd in an unpleasant way; to be malicious and foul-mouthed or over-persistent in begging; to be the daughter of a witch; all these laid the groundwork for classification as a witch, when suspicion was aroused by strange or 'unnatural' events.

More women than men were called witches because witchcraft deals predominantly with the concerns of women and their world was a much more closed and mysterious society to men in the fifteenth century than it is now. Woman was regarded as deficient in the rational faculties—and since she was usually pregnant or nursing (the least intellectual of states) this is an understandable view. Her physical changes and functions were mysterious, particularly that of childbirth, which was assisted by women only, and about which doctors were astonishingly ignorant. Organised religion made little of this most crucial of female concerns till there was a child to be baptised; all the special problems of pregnancy and birth tended to be filed under an *Ave Maria*. Neglected by both religion and science, there is no doubt that women did use charms and spells and imitative magic (i.e. un-locking all the locks in a house) at this time; the queries made at ecclesiastical visitations make it clear that midwives were suspected of witchcraft more frequently than any other women. There still lurks a kind of primitive fear of the midwife; childbirth can never appear to a man (particularly a celibate) quite 'natural' and may therefore be subconsciously associated with the magical. Once the religious or civil laws codify magical acts and produce a unified picture of the witch as rebel to God, a vast number of harmless women can be caught by the simple threads of traditional magic and medicine, enmeshed and finally destroyed by confessions under torture.

The story of the witch-panic in Europe is well known, but will be briefly summarised here.

Witchraft in Europe

The Inquisition, or the Holy Office, was founded in 1199, at a time when the Catholic Church seemed threatened from within rather than without. Many shocks had been provided by the Crusades. As Christians came into real contact with 'the heathen', they often found them superior in the supposedly Christian virtues. For the scholars and priests, the new learning which was to result in the Renaissance and Reformation produced temporarily a terrible pressure as new wine was forced into old bottles. New facts became available before new systems of thought were viable to make sense of them. In its attempts to retain the old category of 'the natural' (which of course included the religious system and man's relationship to it), the Church was forced into outright denial of new discoveries, or into tortured and absurd rationalisations. (The trial of Galileo illustrates a corner of the battlefield.) It cannot be stressed too often that witch-panic appears at the beginning of the Renaissance rather than in the mediaeval age because it is a serious effort to explain, in the only terms available, new insights into the nature of belief and the powers of the mind. Like the ignorant, the learned fell back on magic and demonology as a way of explaining the accumulations of facts and observations that would not fit the pattern.

The major heresies of Europe (Cathars and Waldenses, flourishing in the twelfth and thirteenth centuries) and the minor pantheistic sects had produced the perplexing sight of communities leading apparently blameless and austere lives by the power of a belief felt to be damnable. An analogy to the Inquisition's dilemma may be found in popular perplexity about the early hippy communities, where the service of pot, LSD, and polymorphous perversity apparently produced peace, love and harmony. (The collapse of Haight-Ashbury into squalor and tourism caused almost indecent relief among the middle-aged.) In terms of mediaeval theology, good things done on bad principles exemplify the deceit of that Devil who can appear as an angel of light. All the old horror tales attached to any small and persecuted sect since the days of the early church itself were resurrected as types of the true obscenity of heresy beneath its seeming purity. Bodin, who believed whole-heartedly in religious toleration, has a curiously cool and level passage in *De la République* (Paris 1576) in which he notes how certain tales of orgy and child-murder are routinely ascribed to one disapproved group after another. Yet, as he believed equally whole-heartedly in witches, he fails to connect this tendency with the tales now reported of them.

The heresies and their adherents were exterminated with almost inconceivable brutality, but unease remained. Too many people had seen an alternative to the cynical corruption at the centre of the Church; too many people were tired of physical and spiritual exactions that seemed to have little to do with either love or justice. There were continued small attempts to return to the original purity of the Gospel and continued persecution of these. Rebellion hid, like the serpent in the Tree of Knowledge, beneath a quiet surface; and in the country this was signified by an apparent increase of interest in traditional magic and the remnants of pagan religions, things which up to now the Church had been content to Christianise rather than uproot.

In times of social disturbance (the shaking of the established order of things), there is always such an increase in superstition and unofficial belief. The Inquisitors felt it also, but they felt it as a challenge to combat such belief in others. (In the same way they had felt the power of the Manichaean heresies; they had exterminated the heresies and yet adopted part of the belief themselves, by allocating immensely increased power to the devils, who were credited with inspiring such heresies.)

'Rebellion is as the sin of witchcraft' (I *Samuel* 15: 23)—the text gives sanction to the idea of witchcraft as something organised and deliberate, and it is well known that 'Thou shalt not suffer a witch to live' (*Exodus* 22: 18). The great danger of any feudal system or hierarchy is that, when threatened, it can conceive of opposition only in terms of itself—as an organised entity, as conspiracy. In a series of Bulls, climaxed by that of Innocent the Eighth in 1484, sorcery was gradually identified with heresy.

Sorcery was said to entail beliefs that actively gave aid and encouragement to the Enemy of mankind, beliefs that, like heresies, seemed innocuous and yet entailed an allegiance to the anti-Church, for 'He that is not for me is against me.' Everything that was not of God and His Church must come under the rule of the Devil—an absolutist position that left no room for discovery without the risk of martyrdom.

The Inquisition began to synthesise the various pronouncements concerning witchcraft which had been issued over the last two hundred years; it studied the inquisitorial reports of trials which had already taken place, searched the classics and the Scriptures for precedent. The feudal organisation credited to the heretics was taken over wholesale, with all its ugly tales of sodomy, bestiality and child-eating. Since the heretic was an anomaly in the social and religious structure of things believed to have been ordained by God, all his acts and beliefs were 'unnatural', in essence if not in actuality. Heresy meant belief in the Evil principle expressed in opposition—killing instead of giving life; profaning the Host; parodying the Sacrament with obscene ingredients and rites; giving allegiance by kissing the fundament of a beast instead of the toe of a Pope; having sterile sexual connection with demons, which is regarded as bestiality; even dancing backwards.[9] The witches' meeting to worship was called the Sabbath, perhaps merely because this was the 'Jewish Sunday'.

Unfortunately this theoretical picture had confirmation, not only in the tales told of heretics everywhere, but in Augustine's comments on the powers of witches, and in the classical texts of Horace, Lucan, Apuleius and Virgil received by him and later scholars as authorities. In these decadent aristocratic re-handlings of popular superstitions, the authors presented a hair-raising picture of witches sticking pins in wax images, snatching parts of bodies from the battlefield, raising the spirits of the dead, sacrificing children, invoking Hecate in her blackest incarnation.

European peasant superstition, with its flying demon-owls who sucked the blood of children, ligatures, child-bed magic, love-philtres,

---

[9] Details of the Sabbath and the deeds required of witches by the Devil are found in all the witchcraft handbooks published on the Continent after the mid-fifteenth century. Useful summaries may be found in Rossell Hope Robbins, *The Encyclopaedia of Witchcraft and Demonology* (London and New York, 1959). One of the earliest and most important works has been reprinted in translation several times, and is easily available; *Malleus Maleficarum* (A Hammer for Witches), written by Heinrich Kramer (Henricus Institoris) and James Sprenger in 1486, was translated by the Rev. Montague Summers and first printed in London, 1928.

ghosts and demons, provided many points at which a link with the scholarly, classical picture could be made. The link was obvious enough to impress the peasants themselves for, unlike the heresies but like the crusades, magic touched both rich and the poorest of the poor in every village; an attack on it had the potential of uniting the world-wide Church in fear, as the Crusades had united it in ambition.

Heretics had been men, women and children; the practitioners of country magic were most often women. This simple fact was enough to release in the Inquisitors a violent mixture of anti-feminism and sex-obsession as unexpected as it is nauseating. *Malleus Maleficarum* written in 1486 as a handbook for procedure against witches according to the late Bull is one of the most morally obtuse and pornographically obsessive works existing; by the time the Dominican authors Kramer and Sprenger have finished with witchcraft, every aspect of the subject is emotional dynamite.

Hysterical and psychosomatic states, encouraged by this atmosphere, came under intense observation perhaps for the first time and were 'explained' by further developments in the theories of possession and devil-lore. Even doctors, still caught in the mediaeval view of 'the natural', were forced to accept the reality of witchcraft and devil-caused sickness distinct from ordinary maladies. Under the pressure of all this new observation confined to ludicrously outdated theory and theology, fear and bewilderment exploded into the witch-panic.

It is pointless to consider the Inquisitors' formulation of the witch-craft heresy as a purely cynical undertaking at its inception (though later on, the habit of confiscating the property of the accused brought wealth to both secular and religious judges). Theological language is by its nature highly allusive and metaphorical; it prefers to describe in Biblical terms and analogies the supposed truth of a matter rather than its factual accidents. Unfortunately, the Inquisitors made the common mistake of consuming their own spiritual propaganda in solid form.

And, for all their brilliance, only a few brave and lonely men like the Jesuit Friedrich Spee, a seventeenth-century confessor to tortured witches understood the power of pain to obscure rather than illuminate truth.[10]

[10] Friedrich von Spee, S. J., *Cautio Criminalis, seu de Processibus contra Sagas* (Rinteln, 1631). For a summary of the 1731 edition, see H. C. Lea, *Materials towards a History of Witchcraft*, 3 vols. (repr. New York, 1957), Vol. II, pp. 697–729.

Interrogation

There is nothing particularly novel in the use of torture in the inquisitorial process (first allowed in the fourteenth century); civil systems used it too, and the most horribly inventive torments for witches were produced by civil authorities. Strappado and rack were in use in the Tower of England during Elizabeth's reign, despite pious Protestant horror about the cruelties of the Inquisition.

. However, since witchcraft was declared a *'crimen exceptum'* in 1468, many of the normal limitations on torture were suspended or circumvented. In the zeal of the Inquisitors to get to the bottom of the whole witch-conspiracy, exceptional severity and lack of due process soon became the rule. The events of our own time demonstrate how quickly people with a cause can come to accept unusual brutality as normal, when it seems necessary. The questioners then become trapped in a self-defeating routine which sees any return to more normal methods as weakening, softness or lack of conviction.

Any lack of success in the stepped-up measures then appears to prove that more of the same is demanded, not less; the occasional suspect who defies all torture and refuses to talk is a threat to the whole system and must be forced by any means to submit. Inhuman methods require such private self-justification that it becomes impossible ever to conceive of innocence in those whom one tortures. And indeed, many of the Continental handbooks on witchcraft—used in both civil and ecclesiastical courts—did come to assume that 'common fame' or suspicion was equivalent to proof, that God would not allow the innocent to be wrongly accused.

This process almost guaranteed that no one who was accused could escape without confession, crippling or death—often death by burning alive. As Father Spee recounts: 'A certain religious recently discussed the matter with several judges who had lighted many fires and asked them how an innocent person once arrested could escape; they were unable to answer and finally said they would think it over that night.'[11]

Rack, strappado and thumbscrew produced confessions which were partly the result of leading questions and partly memories of the confessions routinely read at executions. Naturally, there was a great concurrence of evidence in such confessions which seemed to put the fact of an international witch-conspiracy beyond doubt, to priests, people and judges alike. The glaring reason for such consistency occurred,

[11] See above, H. C. Lea, p. 707.

apparently, to very few people; this is very hard to accept or understand, unless we are capable of seeing the fallacies on which we base our own most important actions.

Yet there is one aspect of interrogation which we have learned to understand in this century, and that is the complicity of questioner and questioned. It has received classical expression in *Nineteen Eighty-Four*[12] and *Darkness at Noon*,[13] and scientific assessment in Armed Forces studies of American prisoners in Korea. Brainwashing is essentially a matter of persuading a man to discount his subjective views in favour of more objective and 'correct' ones. The expectations of others are of extreme importance in deciding what we see or remember in the first place—witness some of the retracted evidence in the Warren Report of President Kennedy's assassination.

The interrogator capable of ordering physical punishment or humiliation, trying to alter misconceptions for one's own good, can become a focus for all a child's mixed emotions towards a father. However punitive, he is paying the most flattering attention, and the prisoner cannot help feeling (after a while) the wish to respond in a way which will win approval. When belief rather than fact is the central issue, both questioner and questioned enter a world of emotional double meanings where five fingers really can become four.[14]

On the Continent the interrogators of the Inquisitorial process were priests—authority figures in the highest degree, wardens of a whole world of metaphor and motive in which the layman could find no solid footing, since at any instance the fact itself could be devalued into an illusion or the motive turn into a fact. In one way or another, at some profound level the accused was guilty of everything that mattered. A schizophrenic can establish the same relationship with his doctor, obediently and unconsciously offering up the expected manifestations of a condition assumed by the doctor and thus confirming the diagnosis.[15]

---

[12] George Orwell, *Nineteen Eighty-Four* (London, 1949).

[13] Arthur Koestler, *Darkness at Noon* (published in translation, London, 1941).

[14] George Orwell, *Nineteen Eighty-Four*, ed. cit., Part Three, Ch. II.

[15] This point was dramatically made in *Escape from Sanity*, a documentary on schizophrenia by Hugh Burnett, shot at Shenley Hospital, England, and broadcast on BBC-1, on 9 June 1967. Doctors in the programme stressed 'the infinitely obliging nature of schizophrenia', a characteristic which explains the wild variation in physical signs of derangement observed between one century and another. There is now a strong section of psychiatric opinion which wishes

In England (as opposed to Scotland) we shall see that the examinations of accused witches were first taken by justices of the peace, almost never by figures of religious authority and almost always without torture. Emphasis remained on fact rather than belief and the examination was not usually prolonged. Where, as in the St. Osyth case or the later dealings of Hopkins the Witch-finder, there was deep and repeated interrogation or physical ill-treatment, the confessions begin to follow the Continental pattern; otherwise they are completely different.

The fact that England was no longer Catholic seems to have had nothing direct to do with the more humane nature of its attack on witches. The Protestants on the Continent were as zealous in persecution as the Catholics, and it is an odd fact that, for all their violent rejection of Catholic doctrines, they accepted the principles of *Malleus Maleficarum* as a guide to procedure against witches.

Both Protestants and Catholics believed implicitly that God had let loose the scourge of witches to punish wilful disobedience to 'The Truth'. Each side saw that the world swarmed with devils who could change the very appearance of things—for the opposition could appear pious; the opposition performed the basic rites of Christianity and interpreted its basic Book in error and blindness and must, therefore, be serving evil rather than good. In this ugly controversy between frightened dogmatists, all men lost, and the Devil won hands down.

Pact

It is an odd fact that the absolutely basic adjunct of the Continental idea of a witch was pact, entailing attendance at the Sabbath, sexual orgies and worship of the Devil. There were lists of indications of this state, some favoured by one authority and some by another, but confession of the agreement still was paramount—and it has not the slightest reasonable warrant in Scripture. There were tedious and endless citations of the passages mentioning witches and fortune-tellers, endless exegesis of the incident of the Witch of Endor (I *Samuel* 28), invariable conclusions that 'Thou shalt not suffer a witch to live' (*Exodus* 22: 18). The one quotation which has any bearing at all on pact is skated over lightly, as well it might be, since it has nothing to do

---

to avoid labelling or classifying mental disorders, in order to avoid eliciting supporting symptoms from the patient.

with witchcraft. 'For you have said: We have entered into a league with death: we have made a covenant with hell' (*Isaiah* 28: 15). Yet it is assumed, as William Perkins says[16] (while admitting that 'a manifest Covenant is not so fully set down in Scripture') that 'Covenant is a most evident and certain truth that may not be called in question'.

From the most obvious point of view, pact and some physical sign of it are necessary if witches are to be prosecuted for heresy. The first proves willing adherence to anti-Christian belief, a parody of confirmation and sacrament which is heresy; the second is a physical proof that the spiritual apostasy has taken place, should confession fail. But there is a nexus of traditional belief behind each idea which renders it psychologically as well as practically satisfactory.

It is not always realised that the magician's pact was originally quite distinct from that of the witch. The early books of ritual magic are devoted to the constraint of spirits, many of whom are represented as benign or neutral, and the idea of pact appears first as a contract to be sworn to by the spirit only; not till the sixteenth century do we get agreements sworn to by the magician only.

Legend, on the other hand, had dealt from the earliest centuries with sinners who sold their souls to the devil and gave him a signed contract —magicians who were impatient and wanted immediate results, or young men who desired a particular and ungodly boon (usually the love of a recalcitrant virgin). These legends received an impetus when the church finally asserted that all sorcery and magic were heretical, since, even without sacrifice to the devil, they depended for their success on an implicit unstated pact with him, and the Faustus story is one result of this union of forces. From the sixteenth century on, conjuring manuals begin to show an awareness of the problem of pact (express or tacit), and this starts the downfall of the art magician into Satanism, spiritualism and bad conscience.

The original offering of a cock to the spirit in ritual magic had perhaps had as its intention the luring of the spirit (demon or a spirit of the dead) to the place prepared for it, so that it might drink blood and be helped to put on material form by this infusion of life, as the ghosts in the *Odyssey* were lured to appear and speak when Odysseus sought knowledge of the future.[17] According to Tiresias, they would only speak truth after they drank the blood of the sacrifice. Later, this bribe

[16] William Perkins, *A Discourse of the Damned Art of Witchcraft* (Cambridge, 1608), Cap. 2.
[17] Homer, *Odyssey* XI.

is construed as a sacrifice and becomes a prerequisite, a sign of mortal sin which brings devils eager for the soul of the operator. The shedding of blood is then explicitly an offering to the object of one's worship, according to the Old Testament custom; indeed, the Mass itself is an offering of flesh and blood. Marlowe's Faustus, in a rite even more blasphemous than the conjuration and therefore merely narrated, 'prayed and sacrificed'[18] to the devils before he raises them through ceremonies; there is therefore no doubt that he is really a witch or sorcerer rather than a true art magician—he supplicates and does not adjure the devils.

This offering becomes of paramount importance in the description of the witches' pact. A written bond was out of the question, since few of those accused could write; offerings of murdered babies at the Sabbath, though routinely described, are not quite personal enough; the total depravity of the witch could be summed up only by a mingling of her very nature with the demonic and an offering of her total being. This was provided by the insistence that the witch-cult entailed sexual relations with the Devil himself at the Sabbath and with other incubi and succubi; it was the most loathsome form of bestiality, a parody of the Sacrament in which man receives the nature of God, and an even more intimate mingling of natures than that provided by giving one's blood to a devil.

In many cases, the witch's blood was shed as well; the devil beat his followers unmercifully or produced effusions of blood by painful intercourse. In England, blood sucked by a 'familiar devil' in animal form was the simple and only form of pact till mid-seventeenth century. In Scotland, he baptised the witch with blood from the mark which he bit or pinched into her flesh.

The Mark, and other Proofs

This mark, though not at first of more importance than 'taciturnity' (i.e. ability to withstand torture without confession!) or 'inability to shed tears', or many other indications of witch guilt, gradually becomes the outstanding 'proof' of pact, perhaps because of the comparatively clear-cut nature of the evidence it provides.

The witch was stripped naked, her body hair was shaved and she was searched, particularly in 'secret places' for any unusual or insensible

[18] Christopher Marlowe, *Doctor Faustus*, ed. Irving Ribner (New York, 1963), I. iii. 6 7.

mark or scar. Although some theological writers state that this is indecent, records show that it was done in the majority of cases and the finding of a mark was accorded increasing weight as evidence. Bodin says that the Devil marks only those of whose allegiance he is doubtful, but even this provides a pretext for search and an excuse for *not* releasing those without it.[19]

Many strange and confused ideas lie behind this idea of the unholy brand which the witch carried in her flesh. The Old Testament idea of circumcision signifies an inescapable allegiance to one's tribal God by a physical change. This is replaced in Christian theology by the spiritual rite of baptism and circumcision came to be classed as one of the defects which in the Old Testament rendered a man imperfect, unfit for offering to God as a priest. (In rare cases, Christ signified approval of a saint by granting him the stigmata, the signs in hands and feet, side and head of wounds He received on the cross but this was not regarded as mutilation.) Imperfection was one of the traditional marks of anything created by the Devil in imitation of God—thus his cloven hoof or hidden tail when he appeared in human form. The mutilations by branding or amputation prescribed for various crimes in the civil codes signified, among other things, the separation of the offender from the righteous, so it was fitting that the badge worn by the Devil's followers should be a ritual scar or deformity—at once a mock baptism or stigmata, a marring of God's work, and a sign to the zealous godly for the confounding of sinners. For this mark was happily distinguishable from 'natural' scars; when pins were stuck into it, it did not bleed and the witch remained insensible of pain.

As mysterious as the idea of the mark, and earlier in origin, was the belief that scratching a witch (usually 'above the breath') and so drawing blood, would temporarily break a spell. This was very common in England and apparently rare on the Continent. No one seems to know how this counter-charm worked. Beating a lunatic made the patient's body uncomfortable for the possessing devil, so that he would leave; perhaps her indwelling evil power deserted the scratched witch for the same reason.

Possibly the shedding of the witch's blood, like the burning of one animal from a bewitched flock, was construed as an appeasing sacrifice

[19] Summaries of the books detailing procedure in Continental witch-trials may be found in H. C. Lea, *Materials towards a History of Witchcraft* (Philadelphia, 1939). Bodin's *Démonomanie* (Latin version) is dealt with in Vol. II, pp. 554–74.

or bribe to the evil spirit, which would then agree to depart from the bewitched being. Since in England a witch was supposed to maintain her pact with her familiar spirit, or tame devil, by giving it her blood to drink, scratching her simply offered her familiar an extra meal, for which it was hoped he would desert the body of the bewitched person.

To cut or mark the head could also stand as a symbolic execution—a threat to kill unless the spell was removed, and a demonstration that the witch could not prevent such an attack. (David humiliated Saul in this fashion by sparing his life but cutting off part of his robe in secret. See I *Samuel* 24: 1–11.) Sometimes it was enough to burn thatch from the witch's roof and this even more symbolic gesture would cause her enough pain to bring her to the spot with offers to remove the spell.

The water-ordeal (in which a suspect was trussed up and thrown into a pond to sink, if innocent, or swim, if guilty) is as old as the judicial ordeals of fire or red-hot iron. Early Continental authorities mention it, but under the influence of the Inquisitorial process it was generally replaced by less cumbrous means of torture. However, it remained fixed in folk-belief as an infallible means of discovering a witch, perhaps because it was one of the methods in which the populace at large could have a share. King James accepted the water-ordeal as a proof equal to the mark and rationalised the belief by saying that water would reject the evil creature who had rejected her baptism.[20] One or two judges during his reign made this test semi-official, but it soon reverted to the status of popular superstition; most of the later deaths of witches took place while they were being ducked and beaten by a local mob.

Witchcraft in England

It is necessary to treat witchcraft in England quite separately from witchcraft on the Continent because in the period of most intense persecution abroad from the late fifteenth to late seventeenth centuries, the English belief and practice followed quite different paths. On the Continent, the terror of witches started at the top. The persecution of heretics by both Inquisition and civil authorities shades into the persecution of heretical witches, with much of the original outlook and vocabulary unchanged. The nature of witchcraft was defined by Papal Bulls, inquisitorial reports of trials, theological speculations, and handbooks laying down correct procedures for questioning suspects. Popular

[20] King James I, *Daemonologie* (Edinburgh, 1597), Bk. 3, Ch. VI, p. 80.

literature of the subject, so far as can be determined, occurs after this.

In England, however, there were notable cases before there were any scholarly or theological publications devoted to the subject. Since few of these cases share the extremely grim and terrifying nature of prosecutions abroad knowledge of them was spread through the popular rustic ballads, pamphlets and plays. Many of these survive from the 1560s. It was not really until the late 1580s that similar books began to be produced in English and Danaeus[21] and Lavater were translated only in the '70s.[22]

In England the first full-scale treatise was not a *Malleus Maleficarum* (though this was available and known to scholars), but Reginald Scot's sceptical and pugnacious *Discovery of Witchcraft*. Public information came, not through confessions read at executions, sermons or proclamations, but from crude blackletter pamphlets, accounts of trials put forth by enterprising printers. The most impressive statement of official concern was embodied in the secular law of Elizabeth and this, as we shall see, was aimed less at spiritual perils than national dangers.

A surprising number of the surviving Elizabethan pamphlets can be checked in matters of fact against surviving legal records. Fabrication can be seriously suspected in only two cases. Naturally the standard of reporting varies; there is some wretchedly hurried writing, obviously rushed to meet a deadline, and some truly chaotic printing. There are also extremely detailed and careful accounts, where the writer has obviously had access to court records and examinations and, on occasion, the judge, or some party to the case, has been concerned enough to keep the record straight and supervise publication.

Since these pamphlets were for many years the chief written means by which information about witchcraft was circulated and this information was factual rather than theoretical, they provide the best approach to discovering what witchcraft meant in England at this time and how its manifestations changed. In this volume extracts from theoretical treatises have been kept to a minimum since, with a few lively and readable exceptions, the learned authors were more concerned with 'what Austin saith' than with what was going on in their own villages. These scholarly treatises did affect ministers and judges and thus to some extent the conduct of trials; but most judges were still much more interested in precedent—the handling of similar earlier cases—than in

---

[21] Lambert Daneau, *A Dialogue of Witches* (London, 1575).
[22] Lewes Lavater, *Of ghostes and spirites walking by nyght* (London, 1572).

studying the theory for themselves. Scholarly theories of witchcraft affected popular belief only very gradually; the evolving shape of this folk-belief responded much more sensitively to social and political pressures.

(On the Continent, by contrast, the Inquisitors had in effect 'chosen' the form by which social fears and tensions should be discharged. Magical folk-lore and superstition did not naturally develop into the idea of heretical witchcraft embodied in civil and ecclesiastical trials; that picture was formulated by theologians and stamped across the fears of Europe.)

It might have been expected that the prolific Elizabethan literature would have provided an excellent source of material for examining Elizabethan witch-belief; as a matter of fact, there is little sustained reference in prose or poetry; and the de-classed gentlemen who wrote the plays returned with pathetic persistence to their classical learning for most of their supernatural effects, even when they were supposedly dealing with current events. The more serious witchcraft seems in the villages and courts, the less people want to see it treated realistically on stage; the drabber and nastier it gets in reality, the more colourful and melodramatic they want it as entertainment. For this reason, among others, this volume quotes little from drama; texts are easily available, and Miss Katherine Briggs has made a brief but excellent survey of the subject in *Pale Hecate's Team*.

Witchcraft and the Law

Before examining the pamphlets themselves, it will be helpful to examine the laws concerning witchcraft and any factors which affected the way those laws were put into practice.

Laws against various kinds of magical practice had been promulgated from the earliest times; though it is not always easy to be certain exactly what is being prohibited, it is obvious that the practical application of the penalties is intended to discourage the original pagan religions, which are now, of course, spoken of as devil-worship. In troubled times, adherents of 'the old religion' are always regarded as politically unreliable.

It is important to remember that there was never an Inquisition in England, and that attitudes towards the central authority in Rome were usually less than enthusiastic. Thus the ecclesiastical courts tended to be independent rather than unified in their operations; and such

W—B

records as survive (commencing mainly in the thirteenth century) show that magic and sorcery were in general punished lightly by penance or the pillory—even after the Church had classed them as heresy.

As early as the thirteenth century, sorcerers could also be arrested and punished with death by the civil authorities, but very few seem to have suffered in this way unless they had been involved in conspiracy or rebellion. It is surprising how often would-be rebels or claimants to the throne begin their plans by an attempt to have the king's nativity calculated and the probable day of his death forecast; it seems to have been as routine an endeavour as studying the stock-market before buying. But it was punished with great severity as treachery, since it was an obvious cause of unrest and disaffection and a stimulus to that rebellion of which it was the spiritual counterpart.[23]

Political (margin annotation)

Very common, but apparently regarded with leniency, were magical attempts by the poor to be their own doctors. It was noted in the statute of 3 Henry VIII, c. 11. that: ' . . . artificers as smiths, weavers and women boldly and customably take upon them great cures and things of great difficulty in the which they partly use sorcery . . .' And the query of the Ecclesiastical Commission in 1559—'. . . Whether you know any that do use charms, sorceries, enchantments, invocations, circles, witchcrafts, soothsaying or any like crafts or imaginations, invented by the Devil, and specially in the time of women's travail'— merely echoes many earlier ones. But since there were not enough doctors, and childbirth continued to be managed by women, few authorities were hardhearted enough to punish people severely for giving the aid and comfort that could not be obtained elsewhere.

The first secular law against witchcraft appeared in 1542 (33 Henry VIII, c. 8.) for no very definable reason and was repealed without having been put in action more than once. It deals mainly with treasure-seeking. Digging for treasure in tumuli and ruined buildings was time-honoured sport in England, though it was felt to be practical to pay a magical specialist for protection against the spirits of heathen or miserly owners who might be lingering wretchedly around their treasure. It has been suggested that this act, which comes two years after the Six Articles, is a propitiatory gesture towards the Catholics and an attempt to restrain the iconoclasm of the reformers who had joined the treasure-seekers in searching and destroying church monuments. Certainly all the paraphenalia of conjuration mentioned—the 'images and pictures' (of wax, for sticking pins into), the 'crowns, sceptres, swords, rings,

[23] I *Samuel* 15: 23.

glasses' appears in early Papal Bulls against sorcery. All could be used in ceremonies designed to reveal the future; and Henry was no longer young.

This act was repealed under Edward. A new one written under Elizabeth (5 Eliz., c. 16) clarified things considerably, though it repeats some of the same language:

a) Invocation and conjuration of evil spirits for any purpose becomes a felony.

b) Witchcraft, enchantment, charm and sorcery have three gradations:

  i bewitching to death

  ii injuring person or goods or cattle

  iii seeking treasure, looking for lost things, *trying* to provoke unlawful love, or kill, maim, or injure a person.

The first deserves death. The second and third are punished by combinations of prison and pillory for first offences, by death and life imprisonment for second offences.

The intention of a) was spelt out in Clause 5 of 23 Eliz., c. 2, 'An Act against seditious words and rumours . . .' Here witchcraft and conjuration are included with figure-casting, casting of nativities, astrological calculations and prophesying as means of trying to determine the length of the Queen's life, or the succession, two questions of great importance to Catholics.

The act of 1604, 1 Jas. 1., c. 12, not only stiffens the penalties but alters the bearing of the law by amplifying the 'invocation' section to include the keeping of familiar spirits and exhumation of bodies or use of bones for the purposes of 'witchcraft, enchantment, sorcery, charm'. The use of bones, skin etc. from the dead, was more common in Scotland than in England, and few English cases mention it, even after this date. But mention of the familiar, already common in popular English witch-belief as a privately-owned devil in animal form, had the effect of giving formal, legal sanction to the idea that the very existence of a witch's pet was indeed proof of her witchcraft. This led directly to search for the teat at which she supposedly nourished her familiar; this was already the popular English version of the mark, appearing in most trials after 1579 and from then on it was regarded by many judges as most important evidence for the prosecution. (See speech of Lord Anderson 1602.)

Not mentioned in the law, but set down by James in his *Daemonology*, is the idea that the ordeal of swimming a witch provides acceptable testimony as to her guilt. In 1612 we are told that this is often done, apparently without authority, in the North;[24] in the same year it is ordered by justices, to provide legal 'evidence'.[25]

These details of the law were important because, legally speaking, none of the witch-laws was particularly clear in its language. The early legal codes had been in Anglo-Saxon or Latin or French, and the translations between them and into English were far from standard; not only were the varieties of magic hopelessly confused, they were also confounded with other crimes altogether (*veneficium* could mean either poisoning or witchcraft). Most of the Elizabethan legal definitions are in fact quite non-committal—a state of affairs which had its political uses; they stem from Bodin's statement that '*Sorcier est celuy qui par moyens Diaboliques sciemment s'efforce de parvenir a quelque chose.*' ('A sorcerer is one who by devilish means knowingly strives to attain some end.')[26] But Bodin then spends hundreds of pages in fleshing out this definition with the orthodox Inquisitionary picture of witchcraft, which was not then current in England.

Coke says, 'A witch is a person that hath conference with the devil, to consult with him or to do some act.'[27] He then adds some citations of classical poets to define enchanter and sorcerer, all remarkably inappropriate to England. Similarly William West in 1594: 'A witch or hag is she which being illuded by a league made with the devil through his persuasion, inspiration and juggling, thinketh she can design what manner of evil things soever . . .'[28] He then lists the wildest fancies of Continental witchcraft about the Sabbath, all completely alien to England. He has previously defined magic, soothsaying wizards, divination, juggling, enchanting and charming, of which only the last two help with the act of Elizabeth; and here too he is hopelessly vague: 'Enchanters or charmers through certain words pronounced and characters or images, herbs, or other things applied, think they can do what they list . . .'

[24] *Witches apprehended, Examined and Executed, for notable villanies by them committed both by Land and Water . . .* (London, 1613), C2.

[25] *The Witches of Northamptonshire. . . .* (London, 1612), C2.

[26] Jean Bodin, *De la Démonomanie des Sorciers*, ed. cit., opening sentence of Ch. I. In his Latin version, Bodin uses 'magus' to translate 'sorcier' and both to mean (among other things) 'witch'. This extension of meaning seems to have taken place under the influence of the idea that all sorcery is heresy, and damnable.

[27] Sir Edward Coke, *Third Part of the Institutes of the Laws of England* (London, 1797), Ch. VI. 1st edition 1644.

[28] William West, *Symboleography* (London, 1594).

In 1653 Sir Robert Filmer wrote: 'This statute presupposeth that everyone knows what a conjuror, a witch, an enchanter, a charmer and sorcerer is, as being to be learned best of divines; and therefore they have not described or distinguished between them: and yet the law is very just in requiring a *due and lawful conviction*.'[29] But the Church of England was too busy manœuvring between the supernatural heresies of Protestants and Catholics to lay down definitions which could only be a cause of further trouble.

None of the handbooks on witchcraft produced by various divines was clear enough or theologically unexceptionable enough to receive general recognition till that of William Perkins; incorporating pre-1600 sermon material, it was printed only in 1608. Thomas Potts' account of the 1612 Lancashire witch trials was much used, and its conclusions as to the importance of the mark and animal familiar incorporated in later standard works.[30] Till then, those Elizabethan judges who read up on Continental authorities, civil or ecclesiastical—Bodin, Delrio or *Malleus Maleficarum*—found themselves faced with a theological type of argument and evidence foreign to English law, and manifestations of witchcraft which simply did not appear in the accusations preferred before them. In 1563, the year of Elizabeth's first law, there were no clear or unified ecclesiastical precedents and no civil precedents save those in which magic and witchcraft had been mere adjuncts to a trial for treason. Common law procedures were too confused to be of much use.

But instinctively the judges tried to proceed by the ordinary rules governing accusations and evidence; they looked primarily for a case based on physical injury or loss, not on heresy or magical dealing in the abstract. As Sir Robert Filmer noted in 1653, even after the act of James, which made the keeping of a familiar itself a felony, judges tended to take note only of cases in which there was also 'evidence' of murder or injury by these means.[31]

Conjurors and magicians could be accused with the assistance of concrete evidence—books of conjuration, the magical gear described in the act of Henry VIII, or a witness to ceremonies like Nicholas Starkey; midwives and cunning women could be proved to have said certain charms or given certain prescriptions. But to accuse someone

[29] Sir Robert Filmer, *An Advertisement to the Jury-men of England touching Witches* (London, 1653), Bᵛ.
[30] Thomas Potts, *The Wonderfull Discoverie of Witches in the Countie of Lancaster* (London, 1613); ed. G. B. Harrison (London, 1929), pp. 74–7.
[31] See note 29.

of witchcraft meant to accuse them of something which could not be proved by physical evidence (though Brian Darcy in 1582 regards 'mark' as proof),[32] only by circumstantial deduction, or a confession.

The justices who took the examinations were often acquainted with the complainants and therefore believed implicitly those they knew to be honest or well thought of. Consequently, they accepted the '*post ergo propter*' fallacy of frightened witnesses without question. The facts seemed 'beyond nature': the woman was ill thought of and therefore credited with *maleficium*. (It is noticeable that wise women who do not have a bad reputation, who are consulted as aids against the 'bad witches' never seem to get into trouble, because public fear does not operate against them.) The English are not frightened of magic, only of magical injury.

'She threatened me and my child died.' 'Two months after we quarrelled I had three cows die very strangely.' Once the judges were prepared to accept this initial fallacy as argument, the accused were in a very dangerous position, since whatever they did or said was interpreted in hostility. As the guilt of the accused was assumed on the Continent and required proof of innocence, so in England unconscious illogicalities vitiated the system by which proof of guilt was required; the assumption of guilt created proof. Mark and the animal familiar—both popular, and not learned superstitions as we shall see later—were convenient, tangible rationalisations of fear. It is notable that the indispensable familiars—devils in animal form—are never produced in court as evidence, or even found by those supposedly searching a witch's house for them. Their beds and feeding dishes are solemnly produced, but they are always 'vanished away'. The idea is more important than the actuality (though it may be imagined that most constables would have been too afraid to touch any such creatures even if they had seen them). It is notable that Brian Darcy, in his efforts to emulate Bodin in Essex, follows his procedure in allowing testimony from very young children, making and breaking promises of clemency for confession, etc.—yet still lays the greatest stress upon animal familiars as 'proof', an element not to be found in Bodin's accounts of witchcraft. It seems that the law was almost fatally responsive to the common opinion of its time in

[32] W. W., *A true and just Recorde . . . of all the Witches taken at St. Oses in the countie of Essex* (London, 1582). Brian Darcy was the J.P. who took the initial examinations.

interpretation of its provisions, a condition which Filmer notes with regret:

> To have nothing but the public faith of the present age is none of the best evidence, unless the universality of elder times do concur with these doctrines which ignorance in the times of darkness brought forth, and credulity in these days of light hath continued.[33]

The minor legal changes brought about by James, then, were important in laying down a pattern which helped to reinforce witch-fear; not: 'She wished me ill and my child died, therefore she is a witch', but: 'She has a mole on her cheek and keeps an ugly dog, and I must be careful because this is the description of a witch.' But this attitude was never enough for the law, which continued to cling to deed rather than belief as its province, and, very gradually, legal process freed itself from the heated misconceptions of those who feared themselves bewitched.

Several disastrous mistakes and discredited accusations by possessed children made the more thoughtful judges wary, removing them a little from the atmosphere of complete belief which vitiated evidence at the trials; James himself, while credulous in theory, was shrewd within the limitations of his beliefs, and judges as zealous as the *Daemonologie* seems to require were often disconcerted by a royal intervention to prove them asses. Judges who hanged nine witches on the accusation of a 'possessed' boy in 1616—a proceeding in no way strange according to James' book—must have been flabbergasted to be disgraced by the king after he had reviewed the case; he pronounced the boy a fraud.[34] Edward Fairfax, a man of some importance, was unable to get a conviction in the case of his bewitched children in 1621, despite a record as complete and detailed as that of the Throckmortons at Warboys.[35]

There seems to have been a slight lull in prosecutions during the reign of Charles I, though such cases as exist show that the more spectacular incidents of Continental witchcraft are becoming popularly known and forming the substance of popular accusations. The transformations and Sabbath of the case of the Lancashire witches in 1633-4,

---

[33] Sir Robert Filmer, *An Advertisement to the Jury-men of England touching Witches*, ed. cit., A2–A2^v.

[34] See John Nichols, *History and Antiquities of the County of Leicester* (London, 1795–1815), II, pt. ii, 471.

[35] Edward Fairfax. *A Discourse of Witchcraft As it was acted in the Family of Mr. Edward Fairfax of Fuystone in the County of York, in the year 1621*. MS. edited by R. Monckton Milnes, *Miscellanies of the Philobiblon Society*, Vol. V (London, 1858-9).

though apparently due to spite and imagination rather than real fear (at least in the beginning), display this clearly.[36]

During the troubled years of 1644–6 England for the first and last time suffered under the attentions of a professional witch-finder who was able to use torture in his examinations; the assizes had been suspended and trials were had before the justices of the peace. Matthew Hopkins and his co-worker John Stearne had the insight to make their services valued by charging highly for them. Their methods were simple; the accused was searched for the Devil's marks, which were usually found. She was then 'watched' or kept waking for a minimum of twenty-four hours, strapped naked and cross-legged to a stool or table, while her accusers waited for the appearance of her familiars, which could be any kind of animal, bird or insect. If this did not produce confession, the accused was walked or run up and down her cell by relays of helpers till she was exhausted.

The wildest utterances, solemnly recorded as evidence, were produced by this means; it is noteworthy that the Devil begins to figure in these confessions as a witch-master and lover in the Continental fashion. But with the resumption of assizes and regular juridical procedure, this horrible episode ended; not before one to two hundred people had been executed and as many arrested and tortured.[37]

After this date convictions become less and less frequent, though there are still a great many accusations, many of the wildest and most fantastic nature. It is curious to see the horrors of the Sabbath and the sexual relationship with devils appearing in the English countryside; yet they are quite without the shuddering horror at the heresy of the proceedings which rendered the Continental cases so lurid. Whenever, as with the cases of Puritan possession, the events are fired with genuine religious feeling, or with any of the human emotions which naturally express themselves in religious terms, the evidence touches something basic and frightening in man.

Without belief in an ordered mediaeval universe, genuinely threatened by an evil 'outside nature', the witch-belief trickles away into superstition and fairy-stories about the Black Man which cannot be

[36] There are several MS. sources for this. C. L'Estrange Ewen lists them and gives a cogent account of the case in *Witchcraft and Demonianism* (London, 1933), pp. 244–51.

[37] C. L'Estrange Ewen, *Witchcraft and Demonianism*, ed. cit., pp. 254–314, lists and summarises the many pamphlets dealing with the activities of Hopkins and Stearne.

taken seriously by the educated. People are frightened, but of inconvenience, not hell; yet they still believe in *maleficium* and this fear can be roused into ugliness.

But after the latter part of the seventeenth century, people are no longer so quick to invoke the protection of the law because the law is sceptical, and sometimes turns on those who handle a suspect roughly. Instead of taking witches to court, the bewitched gather neighbours to 'swim' them, occasions which turn into orgies of brutality and often end in death. As the subject drops out of the courts, it returns to the primitive, disconnected, state of magic and tradition and brutality from which it first arose. But it does not die. In times of great fear and uncertainty, it rises in a new shape—political or racist—and sweeps with it the wisest, the godliest and the most reasonable.

The Witch

The portrait of the English witch which emerges from pamphlets between 1566 and 1618 has nothing to do with the Continental one. The English witch is almost invariably a woman (more frequently than on the Continent), usually poor, though there are exceptions, and usually elderly. In most cases she has a bad reputation from the beginning—often for unchastity as well as malice—and this is transferred to her descendants. (One phenomenon of English witchcraft is the extent to which it remains localised, occurring over and over again in the same villages and even the same families; other areas appear to be free of any serious manifestation for centuries.)

The witch may know other witches, but quite often she acts alone; her motive is almost invariably revenge for supposed injury, and revenge takes the form of spoiled brewings and bakings, dying cattle, possession of children by spirits, illness and—increasingly as time passes—death. The Sabbath is almost entirely absent until mid-seventeenth century; a remarkably prosaic feast of mutton and beef in 1612 is our only suggestion of a true community of witches.[38]

The witch almost never sees the Devil, and if she should meet him, it is alone; and his guise is that of a vagrant or an unremarkable animal. Most characteristically, the witch is given or adopts an animal which becomes her familiar, and executes her evil wishes. Her 'pact' with it consists in giving it a living thing at intervals and allowing it to suck

[38] Thomas Potts, *The Wonderfull Discoverie of Witches in the Countie of Lancaster*, ed. cit.

her blood. 'Pact' and 'mark' become confused in the concept of an unnatural teat somewhere on the body from which the animal is regularly suckled on blood. These ideas of the animal familiar and the supernumary teat are so very nearly unique to England that they must be given further discussion.

The Familiar Spirit

'The familiar' is in itself a rather puzzling concept, quite unknown to the Bible and scarcely found on the Continent, where the witches might have particular demons as lovers, but in general met them only at the Sabbath or just before, when they took animal shape to carry the witch through the air to the place of meeting. Incubi and succubi were not 'kept' by those they molested, even when these persons assented to their embraces, though folk-lore has tales of permanent unions between man and spirit. Witches are sometimes found with toads, which they baptise and feed with a stolen Host, or which they use as ingredients for the gruesome ointments and powders by which they bring about death and disease. But these reptiles are part of their equipment for sorcery, not demon-pets.[39]

The Witch of Endor (I *Samuel* 28) was reputed to have a familiar spirit (Vulgate: pythonem), though the only supernatural being she materialised appeared as the dead worthy Samuel. Generations of theologians puzzled over this, generally deciding that she was the type of witch who prophesied by ventriloquy or the voice of a demon *within* her; with the aid of this she could also conjure up evil spirits. The woman of *Acts* 16: 16–18 was possessed by her spirit rather than the possessor of it, and apparently had no control over it at all; but in neither case does 'familiar spirit' appear to mean what it does in England, though the quotations were used as 'proof' that there were 'familiars'.

The magician in folk-lore and common gossip was sometimes supposed to have enough power to compel a devil to be his servant, suitably clad in human form; in the Faustian type of this story there is a nasty suggestion that the 'servant' is attending his master in order to watch over him and prevent him from repenting; he circles the soul that is to be his like a hungry dog circling an inaccessible bone.

And here we may note that, simplistic as it may sound, the supposed

[39] Bodin mentions one case of dog-familiars. See H. C. Lea, *Materials towards a History of Witchcraft*, ed. cit., p. 569.

size of the supernatural beings who attend on human lives is an indication of the force they are supposed to possess. The really sinister fairies, for instance, are at least full sized; others of uncertain benignity are like children and the diminutive ones can do nothing worse than pinching the unchaste. Demons controlled by art magicians are usually at least their equal in size, signifying the real tension and struggle of powers between them (for even the damned magician has at hand the weapon of repentance). Cornelius Agrippa's black dog, however damnable, was obviously well under control. (But here the legend starts from reality; Agrippa really had a much-indulged pet dog and Wierus, his pupil and a notable opponent of the witch-panic, says that he put the dog on a leash and led it away after his master's death.)[40]

Diminutive demons as portable property appear in England at a very early stage, and continue till well past the date of *The Alchemist*.[41] Flies or bees were the common form of these rather sinister mascots, and they were often supposed to ensure luck at cards. They were bought from someone who obviously took all the risk of procuring the demon and enclosing him in fly-form; this, plus their miniature size, made even the prescribed rite of feeding them with a drop of blood ludicrous rather than fearful. The man who was Master of Balliol between 1571 and 1580 cheated some countrymen by selling them flies supposed to guarantee success in play; the men trusted in these mascots and were ruined. The Master did not lose his position and does not seem to have suffered any of the penalties prescribed in the Act of 1563 for those who invoked spirits.[42]

The Continental witch owned nothing and controlled nothing. She had sold herself on emotional grounds and by a poor bargain, to beings over whom she had no power. She was the slave of the Devil and had become so because her desire to do evil drew her to him as the desire for good drew others to Christ. The typical form of the Devil here was that of the huge black man or the monstrous goat, creatures to whom she submitted humbly.

In England, the Devil gave a more practical bargain, a magic possession which did what was asked of it if properly maintained. On the Continent, the ability of the witch to transform herself and others into

---

[40] Johann Weyer (Wierus), *De Praestigiis Daemonum et Incantationibus ac Veneficiis* (Basle, 1563), Liber II, ca. V; 11, 12.

[41] Ben Jonson, *The Alchemist* (London, 1612).

[42] Ben Jonson, *Works*, ed. C. H. Herford and P. Simpson (Oxford, 1954), Vol. X, p. 62.

animals was the object of most heated argument; most authorities conceded that it was possible. In England at this date, despite its prevalence later, this belief occurs only once and receives little attention.[43] Again practical and prosaic, the English separated the animal from the witch and let it do her errands as a separate entity, perhaps because they *did* see old women with pets. The witch's pact was with the subsidiary, the minor devil who lived with her as cat or dog or toad, a being small enough to be in some degree in her control, yet large enough to demand some services.

The element of affection in the alliance, which, on the Continent, took the form of surrender and worship, and bestiality with demons was in England expressed by the cosy, slightly perverted relationship of a lonely and poverty-stricken woman to her pet animal. The witch fear expressed itself through something seen rather than postulated (however misinterpreted); the alliance involved commerce rather than feudal allegiance and the emotions surrounding it were not religious (though they drew strength from incidents involving religious controversy), but social and personal. People who denounced a witch did so not at all because of her heretical opinions, but because they thought she had offered them personal injury.

Possession

Another peculiarly English form of witchcraft was the sending of spirits to 'possess' and torment others, usually children. On the Continent this happened mainly in convents, for reasons easy enough to understand. The lurid case of the handsome priest Urbain Grandier, burned for bewitching the nuns of Loudun, exemplifies this well.[44] In England, where the nuns had been turned into the world, it was not nuns but children who were troubled and cried out on the witches who had sent their spirits to invade them.

This condition was extremely distressing to witness, even if we apply psychiatric rather than theological labels. The sudden emergence, in a docile and amenable child, of a personality which raves, screams, roars with laughter, utters dreadful blasphemies and cannot bear godly

---

[43] See *A Rehearsall both straung and true, of hainous and horrible actes . . . at winsore in the Countie of Barks . . .* (London, 1579).

[44] 1634. Rev. Montague Summers lists many French pamphlets dealing with this case in *The History of Witchcraft* (2nd edition New York, 1956), p. 341. See also Aldous Huxley, *The Devils of Loudun* (London, 1952).

utterances—or alternatively, withdraws into complete blankness—seems, even today, like the invasion of an alien being. In addition, the Elizabethan children suffered from frightening physical convulsions which seemed totally 'beyond nature', vomited strange substances and had the wildest of hallucinations. Various religious sects had different attitudes towards these phenomena.

Possession without the agency of a witch had occurred early among the Puritan sects and still survives among the ecstatic and evangelical cults. Publicity seems to make it more common; and cases begin to appear in England more and more frequently towards the end of the sixteenth century.

Catholics, secure in the rites of exorcism, declared themselves the True Church on the strength of their cures of possessed girls—cases which made a great impression on the heretical majority. Since their position was so dangerous already, they very wisely refrained from accusations of witchcraft in the courts.

Puritans contended furiously that miracles had ceased and that programmes of prayer and spiritual exercise, with no guarantee of success, were all that could legitimately be indulged in. Puritans and Catholics accused each other of fraud, pretended illness and pretended cure. But, perhaps feeling themselves at a disadvantage without the ritual of exorcism, Puritan clergymen took to questioning the invading spirits for information on the witches whose malice had caused them thus to attack the godly. At this point, leaders of the Church of England intervened roughly and decisively. Children were removed from their parents, whisked before bishops and subjected to considerable pressure to make them confess themselves fraudulent; some, at least, of those who did so seem to have been genuine hysterics and epileptics and not consciously to blame at all. But at least the development of the profession of witch-finder was delayed for more than half a century by these means.

Samuel Harsnett's unecclesiastically vigorous attacks on both Puritan and Catholic exorcists are highly entertaining reading.[45] His apparent scepticism is vividly displayed by the recurrent metaphors of acting and the stage which enliven his scornful accounts of famous cases. Yet it is noteworthy that, except for one remark about this 'silly book', he passes over the most notable case—that at Warboys—in silence. The

[45] Samuel Harsnett, *A Discovery of the fraudulent practises of John Darrell, Bacheler of Artes* ... (London, 1599); *A Declaration of egregious Popish Impostures* (London, 1603).

care and reasonableness displayed in the presentation of this case and the daunting number of witnesses seem to have left even him at a loss for an effective way of attack. [46] This more than any other was the book which fixed the unhappy tradition of Puritan witchcraft—a tradition still valid and unchanged at Salem in the seventeenth century.

Trickery

It may seem surprising that children should fake possession, as some undoubtedly did, to the point of allowing women to be executed for bewitching them. Yet many of their elders used fraud in supernatural matters, usually to improve their social or financial positions, though some highly ingenious fake miracles had been discovered at the dissolution of the monasteries—images with eyes movable by strings, for instance—and Scot recounts later examples of 'Popish tricks' with relish. [47] At the highest levels of society, there are Star Chamber records of quite fantastic swindles carried out for pecuniary advantage. [48] Women were frightened into second marriages by the 'ghosts' of dead husbands; disputed property was most ingeniously haunted by devils till it acquired an evil reputation. Most astonishing of all, many substantial citizens lost large amounts of money to gypsies and confidence tricksters because these promised to win for them the favour of the Queen of the fairies. The same story turns up many times in the pamphlets as well as in unimpeachable court records. [49] It seems that some of the jugglers and swindlers who had once pretended to familiarity with spirits (Thomas Ady described how some of them fixed stuffed vermin to small springs hooked into their clothes and called them 'familiars'), [50] became aware of their danger from the law of 5 Elizabeth

[46] *The most strange and admirable discoverie of the three Witches of Warboys, arraigned, convicted and executed at the last assises at Huntington* . . . (London, 1593).

[47] Reginald Scot, *Discovery of Witchcraft*, ed. cit., Bk. 7, Ch. 6.

[48] C. L'Estrange Ewen, *Witchcraft in the Star Chamber*.

[49] *The Brideling, Sadling and Ryding of a rich Churle in Hampshire, by the subtill practise of one Judeth Philips, a professed cunning woman, or Fortune teller* (London, 1595). For this case, see also *Historical MSS. Commission*, Hatfield House, Vol. V (1894), pp. 81–3. The trick used is basically the same as that in *The Alchemist*, III, 5, which seems to be based on another contemporary case of the same kind. Later but similar is *The severall Notorious and lewd Cousnages of John West, and Alice West, falsely called the king and Queene of Fayries* (London, 1613).

[50] Thomas Ady, *A Candle in the Dark* (London, 1655), F2ᵛ.

and hastily improved the supernatural company they kept (nobody, it seems, ever thought of legislating against the fairies).

Some of the less professional swindlers must often have slipped back and forth over the borderline of pretence, for it is the occupational hazard of the juggler and the mindreader to believe in his pretended powers. Orson Welles, interviewed in the *Observer*, April 1967, mentions the fortune-teller's dread of becoming a 'shut-eye'; he left such a job when he found himself developing unconscious, rather than conscious powers of deduction about his clients.

Welles' account casts some light on those cases in which facts apparently capable of a simple but discreditable explanation precipitate a confession of elaborate and evil witchcraft. In other words, what starts in trickery may end in belief, whether the person concerned is accuser or accused; it is not only victims who are credulous.

Emotional Factors in the Witch-belief

We have suggested that in England witch-belief developed from the ground up, as the result of popular fears stemming from the social and political situation, rather than as a response to an imposed pattern. There were several unique factors in the English situation which shaped this growth and the religious conditions will be discussed first.

In the light of hindsight we have come to regard very lightly the changes which brought about the establishment of the Church of England. It is worth trying to imagine what it must have been like to live through them. Henry VIII came to the throne in 1509, when the War of the Roses had been ended for less than 40 years; the rebellions of Buckingham in 1521 and the Maid of Kent in 1533—both encouraged by prophecies—revived terrible memories and traditions. Agricultural misery continually increased as 'the sheep ate up the men' and vagabondage became a serious problem.

The first of the Acts by which Henry, almost against his will, was to create the Church of England, came in 1532. The Acts of Succession and Supremacy in 1534 widened the split with Rome beyond healing and Henry began the long series of manœuvres which led the country step by step into a new and bewildering world.

During the next 30 years there were eight major religious changes requiring oaths from teachers, ministers and public officials. There were four total reversals of religious practice, enforced by law and by death-sentences. What must this have meant to those who lived through them?

There were many martyrs to conscience and many brave men who could temporise only so far, as Thomas More did; but these men were not typical. The historian Green has well remarked that, of all the heroes, the one who most took the English imagination was the pliant and vacillating Cranmer who, caught at last, signed one recantation after another without avail, then confessed with naked honesty at the end, '. . . the setting abroad of writings contrary to the truth . . . things written by my hand contrary to the truth which I thought in my heart, and written for fear of death, to save my life if it might be'.

In this fear most men swore and swore again, with a simple belief in authority, self-deceived, with mental reservations, or falsely. Many must have found themselves in the position of the turncoat below, who killed himself when the visitation of 1559 was at hand with one more change:

> This boy called Blind Tom was brought afore the said Doctor Williams the chancellor, and John Barker alias Taylor the registrar in the consistory by the south door in the nether end of the church. The officers in whose custody the boy remained, by commandment of the chancellor presented the poor boy before the judge.
>
> Then Dr. Williams examined him upon sundry articles magisterial and usual among the tormentors at that time [reign of Mary] as ye may find . . . in Mr. Foxe. And namely he urged the article of transubstantiation.
>
> *Williams* Dost you not believe that after the words of the consecration of the priest that there remaineth the very body of Christ?
>
> *Tom* No, that I do not.
>
> *Williams* Then you are an heretic and shalt be burnt. Who taught thee this heresy?
>
> *Tom* You, Mr. Chancellor.
>
> *Williams* Where, I pray thee?
>
> *Tom* When in yonder place (pointing with his hand and looking as it were toward the pulpit, standing upon the north side of the church).
>
> *Williams* When did I so teach thee?
>
> *Tom* When you preached there (naming the day) a sermon to all men as well as to me, upon the sacrament. You said the sacrament was to be received spiritually by faith, and not carnally and really as the papists have heretofore taught.
>
> *Williams* Then do as I have done, and you shalt live as I do, and escape burning.

Tom Though you can so easily dispense with your self, and mock
with God, the world and your conscience, I will not do so.
Williams Then God have mercy upon thee, for I will read the
condemnatory sentence.
Tom God's will be fulfilled!

Here the registrar stood up and said to the chancellor, 'Fie for
shame, man! Will ye read the sentence and condemn yourself?
Away, away! and substitute another to give sentence and judgment'.

Williams Mr. Registrar, I will obey the law and give sentence
myself according to mine office.

And so he read the sentence with an unhappy tongue and more
unhappy conscience.[51]

There is no more dangerous age than that in which such dilemmas
are common, and every man knows almost for certain that at some
point he will be forced to betray the beliefs that are most essential to
him. It is an age of frenzied revivalism, or of secularism, with night-
mares. Underneath all the splendours of the Elizabethan age and its
aggressive love of this world is a growing melancholy, an imbalance
that can topple into hysteria.

Part of the longing for the simple life, the golden age and lack of
choice, is beyond a mere literary convention. Shakespeare's plays are
full of set-pieces on the terrible responsibilities of power, the realisation
that any addition to one's scope for action involves also a diminution
of freedom; any choice involves acceptance but also rejection of possibilities. The political plays above all show how any compromise
demands further compromises, because experience is adhesive, and
changes the shape of one's intention. To uphold an oath taken doubt-
fully or against one's conscience involves one in dilemmas not foreseen
when the oath was taken. Part of the Elizabethan interest in words—
the puns, euphuisms, alliterations and double meanings—and in
'equivocations', shows an intense concern with the meaning of meanings, the numberless contradictory possibilities of experience contained
in a single word.

The Elizabethans, who must all at some date between reigns have
heard themselves classed as heretics, clung desperately to appearances
which they knew capable at any moment of turning into their opposites.
They were cynical about official professions of belief, yet flung

[51] Reminiscences of John Louthe in *Narratives of the Days of the Reformation*,
Camden Society Publications No. 77 (London 1859), pp. 18–22.

themselves desperately into drum-beating nationalism, into the new learning, or into superstition and half-crazed sectarianism. Formal religion compromised, bandied back and forth, had become a subject for argument rather than belief.

The new middle classes were frenetically class-conscious, extravagant and social-climbing to an extent that provoked jeers from all sides; their predominantly Protestant and Puritan bias rendered this inevitable. The independent new man, who insisted on reading his own Bible and arguing with his ministers, believed that social mobility was a positive virtue; that, far from God wishing him to know his place, God wished him to make his own way, and would materially bless the good man and help him to thrive. Success would not spoil Adam Smith; it would signify the triumph of the just and help him to improve the world for the faithful.

But such an attitude has its own secret terrors, particularly when feudalism is not far behind, and the great exempla of worldly success, like Wolsey and Thomas Cromwell, teach an ambiguous moral. These fears can be summed up in Jules Feiffer's cartoon of the successful man brooding in his office: *'Some day they'll come and take it all away'* . . . And such a man is harsh and suspicious towards 'them'—the havenots, the ones whom he has left behind in poverty, whom he credits with envy and jealousy. The very trials of life seem no longer the chastenings of God but devices of an enemy, human or demonic. Witchcraft enacted against him answered such a man's need for self-justification in his tribulations.

The illiterate, the poverty-stricken, the country-dwellers felt the same tides of change, but without the busyness of prosperity to console them. The answers had all been discredited, but their questions remained. Required observances of the Catholic Church had by their very existence defined a minimum standard for salvation and protection; the new church, by insisting on individual care of the conscience, placed a terrible burden of worry upon minds often ill-equipped to bear it.

The comfortable ritual with its magical, celibate priest was gone; familiar prayers were Englished and made strange. The Pope, who had encouraged the persecutions of Mary, made the impossible demand that Catholic sympathisers not only spurn the rites of the new church, but turn political traitor, one more excruciating dilemma which left many feeling deserted and betrayed in their time of greatest need. The Puritans were contentious and self-righteous; the new stop-gap priests were all too often greedy and unqualified, and the hungry sheep did not even know in which direction to look up.

In such a situation it was inevitable that superstition and magical thinking should return in full force. The forbidden Latin prayers became spells by which people strove to control their own fate; the unlearned flocked to those who could read the unimaginable future, or relieve their terrible anxieties—anxieties that took shape through the accustomed imagery of angels and devils, forgiveness and punishment. Nothing could be trusted and anything might be true. William Fulke inveighs against astrologers in a book of 1560, not only because their weather predictions led farmers to withhold grain in the expectation of scarcity, but because he believes they cause the spirit of terror and superstition of which he is conscious in the country:

> What—is it to be kept in science, how slowly and coldly the people in the last year, seduced by the foolish prophecy of Nostradamus, addressed themselves to set up the true worshipping of God and his religion? Good Lord, what trembling was there? What fear? What expectation? What horror? lest all things suddenly should be turned upside down, so that none almost of them that gave any credit to prognostications durst be bold to open their faith and religion which they bore in their hearts.
>
> Yea, this Nostradamus reigned here so like a tyrant with his sooth-sayings, that without the good luck of his prophecies it was thought that nothing could be brought to effect. What—shall I speak of the common people's voice? 'This day the Bishop of Rome must be driven out of the parliament'; 'To-morrow the Queen shall take upon her the name of Supreme Head'; 'After 20 days all things shall wax worse'; 'Such a day shall be the day of the Last Judgment' —that except the true preachers of God's holy word had sharply rebuked the people for crediting such vain prophecies, there should have been none end of fear and expectation.[52]

A fear 'lest all things suddenly should be turned upside down'. What could be more natural to a people who had seen a feudal system broken, an agricultural system disrupted, plague, civil war, and four wrenching, forcible changes in their most sacred beliefs? This is perhaps the very heart of the panic in which nothing is planned, where the theory is random and contradictory, and where the brutality is casual, personal

---

[52] William Fulke, *Antiprognosticon that is to saye, an Invective agaynst the vayne and unprofitable predictions of the Astrologians.* Translated by W. Painter (London, 1560).

and unsystematic. Why do men suffer? They suffer because of the Devil, because of their sins, but above all because of each other.

Perception and Metaphor

It is the peculiar power of religions to unify and maintain in unity the system of metaphors by which man brings to light and learns to deal with the intangible facts of his mental life and the obscurer facts of life itself. Metaphors of angels and devils can actually affect perception. When a long-standing religious system—like that of the Catholic Church in Elizabethan England—is shaken or destroyed, disturbance is expressed through the old metaphors, now outcropping violently and haphazardly to create new patterns. Frightened people see shadows in candle-light as unnatural animals; they translate dogs into devils seeking to destroy them and all their troubles are projected onto the outside world in the pictures they know, deprived of the system that made sense of these. Furthermore, the Elizabethans were none too clear about the distinction between things that merely looked like each other (by the principle of sympathy in nature, such things were bound to have affinity). William Fulke learnedly explains how a cloud that looks like a dragon is caused by inequalities of temperature in the air and tells the story of the metamorphosis of one:

> This dragon thus being caused, flieth along in the air, and some-time turneth to and fro if it meet with a cold cloud to beat it back, to the great terror of them that behold it, of whom some call(ed) it a fire drake, some say it is the Devil himself, and so make report to others.
>
> More than sixteen years ago, on May-day when many young folk went abroad early in the morning, I remember by six of the clock in the forenoon there was news come to London that the Devil the same morning was seen flying over the Thames. Afterward came word that he lighted at Stratford, and there was taken and set in the stocks, and that though he would fain have dissembled the matter by turning himself into the likeness of a man, yet was he known well enough by his cloven feet.
>
> I know some yet alive that went to see him and, returning, affirmed that he was indeed seen flying in the air, but was not taken prisoner. I remember also that some wished he had been shoot at with guns or shafts as he flew over the Thames.
>
> Thus do ignorant men judge of these things that they know not; as for this devil, I suppose it was a 'flying dragon' whereof we

speak, very fearful to look upon, as though he had life because he moveth, whereas he is nothing else but clouds and smoke. So mighty is God that he can fear his enemies with these and suchlike operations, whereof some examples may be found in holy scripture.[53]

In addition to differences of perception, there are always differences of description in other ages, and these turn usually upon the use of image. It is not always easy to define when a metaphor is a literary device and when it is to be accepted as in part 'solid' or descriptive fact. For instance, Strype describes a woman in 1581 who kept money entrusted to her, conveyed it out of the house and swore she never had it; she 'did bequeath herself to the Devil, both body and soul, if she had the money or ever saw it'. The money was found and she was sent to Bridewell and whipped. 'It was observable what she said then, that the Devil stood at her elbow in the Recorder's study, and willed her to deny it; but as soon as she was upon the cross to be punished, he gave her over.'[54]

There is no suggestion here that the woman's speech is regarded as more than a way of describing her mental state, though the Devil might have been considered to be providing the mental temptations and obduracy so rapidly cured by punishment. But had she been a suspected witch, this would have been taken with deadly literalness, and someone would probably have 'seen' her familiar, or noted that her witch-mark looked freshly sucked.

When the person is suspected, as in a Catholic suicide about this time, the vocabulary used imparts the idea of unlawful dealing: 'In her youth she was bred up in Sir Thomas More's family, in which place she learned idolatrous toys (I transcribe from the Recorder's letter) and usages in the night, so as thereby she was led by evil spirits sometimes to hang herself and sometimes to drown herself as she did at last. Some part of her lewd demeanour was in the exercise of *necromancy*—that is to say, in conferences and speeches had (as she thought) with dead bodies, being of her old acquaintance.'[55] In a Protestant, this pitiful senility would most probably have been

---

[53] William Fulke, *A Goodly Gallerye with a most pleasaunt Prospect into the garden of naturall contemplation, to behold the naturall causes of all kynde of Meteors* ... (London, 1563), B2–B2ᵛ.

[54] John Strype, *Annals of the Reformation*, ed. cit., Vol. III, Bk. 1, Ch. 6, pp. 63–4.

[55] Reference as above.

described in far less 'loaded' words. It is quite possible that literal mis-interpretation of the Biblical phrase 'She hath a devil' (signifying possession or, metaphorically, extreme wickedness) might have had something to do with the growth of the idea that a witch owned a devil.

One particular complication of vocabulary is caused by the deliber-ate attacks of the reformers on priests in the terms of conjuration (the Mass involved Latin, ceremonies, consecration and materialisation of substances; and so did conjuration). Many priests had been linked with plots to dethrone Elizabeth, and numbers of them had doubtless taken the routine step of consulting her nativity, and attempting a prognosti-cation of events concerned with the rebellion; the convenient vagueness of the witchcraft law made it quite possible to accuse priests for the crime of conjuration, a deliberate kind of smear campaign which could become serious if their skills could be made to seem a magical attack on Elizabeth.

About 1577 Edward Phaer, in a singularly nasty attempt to win pardon for coining by turning in all his old friends, shows the assimi-lation of 'mass matters and conjuration'. 'For *Magic*, I can find out as many that way. And if I might speak with my old companions (and many of them are in this town) I would hunt out a marvellous pack of them, with their books and relics. Yea, and with their art goeth many a filthy ceremony, as mass, sacrifice, and their service of the Devil. Also, my acquaintance, supposing me to be the same I was before, would disclose their minds unto me, whereby I should understand that which now my conscience and bounden duty would not permit me to conceal. . . .'[56] All these possibilities must be kept in mind when we consider an Elizabethan account of a witch-trial. Yet, given all these difficulties in entering into the minds of those we meet in these ac-counts, it is avoiding the main issue to refuse some speculation as to what may have happened in a given case; one cannot fall back on the comforting explanation of 'torture' when events in the English trials become too bizarre; and 'senility' or 'mental disturbance' will not work every time. Speculations in this area should be made by a doctor, a psychiatrist and a social scientist, working jointly. In their absence I shall be rash enough to make some suggestions, having checked their plausibility with specialists.

[56] John Strype, *Annals of the Reformation*, ed. cit., Bk. 2, Appendix, No. 11, pp. 114–15.

What really happened?

The overwhelming impression one carries away from the witch-pamphlets is one of consternation at the human predicament. Through these pages we come to know the desperation of lives played out in restricted surroundings, and to feel the helplessness of people before a succession of natural catastrophes which they did not in the least understand. Precious brewings and bakings are lost; treasured livestock suffer from inexplicable sicknesses; crippling diseases strike; and over and over again, children scream and suffer helplessly and die. There are very few literate people today who can enter into an existence in which one bears ten children and watches five of them die in infancy; but such an existence is at the basis of witch-belief.

The women who suffered these things were ill-nourished, overworked and almost continually pregnant and nursing. The profound mental effects caused by any of these states, the obsessions and mental peculiarities, are very much part of the story of witchcraft. Bessie Dunlop, in Scotland, first met the Devil as she stumbled on an errand, weeping from the pain and weakness of recent childbirth, and in terror that her husband's illness was mortal.[57] Similar circumstances exist for many of the women who accuse their neighbours and doubtless for many of those whose background we do not learn. Bitterness, resentment and pain that can no longer be discharged through familiar religious channels will almost inevitably be turned upon others; and in their delusions, such women were aided by the learned and by the religious terms in which they continued to think. Witchcraft is, after all, a reason for suffering and one which leaves a possibility of remedy.

The suspicion that certain diseases of people and cattle were not 'natural' was an easy one to make, since, even among doctors, there was little concept of specific disease. There were types and groups of disorders, and symptoms pointing to an imbalance of one humour or another, but not, in our terms, cancer, typhoid, tuberculosis or measles. (Plague was known to be infectious, but not quite in our sense; infection was in the environment rather than in people.)

Infectious diseases of animals were even less understood, and something like foot-and-mouth or anthrax appears to have been prevalent. Sheep suffer some unusually complicated disasters and sows lose their farrow for no apparent reason. Chickens, then as now, are fragile. The

[57] Robert Pitcairn, *Criminal Trials* (Edinburgh, 1833), Vol. I, pp. 49–58.

odd custom of unwitching one's livestock by burning one—usually
the last to sicken—may occasionally have had the effect of a primitive
form of quarantine, breaking a chain of infection.

Next to destruction of poultry and cattle, the most usual bewitch-
ments were of babies and young children, who are 'strangely taken',
afflicted with screaming and writhing, thrown into convulsions, or
quietly wasted away. Some of the violent and painful diseases that
produce death in a day or two sound like meningitis or pneumonia;
others, which are frightening and recurrent but not fatal, seem to be
fits, either epileptic or a result of bad diet. Even fifty years ago, it was
regarded as quite normal for a baby to have fits occasionally, particularly during teething.

A diet deficient in calcium can produce rickets, and also a nervous
irritability that predisposes one to convulsions. *The Birth of Mankind,*
a popular book for midwives (1545), suggests that children should be
nursed for two years, but says that one year is more common in
England. Among the poor, babies were often put out to nurse while
the mother went back to work, and there is a faint suggestion that
some of the poor infants who 'consumed away' were simply underfed
by ignorant and undernourished women.

Babies were weaned on 'pap', a sort of flour paste, and 'a bit of what
we eat ourselves, doctor'. Maslin, a very coarse bread, was a staple
of adult diet, and there is a hint that it was sometimes made with rye.
Bread containing rye actively reduces the calcium available in the diet,
so the children of the poor must often have suffered from a combination of calcium and protein deficiency, lack of vitamins (fruit was
available only in season and vegetables do not seem to have been much
eaten), excess of roughage and the insanitary habits that encourage
worms.

Babies were tightly swaddled when young, to keep their limbs
straight, and clothed in a version of coarse, heavy adult garments when
older; girl children, particularly, must often have been severely uncomfortable. Most of the infants do not seem to have been unduly
neglected (though tipping over the cradle and falling into the fire were
common accidents, often attributed to witchcraft); but there is not a
single mention of a sick baby receiving any kind of medical treatment
except 'unwitching'. Not even doctors knew how to treat them; they
got better or they died, on their own.

Older children suffered from many unspecified ailments, many of
which seem to have been regarded as routine. (For instance, tuber-

culosis must have been rife, yet it is not mentioned except in the form of 'consuming away'; but several times, as a most casual afterthought to the description of other symptoms, writers will note that the child also spat blood on occasion.) The most commonly noted symptoms are the oddest—a sort of generalised hysteria with tremors, rigidity and convulsions.

One manifestation of this, three times mentioned, is the turning of a hand backwards 'so that the back stood where the palm should be'. The witch does this by threats and is afterwards able to undo it. Unlike the shoulder or knee joint, the wrist is not easily dislocated, and this sounds impossible. However, one of the classic positions of tetany (a nervous instability sometimes brought on by lack of calcium, overbreathing, as in fright, and other factors) is *'main d'accoucheur'*—forearms stretched out horizontally and hands turned upward at right angles, palms towards the face. If one assumes this position from any normal angle, moving the hands last, it will be seen that there is a twist in the whole forearm from the elbow; but to a spectator it looks as though the rotation occurs in the wrist.

Many less specific manifestations (part emotional, part physiological) can be worked out in terms of tetany and general hysteria. Symptoms include muscle spasm, unnatural rigidity, temperature variation, distension of the stomach, flatulence and vomiting and obsessive tics. These things occur mostly between seven and seventeen, and quite often in epidemic form, when children near in age are in close contact. Sometimes they are the result of fright, sometimes they seem to begin deliberately and then become impossible to control.

Such episodes still occur today, particularly in schools. *The British Medical Journal* for 26 November 1966 has an article on an epidemic of 'overbreathing due to emotional tension', which produced alarming symptoms and collapse in over 100 pupils at one school. The outbreak was very carefully studied for possible physical causes, which were discounted, and 'It was considered that the epidemic was hysterical, that a previous polio epidemic had rendered the population emotionally vulnerable, and that a three-hour parade, producing 20 faintings on the day before the first outbreak, had been the specific trigger. The younger girls proved more susceptible, but disturbance was more severe and lasted longer in the older girls.' The authors of the article add in their final paragraph: 'This epidemic received a great deal of publicity as a "mysterious illness". It was initially both mysterious and frightening for the girls affected ... we do not wish to suggest that the whole episode was "nonsense". The girls were certainly not malingering: the original observers were not "fooled". The picture of acute hysterical collapse can be exceedingly alarming and, physically, extraordinarily convincing.'

A follow-up letter on 25 February 1967, adds the following: '. . . It is of interest to note that one of the "victims" applied for work at my factory a year later and volunteered at medical interview that she and some of her friends started to feign illness "as a joke", but then found that they could not control their subsequent actions or mental state.'

Odd and repellent as most of these manifestations seem, they are nearly all perfectly recognisable to any one who has taught in a strict and old-fashioned boarding-school. They are an unconscious way of escaping pressures without challenge to an overwhelming authority, a way of forcing people to stop organising one's life and take notice.

There is also, with the growing self-consciousness of pre-adolescence and adolescence itself, a deliberate experiment with one's physical powers. Simone de Beauvoir and Colette have both noticed the bizarre, obscene and senseless things done by quite normal children at this stage—sticking pins in their hands, drinking loathsome mixtures, and so on—and asserted that they are commoner than supposed. Adolescence is a peculiarly unpleasant stage of one's life to recall, because things one does then seem to have no relation to what one was or what one becomes, and most of us very carefully, if not quite completely, forget such episodes in our own lives and afterwards regard them as 'unnatural'.

The strict surveillance given to possessed children brings them to light, and also stresses other characteristics of growing-up children; for instance, the extent to which they are genuinely distressed by someone else's habits of eating, talking and behaving. The senses seem preternaturally acute, and the ability of some of the children to know with closed eyes when the witch is present may simply indicate an awareness of the woman's breathing, the sound of her clothes or her smell. Other stranger abilities to know things at a distance may point to an intensification of the senses which has not yet been reputably studied.

The late sixteenth and early seventeenth centuries appear to have been peculiarly difficult years for children. Considerable guilt and uncertainty in a compromised generation of parents led them to be abnormally strict and pious in the organisation of their children's lives. We may take from Aubrey a quotation showing the kind of forced respect which was demanded by the heads of families. One of the main reproaches of the Throckmorton children to the witch Mother Samuel—doubtless picked up from parents—was that she allowed her daughter to dominate her. The outrageous demands they made on their relatives in their fits, and the curious ambiguous affection they appear to have conceived for the old lady they tormented perhaps indicate that they too suffered from an excess of submissiveness, as they certainly suffered from an excess of family piety.

'From the time of Erasmus till about 20 years past, the learning was downright pedantry. The conversation and habits of those times were as stiff and starched as their bands and square beards; and Gravity was then taken for Wisdom. The very Doctors of those days were but old boys, when quibbles passed for wit, even in the pulpits.

The gentry and the citizens had little learning of any kind, and their way of breeding up their children was suitable to the rest; for whereas one's child should be one's nearest friend, and the time of growing-up should be most indulged, they were as severe to their children as their schoolmaster, and their schoolmasters as masters of the house of correction. The child perfectly loathed the sight of his parents, as the slave his torturer. Gentlemen of 30 or 40 years old, fit for any employment in the commonwealth were to stand like great mutes and fools bare headed before their parents; and the daughters (grown women) were to stand at the cupboard's side during the whole time of their mother's visit, unless (as the fashion was) 'twas desired that leave, forsooth, should be given to them to kneel upon cushions brought them by the servingman, after they had done sufficient penance standing.'[58]

When we come to the adults, the sicknesses are in general much less confusing. There are internal disorders, particularly among women; there are tumours and dropsies. There is a great deal of bone-ache, lameness and stiffness—all the signs of rheumatism and arthritis, together with fevers and a kind of 'flu'. The countryside at this date was exceedingly damp, particularly Essex, where most of the notable trials took place. (One parsonage not far from Chelmsford was known as Kill-priest, according to Aubrey; its neighbour lost seven priests in ten years through ague and fever.)[59] Huts of the poor were often earth-floored, and infested with vermin of all kinds (this explains the many

[58] *Aubrey's Brief Lives*, ed. Oliver Lawson Dick (Ann Arbor, 1949), pp. xxxii-xxxiii.
[59] Reference as above, p. 231.

visits from toad-familiars; toads and frogs were just naturally around). No one in winter can ever have been quite dry or quite warm except when sitting next to the fire; and the cradle was kept in the chimney-corner.

Even in substantial households it appears that parents and children and visitors shared not only the same bedroom but the available beds because of the cold. Childbirth was the occasion for family parties and visits, with everyone congregating around the mother and handling the new baby with most unsterile hands: 'rheums' must have been like tuberculosis, too common to mention.

This extreme togetherness and lack of privacy must also have had some responsibility for the hysterical afflictions which appear among adults too, mostly in the form of temporary paralysis or hallucination. By contrast, those old ladies finally left to live alone must have suffered abominably from loneliness; no wonder they made pets of anything they could persuade to inhabit the house; and no wonder they made nuisances of themselves with constant visits to borrow things.

This was another source of friction for everyone as well; village life seems to have been very much a matter of borrowing and barter, with few outright sales for money, and many quarrels and enmities grew up over loans refused, or things borrowed and not returned. And perhaps the worst problem of all came from the fact that people could not get away; once they had acquired a bad reputation through meanness or malice or misfortune, they were condemned to stay in the same village and play out the part the community had cast them in till they died; and then their children inherited that legacy.

England is a place of legend rather than myth. Unlike Scotland, Ireland and Wales, it is not a very good place for 'pure' folk-lorists in search of archetypes. Stories are named and dated and given a local habitation by their tellers; ghosts and devils cling closely to their home-ground. The nature of England's witch-delusions tends to follow this pattern for, over hundreds of years, these delusions stay in much the same places, and the same stories are told of dead and gone practitioners, and the same fear clings to their families.

The tension in some of these haunted villages of Essex must have been extremely high; and such a heated atmosphere is in itself the most certain guarantee that strange things will happen, or that people will look intently at familiar things in a light of fear and be suddenly overwhelmed by a sense of strangeness. When there is no clear sense of what is natural, this feeling is the very essence of 'being bewitched'; quite a lot of evidence in the pamphlets seems to stem from some such psychological experience.

It must also be remembered, on the practical level, that home-brewed beer was a staple item of diet for all.

Witches' Confessions

There does not seem any necessity to examine the delusions of self-confessed witches separately from those of their accusers; the same factors produced both. Some of the witches were undoubtedly senile or crazed; some were truly malicious, and it seems very likely that they might have carried out minor acts of magic (people still stick pins in wax images of enemies). Suppose chance then brought about the desired result? Witchcraft is, like the child's sense of omnipotence which leads him to feel guilty about mere wishes, a secret sense of power and superiority which can never really be tested or disproved.

If neighbours also attribute evil powers to a woman, she may easily begin to believe in them herself, and even to trade on them. If she is then arrested, and neighbours depose that her dog is a devil, the shock of seeing her relationship with what she thought was an animal 'turned upside down' may make her break down completely. She sees her life as others see it and confesses its unfamiliarity in their terms.

Although we have spoken mainly of witches who were poor or otherwise rejects of society, it must be remembered that there were others, like the well-to-do Nutters in the 1612 Lancashire case, who also confessed to deeds beyond nature and to service of the Devil. As time went on, and the panic fear of witches became acclimatised, social position ceased to be a protection against accusations of witchcraft, or against confession to it. It became one of the shapes which depression or mental upset took, one of the forms by which formless guilts and fears declared themselves.

That there was any reality behind the few stories of witch-conspiracy seems unlikely; though, given the fact that many modern ladies conduct séances or address themselves to the *ouija* board in their spare time, there may have been, even in the country, rather advanced parties at which people played supernatural games, without much belief in them, just as some of the poor witches seemed to think of their familiars as lucky mascots rather than anything else.

Anyone who could give a likely explanation to fit all the cases in these pamphlets would find himself with a key to all the 'extraordinary popular delusions' in history, and perhaps with a means of forestalling and preventing them. But, after all, this was the very key that the judges and the Inquisitors believed they held. We are not much further forward now heresy has turned into political difference, and man has taken from the Devil the power that the Devil took from God.

Laws and Punishments

Savage as the following Acts may sound, their application was limited and far from uniform—indeed, numerous prefaces to witch-pamphlets make impassioned appeals for the implementation of existing laws and a more aggressive attitude to the problem on the part of the public. There were brief spasms of intense persecution during periods of public anxiety; the last few years of Elizabeth and the first of James were dangerous for witches, and there was a brief and dreadful interlude during the 1640s, when regular courts were suspended and England had a self-appointed Witch-finder General. But on the average, four out of five of those accused were acquitted, or sentenced only to prison and pillory.

Most suspected witches were brought before Justices of the Peace, either at the Quarter Sessions, or informally. Examinations of the accused and testimony of the witnesses were recorded and certified to the travelling Justices of gaol delivery, who acted as judges at the Assizes held twice every year, where juries were sworn in a) to determine whether a case existed and b) to decide on the cases accepted.

Rules of evidence, as we shall see, were startlingly lax; the age of reason was supposed to be fourteen, but much younger children were accepted as key witnesses in these felony trials. Hearsay evidence was allowed, and the word of an honest witness who believed that a certain illness was sent by a certain person as a result of prior disagreement was accepted without question. Visions of witches by the bewitched were treated as circumstantial evidence; so was the account by one witch of what her familiar had told her of the doings of another witch! Enormous importance was attached to confession, and usually it was regarded as an absolute proof of guilt.

The familiar (or pet animal), the unnatural teat at which it was suckled, and the insensible marks given by the Devil were from the beginning regarded as damning physical evidence against the accused. Other indications of guilt which are sometimes used as 'proofs' are: inability to say the Lord's Prayer correctly in English, the swimming test, inability to weep in court, and the behaviour of the bewitched when confronted by the witch.

Most of the judges seem to have been confident that their office protected them from the malice of the arrested witches; Queen Elizabeth showed no personal fear of the magical fifth column. However, members of her government were desperately afraid of magical arts being exercised against her; magic, poisoning and Popish plots were all linked together in their minds as things to be guarded against with the utmost care and the State Papers record many examples of governmental interest in trials which *might* touch on the treasonable use of the black arts. Sometimes particularly important judges were directed to conduct quite minor trials if these seemed likely to deal with image-magic or attempts to foretell the future.

The penalty for felonious witchcraft or conjuration was hanging, unless these also involved treason (and much Catholic activity was punished as treason, to avoid the appearance of persecuting for religion). For treason the sentence ran '. . . ye shall be drawn through the open City of London upon hurdles to the place of execution, and there be hanged and let down alive, and your privy parts cut off, and your entrails taken out and burnt in your sight; then your head to be cut off and your body divided into four parts, to be disposed of at her Majesty's pleasure'. For petty treason (the murder of a husband by a wife, or of master or mistress by a servant), the sentence was burning alive, and a very few women who had killed husbands or employers by witchcraft were executed in this way. The memory of the Marian burnings for heresy was very much alive in Elizabeth's reign, and many people still had a confused idea that this was the appropriate penalty for a witch in England, as it was on the Continent.

But the ecclesiastical courts confined themselves to the examination of minor cases of sorcery and witchcraft only, sometimes in an apparent effort to forestall legal complaints which might create a panic. In most of the possession cases the possessed and the exorcisers were examined by bishops, in order to determine whether or not they were shamming, and the witches were left to the secular courts; frauds could be imprisoned and severely disciplined.

The secular punishments of pillory and prison were highly unpleasant and sometimes dangerous. In the pillory a prisoner stood on a raised platform with head and hands thrust through holes in a split board and acted as a kind of 'Aunt Sally' for fairgoers and disgruntled neighbours. Gaol could mean slow starvation if the gaoler was rapacious; not only privileges but necessities had to be bought, or begged from the public. Filth, cold and rats bred all kinds of disease, and there were frequent epidemics of typhus or 'gaol fever'. Furthermore, delivery from gaol at the end of a sentence was often unreasonably delayed. Without friends in the outside world, a prisoner could literally be forgotten by the law, and several records cease with unanswered petitions from gaol.

The Laws

A.D. 1542. 33 Hen. VIII, c. 8.[1]

The Bill against conjurations and witchcrafts and sorcery and enchantments.

Where divers and sundry persons unlawfully have devised and practised invocations and conjurations of spirits, pretending by such means to understand and get knowledge for their own lucre in what place treasure of gold and silver should or might be found or had, in the earth or other secret places, and also have used and occupied witchcrafts, enchantments and sorceries to the destruction of their neighbours' persons and goods; And for execution of their said false devises and practices have made or caused to be made divers images and pictures of men, women, children, angels or devils, beasts or fowls, and also have made crowns, sceptres, swords, rings, glasses and other things, and giving faith and credit to such fantastical practices have digged up and pulled down an infinite number of crosses within this realm, and taken upon them to declare and tell where things lost or stolen should be become; which things cannot be used and exercised but to the great offence of God's law, hurt and damage of the King's subjects, and loss of the souls of such offenders, to the great dishonour of God, infamy and disquietness of the realm: FOR REFORMATION whereof be it enacted by the King our sovereign lord with the assent of the Lords spiritual and temporal and the Commons in this present Parliament assembled and by authority of the same, that if any person or persons, after the first day of May next coming, use, devise, practise or exercise, or cause to be used, devised, practised or exercised, any invocations or conjurations of spirits, witchcrafts, enchantments, or sorceries, to the intent to get or find money or treasure, or to waste, consume or destroy any person in his body, members or goods, or to provoke any person to unlawful love, or for any other unlawful intent or purpose, or by occasion or colour of such things or any of them,

[1] *Statutes of the Realm*, Vol. iii, p. 837.

w—c

or for despite of Christ, or for lucre of money, dig up or pull down any cross or crosses, or by such invocations or conjurations of spirits, witchcrafts, enchantments, or sorcery, or any of them, take upon them to tell or declare where goods stolen or lost shall become, That then all and every such offence and offences, from the said first day of May next coming, shall be deemed accepted and adjudged felony; And that all and every person and persons offending as is abovesaid, their counsellors, abettors, and procurers, and every of them from the said first day of May shall be deemed, accepted, and adjudged a felon and felons; And the offender and offenders contrary to this Act, being thereof lawfully convict before such as shall have power and authority to hear and determine felonies, shall have and suffer such pains of death, loss and forfeitures of their lands, tenants, goods and chattels, as in cases of felony by the course of the common laws of this realm, And also shall lose privilege of clergy and sanctuary.

This law was repealed in 1547, by I Edw. VI, c. 12. and not replaced for 16 years. The Act of Elizabeth was introduced in 1559 but did not pass in both Houses till 1563.

A.D. 1563. 5 Eliz., c. 16.[2]
An Act against conjurations enchantments and witchcrafts.

Where at this present, there is no ordinary nor condign punishment provided against the practisers of the wicked offences of conjurations and invocations of evil spirits, and of sorceries, enchantments, charms and witchcrafts, the which offences by force of a statute made in the xxxiii year of the reign of the late King Henry the Eighth were made to be felony, and so continued until the said statute was repealed by the Act and Statute of Repeal made in the first year of the reign of the late King Edward the VIth; since the repeal whereof many fantastical and devilish persons have devised and practised invocations and conjurations of evil and wicked spirits, and have used and practised witchcrafts, enchantments, charms and sorceries, to the destruction of the persons and goods of their neighbours and other subjects of this realm, and for other lewd intents and purposes contrary to the laws of Almighty God, to the peril of their own souls, and to the great infamy and disquietness of this realm: FOR REFORMATION whereof be it enacted by the Queen's Majesty with the assent of the Lords spiritual and temporal and the Commons in this present Parliament assembled, and by authority of the same, That if any person or persons after the first

[2] *Statutes of the Realm*, Vol. iv, pt. 1, p. 446.

day of June next coming, use practise or exercise any invocations or conjurations of evil and wicked spirits, to or for any intent or purpose; or else if any person or persons after the said first day of June shall use practise or exercise any witchcraft, enchantment, charm, or sorcery, whereby any person shall happen to be killed or destroyed, that then as well every such offender or offenders in invocations or conjurations as is aforesaid, their counsellors and aiders, as also every such offender or offenders in witchcraft, enchantment, charm, or sorcery, whereby the death of any person doth ensue, their aiders and counsellors, being of either of the said offences lawfully convicted and attainted, shall suffer pains of death as a felon or felons, and shall lose the privilege and benefit of sanctuary and clergy: Saving to the wife of such person her title of dower, and also to the heir and successor of such person his or their titles of inheritance succession and other rights, as though no such attainder of the ancestor or predecessor had been had or made.

And further be it enacted by the authority aforesaid, That if any person or persons, after the said first day of June next coming, shall use, practise, or exercise any witchcraft, enchantment, charm, or sorcery, whereby any person shall happen to be wasted, consumed, or lamed in his or her body or member, or whereby any goods or chattels of any person shall be destroyed, wasted, or impaired, then every such offender or offenders, their counsellors and aiders, being thereof lawfully convicted, shall for his or their first offence or offences, suffer imprisonment by the space of one whole year, without bail or mainprise,* and once in every quarter of the said year, shall in some market town, upon the market day, or at such time as any fair shall be kept there, stand openly upon the pillory by the space of six hours and there shall openly confess his or her error and offence; and for the second offence, being as is aforesaid lawfully convicted or attainted, shall suffer death as a felon, and shall lose the privilege of clergy and sanctuary: saving to the wife [*as above*].

Provided always, That if the offender, in any of the cases aforesaid for which the pains of death shall ensue, shall happen to be a peer of this realm, then his trial therein to be had by his peers, as it is used in cases of felony or treason and not otherwise.

And further to the intent that all manner of practice, use, or exercise of witchcraft, enchantment, charm, or sorcery, should be from henceforth utterly avoided, abolished and taken away; Be it enacted by the authority of this present Parliament that if any person or persons shall from and after the said first day of June next coming, take upon him or them, by witchcraft, enchantment, charm, or sorcery, to tell or declare in what place any treasure of gold or silver should or might be found or had, in the earth or other secret places, or where goods or things lost or stolen should be found or become, or shall use or practise any sorcery, enchantment, charm, or witchcraft, to the intent to provoke any person to unlawful love, or to hurt or destroy any person in his or her body, member or goods; that then every such person or persons so offending, and being thereof lawfully convicted, shall for the said offence suffer imprisonment by the space of one whole year without bail or mainprise, and once in every quarter of the said year shall in some market town, upon the market day, or at such time as any fair shall be kept there, stand openly upon the pillory by the space of six hours, and there shall openly confess his or her error and offence; And if any person or persons, being once convicted of the same offences as is aforesaid, do eftsoons* perpetrate and commit the like offence, that then every such offender being thereof the second time convicted as is aforesaid, shall forfeit unto the Queen's Majesty, her heirs and successors, all his goods and chattels and suffer imprisonment during life.

One application of this Act was developed and rendered explicit in Clause 5 of a later statute, reprinted below.

A.D. 1580–1. 23 Eliz., c. 2.[3]

An Act against seditious words and rumours uttered against the Queen's most excellent Majesty.

. . . And for that divers persons wickedly disposed, and forgetting their duty and allegiance, have of late not only wished her Majesty's death, but also by divers means practised and sought to know how long her Highness should live, and who should reign after her decease, and what changes and alterations should thereby happen; To the intent that such mischiefs and inconveniences as may thereby grow in the commonweal, to the great disturbance of the same, may be cut off and prevented; Be it also enacted by the authority aforesaid, That if any person or persons, of what estate, condition, or degree soever he or they be, at any time, after the end of the said forty days, and during the life of our said sovereign lady the Queen's Majesty that now is, either within her Highness's dominions or without, shall by setting or erecting of any figure or figures, or by casting of nativities, or by calculation, or by any prophesying, witchcraft, conjurations, or other like unlawfull means whatsoever, seek to know, and shall set forth by express words, deeds, or writings, how long her Majesty shall live or continue, or who shall

---

[3] *Statutes of the Realm*, Vol. iv, pt. i, p. 659.

reign as King or Queen of this realm of England after her Highness' decease, or else shall advisedly and with a malicious intent against her Highness, utter any manner of direct prophecies to any such intent or purpose, or shall maliciously by any words, writing, or printing, wish, will, or desire the death or deprivation of our sovereign lady the Queen's Majesty (that now is) or any thing directly to the same effect, That then every such offence shall be felony, and every offender and offenders therein, and also all his or their aiders procurers and abettors in or to the said offences, shall be judged as felons and shall suffer pains of death and [forfeit] as in case of felony is used, without any benefit of clergy or sanctuary.

A general pardon in the same year did *not* include offences of 'invocations conjurations witchcrafts sorceries enchantments and charms'.

A.D. 1604. 1 Jac. I, c. 12.[4]

An Act against conjuration witchcraft and dealing with evil and wicked spirits.

Be it enacted by the King our sovereign Lord the Lords spiritual and temporal and the Commons in this present Parliament assembled, and by the authority of the same, That the Statute made in the fifth year of the reign of our late sovereign lady of most famous and happy memory Queen Elizabeth, intituled An Act against conjurations enchantments and witchcrafts, be from the Feast of St. Michael the Archangel next coming, for and concerning all offences to be committed after the same Feast, utterly repealed.

And for the better restraining the said offences, and more severe punishing the same, be it further enacted by the authority aforesaid, That if any person or persons, after the said Feast of St. Michael the Archangel next coming, shall use practise or exercise any invocation or conjuration of any evil and wicked spirit, or shall consult, covenant with, entertain, employ, feed, or reward any evil and wicked spirit to or for any intent or purpose; or take up any dead man, woman, or child out of his, her, or their grave, or any other place where the dead body resteth, or the skin, bone, or any other part of any dead person, to be employed or used in any manner of witchcraft, sorcery, charm, or enchantment; or shall use, practise, or exercise any witchcraft, enchantment, charm, or sorcery, whereby any person shall be killed, destroyed, wasted, consumed, pined, or lamed in his or her body, or any part thereof; that then every such

---

[4] *Statutes of the Realm*, Vol. iv, pt. 2, p. 1028.

offender or offenders, their aiders abetters and counsellors, being of any the said offences duly and lawfully convicted and attainted, shall suffer pains of death as a felon or felons, and shall lose the privilege and benefit of clergy and sanctuary.

And further, to the intent that all manner of practise, use, or exercise of witchcraft, enchantment, charm, or sorcery, should be from henceforth utterly avoided, abolished and taken away, Be it enacted by the authority of this present Parliament, That if any person or persons shall, from and after the said Feast of St. Michael the Archangel next coming, take upon him or them by witchcraft, enchantment, charm, or sorcery, to tell or declare in what place any treasure of gold or silver should or might be found or had, in the earth or other secret places, or where goods or things lost or stolen should be found or become; and to the intent to provoke any person to unlawful love, or where any chattel or goods of any person shall be destroyed wasted or impaired, or to hurt or destroy any person in his or her body, although the same be not effected and done; that then all and every such person and persons so offending, and being thereof lawfully convicted, shall for the said offence suffer imprisonment by the space of one whole year, without bail or mainprise,* and once in every quarter of the said year, shall in some market town, upon the market day, or at such time as any fair shall be kept there, stand openly upon the pillory by the space of six hours, and there shall openly confess his or her error and offence; And if any person or persons being once convicted of the same offence as is aforesaid, do eftsoons* perpetrate and commit the like offence, that then every such offender, being of any the said offences the second time lawfully and duly convicted and attainted as is aforesaid, shall suffer pains of death as a felon or felons, and shall lose the benefit and privilege of clergy and sanctuary: Saving to the wife of such person as shall offend in any thing contrary to this Act, her title of dower; and also to the heir and successor of every such person, his or their titles of inheritance, succession and other rights, as though no such attainder of the ancestor or predecessor had been made; Provided always, That if the offender in any of the cases aforesaid shall happen to be a peer of the realm, then his trial therein to be had by his peers, as it is used in cases of felony or treason and not otherwise.

II Early Days

Fault in the Stars

A short treatise declaringe the detestable wickednesse of magicall sciences, as Necromancie, Conjurations of spirites, Curiouse Astrologie and suche lyke. Made by Francis Coxe. London, [1561]

Francis Coxe was a man of considerable resourcefulness, and a perfect example of the kind of urban magician aimed at in the laws of Henry and Elizabeth quoted above. He lived by astrology, assisting his skill by conjurations; both these practices led him inevitably to involvement with the shabby underworld of Elizabethan politics and family rivalries.

Arrested for some kind of complicity in an obscure plot to poison Lady St. Loe (later 'Bess of Hardwick'), he was convicted of conjuration, and stood in the pillory on 15 June 1561. Not only did he take the required oath of abjuration, but he improved the occasion by publishing a very handsome broadside, still extant, titled *The unfained retractation* [sic] *of Frauncis Coxe*, and containing a confession of 'sinistral and divelysh artes'.

Later in the year, he capitalised on his own notoriety (but safely) by publishing the 'short treatise' from which extracts are reprinted below. Much of this is cribbed from William Fulke's *Antiprognosticon* (1560) but there are some lively passages of personal comment and illustration, where he speaks of the art of conjuration with first-hand knowledge.

This orgy of repentance does not seem to have damped his spirits unduly, for five years later he is back at his old trade with *A Prognostication for 1566*. Like many of his fellow Elizabethans, Francis had a superb talent for turning the vicissitudes of existence to his own advantage, and a large-minded disdain for consistency.

It is interesting to compare the fate of Francis Coxe with that of John Walsh, whose interrogation is printed next. Francis was picked up by the authorities even before there was a civil law in force to convict him; John, a country wise man, does not seem to have been tried, though his actual conjuring practices were very like those described by Francis.

[Of astrologers and fortune-tellers] . . . The God of Gods, Who suffereth no good deed to be unrewarded, no wicked offence unpunished—which hath said heaven and earth shall perish, but His word shall endure—hath not only manifestly in divers and sundry places of the scriptures forbidden the use and exercise of such curious sciences, but also hath appointed sharp punishment to the users thereof; that is, no less than death.

This godly and wholesome law was in time past executed within this realm, by the terror whereof many were feared from these practices. But now, whilst this law for lack of execution hath lain asleep, and the offenders nothing punished, it was in such sort increased that it was made a very handicraft, so that many lived thereby—yea, and thought they did as honestly get and gather their substance as he which daily sweat for the same. . . .[1]

. . . For the stars and skies are not sufficient for their future prediction, but they must adjoin thereunto most detestable parts or society with spirits. Which thing, when they go about and would have anything brought to effect, they do it by one of these 2 means: either, besides the horrible and grievous blasphemies they commit in their conjurations, they must fall to some composition with the Devil, that is, to promise him for his service he will abstain from wines, or some certain meats, or drinks.

As I myself knew a priest not far from a town called Bridgewater which, as it is well known in the country, was a great magician; in all his lifetime after he once began these practices, he never would eat bread, but instead thereof did always eat cheese, which thing, as he confessed divers times, he did because it was so concluded between him and the spirit which served him, for at what time he did eat bread he should no longer live. Yea, he would not blush to say that after a few years he should die, and that the Devil for his pains that he took with him should have in recompense his soul. . . .[2]

The second way, which is as evil as the first, or rather worse, is thus: for when the spirit is once come before the circle, he forthwith demandeth the exorcist a sacrifice, which most commonly is a piece of wax consecrated or hallowed after their own order (for they have certain books called 'books of consecration'); or else it is a chicken, a lapwing, or some living creature which, when he hath received, then doth he fulfil the mind of the exorcist, for unless he hath it, he will neither do nor speak anything.

Of this testifieth Bacon in his book of Necromancy, where he telleth also this story. After so long time travelled in these sciences, at last [he] joined himself with a Turk, which was most excellently seen therein and, long conferring together, they went about to call a certain she-devil named Ægippia, which spirit would by no means make them answer to any their demands. Whereupon Bacon, which knew that nothing could be done without sacrifice, causeth the Turk to be baptised and, after his baptism, they both entered the circle and called the

[1] A5v–A6.   [2] A7v–A8.

spirit which, when she came, for all their conjurations, she would not speak; until the Turk, by the advice and counsel of Bacon, pricking one of his fingers with a knife, took the blood, spread it on a piece of bread, and so cast the same to the spirit, which weepeth and washeth the same with her tears, and so eateth it and, that eaten, she maketh them direct answers to their demands. . . .[3]

I mind not here to speak of the trumpery which they have in this their work, as hallowed chalk, water and palm, circle, pentacles and plates used for defence, crown, sword and sceptre as a token of power, fine oils and powders to make fumigations; of their tedious fasts, washings and shavings, of the consecration of their invocations, constructions, ligations [libations?] maledictions, and other their foresaid instruments, wherein is contained such horrible blasphemies as my heart quaketh to think thereon. But even as ye see their beginning is most detestable, so is their ends according to the same. For Almighty God of His justice can neither leave the work-master, neither yet him that seeketh to any such for help unpunished. For as well deserveth he execution that seeketh to them as they themselves. . . .[4]

[3] A8ᵛ–B.   [4] Bᵛ–B2.

Witches and Fairies

The Examination of John Walsh, before Maister Thomas Williams, Commissary to the Reverend father in God William bishop of Excester, upon certayne Interrogatories touchyng Wytchcrafte and Sorcerye, in the presence of divers gentlemen and others, the XX of August, 1566.

This blackletter pamphlet was printed on 23 Dec. 1566, and deals with the records of an ecclesiastical examination, not a secular trial; the sequel is not known. All the most primitive elements of Elizabethan magic co-exist here—black witches, white witches, fairies, spirit-worship, magic herbs—and all the new pressures are present too. There is a bishop's commissary eager to classify John's spirits, a printer with Continental stories about conjuring popes, a constable who confiscates the magic book, and the 'scientific' habit of mind which suspects John's cures of being unnatural because John does not know the medical theory of his day.

The running title calls John a sorcerer, but under the secular law of 1563 he would certainly have qualified as a conjurer, guilty of invoking spirits. John remains totally unperturbed and quite confident in his reputation as a healer. Obviously it never crosses his mind that his activities could be classed with those of the 'hurting witches'; in his own eyes he is a professional, with an accepted place in the community, and in all the trials to follow, this attitude to the 'healing witch' is never quite overlaid by terror or instruction.

The Printer to the Christian Reader

Here hast thou, gentle reader, the examination of John Walsh of Netherbury in Dorsetshire, touching sorcery and witchcraft, which he learned (as hereafter is shewed) of a certain priest named Sir Robert of Drayton.[1] Wherein thou mayest see the fruits of Papists and Papistry, and their ill exercises of their idle lives, which hath been no small hurt to all commonweals. For hereby not only the simple people have been falsely seduced and superstitiously led, but all estates have been sore grieved and troubled by these their practices of sorcery and witchcraft.

It would be tedious to show but a few histories of their devilish practices, and too, too horrible facts* in murders and other mischiefs;

[1] Probably Drayton in Somerset.

Wizard performing magical acts
Newes from Scotland 1591–2

which not only the fat belly-fed monks, flattering friars, and idle lusty priests practised and used, but also the holy fathers themselves, popes, cardinals and bishops, were chiefly and wholly given to the study and exercise of these most wicked and devilish sciences, and by these means did work to come to the papal seat, high dignities, and great wealth. Which was, as the histories declare, with the murdering and poisoning privily one of another.

As first Pope Alexander the sixth, having society with wicked spirits and devils gave himself body and soul unto them, upon condition he might attain to the pope's seat and dignity, which they promised him and fulfilled, but he enjoyed it not long, contrary to his expectation. For he, being privily conveyed into a chamber in a certain place called Mount Cavillus, and their questioning with his demon how long he should reign pope, was answered that he should reign 11 and 8, which this holy father understood to be so many years; but he was deceived.

For after he had reigned pope 11 years and 8 months, this devil would no longer be without his prey, but straight came to the pope's court decked like a courtier, and at the pope's chamber door did knock very loudly, saying that he must needs speak with his Fatherhood. The door being opened, he came and spake with the pope, all others being bid to avoid.*

But they were so earnestly talking together that many did rightly conject* that they were at contention. For the pope stoutly affirmed his time not to be expired 'for,' said he, 'I had promised me 19 years (for 11 and 8 is 19) and of these 19 years I have reigned but 11 years and 8 months.' But this courtier-like devil replied and said that he mistook his words 'for I said not' said he, '19 years, but I meant 11 years and 8 months, and therefore now thou must needs die.' Whereat the pope being abashed fell to entreating, but all was in vain.

For as soon as this devil was gone, the soul of this pope departed miserably from his body with horrible cries, fearful groanings and deadly bewailings. In this sort died this horrible sorcerer, as sayeth Hieronimus Marius[2] in his work entitled *Eusebius Captivus*; in which work the history of this wicked Pope Alexander is very lively set forth, both as touching his wicked living and horrible facts, whose terrible end may be an example to all sorcerers, conjurors, and witches.

Like unto him was Pope Gregory 7, otherwise called Hellybrand (Hildebrand, I should say), who was also a great sorcerer and nigromancer,* as Benno[3] the cardinal doth declare in his work of this Gregory's life; saying that he also had a familiar spirit whereby he wrought many mischiefs in the commonweal of Rome, as well for the satisfying of his fleshly and beastly lust as also for to increase his riches and dignity.

Platina[4] also writeth the like of Pope John 8, Pope Sylvester, Pope Benedict 8, with divers others which were better practised in these devilish sciences than in godly divinity.

Much like to these was Pope Paul the third who, as Sleidan[5] declareth, exercised sorcery and witchcraft, and thereby committed 2 horrible murders, and poisoned his mother and nephew, that he might enjoy

[2] Hieronymus Massarius, *Eusebius Captivus*, Basle (1553?). One of two editions in the British Museum calls him Hieronymus Marius.

[3] St. Benno, 1010–1106.

[4] Bartholomaeus Sacchi de Platina, author of an extremely popular work on the Lives of the Popes (Venice 1479).

[5] Johannes Sleidanus, 1505–56, annalist of the Protestant Reformation.

his inheritance the sooner. He poisoned also his own sister's husband, that he more freelier might have her at his wicked commandment.

Pope Clement the 8 was also of this fraternity, as in the Commentaries upon the Articles of the Doctors of Paris is declared, where his style is thus set forth: that he was a bastard, empoisoner, homicide, bawd, simoniac,* sodomite, perjurer, whoremaster, necromancer, church robber, and a practiser of all kinds of wickedness.

These, with a great many more of that abominable sea of Rome, were thus occupied, whose ends were most terrible, as their lives were most wicked. And these faculties their inferior sort (as monks, friars and priests) also used, and would teach the same witchcrafts and sorceries to such men and women as they had committed evil with; as of late was confessed of a woman which used witchcraft and sorcery, that she learned the same of a priest whose harlot she had been many a year.

I exhort all men therefore to flee from them and these devilish practises as from devils incarnate, lest in following them with living here pleasantly a little while, they be tormented with them in hell perpetually. Which God for His Christ's sake withdraw and let* now and ever. Amen.

Finis

The Examination of John Walsh of Dorsetshire, Touching Witchcraft and Sorcery

The Tuesday being the 20 day of August 1566, there was examined before Master Thomas Williams (commissary to the reverend father in God William, Bishop of Exeter) one John Walsh, upon certain interrogatories touching witchcraft, in the house of Master Thomas Sinkeler, keeper of the Sheriff's ward, in the presence of John Butler and Robert Buller, gentlemen, William Blachford and John Bordfield.

He being first demanded of his habitation, he said that he dwelt in a parish called Netherbury in Dorsetshire.

Secondly, being asked whether he were ever Sir Robert Drayton's man, he said that he was retaining unto him by the space of 7 years.

Thirdly, being demanded whether he did practise any physic or surgery, he said that he doth practise both for the tisick* and the agues*, and that he hath practised this physic by the space of these 5 years, since his master Sir Robert Drayton died.

Fourthly, being demanded of whom he learned his physic and surgery, he answered that he learned it of his master Sir Robert Drayton.

Fifthly, being demanded whether he doth it by art, naturally, or else by any other secret or privy means, he answered that he useth his physic or surgery by art, naturally practised by him as he saith, and not by any other ill or secret means. And yet he being demanded whether he knew the natural operation of the herbs, as whether they were hot or cold,[6] and in what degree they were hot or cold, he answered 'he could not tell'.

Sixthly, he being demanded whether he had a familiar or not, he answered and denied utterly that he had none about him, neither in any other place of this world, either above the ground, or under the ground, either in any place secret or open.

Seventhly, he being demanded how he knoweth when any man is bewitched, he saith that he knew it partly by the fairies, and saith that there be 3 kinds of fairies, white, green and black,[7] which, when he is disposed to use he speaketh with them upon hills whereas there is great heaps of earth,[8] as namely in Dorsetshire. And between the hours of 12 and one at noon, or at midnight[9] he useth them, whereof, he saith, the black fairies be the worst.

Also he saith that he had a book of his said master which had great

[6] The four elements of the universe and the four humours in man were made out of various combinations of four qualities, hot, cold, moist and dry. The predominant qualities of various herbs could be used to redress the balance of qualities in man, when that balance was disturbed by sickness, so the classification of herbs was essential knowledge for a physician.

[7] The question of fairy colour is an exceedingly complex and mysterious subject which cannot be discussed here. The colours most frequently mentioned at this date are white or gray, green, black and red (blue does occur). Such a colour-scheme could fit into a classification of elemental spirits such as Cornelius Agrippa describes—air, water, earth and fire; earth spirits are usually described as the most malicious and dangerous, and black would be suitable to them.

[8] Netherbury is not many miles distant from an area full of tumuli and barrows, or burial mounds ('heaps of earth', often 'upon hills'). Maiden Castle, with its history of battles dating back to prehistoric times, is less than thirty miles away. Not only did those who died violently haunt the place of their death, but Lewis Spence, in *British Fairy Origins*, made out an excellent case for the idea that the fairies are connected with ancestor-worship and the spirits of the dead, half-helpful and half sinister when they impinge on the human world.

[9] Mid-day, when shadows vanish and the rising sun begins to sink, is traditionally a 'time out of time' when demons may have power. (There is even a mid-day demon, Meridiana.) Midnight is similarly a transitional moment when worlds may mingle, and humans must be on their guard; among the gypsies, darkness and the precise moment of noon belong to the vampire dead (*The Gypsies*, Jean-Paul Clébert, 1961, trans. Charles Duff, 1963, for Vista Books, London).

circles[10] in it, wherein he would set two wax candles across of virgin wax, to raise the familiar spirit, of whom he would then ask for anything stolen—who did it, and where the thing stolen was left; and thereby did know, and also by the fairies he knoweth who be bewitched.

Eighthly, he being demanded whether he had ever any familiar[11] or no, he saith that he had one of his said master. Which familiar (after his book of circles was taken from him by one Robert Baber of Crewkerne then being constable, in the year 1565) he could never do anything touching his familiar nor the use thereof, but his familiar did then depart from him and will never come to him again, as he saith. And further he saith upon his oath, that his familiar would sometime come unto him like a gray-blackish culver,* and sometime like a brended* dog, and sometime like a man in all proportions, saving that he had cloven feet.

Ninthly, he being demanded how long he had the use of the familiar, he said 'one year by his said master's life and 4 years after his death'. And when he would call him for a horse stolen, or for any other matter wherein he would use him, he saith he must give him some living thing, as a chicken, a cat or a dog; and further he saith he must give him two living things once a year. And at the first time when he had the spirit, his said master did cause him to deliver him one drop of his blood, which blood the spirit did take away upon his paw.[12]

Tenthly, he saith that when the familiar should do anything at his commandment, in going any errand, he would not go except first two wax candles of virgin wax should first have been laid across upon the circle with a little frankincense and St. John's wort,[13] and once lighted, and so put out again; which frankincense must be laid then at every end of the candle[s] (as he saith, across), and also a little frankincense with St. John's wort burned upon the ground or ever the familiar

[10] Since this is overtly an anti-Catholic pamphlet, we may feel a little suspicious of the conjuring taught to John by his Catholic master, especially as he regards it as secondary in importance to the fairies. Many mathematical books 'which had great circles' were destroyed by zealous Reformers, who thought they were conjuring manuals. Queries 7 to 10 elicit suspiciously Continental-sounding material—which may, of course, come from Sir Robert rather than the questioner.

[11] This is not a witch's familiar, but a conjurer's; it comes only in response to ceremonies, and then in differing shapes.

[12] Clear instance of pact.

[13] In folk-lore St. John's wort drives away demons, and it was generally used for its protective qualities.

would go, and that would force him to go the message and return again at the hour appointed.

Eleventhly, he being asked whether they that do good to such as are bewitched cannot also do hurt if they list;* whereto he answered, he that doth hurt can never heal again any man, nor can at any time do good. Howbeit, he saith that he which hath but the gift of healing may do hurt if he list, but his gift of healing can never return again to any other person's use.

Twelfthly, he being demanded whether that any of the three kinds of fairies, when they did hurt, did it of their own malignity or of the provocation of any wicked man; he answered that they do hurt of their own malignity and not provoked by any man, and that they have power upon no man but upon such as only do want faith, which is the cause why they have power more of some persons than of any others.

Furthermore, he being demanded to what end the familiar did serve them? he answered that he serveth for no purpose but to search out things theft-stolen, and for no other purpose at all.

He being further demanded to what end the spirits in the likeness of toads, and the pictures of man or woman made in wax or clay do serve? he said that pictures made in wax will cause the party for whom it is made to continue sick two whole years, because it will be two whole years ere the wax will be consumed. And as for the pictures of clay, their confection is after this manner: They use to take the earth of a new-made grave, the rib bone of a man or woman burned to ashes (if it be for a woman, they take the bone of a woman, if for a man, the bone of a man), and a black spider, with an inner pith of an elder, tempered all in water,[14] in the which water the said toads must first be washed. And after all ceremonies ended, they put a prick (that is, a pin or a thorn) in any member where they would have the party grieved; and if the said prick be put to the heart, the party dieth within nine days. Which image they bury[15] in the most moistest place they can find.

And as touching the using of the toads, the which he saith have several names: some they call Great Browning, or Little Browning, or Bon, Great Tom Twit,[16] or Little Tom Twit, with other like names:

[14] These are all ingredients of traditional magic or sorcery.
[15] The text 'burne' seems unlikely, considering the rest of this paragraph, and query 13.
[16] Probably 'Tom Tit'.

which toads being called, the witches strike with 2 withy spurs* on both sides of the head and saith to the spirit their Pater noster backward, beginning at the end of the Pater noster (but they will never say their Creed). And when he is stricken, they command the toad to hurt such a man or woman as he[17] would have hurted.

Whereto if he swell, he will go where he is appointed, either to the dairy, brewhouse, or to the dry kill* of malt, or to the cattle in the field, to the stable, to the sheepfold, or to any other like places, and so return again to his place. The bodies of men or women be hurt by the images before named, and men's goods and chattels* be hurt by the toads in commanding and using them as aforesaid, as he saith. And if the toad called forth as aforesaid do not swell, then will the witch that useth them call forth another to do the act, which if he do not, then will they spy another time when they may cause the party to be found lacking faith, or else to be more void of grace, where he or they may be hurt. Furthermore he saith, that whoso doth once a day say the Lord's prayer and his Creed in perfect charity, the witch shall have no power on his body or goods for that day.[18]

13. He being demanded whether that those which do heal men or women being hurted by witches, can find out those images under ground wherewith they were tormented? he affirmeth they can.

And 14, he being demanded whether he himself either hath or had at any time any such toad, or that ever he made any such images to hurt man, woman or child? he affirmeth by the oath which he hath taken, that he never had such toads, or ever made such images.

And 15. he being demanded whether that ever he did any hurt to man, woman or child, or to their goods or chattels? he saith by the oath that he hath taken, that he never did any such hurt either in body or goods.

[17] he = the sender of the toad.

[18] Early Catholic theologians believed that the Devil was easily repelled by simple observances and a sound faith. After the fifteenth century, experience led them to conclude that 'by the permission of God' anyone might be afflicted.

Witches at Chelmsford

The examination and confession of certaine Wytches at Chensforde in the Countie of Essex before the Quenes majesties Judges, the XXVI daye of July Anno 1566.

This unique blackletter pamphlet was printed in three parts dated, 13 August, 13 August, 23 August 1566, and is thus the earliest published account of a trial. C. H. L'Estrange Ewen has printed the records of the indictments from the Public Records Office, which support the account given here. The pamphlet is introduced by an epistle in impenetrable prose, a preface in metre, and a metrical 'exhortation to all faithful men . . . annexed to the same' by John Phillips. The author of the preface lays serious claim to consideration as the worst poet of the entire Elizabethan era, and few would quarrel with his assertion that

> The dolour now so doubtful is
> that scant my warbling pen
> Can forth express the sense thereof
> unto the sons of men.

But the length and impressiveness of the build-up are unusual, as is the care taken in the illustrations, where the artist has gone to considerable lengths to differentiate the witches and at least give the impression that the pictures are portraits. We are intended to feel that this is not a catchpenny book, but a painstaking report of something important.

As in the report of John Walsh, ungraspable primitive superstitions hover in the background; Mother Eve's cat is half a mascot and half a hearth-god, and one would give a good deal to know in what words she 'renounced GOD and His word'. There is the same anti-Catholic bias; Mother Waterhouse goes to church, but she prays as she was taught in Latin, and she commands her familiar by the Pater noster, not backwards, but in Latin. The old prayers are already becoming weapons of the Enemy, in the public view, not a superseded good but a positive evil.

The reporting is extremely vivid and convincing, particularly as concerns Agnes Brown, where the prose has that breathless wide-eyed glibness of the born liar—one of those pious, polite little girls whose hysterical spiritual dramas land her centre stage with a halo every time. Her afflictions foreshadow those of the later possessed children (she is lamed, and continually haunted by the familiar, according to the indictment) but no-one seems to have thought of exorcism at this date.

The Preface.

A3ᵛ   . . . Of late in Chelmsford town, dear friends,
      before the noble rout
Of judges just placed in that seat
      by our most famous Queen
Judgment to give as justice leads
      as daily well is seen—
The sessions there by order kept
      offenders to correct,
Three feminine dames attached were
      whom Satan had infect
With Belial's[1] sprite, whose sorcery did
      the simple so molest
That, when they would, with present death
      they were full soon oppressed.
Hereafter shall succeed the acts
      that they themselves have wrought,
As they themselves confessed have
      to judgment being brought;
Which thing when thou has viewed well,
      good reader, do thou pray
To God the Lord, that he from us
      would witches take away.
And thus I end, hoping thou wilt
      my travail well accept,
And judge the truth when thou hast heard
      of this the full effect.

A6. *The examination of them with their confession before Doctor Cole and Master Fortescue at the same Assize verbatim, as near as could be gathered; and first of Elizabeth Francis, who said as here followeth.*

First, she learned this art of witchcraft at the age of 12 years, of her grandmother, whose name was mother Eve of Hatfield Peverel, deceased.

Item: when she taught it her, she counselled her to renounce GOD

[1] In the Old Testament, 'sons of Belial' means simply 'those given to profligacy'. In conjuring books and popular lore, Belial is personified as a leader among the fallen angels, proud and inventive in wickedness; here, as in II *Corinthians* 6: 15, he is a symbol of idolatry and false belief.

Elizabeth Francis and
her grandmother Eve
*The examination and
confession of certaine
Wytches at Chensforde*
1566

and His word, and to give of her blood to Satan (as she termed it), which she delivered her in the likeness of a white spotted[2] cat, and taught her to feed the said cat with bread and milk, and she did so. Also she taught her to call it by the name of Satan,[3] and to keep it in a basket.

When this Mother Eve had given her the cat Satan, then this Elizabeth desired first of the said cat (calling it Satan) that she might be rich, and to have goods, and he promised her she should, asking her what she would have, and she said 'Sheep' (for this cat spake to her, as she confessed, in a strange hollow voice, but such as she understood by use); and this cat forthwith brought sheep into her pasture to the number of 18, black and white, which continued with her for a time, but in the end did all wear* away, she knew not how.

Item: when she had gotten these sheep, she desired to have one Andrew Byles to her husband, which was a man of some wealth, and the cat did promise she should, but that he said she must first consent that this Andrew should abuse* her, and so she did.

And after, when this Andrew had thus abused her, he would not marry her, wherefore she willed Satan to waste his goods, which he forthwith did; and yet not being contented with this, she willed him to touch his body, which he forthwith did, whereof he died.

Item: that every time that he did anything for her, she said that he required a drop of blood, which she gave him by pricking herself, sometime in one place and then in another, and where she pricked herself there remained a red spot which was still to be seen.

Item: when this Andrew was dead, she, doubting* herself with

[2] John Aubrey, speaking of Archbishop Laud's fondness for cats, says that tabby cats were introduced into England about 1637 or 1638 and quickly affected the native breed. 'I doe well remember that the common English Catt, was white with some blewish piedness: sc. a gallipot blew. The race of them are now almost lost.' (*Aubrey's Brief Lives*, edited by Oliver Lawson Dick, ed. cit., p. xxxvi.)   [3] Here and throughout spelt 'Sathan'.

child, willed Satan to destroy it, and he bade her take a certain herb and drink it, which she did, and destroyed the child forthwith.

Item: when she desired another husband he promised her another, naming this Francis whom she now hath, but said 'He is not so rich as the other', willing her to consent unto that Francis in fornication, which she did, and thereof conceived a daughter that was born within a quarter of a year after they were married.

After they were married they lived not so quietly as she desired, being stirred, as she said, to much unquietness, and moved to swearing and cursing; wherefore she willed Satan her cat to kill the child,[4] being about the age of half a year old, and he did so, and when she yet found not the quietness that she desired, she willed it to lay a lameness in the leg of this Francis her husband, and it did in this manner:

It came in a morning to this Francis' shoe, lying in it like a toad, and when he perceived it, putting on his shoe, and had touched it with his foot, he being suddenly amazed asked of her what it was, and she bade him kill it, and he was forthwith taken with a lameness whereof he can not [be] healed.[5]

After all this, when she had kept this cat by the space of 15 or 16 year, and, as some say (though untruly) being weary of it, she came to one Mother Waterhouse[6] her neighbour, a poor woman, when she was going to the oven, and desired her to give her a cake, and she would give her a thing that she should be the better for so long as she lived; and this Mother Waterhouse gave her a cake, whereupon she brought her this cat in her apron and taught her as she was instructed before

---

[4] It is an odd fact that most of the witches kept their familiars hidden away, however innocent and ordinary they might be in appearance; the comfortable, sleeping animal is a symbol of all its owner's guilty wishes, dangerous only when it gets out. When disaster overtakes the object of her hatred or impatience, the witch, like a child, feels guilt, but fixes physical responsibility elsewhere. The familiar, indeed, often serves the same function as the invisible playmate through whom children separate themselves from their anti-social acts and desires.

Very many grotesque confessions are a result of this attempt to translate into the prosecutor's terms the 'magical thinking' in which thoughts are as effective as deeds. As one witch said simply when asked if she killed her husband 'she wished ill wishes to him and whatsoever she wished came to pass'. (*Witch Hunting and Witch Trials*, C. H. L'Estrange Ewen, ed. cit., p. 298; quoted from Brit. Mus. Add. MSS. 27402 fos. 104–21.)

[5] Destroying the agent of a spell often broke the spell, but sometimes fixed it irrevocably, as it did in the case of the Earl of Derby (q.v.).

[6] According to the second Chelmsford trial in 1579, Mother Waterhouse was the sister of Elizabeth Francis.

by her grandmother Eve, telling her that she must call him Satan and give him of her blood, and bread and milk as before; and at this examination would confess no more.

Mother Waterhouse of Hatfield Peverel, of the age of 64 years, being examined the same day, confessed as followeth, and the 29 day suffered.

First, she received this cat of this Francis' wife in the order as is before said, who willed her to call him Satan, and told her that if she made much of him, he would do for her what she would have him to do.

Then, when she had received him she (to try him what he could do) willed him to kill a hog of her own, which he did; and she gave him for his labour a chicken, which he first required of her, and a drop of her blood. And this she gave him at all times when he did anything for her, by pricking her hand or face and putting the blood to his mouth, which he sucked, and forthwith would lie down in his pot again, wherein she kept him; the spots of all the which pricks are yet to be seen in her skin.

Also she saith that another time, being offended with one Father Kersey, she took her cat Satan in her lap and put him in the wood before her door, and willed him to kill 3 of this Father Kersey's hogs; which he did, and returning again told her so, and she rewarded him as before, with a chicken and a drop of her blood, which chicken he ate up clean as he did all the rest, and she could find remaining neither bones nor feathers.

Also she confessed that, falling out with one Widow Goodday, she willed Satan to drown her cow and he did so, and she rewarded him as before.

Also, she falling out with another of her neighbours, she killed her three geese in the same manner.

Item: she confessed that because she could have no rest, which she required, she caused Satan to destroy the brewing at that time.

Also, being denied butter of another, she caused her to lose the curds 2 or 3 days after.

Item: falling out with another of her neighbours and his wife, she willed Satan to kill him with a bloody flux,* whereof he died, and she rewarded him as before.

Likewise she confessed that, because she lived somewhat unquietly with her husband, she caused Satan to kill him, and he did so about 9 years past, since which time she hath lived a widow.

Also she said that when she would will him to do anything for her, she would say her Pater noster in Latin.

Item: this Mother Waterhouse confessed that she first turned this cat into a toad by this means: she kept the cat a great while in wool in a pot, and at length being moved by poverty to occupy* the wool, she prayed in the name of the Father and of the Son and of the Holy Ghost that it would turn into a toad, and forthwith it was turned into a toad, and so [she] kept it in the pot without wool.

Also she said that, going to Braxted a little before her apprehension, this Satan willed her to hie her home, for she should have great trouble, and that she should be either hanged or burned[7] shortly; more at this time she would not confess.

Joan Waterhouse, daughter to this Mother Waterhouse, being of the age of 18 years, and examined, confesseth as followeth.

Joan Waterhouse, daughter of Agnes
The examination and confession of certaine Wytches at Chensforde 1566

First, that her mother this last winter would have learned her this art, but she learned it not, neither yet the name of 'the thing'. She saith she never saw it but once in her mother's hand, and that was in the likeness of a toad, and at that time coming in at a sudden when her mother called it out to work something withal, she heard her to call it Satan; for she was not at any time truly taught it, nor did never exercise it before this time as followeth:

Item: she confessed that when her mother was gone to Braxted, in her absence lacking bread, she went to a girl, a neighbour's child, and desired her to give her a piece of bread and cheese. Which, when [she] denied and gave her not, or at the least not so much as would satisfy her, she going home did as she had seen her mother do, calling Satan, which came to her (as she said) she thought out of her mother's shoe from under the bed in the likeness of a great dog, demanding what she would have.

---

[7] The punishment for a wife killing her husband. She was actually indicted for killing William Finney, a neighbour, perhaps the one with 'the flux'.

Wherewithal she being afeared, said she would have him to make such a girl afeared (naming this girl); then asked he her what she would give him, and she said 'A red cock', then said he 'No, but thou shalt give me thy body and soul;' whereby she being sore feared and desirous to be rid of him, said she would. And herewith he went to this girl in the likeness of an evil-favoured dog with horns on his head, and made her very much afeared, and doth yet haunt her; now can not these witches (as they say) call him in again, because they did not let him out.[8] And more, saith she, she never did, but this her doing was the revealing of all the rest.

Finis.

Devil-dog
The examination and confession of certaine Wytches at Chensforde 1566

The second examination and confession of Mother Agnes Waterhouse and Joan her daughter upon her arraignment,[9] with the questions and answers of Agnes Brown the child, on whom the spirit haunteth at this present, deliberately declared before Justice Southcote and Master Gerard the Queen's attorney, the 27 day of July, Anno 1566, no less wonderful than most true.

The confession of Agnes Waterhouse the 27 day of July in Anno 1566 at Chelmsford before Justic Southcote and Master Gerard the Queen's attorney.

[8] This curious idea has more to do with folk-lore and fairy-tale than with any accepted theory of witchcraft.
[9] i.e. when brought to trial.

First, being demanded whether that she were guilty or not guilty upon her arraignment of the murdering of a man, she confessed that she was guilty; and then upon the evidence given against her daughter Joan Waterhouse, she said that she had a white cat, and willed her cat that he should destroy many of his neighbours' cattle,* and also that he should kill a man, and so he did. And then, after, she must go 2 or 3 mile from her house, and then she took thought how to keep her cat; then she and her cat concluded that he the said cat would become a toad, and then she should keep him in a close house and give him milk, and so he would continue till she came home again.

And then being gone forth, her daughter, having been at a neighbour's house thereby, required of one Agnes Brown, of the age of 12 years or more, a piece of bread and cheese, and the said Agnes said that she had none, and that she had not the key of the milkhouse door. And then the said Joan went home and was angry with the said Agnes Brown and she said that she remembered that her mother was wont to go up and down in her house and to call 'Satan, Satan'. She said she would prove the like, and then she went up and down the house and called 'Satan', and then there came a black dog to her and asked her what she would have.

And then she said she was afeared, and said, 'I would have thee to make one Agnes Brown afraid;' and then he asked her what she would give him and she said she would give him a red cock, and he said he would have none of that. And she asked him what he would have then, and he said he would have her body and soul; and so upon request and fear together she gave him her body and soul.

And then said the Queen's attorney 'How wilt thou do before God?' 'Oh my lord, I trust God will have mercy upon me' [she said], and then he said 'Thou sayest well.' And then he [the dog] departed from her, and then she said that she heard that he made the said Agnes Brown afeared.

The said Agnes Brown was then demanded and called for, and then she came in, and being asked what age she was of, she said she thought she was 12 years old. And then the Queen's attorney asked her what she could say; and then she said that at such a day (naming the day certain) that she was churning of butter, and there came to her a thing like a black dog with a face like an ape, a short tail, a chain and a silver whistle (to her thinking) about his neck, and a pair of horns on his head.

And [he] brought in his mouth the key of the milkhouse door 'and then, my lord' she said, 'I was afeared, for he skipped and leaped to and fro, and sat on the top of a nettle, and then I asked him what he would have, and he said he would have butter, and I said I had none for him, and then he said he would have some or* he went.

And then he did run to put the key into the lock of the milkhouse door, and I said he should have none, and he said he would have some, and then he opened the door and went upon the shelf, and there upon a new cheese laid down the key. And being awhile within he came out again, and locked the door, and said that he had made flap butter[10] for me, and so departed.' And then, she said, she told her aunt of it, and then she sent for the priest, and when he came he bade her to pray to God and call on the name of Jesus.

'And so the next day, my lord, he came again to me with the key of our milkhouse door in his mouth, and then I said, "In the name of Jesus, what hast thou there?" and then he laid down the key and said that I spake evil words in speaking of that name, and then he departed. And so my aunt took up the key, for he had kept it from us 2 days and a night, and then we went into the milkhouse, and there we did see the print of butter upon the cheese. And then within a few days after he came again with a bean pod in his mouth——'

And the Queen's attorney asked what that was, and so the other justices declared, and then she said, 'My lord, I said "In the name of Jesus, what hast thou there?" and so then he laid it down, and said I spake evil words, and departed, and came again by and by with a piece of bread in his mouth.[11] And I asked him what he would have, and he said butter it was that he would have, and so he departed; and, my lord, I did not see him no more till Wednesday last, which was the 24 day of July.'

'Why' said the Queen's attorney, 'was he with thee on Wednesday last?' 'Yea', she said. 'What did he then to thee?' said he. 'My lord', said she, 'he came with a knife in his mouth and asked me if I were not dead; and I said, "No, I thanked God," and then he said if I would not die that he would thrust his knife to my heart but he would make me to die. And then I said, "In the name of Jesus, lay down thy knife,'

---

[10] 'Flap' usually connotes something worthless or topsy-turvy in dialect use. We learn a few lines later that the cheese appeared to be marked with the butter-moulder, i.e. a board with a distinctive incised pattern which was transferred to each block of butter as it was made up.

[11] Apart from his horns, and his powers of conversation, this dog sounds exactly like someone's mischievous and half-trained pet.

and he said he would not depart from his sweet dame's knife as yet. And then I asked of him who was his dame, and then he nodded and wagged his head to your house, Mother Waterhouse.'

Then the Queen's attorney asked of the said Agnes Waterhouse what she said to it; then she demanded what manner knife that it was, and Agnes Brown said it was a dagger knife. 'There thou liest,' said Agnes Waterhouse. 'Why?' quoth the Queen's attorney. 'Marry, my lord', quoth she, 'she saith it is a dagger knife and I have none such in my house but a great knife, and therein she lieth.' 'Yea, yea, my lord', quoth Joan Waterhouse, 'she lieth in that she saith that it had a face like an ape, for this that came to me was like a dog.'

'Well', said the Queen's attorney, 'well, can you make it come before us now? If ye can, we will despatch you out of prison by and by.'[12] 'No, faith,' said Agnes Waterhouse, 'I can not, for in faith if I had let him go as my daughter did I could make him come by and by; but now I have no more power over him.' Then said the Queen's attorney 'Agnes Waterhouse, when did thy cat suck of thy blood?' 'Never', said she. 'No?' said he, 'let me see.' And then the jailer lifted up her kercher* on her head and there was divers spots in her face and one on her nose. Then said the Queen's attorney 'In good faith, Agnes, when did he suck of thy blood last?' 'By my faith, my lord', said she, 'not this fortnight;' and so the jury went together for that matter.

The end and last confession of Mother Waterhouse at her death, which was the 29 day of July, Anno 1566.

First, being ready prepared to receive her death, she confessed earnestly that she had been a witch, and used such execrable sorcery the space of 15 years, and had done many abominable deed, the which she repented earnestly and unfeignedly, and desired Almighty God's forgiveness in that she had abused His most holy name by her devilish practices, and trusted to be saved by His most unspeakable mercy.

And being demanded of the bystanders, she confessed that she sent her Satan to one Wardol, a neighbour of hers being a tailor (with whom she was offended) to hurt and destroy him and his goods. And this her Satan went thereabout for to have done her will, but in the end he returned to her again, and was not able to do this mischief. She asked the cause, and he answered, 'Because the said Wardol was so strong in faith that he had no power to hurt him.'[13] Yet she sent him divers and sundry time, but all in vain, to have mischiefed him.

---

[12] A very equivocal offer.   [13] John Walsh held the same belief.

Mother Waterhouse.

Agnes Waterhouse (probably sister of Elizabeth)
The examination and confession of certaine Wytches at Chensforde 1566.

And being demanded whether she was accustomed to go to church to the common prayers or divine service, she said, 'Yea'; and being required what she did there, she said she did as other women do, and prayed right heartily there. And when she was demanded what prayer she said, she answered, 'The Lord's Prayer, the Ave Maria, and the Belief'.[14] And then they demanded whether in Latin or in English, and she said, 'In Latin'.

And they demanded why she said it not in English but in Latin, seeing that it was set out by public authority and according to God's word that all men should pray in the English and mother tongue that they best understood, and she said that Satan would at no time suffer her to say it in English, but at all times in Latin;[15] for these and many other offences which she hath committed, done and confessed, she bewailed, repented and asked mercy of God, and all the world forgiveness. And thus she yielded up her soul, trusting to be in joy with Christ her Saviour, which dearly had bought her with His most precious blood. Amen.

[14] Belief, i.e. Creed.

[15] 'Satan' is the only explanation open to people who cannot understand the mental blocks which prevent them from following socially approved custom. It must have been very difficult for elderly people brought up on Latin prayers to make the change to an English form, which had none of the associations of lifetime habit.

Witches at Windsor

Witch feeding familiars
A Rehearsall both straung and true . . . at winsore 1579

A Rehearsall both straung and true, of hainous and horrible actes committed by Elizabeth Stile, Alias Rockingham, Mother Dutten, Mother Devell, Mother Margaret, Fower notorious Witches, apprehended at winsore in the Countie of Barks. and at Abbington arraigned, condemned, and executed on the 26 daye of Februarie laste Anno. 1579. (London, 1579.)

This case aroused disproportionate concern in the government of the day, mainly because the witches were rumoured to have engaged in the kind of magic to which Elizabeth was felt to be most vulnerable—image magic. Late in August of 1578, three female wax figures were found buried in a dunghill in London, with bristles stuck in the site of the heart. This caused widespread gossip and dismay, of which even the Spanish Ambassador took note. Four months later, the Privy Council heard of the evidence to be offered at the Windsor trials, and wrote a letter (16 January 1578–9) to Sir Henry Neville and the Dean of Windsor asking them to study the wider implications of the witches' activities, particularly with regard to image making 'as there hath been lately discovered a practice of that device very likely to be intended to the destruction of Her Majesty's person'. (*Privy Council Register*, New Series, vol. 2, p. 22.)

Apparently it was felt that no treason was involved in the Windsor case, but all four witches were executed within a month of the first arrest. One would like to know how Father Rosimond the 'wiseman' escaped; he seems as deep in sorcery as the rest.

The Reader

Among the punishments which the Lord God hath laid upon us, for the manifest impiety and careless contempt of His word abounding in these our desperate days, the swarms of witches and enchanters are not the last nor the least. For that old serpent Satan, suffered to be the scourge for our sins, hath of late years greatly multiplied the brood of them and much increased their malice. Which practice he hath the more easily performed for that wholesome remedies, provided for the curing of such cankers, are either never a whit, or not rightly applied. For albeit the justices be severe in executing of the laws in that behalf, yet such is the foolish pity, or slackness, or both, of the multitude and under-officers that they most commonly are winked at, and so escape unpunished, to the dishonour of God and imminent danger on her Majesty's liege people. Nay, the fondness and ignorance of many is such that they succour those devilish imps, have recourse to them for the health of themselves or others, and for things lost, calling them by the honorable name of 'wise women'. Wherein they know not what honour they do to the devil.

For it is Satan that doeth all, that plagueth with sickness, that maimeth, murdereth, and robbeth, and at his lust restoreth. The witch beareth the name, but the devil dispatcheth the deeds—without him the witch can contrive no mischief. He without the witch can work treason too much, too oft, and too soon.

If then by the law of the Lord of life witches and enchanters are accounted unworthy to live; if by the law of this land they are to be done to death, as traitors to their prince, and felons in respect of her Highness' subjects—whosoever thou be, beware of aiding them! Go not with *Saul* the reprobate to ask council of them, neither, for Christianity sake, seem to be more slack in a good purpose than *Cicero* the Ethnic, who plainly adviseth that witches, poisoners etc. are to be rather shut up in prison and tied with fetters, than moved to amend with council and persuasions, only afterwards suffered to escape, whereby they may renew their malicious and treasonable drifts.

1579
January the 28 day

The true examination and confession of Elizabeth Stile, alias Rockingham, uttered at the Jail of Reading, in the county of Barks. immediately after her apprehension in the presence of the persons hereafter mentioned.

Elizabeth Stile alias Rockingham, late of Windsor, widow, of the age of 65 years or thereabout, being apprehended at Windsor aforesaid and brought personally before the right worshipful Sir Henry Neville, knight, being by him examined and found by manifest and undeniable proofs of her honest neighbours to be a lewd, malicious and hurtful woman to the people and inhabitants thereabouts, was thereupon committed to the common jail of Reading, there to remain until the next great assizes there to be holden, that her offence might be more straitly sifted, and she the offender to receive the guerdon due for her demerits.

Whither when she was come and moved by the jailor there named Thomas Rowe to turn herself to God, from whom she had notoriously fallen, and mildly to bear the punishment belonging to her deeds past; and therewithal urged in sign of her repentance to confess her former follies and facts,* she seemed to have some remorse in conscience and desired to have some talk with the said Thomas Rowe. To whom with one John Knight the constable, John Griffith an innholder, and one William Printall, being all four present, she confessed as followeth.

And first concerning those persons that practise the damnable art of witchcraft, sorcery or enchantment, of her own certain knowledge and voluntary motion she uttered to this effect ensuing.

Imprimis: that one Father Rosimond dwelling in Farnham[1] parish, being a widower, and also a daughter of his, are both witches or enchanters, which Rosimond she saith hath and can transform himself by devilish means into the shape and likeness of any beast whatsoever he will.

2. Item: that one Mother Dutten dwelling within one Hoskins' in Clewer parish can tell everyone's message as soon as she seeth them approach near to the place of her abode and further, she keepeth a spirit or fiend in the likeness of a toad, and feedeth the same fiend (lying in a border of green herbs within her garden) with blood which she causeth to issue from her own flank.

[1] Probably Farnham Royal in Bucks.

3. Item: that one Mother Devell, dwelling nigh the pond in Windsor aforesaid, being a very poor woman, hath a spirit in the shape of a black cat and calleth it Jill, whereby she is aided in her witchcraft; and she daily feedeth it with milk, mingled with her own blood.

4. Item: that one Mother Margaret dwelling in the almshouse at Windsor goeth with two crutches, doth feed a kitling* or fiend by her named Jenny with crumbs of bread and her own blood.

5. Item: the said Elizabeth Stile, alias Rockingham, of herself confesseth that she the same Elizabeth until the time of her apprehension kept a rat (being in very deed a wicked spirit) naming it Philip; and that she fed the same rat with blood issuing from her right-hand wrist, the marks whereof evidently remain, and also that she gave her right side to the devil, and so did the residue of the witches before named.

And thus far forth touching the persons aforementioned in general, now resteth her declaration of their detestable drifts[2] and devices in particular.

6. Furthermore, she confesseth that when she was apprehended Mother Margaret came to her and gave her money, charging her in any wise not to detect their secrets; which if she this prisoner did, the said Mother Margaret threatened that she should be hardly entreated.

7. And moreover, she saith that Father Rosimond with his daughter, Mother Dutten, Mother Devell, Mother Margaret, and herself the said Elizabeth Rockingham, did accustom to meet within the backside of Master Dodge's, in the pits[3] there, and did in that place conclude upon heinous and villainous practices, such as by them or any of them, before had been devised or determined.

8. Also she saith and confesseth that they all purposed and agreed, by their sorceries and enchantments to despatch privily one Langford a farmer, dwelling in Windsor by the Thames side, and that they murdered him accordingly.

9. They also by their devilish art killed one Master Gallis,[4] who in times past had been Mayor of Windsor.

10. The like they practised against one of the said Langford's maids, whom by the mischievous means above expressed they bereft of life.

[2] An echo of this phrase is used as title for the pamphlet describing the trial at Chelmsford in 1579; that work and the present one were both published by Edward White. (See *A detection of damnable driftes* . . .)

[3] Shakespeare's *Merry Wives of Windsor* speaks of a 'sawpit' in the forest; this may be the same kind of pit.

[4] He obviously had time to write a book about the witches before he died; Reginald Scot mentions it with extreme scorn (*Discovery of Witchcraft*, ed. cit., Bk. 1, Ch. 8).

11. Likewise a butcher named Switcher[5] escaped not their treachery but was by their witchcraft brought to his grave.

12. Another butcher named Mastlin was by them handled in such sort that he consumed away.

13. The manner of their enchantments, whereby four of the persons aforenamed were murdered, was thus:—Mother Dutten made four pictures[6] of red wax, about a span long, and three or four fingers broad, for Langford, for his maid, for Master Gallis, and for Switcher; and the said Mother Dutten, by their council and consent, did stick an hawthorn prick against the left sides of the breasts of the images, directly there where they thought the hearts of the persons to be set whom the same pictures did represent, and thereupon within short space, the said four persons, being suddenly taken, died.

14. As for Mastlin the fifth man, she confesseth that he was bewitched, but how or whether he died or no, she uttereth not.

15. Further, the same Elizabeth saith that herself did kill one Saddock with a clap on the shoulder, for not keeping his promise for an old cloak to make her a safeguard,* who presently went home and died.

16. Further she saith, that she and every of them did overspeak one Humphrey Hosey and his wife, and one Richard Mills, and one John Mathinglise, that they lay sick in a strange order a long time, but they were recovered again.

17. Further she saith, that Mother Devell did overspeak one William Foster, a fisher, and one Willis' wife, a baker.

18. Further she saith, that Mother Dutten did give one picture, but she knoweth not whether it was of a man or of a woman; and the man that had it of her she thinketh to be dead, but she knoweth not his name.

19. Further she saith, that one George Whitting, servant to Matthew Glover of Eton, had one picture of herself for one Foster, for that the said George and Foster fell out at variance; and the picture was made in Mother Dutten's house and that Mother Dutten, Mother Devell and herself were at the making; and that Mother Devell did say to her Bun[7] or evil spirit 'Plague him and spare him not!' and she did thrust a hawthorn prick against the heart of him, and so he lay at the point of death a long time, but Mother Dutten recovered him again.

---

[5] Possibly 'Switzer', or man from Switzerland. Judging by the names, there was a considerable foreign colony at Windsor.

[6] pictures, i.e. images or statues.

[7] Pet name for cat or rabbit; cf. 'Bunny rabbit'.

20. And in the end they killed a cow of his by their witchcraft.

21. And further she saith, that they and every of them, if any had angered them, they would go to their spirits and say 'Such-a-one hath angered me, go do them this mischief' and for their hire would give them a drop of their own blood; and presently the party was plagued by some lamentable casualty.

22. Elizabeth Stile also confesseth that she herself hath gone to Old Windsor, to the bedmakers there, to beg a mess of milk, which she could not have for that the maid was then milking, but her rat had provided for her both milk and cream against her coming home.

23. Elizabeth Stile, touched with more remorse, saith that Mother Dutten and Mother Devell were her first enticers to folly; and that she and every of them did meet sometimes in Master Dodge's pits, and sometime about eleven of the clock in the night at the pound, and that Mother Dutten and Mother Devell did persuade her to do as they had done in forsaking God and His works and giving herself to the devil.

24. Elizabeth Stile confesseth herself often times to have gone to Father Rosimond's house, where she found him sitting in a wood not far from thence, under the body of a tree, sometimes in the shape of an ape and otherwhiles like an horse.[8] She also confesseth herself to have turned a child's hand in Windsor clean backwards, which was returned to the right place by Mother Dutten.

25. Further she saith, that she will stand unto her death to all and every article before rehearsed, and that Father Rosimond can transform himself into the likeness of an ape or a horse, and that he can help any man so bewitched to his health again, as well as to bewitch.

26. Further she saith, that Mother Seder dwelling in the almshouse was the mistress witch of all the rest, and she is now dead.

27. Further she saith, that if she had been so disposed, four or five or more of the best men in Windsor should not have brought her to the jail, but that she came of her own accord; and by the way as she came with John Brome, who brought her to the jail, her Bun or familiar

---

[8] *The Merry Wives of Windsor* uses the legend of Herne the Hunter, who walks in the forest with horns on his head and bewitches both cattle and crops. This tale may have been used in a local mummer's play, with appropriate costumes; or Father Rosimond may simply have liked to trick and mystify his superstitious neighbours. There is no other reference in early witch pamphlets to the witch's supposed powers of transformation, and it is not taken seriously here, for Father Rosimond apparently gets off scot free.

came to her in the likeness of a black cat and would have had her away, but she banished him, hoping for favour.

Memorandum, that besides the examination and confession aforesaid, there was given in evidence *viva voce* at the arraignment of the said witches, one special matter by an ostler of Windsor, who affirmeth upon his oath that the said Mother Stile, using to come to his master's house, had oftentimes relief given her by him. And on a time not long since she coming to his master's house when there was little left to be given her, for that she came somewhat late, yet he giving her also somewhat at that time, she therewith not contented went her ways in some anger and, as it seemed, offended with the said ostler for that she had no better alms; and by the sequel, so it appeared.

For not long after, he had a great ache in his limbs that he was not able to take any rest nor to do any labour, and having sought many means for remedy thereof, could find none. At the last he went to a wiseman, named Father Rosimond, alias Osborne, who told him that he was bewitched and that there was many ill women in Windsor, and asked him whom he did mistrust, and the said ostler answered 'One Mother Stile,' one of the witches aforesaid. 'Well,' said the wiseman, 'if you can meet her, and all to-scratch her so that you draw blood of her, you shall presently mend.' And the said ostler upon his oath declared that he watching her on a time did all to-scratch her by the face, that he made the blood come after, and presently his pain went away so that he hath been no more grieved since.

Moreover, on a time a man's son of Windsor coming to fetch water at a well which was by the door of the said Mother Stile, and by chance hurling a stone upon her house, she was therewithal much grieved, and said 'she would be even with him', and took his pitcher which he had brought from him. The boy, coming homewards, happened to meet with his father, and told him how that Mother Stile had taken away his pitcher from him.

'Well,' said his father 'you have done her some unhappiness;* come on with me and I will go speak with her.' And so the boy going with his father towards her house did suddenly cry out 'Oh, my hand, my hand!' His father therewithal looking back and seeing his son's hand to turn and wend backwards, laid hold thereupon, but he was not able to stay the turning thereof. Besides, a neighbour of his being in his company at that time did also lay hold thereon, and notwithstanding both their strengths, the child's hand did turn backwards, and the palm thereof did stand where the back did, to the grievous torment of the said child and vexation of his father. The which hand was turned again to his right place either by the said Father Rosimond or the said Mother Devell.[9]

Also this is not to be forgotten, that the said Mother Stile, being at the time of her apprehension so well in health of body and limbs that she was able, and did, go on foot from Windsor unto Reading unto the jail, which are twelve miles distant; shortly after that she had made the aforesaid confession, the other witches were apprehended and were brought to the said jail, [where] the said Mother Devell did so bewitch her and others (as she confessed unto the jailer) with her enchantments, that the use of all her limbs and senses were taken quite from her, and her toes did rot off her feet, and she was laid upon a barrow, as a most ugly creature to behold, and so brought before the judges at such time as she was arraigned.

Finis.

Reginald Scot, The Discovery of Witchcraft, *ed. cit., Bk. 16, Ch. 3.*

Were there not three images of late years found in a dunghill, to the terror and astonishment of many thousands? Insomuch as great matters were thought to have been pretended to be done by witchcraft. But if the Lord preserve those persons whose destruction was doubted to have been intended thereby [i.e. Queen Elizabeth] from all other the lewd practices and attempts of their enemies, I fear not but they shall easily withstand these and such like devices, although they should indeed be practised against them. . . .

But to return to the discovery of the aforesaid knavery and witchcraft. So it was that one old cozener, wanting money, devised or rather practised (for it is a stale device) to supply his want by promising a young gentleman, whose humour he thought would that way be well served, that for the sum of forty pounds he would not fail by his cunning in that art of witchcraft to procure unto him the love of any three women whom he would name, and of whom he should make choice at his pleasure. The young gentleman, being abused with his cunning devices, and too hastily yielding to that motion, satisfied this cunning man's demand of money which, because he had it not presently to disburse, provided it for him at the hands of a friend of his.

Finally this cunning man made the three puppets of wax etc., leaving nothing undone that appertained to the cozenage until he had buried them, as you have heard. But I omit to tell what ado was made hereof,

[9] See introduction, p. 45.

and also what reports and lies were bruited; as what white dogs and black dogs there were seen in the night season passing through the watch, maugre* all their force and preparation against them etc.

But the young gentleman who for a little space remained in hope mixed with joy and love, now through tract of time hath those his felicities powdered with doubt and despair. For instead of achieving his love he would gladly have obtained his money. But because he could by no means get either the one or the other (his money being in huckster's handling, and his suit in no better forwardness), he revealed the whole matter, hoping by that means to recover his money; which he neither can yet get again, nor hath paid it where he borrowed. But till trial was had of his simplicity or rather folly herein, he received some trouble himself hereabouts, though now dismissed.

Chelmsford Witches Again

A Detection of damnable driftes, practized by three Witches arraigned at Chelmisforde in Essex, at the laste Assises there holden, which were executed in Aprill 1579.

This dreary record of misery and superstition shows echoes of the trial of 1566 still lingering. The inhabitants of Hatfield Peverel, Maldon, and the surrounding countryside appear to have lived in absolute terror of bewitchment; the slightest mischance or illness was thought to have inception in the malice of one of the poor women who survived by pestering their neighbours for food and goods. (No member of a Welfare State could ever have taken her right to assistance more for granted than these women who depended on personal charity; the most reasonable refusal leaves them filled with resentment and anger.)

Mother Staunton, the most genuinely malicious of the group, was the only one who escaped hanging. There was no charge of murder against her, and for some reason she was not charged with the injuries to persons here testified against her; the indictment charging her with the bewitchment of beasts was incorrectly drawn, and therefore found insufficient.

The address to the reader (not reprinted here) asserts its moral purpose, but also sounds an ominously practical note. 'And if in time past he hath escaped their sorceries, let him not the less fear the harms that may hereafter ensue. For the Devil by the sufferance of Almighty God is as well able to plague the person that most presumeth of safety as any have been who in this treatise are mentioned. ... If, therefore, thou be assured that thy neighbour either in body, family or goods, is impaired by damnable witchcraft, or perceivest by information or otherwise of such devices intended to be practised, or likely presumption of such devilish deeds contrived, for charity to thy Christian brother and tender regard of thine own state, prevent or stop the mischief by all possible means.' (A2v–A3v).

The confession of Elizabeth Francis, late of Hatfield in Essex.

Imprimis: The said Elizabeth Francis[1] confessed that about Lent

---

[1] Elizabeth Francis had been sentenced to a year's imprisonment and pillory for bewitching a child in 1566; in 1572 she was convicted of making a woman ill by witchcraft, and punished with the same sentence, though the law required death for a second offence. This present Elizabeth Francis, who seems to be the same, though there is no mention of a husband in the indictment, was executed for the death of Alice Poole. (C. H. L'Estrange Ewen, *Witch Hunting and Witch Trials*, ed. cit., pp. 120, 125, 138.)

Hedgehog?
A Detection of damnable driftes . . . at Chelmisforde 1579

last, as she now remembereth, she came to one Poole's wife, her neighbour, and required some old yeast of her; but being denied the same, she departed towards one Goodwife Osborne's house (a neighbour dwelling thereby) of whom she had yeast, and in her way, going towards the said Goodwife Osborne's house, she cursed Poole's wife and bade a mischief to light upon her for that she would give her no yeast.

Whereupon, suddenly in the way she heard a great noise, and presently* there appeared unto her a spirit of a white colour, in seeming like to a little rugged* dog, standing near her upon the ground, who asked her whither she went. She answered 'for such things as she wanted', and she told him therewith that she could get no yeast of Poole's wife, and therefore willed the same spirit to go to her and plague her, which the spirit promised to do; but first he bade her give him somewhat.

Then she having in her hand a crust of white bread did bite a piece thereof and threw it upon the ground, which she thinketh he took up and so went his way; but before he departed from her she willed him to plague Poole's wife in the head. And since then she never saw him, but she hath heard by her neighbours that the same Poole's wife was grievously pained in her head not long after, and remaineth very sore pained still, for on Saturday last past this examinate talked with her.

2. Item: this Elizabeth Francis saith further, that she knoweth one Elizabeth Lord, a widow dwelling in the same parish of Hatfield and so hath done of long time, of whom she heard that about seven or eight years past she brought drink in a cruse and gave it to one John

Frances, servant to Goodman Soame of the same parish, shortly after the taking of which drink he sickened and died.

3. Item: she further confesseth that she likewise knoweth that the same Widow Lord was said to have bewitched one Joan Roberts, servant to old Higham, in a piece of apple cake which she gave her, upon the eating whereof she presently sickened and not long after died.

4. Item: she also confesseth that she knows one Mother Osborne, a widow in the same town, to be a witch, and that she hath a mark in the end of one of her fingers like a pit, and another mark upon the outside of her right leg, which she thinketh to be plucked out by her spirit;[2] and that one Mother Waterhouse, her own sister[3] (long since executed for witchcraft) had the self same marks which she termeth 'nips'.

And she saith that this Mother Osborne lying lame, and complaining of her sore leg, she the said Elizabeth Francis came unto her and required to see her leg, which being showed unto her, she the said Elizabeth bade to put it into the bed again, saying that she herself knew that the same came by want of well serving of God. And thus much for Elizabeth Francis.

The evidence given against Ellen Smith of Maldon

There was one John Chandler dwelling in Maldon whose wife, named Alice Chandler, was mother unto this Ellen Smith, and for witchcraft was executed long before; after whose execution he went unto his daughter-in-law[4] Ellen Smith and demanded certain money of her which she had received of her mother his wife. By means of which money they fell out, and in falling out the said Ellen in great rage said unto him that it had been better for him he had never fallen out with her, and so it came to pass; for the same John Chandler confessed before his death that after the same hour that she had said so unto him, he never ate any meat that digested in him, but ever it came up again as soon as it was down,[5] by which means he consumed and wasted away to his death.[6]

---

[2] Possibly a bad varicose vein.

[3] Ewen thinks that this means that Mother Waterhouse was sister to Mother Osborne; Notestein takes it that Mother Waterhouse was sister to Elizabeth Francis, which seems marginally more likely in view of the phrasing here and in the next paragraph (her *own* sister; she *herself* knew . . .), although the relationship is not mentioned in the 1566 pamphlet (q.v.).

[4] 'Daughter-in-law' could also mean, as here, 'step-daughter'.

[5] 'down'—original pamphlet has 'done'.

[6] Suspension of the normal processes of digestion was often regarded as a sign

2. The son of the foresaid Ellen Smith of the age of thirteen years or thereabouts, came to the house of one John Eastwood of Maldon for to beg an alms; who chid the boy away from his door, whereupon he went home and told his mother, and within a while after the said Eastwood was taken with very great pain in his body. And the same night following, as he sat by the fire with one of his neighbours, to their thinking they did see a rat run up the chimney, and presently it did fall down again in the likeness of a toad, and taking it up with the tongs, they thrust it into the fire and so held it in forcibly. It made the fire burn as blue as azure, and the fire was almost out; and at the burning thereof the said Ellen Smith was in great pain and out of quiet,[7] whereupon dissemblingly she came to the house of the foresaid John Eastwood and asked how all that were there did, and he said 'Well, I thank God', and she said 'I thought you had not been well, and therefore I came to see how you did', and so went her way.

3. Also it was avouched, and by this prisoner confessed, that whereas her daughter and the daughter of one Widow Webb of Maldon aforesaid did fall out and fight, the same Ellen Smith, offended thereat, meeting Goodwife Webb's daughter the next day, gave her a blow on the face, whereupon so soon as the child came home she sickened and, languishing two days, cried continually 'Away with the witch! Away with the witch!' and so died. And in the morning immediately after the death of the same child, the said Goodwife Webb espied, as she thought, a thing like to a black dog go out at her door, and presently at the sight thereof she fell distraught of her wits.

4. Besides, the son of this Mother Smith confessed that his mother did keep three spirits, whereof the one called by her Great Dick was enclosed in a wicker bottle, the second, named Little Dick, was put into a leather bottle, and the third, termed Willet, she kept in a wool-pack;[8] and thereupon the house was commanded to be searched. The bottles and pack were found, but the spirits were vanished away.

---

of the presence of demons, as was the vomiting of stones, pins, hair etc. Francis Coxe records with gloomy relish that '[Roger] Bacon's end was much after the like sort for, having a greedy desire unto meat, he could cause nothing to enter his stomach, wherefore thus miserably he starved to death.' (*A short treatise declaringe the detestable wickednesse of magicall sciences* . . . London, 1561) B3ᵛ. Roger Bacon was still regarded as a magician rather than a scientist.

[7] In order to torment a witch and bring her to the spot, it was usual to boil her urine, or to burn thatch or a tile from her roof (as in the case of Joan Cason, q.v.); here the sufferings inflicted on her familiar serve the same purpose.

[8] Mother Waterhouse kept her cat in a pot full of wool (Chelmsford, 1566);

The effect of the evidence against Mother Staunton, late of Wimbish in Essex, who was arraigned but not executed, for that no manslaughter or murder was objected against her.

Imprimis: this Mother Staunton, late of the parish of Wimbish in Essex, came to the house of one Thomas Pratt of Brook Walden, John Ferrer of Littlebury being present and one Thomas Swallow; and the said Mother Staunton being demanded by one of them how she did, she answered that a knave had beaten her, saying she was a witch. Then said he again 'In good faith, Mother Staunton, I think you be no witch.' 'No, master', quoth she, 'I am none indeed, although I can tell what belongeth to that practice.' Of which words the goodman of the house took witness of the aforenamed parties, and delivered a bill subscribed with their hands thereof to Master George Nicolls.

2. Item: the said Mother Staunton came to his house another time, and after certain words of anger between him and her, he raced* her face with a needle.[9] 'What', quoth she, 'have you a flea there?' and the next night after, the said Pratt was so grievously taken with torment of his limbs that he never thought to have lived one hour longer; which also was subscribed and sent.

3. Item: she came the third time by his door with grains, and he demanding a few of her, she asked what he would do with them. 'I will give them' said he 'to my chickens', and, snatching a handful from her, did so. But after they had tasted of them, three or four dozen of them died, and only one chicken escaped of them all.

4. Item: she came on a time to the house of one Richard Saunder of Brook Walden, and being denied yeast which she required of his wife, she went her way murmuring, as offended with her answer. And after her departure, her young child in the cradle was taken vehemently sick, in a marvellous strange manner, whereupon the mother of the child took it up in her arms to comfort it; which being done, the cradle rocked of itself six or seven times, in presence of one of the Earl of Surrey's gentlemen who, seeing it, stabbed his dagger three or four times into the cradle ere it stayed, merrily jesting, and saying that he would kill the Devil if he would be rocked there.

Rachel Pinder was troubled by a devil like five cats, among other things (See *The disclosing of a late counterfeyted possession*, 1574) and Mildred Norrington in the same year was possessed by a devil kept in two bottles (Reginald Scot, *The Discovery of Witchcraft*, ed. cit., Bk. 7, Ch. 1).

[9] Here the scratching does not seem to have any curative purpose, but is mere brutality, or an attempt to drive the evil power out of the witch by ill treatment.

5. Item: the said Mother Staunton came on a time to the house of one Robert Petty of Brook Walden and, being denied by his wife divers things which she demanded at once, and also charged with the stealing of a knife from thence, she went her way in great anger. And presently after her departure the little child of the said Petty fell so strangely sick as for the space of a week nobody thought it would live.

6. Item: the said Staunton's wife came also to William Turner's house of Brook Walden upon a Friday, as she had done often in times past, and being denied of certain things which she craved (as a piece of leather, etc.) she asked the goodwife how many children she had, who answered 'One'. Which child, being then in perfect health, was presently taken with such a sweat and coldness of body, and fell into such shrieking and staring, wringing* and writhing of the body to and fro, that all that saw it were doubtful of the life of it.[10]

7. Item: she came on a time to the house of Robert Cornell of Seward's End, and craved a bottle of milk of his wife; but being denied it, she departed for a little while, leaving her own bottle behind her, and took another with her that belonged to the aforesaid Cornell. After three days she came again and requested her own bottle and restored the other, craving milk as before. The wife of the house, always suspecting her to be a witch, denied her request and barred the doors against her; whereupon she sat down upon her heels before the door and made a circle upon the ground with a knife.

After that, she digged it full of holes within the compass, in the sight of the said wife, her man and her maid, who, demanding why she did so, she made answer that she made a shitting-house for herself after that sort, and so departed. The next day the wife coming out at the same door was taken sick,[11] and began to swell from time to time as if she had been with child; by which swelling she came so great in body as she feared she should burst, and to this day is not restored to health.[12]

[10] This is a very vivid description of violent 'ague', or the malarial fever still prevalent in the low-lying parts of England at this date. (Much of Essex was notoriously unhealthy.)

[11] Kittredge notices a peculiar case of 1601, where one Alice 'threw water' on her landlady's stairs, but forgetfully walked up them before she did, and suffered the consequences of the spell—gangrened fingers and toes. (G. L. Kittredge, *Witchcraft in Old and New England*, ed. cit., p. 17, cited from MS. 24241·5 in Harvard College Library.)

[12] Possibly ovarian cyst. It is likely here, as in many other cases, that the witch's curse focused attention on symptoms already present, and made the sufferer conscious of the development of a disease over a period of time.

8. Item: she came often to the house of one John Hopwood of Walden, and had continually her requests. At the last, being denied of a leathern thong, she went her way offended, and the same night his gelding in the stable, being the day before in very good case, died suddenly; and afterward, being burdened with all, she never denied it.

Item: she coming to the house of John Cornell the younger of Wimbish, and being denied her demand, she took offence, and immediately after his cattle, instead of sweet milk yielded gore stinking blood,[13] and one of his kine fell into such miserable plight that for a certain space he could by no means recover her.

Item: she came on a time to the vicar's house at Wimbish and, being denied her errand by his wife (he being as then from home) his little son in the nurse's lap was taken with such vehement sickness that the beholders supposed no less but it would straight have died; the said Mother Staunton sitting by, and having touched the child before it grew sick. But within one hour after the vicar came home, the child recovered perfectly and played as before.

Item: also she came on a time to the house of one Robert Lathbury of the same town who, disliking her dealing, sent her home empty; but presently after her departure his hogs fell sick and died to the number of twenty, and in the end he burned one, whereby, as he thinketh, he saved the rest. He also had a cow strangely cast into a narrow gripe* and, being holpen out in the presence of Master Henry Mordaunt, notwithstanding the diligent care that was taken of her, she was in few days three times like to be lost in the mire. And thus much for Mother Staunton.

The effect of the evidence given in against Mother Nokes, late of Lambourne parish in Essex.

A certain servant to Thomas Spicer of Lambourne End in Essex, yeoman, sporting and passing away the time in play with a great number of youth, chanced to snatch a pair of gloves out of the pocket of this Mother Nokes' daughter, being a young woman of the age of 28 years, which he protesteth to have done in jest. Her mother, perceiving it, demanded the gloves of him, but he giving no great ear to her words, departed towards the fields to fetch home certain cattle.

Immediately upon his departure quoth the same Mother Nokes to her daughter, 'Let him alone, I will bounce him well enough;' at what time he, being suddenly taken and reft of his limbs, fell down. There

---

[13] Mastitis?

was a boy then in his company by whom he sent the gloves to Mother Nokes; notwithstanding, his master was fain to cause him to be set home in a wheelbarrow, and to be laid into a bed, where with his legs across[14] he lay bedrid eight days, and as yet hath not attained to the right use of his limbs.

Further it was avouched that Mother Nokes had said that her husband lay with one Taylor's wife of Lambourne End, and with reproachful words reviled her, saying at last 'Thou hast a nurse child, but thou shalt not keep it long;' and presently thereupon the child died.

Another affirmed that when he had reproved the said Taylor's wife and Mother Nokes as they were at church, and willed them to agree better, the same Mother Nokes in a fume answereth that she cared for none of them all as long as Tom held on her side; meaning her fiend.

The same man having a servant of his at plough, this Mother Nokes going by asked the fellow a question, but getting no answer of him, she went her way. Forthwith one of his horses fell down. At his coming home to dinner he told his master how the same horse was swollen about the head.[15] His master, at first supposing that it came by a stripe,* was greatly offended at the ploughman; but afterwards, understanding of Mother Nokes' going by, and the circumstance aforementioned, went to the said Mother Nokes and chid and threatened to have her to her answer;[16] howbeit the horse died.

[14] A classic position of certain kinds of hysteria.
[15] Glanders?
[16] 'Have her to her answer'—i.e. bring her into court.

III Law Tricks

Witches at St. Osyth

W.W., A true and just Recorde, of the Information, Examination and Confession of all the Witches, taken at S. Oses in the countie of Essex; whereof some were executed, and other some entreated according to the determination of lawe. Wherein all men may see what a pestilent people Witches are, and how unworthy to lyve in a Christian Commonwealth. Written orderly, as the cases were tryed by evidence, By W.W. 1582.

This pamphlet consists mainly of the pre-trial examinations taken before a justice of the peace, and certified to the Assizes, where they formed a basis for deciding whether the case should be brought to trial. Thus such examinations represent fairly accurately the evidence to be offered in court, though there were usually additional items and confessions which were taken later, in jail or in court.

Brian Darcey, esquire, the Justice of the peace who figures so largely in this book, was the late-born son of a third wife, a fairly well-to-do man living in the shadow of elder brothers and their children, and an ennobled branch of the family. He did his best; he rebuilt Tiptree Priory into a comfortable manorhouse; he got many children and trained at least one of them up in the law; he entertained widely, was notably charitable, and had at least one devotional book dedicated to him (jointly, with a relative). He was justice of the peace in 1580, county sheriff in 1585, a knight after the Cadiz voyage, and dead in 1587.

By 1580, Essex had already become notorious for witches and Protestant zeal, and some JPs had been reprimanded by the Privy Council for over-conscientiousness. But there continued to be a brisk exchange of letters with the councillors concerning suspected conjurors who were to be sent to London for examination. Such extreme precautions were taken to seize their books and papers, to prevent their escape, and even to keep them incommunicado (*Acts of the Privy Council*, New Series, ed. cit., Vol. 12, p. 23) that it seems likely that the government was really looking for a Catholic plot ('conjuration' was a useful blanket term both for the mass and for attempts to foretell the future and, as the Jesuits remarked, the government preferred to make accusations not directly connected with the practice of religion). This supposition is strengthened by a 'search and seize' warrant for Richard Topcliff, Catholic-hunter extraordinary, sent to Essex JPs in April 1582, immediately after the witch-trial recorded here.

Whatever the real state of affairs, Brian Darcey regarded the preparations for the 1582 trial as his big chance. It is obvious from the many first-person passages that he supervised the writing of the account as well as the examinations; the whole work is planned to display his superlative cleverness and efficiency. One hates to admit it, but he was successful in his aim; the book *was* influential and still remains, in its obsessive, niggling care, its breathless savouring of the big moments that produced confessions, a unique record of a community and personalities caught up in a witch-scare.

It seems inevitable that in every witch-story there shall be one ambitious, well-intentioned meddler—one man who finds public duty an excuse for self-dramatisation: John Darrell, Jesse Bee, Sir Gilbert Pickering—and Brian Darcy, perhaps the ultimate example of this petty, dangerous, necessary man. Darcy was more dangerous than most, because he made a conscious and determined effort to adapt Continental procedures in witch-trials to the English court.

The techniques of interrogation, with their confrontations, changes of tone, threats and promises, are far subtler than anything seen before in the pamphlets, and depend directly on the recommendations of Jean Bodin in his *Démonomanie* (see note 24). The use of very young children, which disgusted Reginald Scot so deeply, is new. Worst of all, we can see from the careful records how an innocent word or action, in the light of the 'presumption of guilt' so casually applied to those rumoured to be witches, could become a hanging matter. The demand that one prove innocence of a charge was routine on the Continent, but foreign to English law; yet the acting upon such a principle in gathering pre-trial evidence could have a deadly effect on shaping that evidence towards guilt in the minds of a jury.

The material confessed in these examinations gets more and more fantastic as justice and suspect act upon each other, and upon witnesses. It does not appear from the records that leading questions were used for the wilder stories; what tales from Darcy's reading in Bodin, discussed over supper with friends, may have circulated in the town and jail, we shall never know. The wonder is that so little took root that was not already common superstition.

To the right honourable and his singular good Lord, the lord Darcy[1] *W. W. wisheth a prosperous continuance in this life to the glory of God, and a daily preservation in God's fear, to his endless joy.*

If there hath been at any time, Right Honourable, any means used to appease the wrath of God, to obtain his blessing, to terrify secret offenders by open transgressors' punishments, to withdraw honest natures from the corruption of evil company, to diminish the great multitude of wicked people, to increase the small number of virtuous persons, and to reform all the detestable abuses which the perverse wit and will of man doth daily devise—this doubtless is no less necessary than the best: that sorcerers, wizards (or rather dizzards), witches, wise women (for so they will be named), are rigorously punished.

[1] Thomas, Baron Darcy of Chiche (i.e. St. Osyth). His father had died a year ago and he was apparently only 16 or 17 at this time. He is listed among justices at the trial.

Revenge for a quarrel: familiar in action
A Rehearsall both straung and true . . . at winsore 1579

Rigorously, said I? Why, it is too mild and gentle a term for such a merciless generation! I should rather have said 'most cruelly executed', for that no punishment can be thought upon, be it in never so high a degree of torment, which may be deemed sufficient for such a devilish and damnable practice. And why? Because all the imaginations, all the consultations, all the conferences, all the experiments, finally, all the attempts, proceedings and conclusions of sorcerers, witches and the rest of that hellish livery, are mere blasphemers against the person of the most high God; and draw so near to the nature of idolatry (for they worship Satan, unto whom they have sworn allegiance) that they are by no means to be exempted from the suspicion of that most accursed defection.

Nay, rather, they are guilty of apparent apostasy, which is more heinous, considering the circumstances of their ordinary actions, than any trespass against the second table;[2] which ugly sins of blasphemy, and gross, or rather devilish, idolatry concurring in no malefactor so roundly as in sorcerers, witches, enchanters etc., in whom the[y] meet with a million of enormities more, as it were in a centre—the magistrates of foreign lands noted so precisely that, weighing the quality of the crime, they kept a due analogy and proportion of punishment, burning them with fire whom the common law of England (with more measure of mercy than is to be wished) strangleth with a rope.

[2] table, i.e. commandment.

An ordinary felon, and a murderer offending against the moral law of justice, is throttled: a sorcerer, a witch (whom a learned physician is not ashamed to avouch innocent, and the judges that denounce sentence of death against them no better than hangmen)[3] defying the Lord God to his face and trampling the precious blood of that immaculate Lamb Jesus Christ most despitefully under feet, is stifled; the one dieth on the gallows and so doth the other. Wherein doubtless there is a great inequality of justice, considering the inequality of the trespass, which deserveth a death so much the more horrible by how much the honour of God is eclipsed, and the glory due to His inviolable name most abominably defaced, even to the uttermost villainy that they can put in practice.

This I speak, Right Honourable, upon a late view of trial taken against certain witches in the county of Essex, the orderly process in whose examinations, together with other accidents, I, diligently observing, and considering their treacheries to be notable, undertook briefly to knit up in a few leaves of paper their manifold abuses; and obtaining the means to have them published in print,[4] for that a number of memorable matters are here touched, to present the same unto your Lordship. Of whose gentle acceptation though I do not doubt, yet will I not be over-bold thereupon to presume, but rather refer the same to your Honour's judgment and patronage by way of humiliation; that, going abroad under covert of your honourable name, the discourse may seem the more credible, your Lordship knowing the grounds of this whole book to be true and justifiable, and therefore the further off from fear of impugning.

But supposing I have been too tedious, and sparing to trouble your Lordship with multitude of words, I build upon hope, and so put forth my book, praying the Lord here to bless your Honour and all

[3] A marginal note here refers to Bodin as the source of the argument. The physician is Wierus, attacked by Bodin for maintaining that witches were mentally ill.

[4] The present pamphlet was put out by Thomas Dawson, who had earlier contacts with Brian Darcy. In 1581 he joined Gregory Seaton in printing *The Christian Man's Closet* by Bartholomew Batty, translated by William Lowth, who dedicated it rather fulsomely to Brian Darcy and his step-nephew, Thomas Darcy esquire. It is possible that William Lowth, who felt deeply indebted to the Darcys, wrote the present pamphlet under the pseudonym W.W. (it was, after all, a hack job); there are stylistic likenesses in the two dedications. If Brian Darcy backed the project financially it is understandable that the dedication is not to him but to the young lord who could advance his ambitions.

about you with the increase of His grace in this life, and with the presence of His divinity in the life to come.

Amen.

Your Honour's to command. W. W.

The 19 day of February, the 24 year of the reign of our Sovereign Lady Queen Elizabeth.

The information of Grace Thurlow, the wife of John Thurlow, taken before me Brian Darcy the day and year abovesaid, against Ursula Kemp alias Grey, as followeth.

The said Grace saith, that about 12 months past, or near thereabouts, her son Davy Thurlow being strangely taken and greatly tormented, Ursula Kemp alias Grey came unto the said Grace to see how the child did; at which time, the child lying upon a bed in the chimney corner, she the said Ursula took it by the hand saying, 'Ah good child, how art thou loden',* and so went thrice out of the doors, and every time when she came in she took the child by the hand and said 'Ah good child, how art thou loden.' And so at her departure the said Grace prayed the said Ursula to come again unto her at night to help her.

And thereupon she the said Ursula replied and said 'I warrant thee, I, thy child shall do well enough'; and that night it fell to rest, the which it did not of a long time before. And the next day the said Grace going to mill-ward, meeting the said Ursula, she asked her how her child did and she said 'It took good rest this night, God be thanked.' 'Aye, aye,' said the said Ursula, 'I warrant thee it shall do well.' Note, that the palms of the child's hands were turned where the backs should be, and the back in the place of the palms.

The said Grace saith also, that about three quarters of a year ago she was delivered of a woman child, and saith, that shortly after the birth thereof, the said Ursula fell out with her, for that she would not suffer her to have the nursing of that child at such times as she the said Grace continued in work at the Lord Darcy's place. And saith, that she the said Grace nursing the said child, within some short time after that falling out, the child lying in the cradle, and not above a quarter old, fell out of the said cradle and brake her neck, and died. The which the said Ursula hearing to have happened, made answer, 'It maketh no matter; for she might have suffered me to have the keeping and nursing of it.'

And the said Grace saith, that when she lay in the said Ursula came unto her, and seemed to be very angry for that she had not the keeping in of the said Grace, and for that she answered unto her that she was provided. And thereupon they entered further into talk, the said Grace saying that if she should continue lame as she had done before, she would find the means to know how it came, and that she would creep upon her knees to complain of them, to have justice done upon them.

And to that she the said Ursula said 'It were a good turn.' 'Take heed,' said Grace, 'Ursula, thou hast a naughty name.' And to that Ursula made answer, though she could unwitch she could not witch; and so promised the said Grace that if she did send for her privily, and send her keeper away, that then she would show the said Grace how she should unwitch herself or any other at any time.

And the said Grace further saith, that about half a year past she began to have a lameness in her bones, and specially in her legs, at which time the said Ursula came unto her unsent for and without request,[5] and said, she would help her of her lameness if she the said Grace would give her 12 pence; the which the said Grace, speaking her fair, promised her so to do, and thereupon for the space of 5 weeks after, she was well and in good case as she was before.

And then the said Ursula came unto the said Grace and asked her the money she promised to her; whereupon the said Grace made answer that she was a poor and a needy woman and had no money.

And then the said Ursula requested of her cheese for it, but she said she had none. And she the said Ursula, seeing nothing to be had of the said Grace, fell out with her and said, that she would be even with her; and thereupon she was taken lame, and from that day to this day hath so continued.

And she saith, that when she is anything well or beginneth to amend, then her child is tormented, and so continueth for a time in a very strange case; and when he beginneth to amend, then she the said Grace becometh so lame as without help she is not able to arise, or to turn her in her bed.

The information of Agnes[6] Letherdale, wife of Richard Letherdale, taken

---

[5] It was necessary to stress this point, as those who consulted witches were in danger of the law if death or injury to others resulted. 'Unwitching' sometimes meant casting a counter-spell to injure the original causer of a disease; though public sentiment was overwhelmingly in favour of this activity of the 'white witch' or 'cunning man', Grace has obviously been coached to keep clear of any suggestion that she was one of Ursula's clients.

[6] Here and throughout, original has 'Annis', which seems to be an obsolete local variant.

*by me Brian Darcy, Esquire, against Ursula Kemp, alias Grey, the
19 day of February.*

The said Agnes saith, that before Michaelmas last, she the said Ursula
sent her son to the said Letherdale's house to have scouring sand,[7] and
sent word by the said boy that his mother would give her the dyeing
of a pair of women's hose for the sand; but the said Agnes, knowing
her to be a naughty beast, sent her none. And after, she the said Ursula
seeing her girl[8] to carry some to one of her neighbours' houses,
murmured, as the said child said, and presently after her child was
taken as it lay very big, with a great swelling in the bottom of the belly
and other privy parts.

And the said Agnes saith, that about the tenth day of February last
she went unto the said Ursula and told her that she had been forth with
a cunning body,* which said, that she the said Ursula had bewitched
her child. To that the said Ursula answered, that she knew she had not
so been, and so talking further she said, that she would lay her life that
she the said Agnes had not been with any; whereupon she requested a
woman being in the house a-spinning with the said Ursula to bear
witness what she had said. And the next day the child was in most
piteous case to behold, whereby she thought it good to carry the same
unto Mother Ratcliffe, for that she had some experience of her skill.
The which when the said Mother Ratcliffe did see, she said to the said
Agnes that she doubted she should do it any good, yet she ministered
unto it, etc.

*The information of Thomas Rabbet[9] of the age of 8 years or thereabouts,
base son to the said Ursula Kemp alias Grey, taken before me Brian
Darcy, Esquire, one of her Majesty's justices, the 25 day of February,
against his said mother.*

The said Thomas Rabbet saith, that his said mother Ursula Kemp
alias Grey hath four several* spirits, the one called Tiffin, the other
Titty, the third Piggin, and the fourth Jack, and being asked of what
colours they were, saith that Titty is like a little grey cat, Tiffin is like a

---

[7] The earliest form of abrasive cleanser for pots, etc.

[8] girl, i.e. an older child than the one afflicted.

[9] Surnames present an inextricable problem at this date, particularly in the
country, where they are still quite often used to reflect locality or occupation as
well as relationship. Nicknames are still used and recorded; woman who marry
two or three times (as many seem to do) retain former names as an alias. Illegiti-
mate children seem to be named at random—perhaps after godparents, or, just
possibly, after their putative fathers, but not after their mothers.

Cat
*The examination and confession of certaine Wytches
at Chensforde* 1566

white lamb, Piggin is black,* like a toad, and Jack is black, like a cat. And he saith, he hath seen his mother at times to give them beer to drink, and of a white loaf or cake to eat; and saith that in the night-time the said spirits will come to his mother and suck blood of her upon her arms and other places of her body.

This examinate being asked, whether he had seen Newman's wife to come unto his mother, saith, that one morning, he being in the chamber with his mother, his godmother Newman came unto her; and saith, that then he heard her and his mother to chide and to fall out, but saith before they parted they were friends. And that then his mother delivered an earthen pot unto her, in the which he thinketh her spirits were, the which she carried away with her under her apron.

And this examinate saith, that within a few days after, the said Newman's wife came unto his mother, and that he heard her to tell his mother that she had sent a spirit to plague Johnson to the death, and another to plague his wife.

The information of Alice Hunt, taken before me Brian Darcy, Esquire, the 24 day of February, against Joan Pechey, widow.
This examinate Alice Hunt saith, that she dwelleth in the next house unto the said Joan Pechey, and that the said Joan two or three days before Christmas last went to the house of Johnson, the Collector appointed for the poor, whereas she the said Joan received beef and bread, the which this examinate saith, she heard to be of the gift of the said Brian Darcy. And this examinate saith, that the said Joan going homewards, murmured and found great fault at Johnson, saying, he might have given that to a girl or another, and not to her; saying, the bread was too hard baked for her, and that she then seemed to be in a great anger therewithal.

This examinate saith, she was at that present in the house of the Widow Hunt, and that there was but a wall between them. The said Joan coming to her house did unlock her door, the which this examinate did see her do; and after she was entered into her house, this examinate saith, she heard the said Joan to say, 'Yea, are you so saucy? are ye so bold? you were not best to be so bold with me. For if you will not be ruled, you shall have Symond's sauce[10]—yea,' said the said Joan, 'I perceive if I do give you an inch you will take an ell.' And saith she is assured that there was no Christian creature with her at that time, but that she used those speeches unto her imps.

And this examinate saith, that she hath heard her mother say, that she the said Joan was skillful and cunning in witchery, and could do as much as the said Mother Barnes, this examinate's mother, or any other in this town of St. Osyth. And further saith, she hath heard her mother to say that the said Joan did know what was said or done in any man's house in this town.

The information of Margery Sammon, sister to the said Alice Hunt, taken before me Brian Darcy, Esquire, the 25 day of February against the said Joan Pechey, as followeth.

The said Margery saith, that she had heard the Widow Hunt to say that the said Joan Pechey should say that she could tell what any man said or did at any time in their houses, when and as often as she listed;[11] and saith, that the said Widow Hunt did tell her that she hath heard the said Joan Pechey, being in her house, very often to chide, and vehemently speaking as though there had been somebody present with her. And saith, that she went in to see to whom the said Joan should speak, but she found nobody but herself, all alone. And saith, that she the said Joan Pechey was with this examinate's mother, Mother Barnes, the day before she departed, where this examinate left them together while she went home to her mistress' house to do her business and work.

[10] 'To have Simondsall sauce' means to have a good appetite, and means here 'to go without food'. This version seems nearer to the original saying, which is based on an obscure story about a greedy clown; 'Simon' (as in 'Simple Simon') is the conventional name in folk stories for a silly fellow. (See M. P. Tilley, *A Dictionary of Proverbs in England in the Sixteenth and Seventeenth Centuries* (Ann Arbor, 1950), p. 585.)

[11] Hearsay of hearsay, but recorded as evidence.

The information of John Tendering of St. Osyth, taken before me Brian Darcy, Esquire, the 26 day of February 1582.

The said John saith, that William Byatt, having occasion to come to this examinate, saith, that after they had conferred and talked, he the said William Byatt did declare to this examinate that, that morning he did tell him that he had a cow which had lain two days or longer in a strange case and had eaten nothing, and was not likely to live; and that he and his servants several times had lifted at the said cow to raise her upon her feet, but they could not make her to arise or stand. Whereupon he told this examinate that he had caused his said servants to fetch straw and to lay the same round about her, and that he himself took an axe, minding to knock her upon the head and so to burn her;[12] and said that the fire being kindled, the said cow of herself start up, and ran her way until it came to a woodstack, and there stood still, and fell a-biting of sticks bigger than any man's finger and after lived and did well.

The information of Phoebe Hunt, daughter-in-law[13] to Alice Hunt, of the age 8 years or thereabouts, taken before me Brian Darcy, Esquire, the 25 day of February against Alice Hunt her mother.

The said Phoebe Hunt saith, that she hath seen her mother to have two little things like horses, the one white, the other black, the which she kept in a little low earthen pot with wool, colour white and black; and that they stood in her chamber by her bedside. And saith, that she hath seen her mother to feed them with milk out of a black trening[14] dish; and this examinate being carried after this confession by the constables to her father's house, she shewed them the place where they stood and the board that covered them.

And this examinate chose out the dish out of which they were fed from amongst many other dishes. She this examinate did also confess that her mother had charged her not to tell anything what she had seen; and if she did, those things would take her. And this examinate saith, that her mother did send them to Hayward of Frowick, but to what end she cannot tell; and she being asked how she knew the same saith, that she heard her mother bid them to go.

---

[12] Perhaps to prevent the deaths of other cattle.
[13] daughter-in-law, i.e. step-daughter.
[14] Probably a variant of 'treen' or wooden.

Lizard (supposedly a toad)
*The examination and confession of certaine Wytches
at Chensforde* 1566; *also A Rehearsall both straung
and true . . . at winsore* 1579

*The information of William Hook, painter, taken before me Brian
Darcy, Esquire, the 23 of February, against Alice Newman.*

This examinate William Hook saith, that he dwelleth in the next
house unto Alice Newman, and saith, that he had heard William Newman her husband to say unto the said Alice his wife, that she was the
cause of her husband's great misery and wretched state; and saith, that
when the said Alice doth give her husband any meat to eat, then presently he the said William said to his wife, 'Dost thou not see? Dost
thou see?' Whereunto, this examinate saith, that he had heard the said
Alice to say 'If thou seest anything, give it some of thy meat.'[15] And
saith further, that he hath heard the said William Newman bid the said
Alice his wife to 'beat it away'.

*The information of Elizabeth Bennett, taken by me Brian Darcy, Esquire,
the 24 day of February 1582, against Alice Newman.*

The said Elizabeth saith, that she never sent any spirit to plague
Johnson or his wife, neither knew she Mother Newman to have sent
any of her spirits to plague him or his wife. She this examinate for her
part saith, she was greatly beholding to the said Johnson and his wife,
but denieth that ever she sent any spirit to hurt him and his wife, or
that she knew Mother Newman to have hurt them. But this examinate
saith, that she being at Johnson's to have wool to spin (he being a
clothmaker of whom she had many times work), at that present Mother

---

[15] Very much what schoolchildren used to say when they found a caterpillar
in the salad. Perhaps Alice was merely a very bad cook and housekeeper.

Newman being come thither, she this examinate saith she heard the said Mother Newman to desire Johnson to give her 12 pence, saying her husband lay sick.

Whereunto she heard him answer that he would gladly help her husband, but that he had laid out a great deal more than he had received; saying, he was a poor man and he, his wife and family, might not want for the helping of her husband; saying that he could not help her with any until he had collected more money. Whereupon she departed, and used some hard speeches unto him, and seemed to be much angry.

The examination and confession of Ursula Kemp, alias Grey, taken at St. Osyth, and brought before me Brian Darcy, Esquire, one of her Majesty's justices of the peace, the 20 day of February 1582.

Condemned.

The said Ursula Kemp saith, that about ten or eleven years past, she this examinate was troubled with a lameness in her bones, and for ease thereof, went to one Cock's wife of Weeley, now deceased, who told this examinate that she was bewitched, and at her entreaty taught her to unwitch herself; and bade her take hog's dung, and charnell,[16] and put them together and hold them in her left hand, and to take in the other hand a knife, and to prick the medicine three times, and then to cast the same into the fire, and to take the said knife and to make three pricks under a table, and to let the knife stick there. And after that to take three leaves of sage, and as much of herb John (alias herb grace)[17] and put them into ale and drink it last at night and first in the morning; and that she taking the same had ease of her lameness.

The same examinate saith, that one Page's wife and one Gray's wife, being either of them lame and bewitched; she being requested and sent for to come unto them, went unto them. And saith that she knew them to be bewitched and at their desires did minister unto them the foresaid medicine, whereupon they had speedy amendment.

The said Brian Darcy then promising to the said Ursula that if she

[16] Reginald Scot (*Discovery of Witchcraft*, ed. cit. Bk. 15, Ch. 31) speaks of witches carrying 'hogs doong and charvill', which seems to be a reference to this passage. 'Charvell', i.e. chervil, a herb, would be much more likely in this context; English witches did not at this date rob graves.

[17] Herb John: St. John's Wort, which drives away demons. Herb grace is rue —a different plant, but equally common in charms.

would deal plainly and confess the truth, that she should have favour; and so by giving her fair speeches she confessed as followeth.

The said Ursula, bursting out with weeping, fell upon her knees and confessed that she had four spirits, whereof two of them were he's and the other two were she's; the two he-spirits were to punish and kill unto death, and the other two she's were to punish with lameness and other diseases of bodily harm, and also to destroy cattle.

And she this examinate, being asked by what name or names she called the said spirits, and what manner of things, or colour they were of, confesseth and saith, that the one is called Titty, being a he, and is like a gray cat, the second called Jack, also a he, and is like a black cat; the third is called Piggin, being a she, and is like a black toad, the fourth is called Tiffin, being a she, and is like a white lamb.

This examinate being further asked, which of the said spirits she sent to punish Thurlow's wife and Letherdale's child, confessed and said, that she sent Titty to punish Thurlow's wife and Piggin Letherdale's child.

And this examinate, without any asking, of her own free will at that present, confessed and said, that she was the death of her brother Kemp's wife, and that she sent the spirit Jack to plague her, for that her sister[18] had called her 'whore' and 'witch'.

And this examinate further confessed, that upon the falling out between Thurlow's wife and her, she sent Tiffin the spirit unto her child which lay in the cradle, and willed the same to rock the cradle over, so as the child might fall out thereof, and break the neck of it.

These foresaid 5 last recited matters, being confessed by the said Ursula privately to me the said Brian Darcy were afterwards (supper being ended, and she called again before me the said Brian) recited, and particularly named unto her, all which she confessed as before in the presence of us, whose names be hereunder subscribed. [But they are not here.]

Also after this examinate's aforesaid confession, the said Thurlow's wife and Letherdale's wife, being then in my house and she the said Letherdale's wife having her child there also, were brought in my presence before this examinate; who, immediately after some speeches had passed between them, she this examinate burst out in tears and fell upon her knees, and asked forgiveness of the said Letherdale's wife, and likewise of Thurlow's wife; and confessed that she caused Newman's wife to send a spirit to plague the child, asking the said Letherdale's

[18] Sister, i.e. sister-in-law.

wife if she were not afraid that night that the spirit came unto the child, and told her about the same hour, and said that she herself by reason thereof was in a great sweat. And this examinate confesseth, that she caused the said Newman's wife to send a spirit to Thurlow's wife, to plague her where that thought good[19] etc.

The said Letherdale's child (being a woman child) at the time of this examination appeared to be in most piteous sort consumed, and the privy and hinder parts thereof to be in a most strange and wonderful case,[20] as it seemed to very honest women of good judgment, and not likely to live and continue any long time.

Note also that it is specially to be considered that the said child being an infant and not a year old, the mother thereof carrying it in her arms to one Mother Ratcliffe's (a neighbour of hers) to have her to minister unto it, was to pass by Ursula this examinate's house; and passing by the window, the infant cried to the mother, 'Woe! woe!', and pointed with the finger to the window-wards. And likewise the child used the like as she passed homewards by the said window, at which she confessed her conscience moved her so as she went shortly after and talked with the said Ursula; whereupon she used such speeches as moved her to complain.

The second confession and examination of Ursula Kemp, taken the 21 day of February.

The said Ursula being committed to the ward and keeping of the constable that night, upon some speeches that she had passed, said that she had forgotten to tell Master Darcy one thing; whereupon the next day she was brought before Brian Darcy, and the second time examined, who confessed and said:

That about a quarter of a year last past, one Alice Newman, her near neighbour, came unto this examinate's house and fell out with her, and said she was a witch, and that she would take away her witchery and carry the same unto Master Darcy. But this examinate saith, she thought she did not mean it; but after they had chidden they became friends, and so she departed, carrying away with her her spirits in a pot, as this examinate saith.

And she further saith, that about Christmas last, she went to the said Alice Newman and declared to her that Thurlow's wife and she

[19] Careful questioning seems to have made it clear that the witches did *not* know in what way their curses would take effect, and would therefore accept the next misfortune to an enemy as their own doing.

[20] Perhaps a cancerous affliction.

were fallen out, and prayed the said Newman's wife to send the spirit called Titty unto her to plague the said Thurlow's wife where that thought good. The which this examinate saith, she did; and at the return of the said spirit it told this examinate that it had punished Thurlow's wife upon her knee. And then it had a reward by sucking blood of this examinate, and so returned, as she saith, to the said Alice Newman.

This examinate saith, that about three months past, she and one John Stratton fell out, and the said John called her 'whore' and gave her other evil speeches; whereupon this examinate saith, that shortly after she sent her boy for spices unto the wife of the said John. But she saith, she sent her none, whereupon this examinate saith, she went unto the said Newman's wife and told her of the falling out between Stratton and her, and requested the said Newman's wife to send Jack the spirit unto Stratton's wife to plague her.

The which the said Alice Newman promised this examinate to do the next night, as this examinate saith she did, and the spirit told this examinate when it returned that it had plagued her in the back even unto death. And the spirit did suck of this examinate upon the left thigh, the which when she rubbeth (she saith) it will at all times bleed. And she saith that then the spirit did return to the said Newman's wife again, and had the like reward of her, as she thinketh.

This examinate saith, that about Friday was sevennight, being about the ninth of February, she went unto the said Alice Newman and did show her that one Letherdale's wife and she were fallen out, and saith, that she prayed her to send one of the spirits unto her young child, whereunto she the said Alice answered 'Well, she would'. And this examinate saith, that at that time she could have no longer talk with her, for that her husband was then present in the house. And this examinate saith, that the said Alice sent the spirit Piggin to plague the said child where that thought good; and after that it had sucked of this examinate, she saith it returned to the said Newman's wife; and more at that time the said examinate confessed not.

The third examination and confession of Ursula Kemp, alias Grey, taken before me Brian Darcy, Esquire, one of her Majesty's justices of the peace the 24 day of February.

This examinate being asked how she knew the said Elizabeth Bennet to have two spirits, saith, that about a quarter of a year past, she went unto Mother Bennett's house for a mess of milk, the which she had promised her. But at her coming, this examinate saith, she knocked at her door and nobody made her any answer, whereupon she went to her chamber window and looked in thereat, saying, 'Ho, ho, Mother Bennett, are you at home?' And casting her eyes aside, she saw a spirit lift up a cloth lying over a pot, looking much like a ferret.[21] And it being asked of this examinate why the spirit did look upon her, she said it was hungry.

This examinate being asked how she knew the names of Mother Bennett's spirits, saith, that Tiffin her spirit did tell this examinate that she had two spirits, the one of them like a black dog and the other red like a lion, and their names were Suckin and Lierd, and saith that Suckin did plague Byatt's wife unto death, and the other plagued three of his beasts, whereof two of them died and the third lay sick[22] or drooping, and not likely to live. Byatt caused his folks to make a fire about her; the cow, feeling the heat of the fire, start up and ran her way, and by that occasion was saved.

This examinate saith, that about the fourteen or fifteen day of January last, she went to the house of William Hunt to see how his wife did; and she being from home, she called at her chamber window and looked in, and then espied a spirit to look out of a potsherd* from under a cloth, the nose thereof being brown like unto a ferret.

And saith, that the same night she asked Tiffin her white spirit what Hunt's wife's spirit had done; and then it told this examinate that it had killed Hayward of Frowick six beasts which were lately dressed of the gargette.[23] And saith, that her said spirit told her that Hunt's wife's spirit had a drop of her blood for a reward, but she saith, that she asked not her spirit upon what place of her body it was.

This examinate saith, that one Michell, a shoemaker of St. Osyth did tell her that he thought that Glascock's wife had bewitched his child, whereof it died. Whereupon, she this examinate saith that she went home and asked Tiffin her white spirit whether the same were so; which told this examinate that she had bewitched the said child, and sent one of her spirits to plague it to the death.

---

[21] Ursula has already accepted the thesis of the examiner, and describes the ferret she saw as the spirit she is assured it must have been.

[22] Original has 'the third leyer fire'. Probably the compositor picked up 'a fire' from the succeeding sentence as he was setting 'lay' since 'fire' and 'sick' would not be too unlike in Elizabethan handwriting.

[23] Gargette—a swelling or inflammation of the throat in pigs and cattle; dressed—prepared by the butcher.

And saith also, that the said Glascock's wife did bewitch the base*
child that Page and his wife have in keeping, and that her said spirit
told her so. And being demanded, how many spirits Glascock's wife
had, and by what names she called them, this examinate saith, that she
asked not her spirit Tiffin any such questions.

This examinate saith, that the said Elizabeth Bennett did send her
spirit Suckin to plague one Willingale, whereof he languished and
died, being sick of an imposthume.*

This examinate saith also, that the said Elizabeth sent the said spirit
to William Willes his wife to plague her, whereof she languished many
years and died.

This examinate saith, that the said Elizabeth (not above three weeks
since) sent her spirit Lierd to plague Fortune's wife and his child.

This examinate saith, that the said Elizabeth did send her spirit
Lierd to Bonner's wife to plague her, the which her said spirit told
this examinate to be done upon the knee.

This examinate saith further, that Alice Newman went unto Johnson
(being Collector for the poor) and did require him to give her 12
pence for her husband which was sick. But he answering her that he
had disbursed more money than he had collected, saying therefore
he could not then help her with any; the said Newman's wife fell out
with him very angerly, and the next day after sent one of the spirits
that she had from this examinate to plague the said Johnson and his wife
unto the death. And that her spirit called Tiffin did tell the same unto
her, and she being asked what words the said Newman's wife used
to Johnson upon the falling out saith, that she asked not her said
spirit.

This examinate saith, that Newman's wife, being at Butler's and
asking a piece of meat, was denied thereof; whereat she went away
murmuring, and then shortly after sent one of her spirits to punish
him upon the back. The which Tiffin her said spirit telleth this examinate was done, whereof he languisheth and is greatly pained.

This examinate being asked, whether her white spirit called Tiffin
did ever at any time tell her any untruths, or whether she had found
it at any time to tell anything contrary to truth, saith, that the said
spirit did ever tell her true in any matter she required of it, and saith,
that she never knew it to tell her otherwise than truth.

This examinate being asked whether she sent any of her spirits to
plague or punish John Stratton's child, confesseth and saith, that the
spirit which plagued Stratton's wife to the death did also punish the

Dog
The examination and confession of certaine Wytches at Chensforde 1566;
also *A Detection of damnable driftes . . . at Chelmisforde* 1579

said Stratton's child; saying, that the said child should not complain
thereof until the mother were departed.

Note, it is to be considered that the said Ursula Kemp in this her
confession hath uttered many things well 'approved and confessed to
be most true; and that she was brought thereunto by hope of favour.

*The examination and confession of Alice Newman, taken before me Brian
Darcy, Esquire, the 21 of February.*

Condemned.

This examinate saith, that she went unto the house where the said
Ursula Kemp, alias Grey, dwelt, and entered into communication
with her, and that they fell out greatly, and confesseth that she said
unto the said Ursula that she knew her to be a witch, but denieth the
residue of the speeches alleged by the said Ursula against this examinate.

The said Brian Darcy, finding this examinate to be obstinate, and
that she could be brought to confess nothing, said to this examinate
that he would sever and part her and her spirits asunder. 'Nay,' saith
she this examinate, 'that shall ye not, for I will carry them with me.'
And hold being taken of her words, after some distance she added 'if
she have any'.

*The information of William Bonner, taken before me Brian Darcy,
Esquire, the 24 day of February.*

The said William Bonner saith, that the said Elizabeth Bennett and
his wife were lovers and familiar friends, and did accompany much to-

gether; and saith that since Candlemas last his wife hath complained of a lameness in her knee, and that since also she hath been much troubled. And saith also that not ten days past the said Elizabeth Bennett being with his wife, she being sickly and sore troubled, the said Elizabeth used speeches unto her, saying 'Ah good woman, how thou art loden,' and then clasped her in her arms and kissed her. Whereupon presently after her upper lip swelled and was very big, and her eyes much sunked into her head, and she hath lain since in a very strange case.

Upon the said information made by Ursula Kemp, alias Grey, against Elizabeth Bennett, I, Brian Darcy, directed my warrant for her apprehension, whereupon she was brought before me the said Brian; whose confession being taken the 22 day of February.

Condemned.

The said Elizabeth Bennett being charged with the foresaid information, denieth the same in general and, after many and sundry demands, being asked whether she had not a pot or pitcher of earth standing under a pair of stairs in her house, and wool in the same, in the which usually the said two spirits did lie, denied the same with many oaths, saying that she was well assured that she had none such. Whereupon it was said to her, 'If it be proved to your face, what will you say to all the other matters you have been charged with? are they true?' To that she made answer and said 'Yea.'

Then was the pot brought before her, the which she then confessed to be her pot, but denied that the wool therein was any of hers. Then I, calling her unto me, said, 'Elizabeth, as thou wilt have favour, confess the truth. For so it is, there is a man of great cunning and knowledge come over lately unto our Queen's Majesty, which hath advertised her what a company and number of witches be within England;[24]

---

[24] Jean Bodin, the great French jurist, published *De la Démonomanie des Sorciers* (in which he advocated the utmost rigour towards witches) in 1580. In 1581 he himself visited England in the train of the Duc d'Alencon, a visit which lasted from November till 1 February 1581/2. We learn from Bodin's additions to his *De Republica* that he visited Parliament, attended the trial of the Jesuit Campion, and made a speech to Elizabeth herself on the necessity of religious toleration (oddly enough, a principle of his). Among those outside the court, it is quite likely that the speech was surmised to concern Bodin's other passion, witchcraft. The preface to the present pamphlet borrows Bodin's arguments and quotes him; Darcy follows his recommendations closely and is, in

whereupon I and other of her justices have received Commission for the apprehending of as many as are within these limits,[25] and they which do confess the truth of their doings, they shall have much favour; but the other, they shall be burned[26] and hanged.'

At which speeches she the said Elizabeth, falling upon her knees distilling tears, confessed as hereafter followeth.

Saying, that one William Byatt dwelt in the next house unto her three years; saying, that the first year they did agree reasonably well, but ere the second year passed, they fell out sundry and oftentimes, both with this examinate and her husband, Byatt calling her oftentimes 'Old trot' and 'Old witch', and did ban* and curse this examinate and her cattle. To the which this examinate saith, that she called him 'Knave,' saying, 'Wind it up, Byatt, for it will light upon yourself.'[27] And after this falling out this examinate saith, that Byatt had three beasts died; whereof he seeing one of them somewhat to droop, he did beat the said cow in such sort (as this examinate saith) that she thought the said cow did die thereof.

This examinate saith further, that Byatt's wife did beat her swine several times with great gibbets,* and did at another time thrust a pitchfork through the side of one of this examinate's swine, the which Durrant a butcher did buy; and for that when he had dressed it, it proved a-measled,[28] this examinate saith, she had nothing for it but received it again etc.

This examinate saith also, that above two years past there came unto her two spirits, one called Suckin, being black like a dog, the

---

this very passage, carrying out one of Bodin's most unpleasant suggestions— he is trying to procure a confession by a promise of mercy which he has no intention of keeping. It is certainly Bodin of whom he is thinking in this condescending, nursery-style threat to the old woman.

[25] Justices of the peace had no special commission to try witches in Quarter Sessions till 1590. However, the records of the Privy Council show that Councillors were kept informed of all suspicious magical dealings, and frequently sent directives to J.P.s for the apprehension of conjurers. (See *Acts of the Privy Council*, New Series (London, 1895), Vol. 12, pp. 23, 29, 34.) After the *Act against seditious words*, 1580/1, and the exemption of witches from the general pardon, Brian Darcy may well have felt that the specific letters of the Privy Council constituted a general warrant to round up witches.

[26] He threatens the punishment he would like to see inflicted, as well as the one in force.

[27] Cf. the way in which Richard III retorts Margaret's curse upon herself. *Works of Shakespeare*, ed. cit. *Richard III*, I. iii. 234.

[28] Original has 'a messell', i.e. a measel or measle—tapeworm disease of swine.

other called Lierd, being red like a lion. Suckin, this examinate saith, is a he, and the other a she. And saith, on a time as this examinate was coming from mill, the spirit called Suckin came unto her and did take her by the coat, and held her that she could not go forward nor remove by the space of two hours, at the which (this examinate saith) she was much amazed.

And she saith, that the spirit did ask her if she this examinate would go with it, whereat she this examinate said, 'In the name of God, what art thou? Thou wilt not hurt me?' At the which speech it said, 'No.' And this examinate saith, that she then prayed devoutly to Almighty God to deliver her from it, at which time the spirit did depart from her until she had gone a good way; and being come within 30 or 40 roods* of her house, this examinate saith, that the said spirit came again unto her and took her by the coats behind, and held her fast, whereat this examinate saith, that she desired God to deliver her from that evil spirit, and then that did depart to the well. And this examinate saith, that within one hour after, the same spirit came again unto her, she being a-sifting of her meal, and saith, the same remained with her until she had laid her leaven, and then departed.

The said examinate saith, that the next day, she being a-kneading of her bread, the said spirit came again unto her, and brought the other spirit with it called Lierd, and that one of them did ask her why she was so snappish yesterday. To that this examinate saith, that she made answer, 'I trust I am in the faith of God, and you shall have no power over me,' at which words, this examinate saith, the said spirits departed.

Then she this examinate saith, that she being a-making of a fire in her oven, the said spirits came again unto her and took her by the leg; this examinate feeling it to take her by the leg saith she said, 'God and the Holy Ghost deliver me from the evil spirits,' at which words, this examinate saith, that the said spirits did depart, to her thinking.

But this examinate saith, that within half an hour after, she having a fire fork in her hand and being a-stirring of the fire in the oven, the spirit called Suckin came unto her and took this examinate by the hips, and said, 'Seeing thou wilt not be ruled, thou shalt have a cause,'[29] and would have thrust this examinate into the burning oven, and so had (as this examinate saith) but for the foresaid fork. But this examinate striving and doing what she could to her uttermost, the said spirit burnt her arm. the which burning is apparent and evidently to be seen; and when it had thus done it did depart.

[29] Thou shalt have a cause, i.e. I will give you a reason to obey me.

And this examinate saith, that about a month after or more, she being a-walking in a croft near unto a barn called Heywood's barn, the spirit called Suckin came and followed this examinate, she spying the same as she looked back. At the sight thereof, this examinate saith, that her eyes were like to start out of her head, then she saith, that she did beseech God to govern and guide her from the evil spirits, whereupon she saith they did depart.

But the same evening she this examinate being set a-milking of a red cow with a white face, saith that Suckin and Lierd came again unto her, and saith, that Suckin appeared at that time in the likeness of a black dog, and Lierd in the likeness of a hare, the one sitting on the one side of her, the other on the other side of her within less than two yards. And saith, that the cow she was then a-milking of snorted and ran away, and brake her pail and spilt all her milk; neither could she get the said cow any more that night to stand still and saith, that for the loss thereof her husband did much chide her, but she would not tell him what was the cause. And she praying to the Father, the Son, and the Holy Ghost, saith that they did depart, and that she saw them not a quarter of a year after, nor above three times since Midsummer last.

The said examinate saith, that about that time they appeared again unto her, and saith, that a little before there was a falling out between her and the said Byatt; whereupon and for that the said Byatt had oftentimes misused her this examinate and her cattle, she saith, that she caused Lierd in the likeness of a lion to go and to plague the said Byatt's beasts unto death; and the spirit returning told this examinate that it had plagued two of his beasts, the one a red cow, the other a black. And saith, that the spirit told her that he plagued the black cow in the back, and the red cow in the head.

This examinate saith further, that about Whitsuntide last past, the spirit called Suckin did come again at that time unto her, saying to this examinate that he had met Byatt's wife two several times, telling this examinate that it met her once in this examinate's yard, and the next day after it said that it met her at the stile, going into her ground. And saith, it told this examinate it had plagued the said Byatt's wife to the death, she this examinate saying it was done by the spirit, but not by the sending of this examinate; the said spirit saying 'I know that Byatt and his wife have wronged thee greatly, and done thee several hurts, and beaten thy swine and thrust a pitchfork in one of them'— the which the spirit said to have done to win credit with this examinate.

And this examinate saith further, that about Lammas* last past, for that the said William Byatt had abused her, in calling her 'Old Trot, old whore,' and other lewd speeches, she this examinate caused the spirit called Suckin to go and plague the said William Byatt where that would; the which the said spirit did, and at the return of it, it told this examinate, that it met Byatt in the barnyard, and that it had plagued him in the hips, even unto death. And saith, she gave it a reward of milk, and saith, that many times they drank of her milk bowl. And being asked how she came by the said spirits, she confessed and said, that one Mother Turner did send them unto her to her house (as she thinketh) for that she had denied the said Mother Turner of milk.[30] And when, and as often as they did drink of the milk, this examinate saith they went into the said earthen pot, and lay in the wool.

The examination and confession of Agnes Glascock, wife of John Glascock, sawyer, taken before me Brian Darcy, Esquire, the 24 of February.

This examinate being charged by Michell the shoemaker that a woman, sometimes fellow with her in the house, should report her to be a naughty woman and a dealer in witchcraft, denieth that she knew any such woman or that any such speeches were made unto her.

This examinate being charged that one Sparrow, being lodged in her house, should hear a strange noise or rumbling since Christmas last, saith, that she made a noise by removing of boards one night, for that she would have him to lie in another chamber.

This examinate saith also, that long since she dwelt by the space of one quarter or more with her brother Edward Wood; and that at several times in that time certain leaden weights and great stones were cast into the house, and divers strange noises of rumblings heard. The which weights and stones came always nearest one Arnold's head, being then a boarder in that house, and saith that Arnold's wife was accompted a witch,[31] and was suspected to cause the same stones to be

---

[30] These unpleasant and disobliging familiars are regarded as a curse or punishment rather than a gift, showing Elizabeth to be hopelessly confused about the whole idea. Nonetheless, she was hanged.

[31] There is an interesting link here with other records and pamphlets. Lowndes' *Bibliographers' Manual* records a pamphlet now lost: *The Examination and Confession of a notorious Witch named Mother Arnold, alias Whitecote, alias Glastonbury at the Assize of Burntwood in July, 1574; who was hanged for Witchcraft at Barking.* Ewen prints an indictment of Cecilia Glasenberye (Gaol delivery roll: 'Glassenbury al[ias] Arnold') which confirms date and place; and Joan Upney, in the Chelmsford trial of 1589 began her career as a witch after being

cast, to the intent to drive her husband from boarding there, being in jealousy of this examinate, she being at that time not above the age of 20 years.

This examinate saith, that by many years past she was much troubled with strange aches in her bones, and otherwise, whereupon she consumed by the space of two or three years. And saith, that she was told that about Sudbury there dwelt one Herring—named to be a caulker—to whom she went; who declared to this examinate that she was haunted with a witch (naming Arnold's wife), and that she should not escape death without she had some remedy. Whereupon this examinate saith, that she prayed the said Herring to help her; and that he then delivered unto her a little linen bag of the breadth of a groat, full of small things like seeds, and willed her to put the same where her pain was most.[32] The which she proved by sewing it upon her garment near the place where her grief was; and after a while, this examinate saith, she recovered and was well.

This examinate denieth that ever she hurt the base child which Page his wife kept, or that there was any falling out between this examinate and her; and said, that she knoweth not whether the said child be a base child or not.

This examinate being charged, that she sent a spirit to plague Michell the shoemaker's child, or that she had bewitched the said child, denied that she had done either or both. And she being asked whether she ever fell out with one Fortune or his wife, or whether she hurt any of their children, saith, that there was no falling out between them, or that she hurt any of his children.

Agnes Letherdale and Margaret Simpson, women appointed to see and view the body of this examinate, said, and affirm upon their credits, that upon the left side of the thigh of this examinate, there be some spots, and upon the left shoulder likewise one or two, which spots be like the sucked spots that Ursula Kemp hath upon her body.

This examinate and the said Ursula Kemp, alias Grey, being brought before me face to face, the said Ursula then charged this examinate to have plagued and punished Michell's child, whereof it died, and also Fortune's wife's child, whereof it languished. At which speeches this

---

given a familiar by 'one Fustian Kirtle, otherwise called White-cote, a witch of Barking', though she dates this around 1580. However, the general vagueness of her evidence makes it quite possible that she or the reporter is ten years out.

[32] Some people still carry a potato in the pocket to cure rheumatism by 'absorbing acids'.

examinate used outrageous words, calling the said Ursula 'whore', saying she would scratch her, for she was a witch and that she was sure she had bewitched her, for that she could not now weep.

The confession and examination of Alice Hunt, the wife of William Hunt, taken before me, Brian Darcy, Esquire, the 24 of February.

The said Alice Hunt being asked, whether there was any falling out between this examinate and Hayward of Frowick or his wife, saith, there was none; but rather she had cause to be beholding unto them, saying that Hayward's wife did christen her a child. And she being charged to have a spirit in a potsherd, which Ursula Kemp had seen, denied that she had any such, or that she had plagued Hayward's cattle with that or with any other spirit.

This examinate being asked, if she never did feed her spirits with milk out of a little trening dish, said 'No'; the which dish was brought by the constable from her house and then showed to this examinate, the which she denied to be her dish, or that she had any such in her house.

This examinate's warrant being made and to her read, and she committed to the constable to be carried to the jail, desired to speak alone with me the said Brian Darcy; whereupon I went into my garden and this examinate followed me; she then falling upon her knees, with weeping tears confessed and said, that she had within 6 days before this examination, two spirits like unto little colts, the one black and the other white. She saith, she called them by the names of Jack and Robin, and that they told her that the said Ursula Kemp would bewray* her this examinate, and willed her therefore to shift for herself. And so they went from her, and since, this examinate saith, she saw them not.

This examinate saith, that her sister, named Margery Sammon, hath also two spirits like toads, the one called Tom and the other Robin; and saith further, her said sister and she had the said spirits of their mother, Mother Barnes, who departed out of this world within 12 days before the taking of this examination.

The examination and confession of Margery Sammon, taken before me Brian Darcy, Esquire, the 25 of February.

The said Margery Sammon, sister to the said Alice Hunt, daughter to one Mother Barnes lately deceased (which Mother Barnes was accompted* to be a notorious witch), saith, that she remained at home with her mother by the space of half a year, and saith she was with her mother several times when she lay sick, and also at the hour of her death; but denieth the having of any spirits of her said mother, or that her mother had any to her knowledge.

The said Margery that night being committed to the ward and keeping of the constable, and the next day brought before me the said Brian in the presence of her sister Alice Hunt; and being charged by her said sister to have two spirits like toads, given her by her mother at her death, utterly denied the same, saying, 'I defy thee, though thou art my sister,' saying she never saw any such. At which speeches her sister, taking her aside by the arm, whispered her in the ear; and then presently after, this examinate with great submission and many tears, confessed that she had two spirits delivered her by her mother, the same day she departed.

And that she this examinate carried them away with her in the evening, they being in a wicker basket more than half full of white and black wool; and that she asking her mother what she should do with them, she bade her keep them and feed them. This examinate asking 'wherewithal?' her mother answered, 'If thou dost not give them milk, they will suck of thy blood,' and saith, she called them by the names of Tom and Robin. And this examinate being asked how often she had given them meat since she had them, saith and confesseth, that she fed them twice out of a dish with milk; and being asked when she fed them last, this examinate said 'Upon Tuesday last past before this examination, and that with milk.'

This examinate saith also, that when she took them of her mother, she said unto her, 'If thou wilt not keep the said spirits, then send them to Mother Pechey, for I know she is a witch and will be glad of them.' And saith further, that she hearing that Ursula Kemp was apprehended, and fearing that she should be called in question, saith thereupon she took the said spirits (being in a basket) and in the evening went into the ground of her Master, and so into Read's ground, and bade them go to the said Mother Pechey. At which words they skipped out of the said basket, and went before this examinate, she this examinate saying, 'All evil go with you, and the Lord in heaven bless me from ye.' And saith, she might see the said spirits going towards a barred stile, going over into Howe Lane; and when they came at the stile, she saith, they skipped over the same stile and went the ready* way to Mother Pechey's house. And saith, she verily thinketh the said Mother Pechey hath them.

The examination and confession of Joan Pechey, widow, taken before me Brian Darcy, Esquire, the 25 of February.

This examinate Joan Pechey, being asked how old she was, saith, she is threescore years and upwards, and saith that she hath dwelt in the town of St. Osyth above 40 years; and saith, she knew Mother Barnes, and she knew her to be no witch, or that she ever heard her to be accompted, or to have skill in any witchery. And she being asked whether she was with her when she lay upon her death-bed, saith that she was not.

This examinate also denieth, that she hath, or ever had, any puppets, spirits, or mommets,* or that she had any spirits which she bought, or were conveyed unto her by Margery Barnes, or sent by any other since the death of Mother Barnes.

This examinate also denieth, that ever she said to any of her neighbours, or to any other person, in secret sort or merely, that she knew or could tell what any man in the town at any time did or said, when she herself listed or would know.

This examinate saith, that she never used any of those speeches which Alice Hunt hath informed against her, as 'Yea, art thou so saucy? art thou so bold? thou were not best to be so bold, for if thou be'st, thou shalt have Symond's sauce.'

This examinate being asked, what she thought of the sudden death of Johnson the Collector, saith, 'He was a very honest man, and died very suddenly.' And saith, she heard that one Lurkin should say, that he heard Johnson to say, that Mother Newman had bewitched him. And being asked of whom she heard it, she answered, she could not tell; and saith, that she herself never used any hard speeches against the said Johnson.

This examinate, being charged to have willed her son Phillip Barrenger, being of the age of 23 years, to lie in bed with her, denieth that she had so done, other than she had willed him at some times to lie upon the bed at her back.

But the said Phillip, being examined, confesseth and saith, that many times and of late he hath lain in naked bed with his own mother, being willed and commanded so to do of her.[33]

---

[33] These rather squalid domestic arrangements seem to reflect those of David and Abishag rather than a true incest. Nothing further is made of this charge, and Joan is discharged from prison without comment. Though Brian Darcy must have been aware of the unnatural orgies attributed to the witches at their Sabbath on the continent, he ignores this lead into the subject. It is as though the English

This examinate being asked, whether she had any cat in her house, saith that she hath a kitten and a little dog. And being asked, what colour the kitten was of, she this examinate said she could not tell, saying 'Ye may go and see.'

The information of John Sayer, one of the constables of Thorpe, taken before me Brian Darcy, Esquire, one of Her Majesty's justices, against Alice Manfield, the 13 day of March.

The said John saith, that above one year since he had a thatcher which was a-thatching of a barn of his near Mother Manfield's house; and that then she the said Alice came unto the thatcher and would have had him to thatch over an oven of hers, whereunto this thatcher made answer and said 'he would do it if his master would let him, but else he would not do it'. Whereunto she said 'He had been as good as to have willed you to do it; for I will be even with him.'

And he saith, that within a while after, he had occasion to come by the house of the said Alice Manfield with his cart well near three-quarters loaden, and being before her door, upon the hard ground, saith, his cart stood, that he could not make it go forward nor backward by the space of one hour and more. The which he saith, he thought to be done by some witchery which the said Alice Manfield then used.

The information of Robert Sannever, taken before me Brian Darcy, Esquire, one of Her Majesty's justices the 14 of March.

The said Robert saith, that about 15 years past, there dwelt with him the daughter of Elizabeth Eustace, and that for some lewd dealings and behaviour by her done, he saith, he used some threatening speeches unto her, being his servant. And that shortly after she went home to her said mother and told her of her master's using of her; and the next day, he saith, as he was a-sitting by his fireside, his mouth was drawn awry, well near up to the upper part of his cheek. Whereupon he saith, he sent presently to one of skill to come unto him, who came unto him; and that he, seeing him in that case, took a linen cloth and covered his eyes, and struck him on the same side with a strong blow, and then his mouth came into the right course. And he saith that he

---

imagination, perfectly capable of seeing a cat as a devil, simply cannot visualise elderly neighbours flying through the sky to dance naked in a field at midnight, and commit nameless indecencies in the chilly night air.

willed this examinate to put away his servant, and that out of hand, the which he saith he did.

This examinate saith, that 3 years since his brother Cross was taken very sickly, and at times was without any remembrance, and that he sent for this examinate, and when he came unto him, he told him that Margaret Eustace had bewitched him and brought him into that weak state he then was at. Whereto this examinate saith, that if that be so, he then wished a spit red hot and in her buttocks, which speeches of his, he saith, was carried by one then in the house unto the said Mother Eustace; and this examinate saith, that she, seeing a neighbour of his going towards this examinate's house, asked her whither she was going, and she answered, 'unto this examinate's house'. Whereunto she the said Mother Eustace should say 'Nay, go not thither, for he saith I am a witch,' and said 'His wife is with child, and lusty, but it will be otherwise with her than he looketh for.' Whereupon this examinate saith, that his wife had a most strange sickness, and was delivered of child, which within short time after died.

This examinate saith, that the summer after he milked 7 milch* beasts, and that all that summer, many and very often-times, his said beasts did give down blood instead of milk, and that he had little or no profit by them. And he saith that about 4 months after, many of his hogs did skip and leap about the yard in a strange sort, and some of them died.

The information of Ursula Kemp, alias Grey, taken at Colchester by Thomas Tey and Brian Darcy, Esquires, two of her Majesty's justices, the 9 of March.

This examinate being charged that she should report to several persons that have comen unto her since her imprisonment, that Alice Newman should send a spirit to plague the late Lord Darcy, whereof he died;[34] and she being asked whether she said so, saith she said, 'that Tiffin her white spirit told her that Alice Newman had sent a spirit to plague a noble man of whom we (meaning the poor) had all relief'. The which she saith, she took to be the said Lord Darcy; and otherwise she said not.

The information of Richard Ross of Little Clacton, taken before me Brian Darcy, Esquire, against Henry Sellis and Cicely his wife, the 1 day of March.

[34] John, Baron Darcy of Chiche, who died on 3 March 1580/1.

The said Richard saith, that about 6 years past, the said Henry Sellis wrought with this examinate in husbandry many and several times; and saith that at one time he the said Henry being at plough in that said Richard's ground with his plough of horses, they being as well and as likely to any man's judgment as any men's horse might be when they began to work—yet before they had gone twice or thrice about the land, two of his likest horses fell down in most strange wise and died.

This examinate saith, that a little before he had denied the said Cicely Sellis of two bushels of malt, which she would have had for three shillings, but he held it at ten groats.* And saith further, that within a while after the said Cicely Sellis did come unto this examinate's wife, bringing with her a poke,* and desired to buy a bushel or a bushel and a half of malt of her, or as much as her bag would hold. But for that she the said Cicely would not give her her price, she departed without having any, using many hard speeches at that time, whereupon they fell out.

This examinate saith also, that his wife finding Sellis his cattle in his ground did hunt them out thereof, which Sellis his wife seeing, was thereat in a great anger and gave her loud speeches; and saith that presently after, many of his beast were in a most strange taking, the which he doth say to be wrought by some witchcraft or sorcery by the said Henry or Cicely his wife.

This examinate saith, that about 12 months and more past, a barn of his standing in his ground a good way off from his dwelling house with much corn therein was in a most sudden sort fired and burned. But, he saith, he cannot charge the said Henry or Cicely his wife to be the doers thereof, other than the youngest son of the said Henry and Cicely should say 'Here is a goodly store of corn!' and a man unknown should answer 'there was the devil's store.'

The information of Henry Sellis, son of the said Henry, taken before me Brian Darcy, Esquire, the said day and year.

The said Henry saith, that he is of the age of 9 years, and that since Candlemas last, one night about midnight, there came to his brother John a spirit, and took him by the left leg and also by the little toe, which was like his sister but that it was all black; at which time his brother cried out and said, 'Father, Father, come help me! There is a black thing that hath me by the leg, as big as my sister.' Whereat his father said to his mother, 'Why, thou whore, cannot you keep your imps from my children?' Whereat she presently called it away from her son, saying, 'Come away! come away!' at which speech it did depart.

This examinate saith, that the next day he told his mother he was so afraid of the thing that had his brother by the leg that he sweat for fear, and that he could scarce get his shirt from his back; his mother answering, 'Thou liest, thou liest, whoreson.' This examinate being asked, wherewith he had seen his mother to feed her imps and wherein, he saith, that she fed them out of a black dish each other day with milk, and saith, that he hath seen her to carry it unto a heap of wood and broom standing under a crab tree by the house. And being asked what their names were, he saith, that one of them is called by two names, which is Herculus, other John or Jack,[35] and that is a black one and is a he, and the other is called Mercury, and is white, and is a she; and that their eyes be like unto goose eyes. And saith, that he hath seen his mother to remove four broom faggots and so to creep into the crabtree root, whereas they stand and lie upon a fleece of wool.

And this examinate saith further, that the same night Ross his maid was taken, when his father came home, his mother told him her husband that she had sent Herculus to Ross his maid, and he answered, 'Ye are a trim* fool.' This examinate saith, that as he and his mother were coming (they being in Ross his broomfield) she said unto him, 'Take heed ye say nothing.'

The information of John Sellis the youngest son of Henry and Cicely, taken before me Brian Darcy, Esquire, the third day of March.

The said John Sellis saith, that he is about the age of 6 years 3 quarters, and saith, that one night there was a black thing like his sister that took him by the leg, and that he cried out saying, 'Father, Father, come help me and defend me, for there is a black thing that hath me by the leg!' At which he saith, his father said to his mother, 'Ye stinking whore, what mean ye? Can ye not keep your imps from my children?' And being asked what colour they were of and what they were called, he saith, that one is black and another is white, and that he hath heard his mother to call them Imps, and that they have eyes as big as himself; and he saith that his father bade his mother put them away or else kill them.

[35] Original has '*herculus* sothe *hons* or *Jack*'; the fold-in sheet at the end of the book transcribes this 'Sotheons Herculus, Jack'. Since the little boy John says his father calls the black imp John to tease him, it might be that this should read 'Herculus, other John or Jack' (Jack as pet-name of John).

And saith, that a while since his mother delivered them to one of Colchester (he thinketh his name is Wedon or Glascock) and saith that Wedon's wife had a cap to dress of his mother's, and saith, that they were carried away in a basket at that time. And being asked, whether his father or mother bade him that he should say nothing, he saith, that his mother said unto him that he should go before a gentleman, and willed him to take heed he told no tales nor lies.

He saith, that his father called one of them, which is the black one, John, which he said his father mocked him because his name was so; and his mother called the white one an Imp. He saith, he hath seen his father to feed them out of a black dish with a wooden spoon, and that he knoweth the same dish, and the last time he fed them it was behind the broomstack at the crabtree. And he saith, that the man which carried them away gave his mother a penny, and that when she should go to him she should have another penny; he saith at that time his brother was from home at one Gardener's house.

And being asked, whether ever he saw his mother to feed them, he saith, that he hath seen his mother to feed them twice, and that out of a dish with a spoon, with thin milk.

Note also, it is to be considered that there is a scar to be seen of this examinate's leg where it was taken, and also the nail of his little toe is yet unperfect.

The information of Joan Smith, wife of Robert Smith, taken before me Brian Darcy, Esquire, the said day and year.

The said Joan saith, that one holy day in the afternoon since Michaelmas last, she had made herself ready to go to church, and took in her arms her young child and, opening her door, her mother (grandmother to the child), one Redworth's wife, and Sellis his wife were at the said door ready to draw the latch, she this examinate telling her mother she was coming out of doors to churchward. Whereat the grandmother to the child took it by the hand and shook it, saying, 'Ah, Mother Pugs,[36] art thou coming to church?' And Redworth's wife looking on it said, 'Here is a jolly and likely child, God bless it.'

After which speech Sellis his wife said 'She hath never the more children for that, but a little babe to play withal for a time.' And she saith within short time after her said child sickened and died. But she saith that her conscience will not serve her to charge the said Cicely

[36] Pet name.

or her husband to be the causers of any such matter, but prayeth God to forgive them if they have dealt in any such sort etc.

The examination and confession of Henry Sellis and Cicely his wife, taken before me Brian Darcy, Esquire, the first day of March.

The said Henry saith, that he hath wrought in husbandry by some long time past with Richard Ross of Little Clacton, and that one time, he being at plough, two of his horses upon a sudden fell down and were in most strange taking, but what the occasion should be thereof, he saith, he knew not. And saith, that he doth not remember that [his wife] would have had any malt of the said Ross at his price, or that there was any falling out between them; and denieth that his child cried out unto him, saying, 'Father, come help me!' or that he called his wife 'stinking whore;' and denieth all the residue of the matters in general informed against him etc.

Condemned.

The said Cicely his wife saith, that she doth not remember that Ross his wife did at any time hunt her cattle, being in her ground, or that she used any hard speeches to his wife thereupon, or that she fell out for that she could not have any malt at her price; but she saith at one time she met Ross his wife, and that there was some talk between them the which she doth not remember more than that the said Ross's wife said, 'I shall see at your end what you are.'

And being asked if she knew not Mother Tredsall, she saith she knew her, but she denieth that she said 'if she were a witch, she learned the same of the said Mother Tredsall;' and denieth that her child cried out in the night to his father, and all the residue of the matters in general informed against her.

Alice Gilney, Joan Smith, and Margaret Simpson, women of credit appointed by me Brian Darcy to view and see the body of the said Cicely say, that she hath upon her body many spots very suspicious, and the said Margaret saith, that they be much like the sucked spots that she hath seen upon the body of Ursula Kemp and several others.

The information of Alice Baxter, servant with Richard Ross, taken by me Brian Darcy, Esquire, one of her Majesty's justices of the peace, the 19 day of March.

The said Alice saith, that about Hallowmass last past, about four of the clock in the afternoon she went a-milking into her master's ground

Cat
A Rehearsall both straung and true . . . at winsore 1579

two closes* off from the house, and that she had eight or nine beasts to milk, and saith that after she had milked all but one, and as she was a-milking of that one, before she had half done the cow start, and struck down her pail, and that she saw all the rest to make a staring and a looking about.

And she saith, as she was a-making an end of milking of that cow, she felt a thing to prick her under the right side, as if she had been stricken with one's hand; and she saith that after, as she was going homewards with her milk, near the stile in the same close there came a thing all white like a cat, and struck her at the heart in such sort as she could not stand, go, nor speak; and so she remained until her said master and two of his workmen did carry her home in a chair. She saith, she saw the said thing to go into a bush by the stile, and that she knew not her master when he came unto her.[37]

Robert Smith saith, that about Hallowmass last past he wrought with Richard Ross, and that about 5 o'clock was called by the said Ross to help him to fetch home his maid, and going then with him, they found the said Alice his maid sitting leaning against the stile and in that case as she could not stand, go, nor speak; and that he and

[37] This sounds like a stroke.

one other with their master's help took her up and brought her home in a chair.

The information of Henry Durrant, taken by me Brian Darcy, Esquire, one of Her Majesty's justices of peace, the 26 day of March, against Alice Hunt.

The said Henry Durrant saith, that about the second day of this present month, he went to Colchester to appear before the justices there to be bound from killing of flesh.[38] And after that he had so done he saith, that he went with several of his neighbours unto the Castle, to see the witches that were committed thither, at which time he saith, he talked with Ursula Kemp alias Grey, who then told him after some demands which he used unto her, that Alice Hunt and her mother, the Widow Barnes, had bewitched his daughter, whereof she died; saying that 'because they were denied of a piece of pork at such time as they came for it, therefore they were offended with you.' And saith further, that he doth remember that they came unto him and would have had a piece of pork, the which, for that it was newly dressed and somewhat hot, he made them answer that he would not cut it out.

The information of Richard Ross and others together, with the confession of Henry Sellis and Cicely his wife.

[Missing.]

The examination and confession of Alice Manfield, taken at Thorpe, and brought before me Brian Darcy, Esquire, one of her Majesty's justices, the 13 day of March.

Condemned.

The said Alice Manfield saith, that she is of the age of threescore and three years or thereabouts, and that about 12 years since one Margaret Grevell came unto this examinate and said, that she should go out of her house that she dwelt in unto another house in the town, and then told her that she had four imps or spirits, the which she would not carry with her to that house, for fear they should be espied or seen; and prayed her this examinate that she would keep them, and also told her what they would do for her (saying she should have them upon condition that she the said Margaret might have them at her

---

[38] Presumably because of Lent.

pleasure, otherwise she should not have them) and with what, and how she should feed them. And at her desire and request she saith that she was contented to keep them; and thereupon, she saith it was concluded and agreed between her and this examinate that she the said Margaret should have them as often and as many times as she would, at her pleasure, and that then she received them.

This examinate being asked what names they were called by, and of what likeness, saith that one of them was called Robin, another Jack, the third William, the fourth Puppet, alias Mommet, and that two of them were he's and the other two were she's, and were like unto black cats. And saith, that she kept them in a box with wool therein, and that they did stand upon a shelf by her bed where she lay.

This examinate saith also, that the said Margaret Grevell hath comen unto her many and oftentimes since the said agreement between them made, and according to the said condition hath received of this examinate the said imps or spirits, she this examinate being told of her sometimes wherefore she would have them, and that sometimes she knew by asking the said imps or spirits where they had been and what they had done when they returned again unto her.

And being asked how often and when to her remembrance, she this examinate saith about 7 years since the said Mother Grevell came unto this examinate and told her that Cheston's wife and she were fallen out, and had chidden very much, and that she gave her evil speeches; whereupon she requested to have the spirit Robin to go to plague his beasts, and then sent it; which said when it returned that Cheston being at plough, leaving work, that it had plagued a bullock of his that was well liking and lusty, whereof it should pine and die.

This examinate saith, that the said Margaret Grevell, well near two years after, sent her spirit Jack to go to plague Cheston upon the great toe unto the death. This examinate saith, that when it returned it told her that it had plagued the said Cheston upon the toe even unto death, and that it had sucked blood of the said Margaret's body, and that besides it had of her beer and bread for the labour; and saith, that she this examinate gave it beer and bread then also, for telling of her.

This examinate saith also, that five years past or thereabouts, her spirit Robin told her that Margaret Grevell had sent the said spirit unto her husband to plague him, whereof he pined above half a year and more, having by that means many and several strange sores, and thereof died. And this examinate saith, that he would eat as much or more than two men would do, and that it sucked blood upon the body of the said Margaret for the labour; she this examinate being asked upon what place saith, the said spirit did not tell her.

This examinate saith, that on a time she went unto the house of Joan Cheston, widow, and desired of her to give her some curds; but she saith, she gave her none, wherefore she saith, that she sent her imp Puppet, alias Mommet to plague her beasts where that would, and so it did. And that when the said imp returned, it told this examinate that it had plagued four of her beasts with lameness, and that it did suck blood upon this examinate's body for a reward.

This examinate saith, that about two years past, one John Sayer did fetch dung out of an orchard from a pit's bank near this examinate's house, and did by reason thereof gull* a green place before her door, whereupon, she saith, she sent her imp called Puppet alias Mommet to stay the cart, being before the door. The which it did, and she saith that she saw him and others to lift at the wheels, and to set his hawser rope, the which did little good, and that the same hawser rope and other of his horse harness burst asunder, and she saith, she gave her said imp beer for the labour.

This examinate saith, that little before Michaelmas last, her said four imps said unto her, saying, 'I pray you, Dame, give us leave to go unto Little Clacton to Sellis,' saying, they would burn barns and also kill cattle; and she saith, that after their return they told her that they had burnt a barn of Ross's with corn, and also told her that Sellis his wife knew of it, and that all they four were fed at Sellis' house by her all the time they were away from this examinate, which she saith was about a sevennight; and that Puppet sucked upon this examinate's left shoulder at their return unto her, and the rest had beer.

This examinate saith, that William, one of her imps, not above a sevennight before her apprehension told her that she should be called in question, and bade her shift for herself, saying, they would now depart from her and go unto St. Osyth unto Mother Grey, Mother Turner, or Mother Barnes' two daughters, but to which of them it was that they would go she doth not now remember. But they told her that they to whom they went had hurt men and women to death, and several men's cattle, and other things.

This examinate saith, that about a quarter of a year since, she went unto the house of Mother Eustace to speak with her, at which time she saith, she saw three imps which she had standing in an earthen pot in the one side of her house next the heath; and saith that one of them was white, the other gray, and the third black, and saith they were like cats. This examinate saith also, that her white spirit told her that Mother Eustace their dame sent her imps to hurt a child, whereof it should pine and become lame, but whose child she remembereth not.

Also this examinate saith, that upon some conference between Mother Eustace and her, she this examinate told Mother Eustace that Mother Grevell did plague her husband, whereof he died, which was done by her spirit Robin; she saith that she also told Mother Eustace that Mother Grevell sent her spirit Jack to plague Cheston to the death, but what answer she the said Mother Eustace then made, she now remembereth not.

This examinate saith, that about a year since the said Mother Grevell told her that she had caused her imps to destroy several brewings of beer and batches of bread; being asked where, she saith 'A brewing at Read's, a brewing at Carter's and a brewing of three or four bushels of malt at Bruce's.'

The said confession being made by the said Alice in manner and form aforesaid, I the said Brian in the presence of the constables and other the townsmen of Thorpe, said as I had several times before unto the said Alice what a danger it was, and how highly she should offend God if she should charge any person with anything untrue, and also told her that her said confession should be read again unto her, willing her that if she heard anything read that she knew was not true, that she should speak and it should be amended; the which being done, she said her confession was true, and the said Margaret and Elizabeth being then also called before me, she affirmed her confession to their faces.

The information of Thomas Death and Mary his daughter, taken by me Brian Darcy, Esquire, one of her Majesty's justices, the 15 day of March.

The said Thomas Death saith, that about two years since, there was a great falling out between this examinate's wife and the said Cicely Sellis, for that one George Battle having put a child of his to the nursing and keeping of the said Cicely, and after he taking the said child away from her and put the same to this examinate's wife to be nursed and kept; whereupon at the next meeting of the said wives, the said Sellis his wife chid and railed at her and said 'Thou shalt lose more by the having of it, than thou shalt have for the keeping of it.' And within one month after, as he now remembereth, he saith that a child of his, of the age of four years, being in good liking and well, went but out of the doors into the yard, who presently fell down dead,[39] and after by help being brought to life, the said child was in a piteous case and so died presently.

This examinate saith, that he had presently after several swine which did skip and leap about the yard in a most strange sort, and then died. And he saith that over night he had a calf which was very fat, and the next morning he found the same dead.

This examinate saith, that having been at sea and newly arrived at Ipswich, a messenger which was newly come from his wife by chance met him, who told this examinate that his daughter Mary was taken very strangely and lay in a most piteous case; saying he had brought her water to carry unto a physician to have his opinion thereof.

Whereupon this examinate saith, that he and the messenger went therewith unto one Bert dwelling in that town, and showed him the same; he saith, he asked him if that his daughter were not bewitched. But he said that he would not deal so far to tell him, whereupon he not satisfied to his mind met after with an acquaintance of his, and asked him where he might go to a cunning man, telling him in what case his daughter lay in; who then sent him to a man whom he knew not, nor his name he now remembereth not, with whom after he had conferred and showed his daughter's said water, this examinate saith, he told him if he had not comen with some great haste to seek help, he had come too late.

And this examinate saith, that he told him that within two nights after, the parties that had hurt his daughter should appear unto her and remedy her; and he saith, that he himself did not then come home, but went to sea. But he saith he sent his messenger home with things that were to be ministered unto his said daughter.

This examinate saith, that when he came home, his wife told him that the next night after his daughter had received the things ministered unto her, that she heard a noise like a groaning, and that she did arise and went unto her daughter and asked her how she did; whereunto her daughter made answer and said, 'Ah mother, that you had comen a little sooner, you should have seen Sellis' wife and Barker's wife here standing before me.'

Mary Death, daughter of the said Thomas Death, saith, that about two years since upon a Sunday, she was taken with an ache or numbness from her neck down her back, all over. And she saith, that after her mother had ministered things unto her sent from a physician, the

[39] dead, i.e. in a swoon.

next night after she saith she heard a voice saying unto her, 'Look up'; at which she saith she lifted up her eyes and then did see Sellis' wife and Barker's wife standing before her in the same apparel that they did usually wear.

And she this examinate saith, she thought they said unto her 'Be not afraid,' and that they vanished away; as she thinketh it was about midnight. And the next day after, this examinate saith, she amended and was in case to rise without help, where afore two or three could scarce turn her in her bed as she lay.

The information of Joan Cheston, widow, John Carter, and other the inhabitants of the town of Thorpe, taken before me Brian Darcy, Esquire, one of her Majesty's justices of the peace, the 13 day of March, against Alice Manfield.

The said Joan saith, that in summer last, Mother Manfield came unto her house and requested her to give her curds. She saith that answer was made that there was none, and so she departed. And within a while after some of her cattle were taken lame and could not travel to gather their meat, so that her servants were constrained to mow down grass for them by the space of eight days.

She saith, that afterwards the said Mother Manfield came again unto her and demanded curds and she saith, that she then told the said Mother Manfield that she had bewitched her cattle; and that she then said unto her that if her cattle did not amend and become well, she would burn her; whereupon she saith, that her cattle did amend and within a very short while after were as well as before.

Lynd's wife saith, that the said Mother Manfield came unto her and asked her a mess of milk, who answered that she had but a little, not so much as would suckle her calf, whereat she departed; and she saith, that that night her calf died, being very lusty and 20 days old.

The information of John Carter and others of Thorpe, taken by me Brian Darcy, Esquire, one of her Majesty's justices, the 20 day of March, against Margaret Grevell.

Continued in prison.

The said John saith, that on a time Margaret Grevell came unto this examinate's house, desiring her to have God's good,[40] which was

[40] Probably 'yeast' in this context, though God's good could also mean (a) property belonging to no one (b) property belonging to the church or God, and therefore alms.

denied her, and saith that within a few days after his folks went in hand with brewing. But of two brewings after they could make no beer, but was fain to put the same to the swill tub, which was half a seam* at a brewing. And saith, that the third time they went to brewing with the like quantity and that his son, being a tall and lusty man of the age of 36 years, was wished to take his bow and an arrow and to shoot to make his shaft or arrow to stick in the brewing vat, and that he shot twice and could not make the same to stick, but at the third time that he shot, he made the same to stick in the brewing vat, and after, he saith, they could brew as well as before.

Nicholas Strickland, butcher, saith, that Margaret Grevell sent her son unto him for a rack* of mutton; he having newly killed a mutton saying the same was hot and that he could not cut it out, and saith, that he bade him come again in the afternoon. And the Monday after, his wife seething milk for the breakfast of his workfolks, the same stank and was bitter; and saith within few days after his wife went to churn her cream that she had gathered and that she was from the morning until ten of the clock in the night a-churning, and could have no butter. The which this examinate seeing, he saith he caused his wife to pour the said cream into a kettle and to set it upon the fire, the which was done; and making a great fire under it, this examinate saith, they could not make it to seethe over.

Then this examinate saith, that he seeing it would not do, he saith he took the kettle off the fire and poured the one half thereof into the fire, and the other half he let stand in the kettle; the which, he saith, stank in such exceeding sort as they could not abide in the house.

And this examinate saith, that the second time that his wife went to churn her cream, she continued a-churning and could have no butter but that it was as the other; the which, he saith, his wife was constrained to put it into the swill tub. And after that this examinate saith, that the head and master cow of five beasts did also cast her calf, and presently after fell a-halting, the which he, fearing that it would have died, saith that he fed it and killed it.

The information of Felice Okey, widow, taken by me Brian Darcy, Esquire, one of her Majesty's justices of the peace, the 20 day of March against Elizabeth Eustace.

The said Felice saith, that she was the late wife of Thomas Cross, and that she on a time finding the geese of Elizabeth Eustace in her ground did drive them out, and that by mischance one of her geese was hurt.

Whereat the said Elizabeth fell out exceedingly with this examinate and gave her hard speeches, saying that 'thy husband shall not have his health, nor that which he hath shall not prosper so well as it hath done,' and that she also said 'Thou hast not had so good luck with thy goslings, but thou shalt have as bad.'

And she saith, that never after that she could have any of them geese which she herself kept; and also the same night she saith that one of her kine gave down blood instead of milk, and after for the space of 8 days.

This examinate saith, that her late husband T. Cross was taken in a strange sort and thereof pined and saith, that on a time as her said husband was a-walking in his ground, he was cast amongst bushes and was in that case that he could neither see, hear, nor speak, and his face all to-bescratched. And she saith, that he being in that strange case, when he came to his memory he would always cry out upon the said Elizabeth even unto his dying day, and would say that since she the said Elizabeth had threatened him he was consumed, and that she had bewitched him.

The examination of Lawrence Kemp taken before me Brian Darcy, Esquire, one of her Majesty's justices, the 20 day of March, against Ursula Kemp.

The said Lawrence saith, that his late wife was taken in her back and in the privy parts of her body in a very extreme and most strange sort, and so continued about three quarters of a year, and then died; and he saith, that his said wife did tell him several times that Ursula Kemp his sister had forspoke her, and that she was the only cause of that her sickness.

This examinate saith, that his said wife did tell him that two years before she met the said Ursula his sister upon Eliot's Heath, and that she fell upon her, and then took up her clothes and did beat her upon the hips, and otherwise in words did misuse her greatly.

This examinate saith, that when his wife lay a-drawing home, and continued so a day and a night, all the parts of her body were cold like a dead creature's, and yet at her mouth did appear her breath to go and come; and that she so continued in that case until the said Ursula came unto her without sending for, and then lifted up the clothes and took her by the arm, the which she had not so soon done but presently after she gasped, and never after drew her breath, and so died.

The examination and confession of Margaret Grevell, taken before me Brian Darcy, Esquire, one of her Majesty's justices of the peace, the 24 day of March.

Continued in prison.

This examinate saith, that she is of the age of 55 years or thereabouts, and being charged with the foresaid information and confession made by the said Alice Manfield against her, denieth the same in general and saith, that she herself hath lost several brewings, and bakings of bread, and also swine, but she never did complain thereof; saying, that she wished her gear were at a stay, and then she cared not whether she were hanged or burnt or what did become of her.

This examinate being asked what falling out was or hath been between Cheston and her, saith, on a time she went to the said Joan Cheston to buy a pennyworth of rye meal,[41] but she would let her have none; and saith, she said that it was pity to do her any good, saying that she this examinate had told Master Barnish that Sheriff's dog did kill a doe of his by the park pale, and saith, that there was none other falling out as she remembereth.

This examinate being viewed and seen by women, say that they cannot judge her to have any sucked spots upon her body.

This examinate and the said Alice Manfield being brought before Brian Darcy, the said Alice did affirm her confession made by her to her face to be true.

The examination and confession of Elizabeth Eustace, taken before me Brian Darcy, Esquire, the 14 day of March.

Continued in prison.

The said Elizabeth Eustace saith, she is of the age of 53 years or thereabouts, and denieth the information and confession made by the said Alice Manfield in general, or that ever she had any imps or mommets, saying 'Out upon her, hath she told anything of me?' And she

---

[41] Bread can be made successfully only with wheat or rye, or 'maslin'—a mixture of these. Rye is subject to a particular blight which renders the grain poisonous, and ergot poisoning has occasionally affected whole communities. Symptoms are loss of circulation and gangrene of the extremities; tingling, loss of sensation, deafness, vision defect, and mental disorders including hallucination. Some of these symptoms are common in accounts of witch trials, and it is possible that ergot poisoning might sometimes have been a factor in the wilder stories of witches and their spirits.

being asked, what conference had been between her and the said Alice Manfield saith, that there was none to her remembrance, other than once she went unto her and carried her ointment to anoint her lameness that she was troubled with, and that then there was no conference which she remembereth.

The said Alice Manfield in my presence did affirm her confession made against the said Elizabeth to and before her, face to face.

The information of John Wad, Thomas Cartwright, Richard Harrison with several others the parishioners of Little Oakley, taken by me Brian Darcy, Esquire, one of her Majesty's justices the 16 day of March.

John Wad saith, that about two month since Agnes Herd said unto him that she was presented into the spiritual court for a witch, and prayed him to be a means to help her, that she might answer the same when the days were longer. Whereunto he said, that he told her that the Register dwelt at Colchester, saying, 'It must be he that therein may pleasure thee;' whereto she said that she would go to John Aldust of Ramsey to speak unto him, for that he goeth to Colchester that he might speak to the officers for her, and so she departed.

This examinate saith, that since that time he drove forty sheep and thirty lambs to a pasture that he had at Tendring, being thereof well near fourscore acres, the which he had spared by some long time, and knew the same to be a good sheep's pasture; and saith, that after they had been there 8 or 9 days, he went to see them (having nevertheless appointed one to look to them). And at his coming he found one to be dead, another to be lame, another to sit drooping and a lamb in the same case by it, which all died; and he found one other with the neck awry, which is in that case to this day, and one other which was so weak that it could not arise.

And this examinate saith, that since he with others that presented her, and since she the said Agnes talked with him, he hath had not so few as twenty sheep and lambs that have died, and be lame and like to die; and he saith, that he hath lost of his beasts and other cattle, which have died in a strange sort.

Thomas Cartwright saith, that after a great wind and snow well near three years since, there was an arm or bough of a tree of his that was blown down, whereof Agnes Herd had removed a piece and laid the same over a wet or dirty place to go over; which being to this examinate unknown, he took the same and the rest and carried it home. The which the said Agnes knowing that he had carried the same away, she said that the churl (meaning this examinate) to a neighbour of hers had carried away the piece of the bough that she had laid to go over, saying that she would be even with him for it.

After which, this examinate saith, within three nights after (there then being a snow) two of his beasts went from all the rest whereas they lay, as he might well perceive by the snow and the head cow fell over a great bank into a ditch on the other side, and there lay with the neck double under her and the head under the shoulder, but alive. And he saith, he got it home by good help and laid it in his barn and saith, that it lay fourteen days in a groaning and piteous sort, but of all that time would eat nothing; whereupon he saith, he took an axe and knocked it on the head. And also the other cow that was with the said cow, being a-calving, in a most strange sort died; the which this examinate saith, that he verily thinketh to be done by some witchery by the said Agnes Herd.

Bennet Lane, wife of William Lane, saith that when she was a widow, Agnes Herd being at her house she gave her a pint of milk and also lent her a dish to bear it home, the which dish she kept a fortnight or three weeks; and then the girl of the said Agnes Herd's came to her house on a message, and she asked the girl for the dish and said, 'Though I gave thy mother milk to make her a posset, I gave her not my dish'—she this examinate being then a-spinning.

And so the girl went home and, as it seemed, told her mother, who by her sent her dish home to her; the which girl having done her errand and being but a while gone, she this examinate saith, she could no longer spin nor make a thread to hold. Whereat she was so grieved that she could not spin, she saith, she took her spindle and went to the grindstone therewith once or twice, and ground it as smooth as she could, thinking it might be by some ruggedness of the spindle that did cause her thread to break; and so when she had ground it as well as she could, she went again to work therewith, thinking that then it would have done, but it would not do no better than it did before. Then she saith, that she remembered herself and took her spindle and put it into the fire and made it red hot, and then cooled it [a]gain and went to work; and then it wrought as well as ever it did at any time before.

This examinate saith, that another time the said Agnes Herd owed her twopence, and the time came that she should pay the Lord's rent,[42] and she being a poor woman was constrained to ask her the twopence,

[42] Lord's rent, i.e. tithe to the church.

and to borrow besides (as she said); whereto she the said Agnes answered, that she had paid eight or nine shillings that week and she had it not now, saying she should have it the next week. Whereto she this examinate said, 'You must needs help me with it now, for this day I must pay the Lord's rent.' Then she said she must go borrow it, and so went and fetched it, saying 'There is your money;' whereunto she this examinate answered and said 'Now I owe you a pint of milk; come for it when you will and you shall have it.' The which she came for the next day and had it with the butter.

This examinate saith, that the next day she would have fleet* her milk bowl, but it would not abide the fleeting, but would rope and roll as it were the white of an egg;[43] also the milk being on the fire it did not so soon seethe but it would quail, burn by, and stink, the which she said she thought might be long of the feeding of her beasts or else that her vessels were not sweet. Whereupon, she saith, she scalded her vessels and scoured them with salt, thinking that might help, but it was never the better but as before.

Then, she saith, she was full of care that she should lose both milk and cream; then she saith it came into her mind to approve another way which was:—she took a horse-shoe and made it red hot and put it into the milk in the vessels and so into her cream; and then, she saith, she could seethe her milk, fleet her cream, and make her butter in good sort as she had before.

Andrew West and Anne saith, that on a time the said Agnes Herd came unto his house saying she had been at mill and that she could get neither meal nor bread; at which her speeches he, knowing her need, saith, he caused his wife to give her a piece of a loaf. And that then he said unto her 'Agnes, thou art ill thought of for witchcraft;' the which she then utterly denied that she could or did any such thing.

Whereunto he saith, his wife said 'We have a sort* of pigs; I wot not what we shall do with them,' saying 'I would somebody had one or two of them.' To that the said Agnes said, that if a poor body should have of them and bestow cost, and that then if they should die it would half undo them; and said if her landlord would give her leave to keep one, she then wished that she would give her one of them, whereunto this examinate said, she should have one.

But for that she came not for it, this examinate saith, that he did think that she cared not for it, and after a while one of her neighbours

---

[43] Reginald Scot gives a learned explanation of this common disaster, often attributed to witches. (*The Discovery of Witchcraft*, Bk. 12, Ch. 21.)

bought two of them; and within 2 or 3 days after the said Agnes came for one. To whom this examinate said, for that they had not heard no more of her, that he thought she would have none; and told her that he had sold two of them, and so the said Agnes departed and went home.

This examinate saith, that his wife the next day sent unto the said Agnes a pound of wool to be spun, and that she said to the boy that brought it, saying 'Can she not have her weeders to spin the same?' and that she then said to the boy, 'Your aunt might as well give me one of her pigs as to Penly.' And this examinate saith, that within two hours after, one of the best pigs that he had fell upon a-crying as they stood all together before the door in the yard, and the rest of the pigs went away from it. At the length the pig that cried followed staggering as though it were lame in the hinder parts, and that then he called his weeders to see in what strange case the pig was in, and asked them what was best to do therewith.

To which some of them said 'Burn it,' other said 'Cut off the ears and burn them,' and so they did, and then the pig amended by and by. And within two days after this examinate's wife met with the said Agnes Herd, and she then burdened her with that she had said to her boy; to the which the said Agnes made answer that she did say so. And then this examinate's wife told the said Agnes in what case her pig was, saying 'Thou saidst the other day thou hadst no skill in witchery.' His said wife then said, 'I will say thou hast an unhappy tongue.'

After which this examinate's wife could not brew to have any drink that was good, so as she was full of care, saying that sometimes she put one thing into her brewing vat, sometimes another thing to see if it could do it any good but she saith, it did none. Then she saith, one gave her counsel to put a hot iron into her mash vat, the which she did, and then she could brew as well as she did before.

Edmund Osborne and Godlife his wife said, that a little before Christmas last past he bought at Manningtree malt, and brought it home and said to his wife, 'Good wife, let us have good drink made of it.' And the next day she went in hand to brew the same, and when she had mashed her first wort* and did let it go, that did very well. Then his said wife having occasion to send her lad to their ground, she bade the lad call at Agnes Herd's for 3 pence the which she owed her for a peck of apples, and that the lad so did. And she answered him very short and said, she had it not now, saying she should have it as soon as the wool-man came; and the lad came home and told his dame what she had said.

And at that time, she this examinate was ready to mash the second time, and when she had done, her mash vat wrought up as the vat doth when it was set a-work with good beer and bare up a handbreadth above the vat, and as they thrust in a stick or any other thing, it would blow up and then sinked again; then she did heat an iron red hot and put the same into it and it rose up no more. And then she let go, and then she did seethe* the wort, and when it was sodden* it stank in such sort as that they were compelled to put the same in the swill tub.

Richard Harrison, Clerk, parson of Beaumont saith, that he and his late wife did dwell at Little Oakley, in a house of his said wife, and that he the said Richard Harrison had also the parsonage of Oakley in farm.[44] And about summer was twelvemonth, he being at London, his wife had a duck sitting on certain eggs under a cherry tree in a hedge; and when the said duck had hatched, his said wife did suspect one Agnes Herd, a light woman and a common harlot, to have stolen her ducklings. And that his said wife went unto the said Agnes Herd and rated her, and all to-chid her, but she could get no knowledge of her ducklings, and so came home and was very angry against the said Agnes.

And within a short time after, the said Richard Harrison went into a chamber and there did read on his books for the space of 2 or 3 hours, bidding his said wife to go to bed with the children and that he would come to her, and she so did. And being awhile laid down in her bed, his wife did cry out, 'Oh, Lord, Lord, help me and keep me!' and he running to her asked her what she ailed; and she said 'Oh Lord, Lord, I am sore afraid, and have been divers times, but that I would not tell you,' and said 'I am in doubt, husband, that yonder wicked harlot Agnes Herd doth bewitch me.' And the said Richard said to his wife 'I pray you, be content and think not so, but trust in God and put your trust in Him only, and He will defend you from her, and from the Devil himself also.' And said moreover, 'What will the people say, that I being a preacher should have my wife so weak in faith?'

This examinate saith, that within two months after his said wife said unto him, 'I pray you, as ever there was love between us (as I hope there hath been, for I have 5 pretty children by you, I thank God), seek some remedy for me against yonder wicked beast (meaning the

---

[44] in farm, i.e. rented out.

said Agnes Herd). And if you will not, I will complain to my father, and I think he will see some remedy for me, for' said she, 'if I have no remedy she will utterly consume me.'

Whereupon this examinate did exhort his said wife as he had before, and desired her to pray to God, and that he would hang her, the said Agnes Herd, if he could prove any such matter; and after he went to the parsonage, and there he saith he gathered plums. And the said Agnes Herd then came to the hedge-side and Anwick's wife with her, and said unto him, 'I pray you give me some plums, sir;' and this examinate said unto her, 'I am glad you are here, you vile strumpet,' saying, 'I do think you have bewitched my wife. And as truly as God doth live, if I can perceive that she be troubled any more as she hath been, I will not leave a whole bone about thee; and besides, I will seek to have thee hanged.'

And saith, he said unto her that his wife would make her father privy unto it, 'and that then, I warrant thee, he will have you hanged, for he will make good friends, and is a stout man of himself.' And saith, that then he did rehearse divers things to her that were thought she had bewitched, as geese and hogs, and as he was coming down out of the tree, she the said Agnes did suddenly depart from him without having any plums.

This examinate saith, after which speeches so by him used unto her, and before Christmas, his said wife was taken sore sick, and was at many times afraid, both sleeping and waking; and did call this examinate her husband unto her not above two days before her death and said unto him, 'Husband, God bless you and your children, and God send you good friends, for I must depart from you; for I am now utterly consumed with yonder wicked creature' naming the said Agnes Herd. Which words he saith were spoken by her in the presence of John Pollin and Mother Pope; and within two days after his said wife departed out of this world in a perfect faith, she divers times in her sickness and before, repeating these words: 'Oh Agnes Herd, Agnes Herd, she hath consumed me.'

John Pollin saith, he was at Master Harrison's when his wife lay sick and near the departing out of this world, and that her husband gave her good counsel for her salvation, and that she then said 'Oh, Agnes Herd, Agnes Herd.'

Brett's wife saith, she heard Mistress Harrison say, that the said Agnes Herd had consumed her even to the death; and that she cried out upon her to the hour of her death.

The information of Agnes Dowsing, base daughter of Agnes Herd, taken before me Brian Darcy, Esquire, one of her Majesty's justices, the 18 day of March.

The said Agnes saith, that she is of the age of 7 years the Saturday before our Lady Day next. And she being asked whether her mother had any little things, or any little imps, she saith that she hath in one box six avices, or blackbirds; being asked of what colour, she saith 'They be white, speckled, and all black.' And she saith, that she hath in another box 6 spirits like cows; being asked 'How big?' she saith they be as big as rats, and that they have little short horns, and they lie in the boxes upon white and black wool. And she saith, that her mother gave unto her one of the said cows, which was called by the name of Crow, which is of colour black and white; and she saith, that her mother gave to her brother one of them which she called Donne, and that is of colour red and white.

And she being asked wherewithal she had seen her mother to feed the avices and blackbirds, she saith, she hath seen her feed them sometimes with wheat, barley, sometimes with oats, and with bread and cheese; and the cows that were like beasts, sometime with wheat straw, sometime with barley straw, oat straw, and with hay. And being asked what she gave them to drink she saith, sometimes water and sometimes beer, such drink as they drunk.

She this examinate saith, that her brother sometimes seeing them the avices and blackbirds to come about him saith, that he saith they keep a-tweetling* and tattling,* and that then he taketh them and put them into the boxes.

She being asked if she saw them suck upon her mother saith, that the avices and blackbirds have sucked upon her hands, and upon her brother's legs; being willed to show the place, she said 'Here sucked Avice, and here sucked Avice, and here sucked Blackbird.' And being asked how one spot upon the back of her hand came so, somewhat like the other, she saith the same was burnt.

The examination and confession of Agnes Herd of Little Oakley, taken by me Brian Darcy, Esquire, one of her Majesty's justices of the peace, the 17 day of March.

Continued in prison.

The said Agnes Herd saith, that she told one of her neighbours that the churl (meaning Cartwright) had carried away a bough which she had laid over a flow in the highway; and said that she was fain to go up to the ankle every step, and that she said, he had been as good he had not carried it away, for she would fetch as much wood out of his fields as that doth come unto. And she saith also, that she remembereth she came unto goodman Wad and told him that she was presented into the spiritual court for a witch, and that then she desired that she might answer the same when the days were longer.

Also she confesseth that Lane's wife gave her a pint of milk, and lent her a dish to carry it home in; and that she kept the dish a fortnight or longer, and then sent it home by her girl, and also that Lane's wife came to her for 2 pence which she owed her.

Also she confesseth that she came to the house of her neighbour West, and told him that she had been at mill, but she could get no meal nor yet no bread, and that he gave her a piece of a loaf; and she confesseth the speeches that then were of the pigs, and that she said to the boy that brought wool, that his aunt might as well have let her have one as Penly. She saith also, that she remembereth that she came to Goodwife Osborne and bought of her 3 pecks of apples, and confesseth that she owed unto her 3 pence, but denieth that the boy or lad came to her for any money.

Also she remembereth that Mistress Harrison charged her to have stolen her ducklings, and that she called her 'harlot' and 'witch'; and confesseth that she came unto Master Harrison, he being at the parsonage a-gathering of plums, and that she prayed him to give her some plums. But denieth that she hath any imps, avices or blackbirds, or any kine called Crow or Donne; and all and every other thing in general, or that she is a witch, or have any skill therein.

The information of Edward Upcher, Thomas Rice, and several others of the inhabitants of Walton, taken by me Brian Darcy, Esquire, the 25 day of March.

The said Edward saith, that he and wife being at Colchester this last week, they went together unto the jail to speak with Ursula Kemp; and then entering into talk with her, saith, he asked her if she could tell what sickness or diseases his wife had. Whereunto the said Ursula then told him, that his wife was forspoken or bewitched; he then asked her by whom, she told him it was by a woman that dwelt in their town, saying that 'the party hath one of her ears less than the other, and hath also a mole under one of her arms, and hath also in her yard a great woodstack.'

Alice Miles saith, that she went to the house of Joan Robinson for a pound of soap, at which time she the said Joan was gone from home. And saith, that her maid Joan Hewett told her that her dame made her nose bleed, and then called her cat to eat the same, saying she did marvel why her dame should call the cat to eat her blood.

Thomas Rice saith, that about 14 days past, Joan Robinson came unto the house of this examinate and desired to borrow a hayer,* the which his wife denied her, saying that she was to use it herself, whereat she departed. And presently after there arose a great wind which was like to have blown down their house. And the next day after one of his kine could not calve without help; it being drawn from her, died, and the cow was in danger and did hardly escape.

And saith also, that his wife hath a brood goose a-sitting that hath been as good for the bringing forth of her brood as any goose in Walton; and saith, that since the said Joan was denied of the hayer, the goose in the night will go from her nest, and will not suffer his wife, nor none of his folk to come near her but she will fly away, so as she hath lost two of her eggs. And saith also, that he thinketh the same to be done by the said Joan by some witchcraft.

Margery Carter saith that about ten years past, the husband of the said Joan came unto this examinate's house, and requested this examinate's husband to hire a pasture for a cow, the which she saith was denied him, with answer that he could not forbear it for fear he might want for his own beasts. And that presently after two of his best and likeliest beasts in a strange sort brake their necks; and saith also that presently after this mischance Joan's husband came unto this examinate's husband William Carter and said, 'God restore you your loss, now you may pasture me a cow,' the which then he did, and then his beasts left breaking of their necks.

And saith also, that about 2 years since, the said Joan's husband would have bought a house and an acre of ground of William Carter her husband, the which he would not sell unto him for that he would not have him his neighbour. And the next day he had a fair ambling mare, for which he might have had £5 often times; the which mare of herself came into the stable and presently was in a great sweat, and did hold her tongue out of her head, and shook and quaked in a strange sort, and presently died; the which when it was flayed, a neighbour's dog came and fed of it, and thereof presently died.

Also she saith, not above 14 days past, the said Joan Robinson came unto this examinate, and requested to borrow a hayer, to which she made answer that she had vowed not to lend the same; and saith that within 3 days after, she had one of her best beasts drowned in a ditch where there was but a little water.

Alice Walter saith, that well near 4 years past, the said Joan came unto her and requested to buy a pig of her; whereto she saith she would lend her one, but sell her any she would not; whereto the said Joan said that she would have none except she did buy it, and so they parted. And presently after the sow would not let her pigs suck, but did bite and fly at them as though she had been mad, when they had sucked above 7 days very well; and she saith that she sold of the pigs, the which Joan Robinson hearing, came unto her and requested to buy one of them, which she had for 3 pence, and told her that her sow did the like, and bade her give them milk as it came from the cow and they would drink; which she approved, and they drank.

This examinate saith, that two years since she going to the house of Joan Robinson found her and her husband sitting by the fire, with whom after she had talked, Joan Robinson required to buy two pigs of her sow that then was to pig; whereto she said she would see first what she should have herself, and would not then promise her any. And the same night her sow pigged two pigs in the cote where she lay, and for the more safety of them, she took a broom faggot and laid a close overthwart the door, because the pigs should not come out. And saith the same night all the farrow of pigs, being ten, came out over the broom sheaf and stood one before another in a tracked place like horses in a team, being all dead to the number of nine, and the tenth was drowned by the pond side being about a rod from the cote.

Alan Duck saith, that about five or six years past the said Joan came unto this examinate, and requested to buy a cheese of his wife; but she made her answer that she could sell none. Yet nevertheless she was very desirous to have one, the which, she saith, she denied her, and that she went away in a great anger. And this examinate saith, that the next day he went with his cart and four horses therein to fetch a load of corn and that his wife and two of her children rid in the cart.

And saith, that as he went towards the field he watered his horses at a weir called the Vicarage weir; which horses when they had drunk he could not get them out of the water, but was fain to wade to the forehorse['s] head (it being about a yard deep) and to take him by the head and to lead him out.

This examinate saith, that the said Joan came unto this examinate's wife at two several times to buy two pigs, whereof he saith she was denied, and presently after he had two pigs that died. And saith, that he assuredly thinketh that the said pigs died of some witchcraft which she the said Joan used, and the like for the staying of his horses, being in the water.

John Bracer saith, that about two years since the said Joan Robinson came unto this examinate's house, and requested to buy a sow-pig to wean, the which was a month old; whereunto he told her he meant to wean it himself, and that he would not let her have it, the which being a fat and a well-liking pig above all the rest, the next day died.

Also this examinate saith, that since Christmas last past, this examinate's wife went unto the said Joan Robinson to pay her money she owed unto her for wares which she had, being due upon scores. And for that his wife would not pay her her own reckoning, she fell out with his wife, and presently after he had a cow that was drowned in a ditch not a foot deep with water; all which he supposeth was done by some witchcraft by the said Joan.

The information and confession of Joan Robinson, taken by me Brian Darcy, Esquire, one of her Majesty's justices of peace, the 25 day of March.[45]

The said Joan saith, she went to the house of T. Rice to borrow a hayer (two days before a flaw of wind) which was denied her; but denieth that she hath any imps or caused his calf to die, or that she hurt her brood goose.

Also she remembereth that her husband went to W. Carter to buy a house and an acre of ground, and to hire a cow pasture, and to borrow a hayer of goodwife Carter. But denieth that she sent any imps to hurt any of his beasts, or his ambling mare, or caused any cow of his to be drowned.

[45] According to public records, the results of the trial were as follows:

Hanged	Elizabeth Bennett, Ursula Kemp
Reprieved after sentence	Agnes Glascock, Alice Newman, Cicely Sellis, Joan Turner (not in pamphlet)
Discharged	Elizabeth Eustace, Joan Pechey
Acquitted	Margaret Grevell, Agnes Herd, Alice Hunt, Alice Manfield
Not in records	Joan Robinson, Margery Sammon

Margery Sammon, daughter of Mother Barnes the witch, may have fled. At Witham Summer Sessions 1583, one Margery Barnes 'late of St. Osyth' was acquitted of helping to kill a man by witchcraft, and tried for keeping three 'imps or spirits', one a black mole called Piggin.

Also this examinate saith, that she went to buy a pig of Alice Walter, but denieth that she required to buy any that was not pigged of her, or of any other at any time; and denieth that she sent any imps or spirits to kill any of her pigs, and all the other matters against her informed she denieth in general.

A Comment on Evidence

George Gifford attended Hart Hall, Oxford, the same college as his contemporary Reginald Scot; he was given a living at Maldon, Essex, in mid-1582. Though suspended from his post when he became a Nonconformist, he continued to live and preach at Maldon till his death in 1620. His first work on witchcraft was *A Discourse of the subtill Practises of Devilles by Witches and Sorcerers* (London, 1587). His second, written in dramatic dialogue form and colloquial vocabulary for the benefit of the uneducated, was *A Dialogue concerning Witches and Witchcraftes* (London, 1593). The following extract is taken from that work; speakers are Samuel, a countryman, and Daniel, a scholar who speaks for the author.

Sam. I was of a jury not many years past when there was an old woman arraigned for a witch. There came in eight or ten which gave evidence against her; I do not remember every particular but the chief, for some things were of small value.

One woman came in and testified upon her oath that her husband upon his death-bed took it upon his death that he was bewitched, for he pined a long time. And he said further, he was sure that woman had bewitched him. He took her to be nought, and thought she was angry with him because she would have borrowed five shillings of him and he denied to lend it her. The woman took her oath also, that she thought in her conscience that the old woman was a witch, and that she killed her husband.

There came in a man that halted; he told a shrewd tale. 'I once' said he 'had both my legs sound. This old woman and I fell out and did chide; she said she would be even with me. Within three days after I had such a pain in my knee that I could not stand, and ever since I go halting of it, and now and then feel some pain.'

There came in another, a little fellow that was very earnest—methinks I see him yet. He took his oath directly that she was a witch. 'I did once anger her', said he, 'but I did repent me, for I looked somewhat would follow. And the next night I saw the ugliest sight that ever I saw; I awaked suddenly out of my sleep and there was, methought, a great face, as big as they use to set up in the sign of the Saracen's Head, looked full in my face. I was scarce my own man two days after'.

Another came in, a woman; and her child died with grievous pain, and she took her oath that in her conscience she [the witch] killed her child. Then followed a man, and he said he could not tell, but he thought she was once angry with him because she came to beg a few pot-herbs and he denied her; and presently after he heard a thing, as he thought, to whisper in his ear 'Thou shalt be bewitched!' The next day he had such a pain in his back that he could not sit upright. He said he sent to a cunning woman, she told him he was bewitched and by a woman that came for pot-herbs. But she said he should recover of it, and so he said he did within some ten days. Then came in two or three grave honest men which testifies that she was by common fame accounted a witch.

We found her guilty, for what could we do less? She was condemned and executed, and upon the ladder she made her prayer and took it upon her death she was innocent and free from all such dealings. Do you think we did not well?

Dan. Nay, what think you? Are you sure she was a witch? May it not be she was innocent, and you upon your oaths shed innocent blood?

Sam. If she were innocent, what could we do less? We went according to the evidence of such as were sworn; they swore that they in their conscience took her to be a witch, and that she did those things.

Dan. If other take their oath that in their conscience they *think* so, is that sufficient to warrant men upon mine oath to say it *is* so?

Sam. Nay, but you see what matters they brought which persuaded them to think so.

Dan. Might not both you and they be deceived in your thinking, or may you upon matters which induce you to *think* so, present upon your oath that you *know* it is so? . . . is this a good proof—the Devil appeareth to a man after he hath displeased a woman, therefore she sent him? Doth not Satan haunt all men continually, and would if he could get leave from God terrify them with such illusions when men are afraid, and have strong imaginations?

What *reason* did the woman show, which took it upon her conscience that the old woman killed her child, to prove that it was so? If she thought so in her conscience, and ten thousand more with her upon bare imagination, was that a warrant for you to swear solemnly that it *was* so? As for the testimony of the cunning woman that he was bewitched which had the pain in his back upon the denial of pot-herbs, it was the testimony of the Devil, as I showed before. And what is common fame grounded upon imagination? . . .

Sam. I was of another jury since, and there was a woman indicted for a witch, but not for killing any man or child. There came in five or six against her. The first was an old woman, and she said she had displeased her, as she thought, and within two or three nights after, as she sat by her fire, there was a thing like a toad, or like some little crab-fish which did creep upon the hearth; she took a besom* and swept it away, and suddenly her body was griped.*

Another fell out with her as she said, and her hens began to die up, until she burned one hen alive. A third man came in and he said she was once angry with him. He had a dun cow which was tied up in a house, for it was in winter; he feared that some evil would follow, and for his life he could not come where she was but he must needs take up her tail and kiss under it. Two or three other came in and said she was by common fame accounted a witch; we found her guilty and she was condemned to prison, and to the pillory, but she stood stiff in it that she was no witch.

Dan. And are you sure she was one? . . .

Sam. But what can you say to the other? The man which could not choose but kiss under his cow's tail?

Dan. I say he was far in love with his cow! Let such men learn to know God, and to expel fantasies out of their minds that the Devil may not have such power over them; for he worketh in the fantasies of man's mind, and the more strongly where they fear him, as it appeareth this man did.[1]

[1] Passages are taken from L3–L3v, L4, M2. Italics are mine.

A Comment on Method

It is likely that the trials at Chelmsford in 1582 were the occasion of Reginald Scot's decision to write *The Discovery of Witchcraft*, which was first published in 1584. There are many scornful asides concerning Brian Darcy throughout the book, and one angry outburst in the course of a discussion proving that devils cannot take corporal form (*A Discourse upon divels and spirits*, Ch. 33, appended to the *Discovery* in the edition of 1584).

Now, how Brian Darcy's he-spirits and she-spirits, Titty and Tiffin, Suckin and Piggin, Liard and Robin, etc.—his white spirits and black spirits, gray spirits and red spirits, devil toad and devil lamb, devil's cat and devil's dam—agree herewithal or can stand consonant with the word of God or true philosophy, let heaven and earth judge. In the meantime, let any man with good consideration peruse that book published by W. W. and it shall suffice to satisfy him in all that may be required touching the vanities of the witches' examinations, confessions, and executions, where, though the tale be told only of the accusers' part, without any other answer of theirs that their adversary setteth down, mine assertion will be sufficiently proved true.

And because it seemeth to be performed with some kind of authority, I will say no more for the confutation thereof, but refer you to the book itself; whereto if nothing be added that may make to their reproach, I dare warrant nothing is left out that may serve to their condemnation. See whether the witnesses be not single, of what credit, sex, and age they are—namely, lewd, miserable, and envious poor people, most of them which speak to any purpose being old women, and children of the age of 4, 5, 6, 7, 8 or 9 years.

And note how and what the witches confess, and see of what weight and importance the causes are; whether their confessions be not won through hope of favour and extorted by flattery or threats, without proof. But insomuch as there were not past seventeen or eighteen condemned at once at St. Osyth in the county of Essex, being a whole parish (though of no great quantity) I will say the less, trusting that by this time there remain not many in that parish.

If any be yet behind, I doubt not but Brian Darcy will find them out, who, if he lack aid, Richard Gallis of Windsor were meet to be associated with him; which Gallis hath set forth another book to that effect, of certain witches of Windsor executed at Abingdon. But with what impudency and dishonesty he hath finished it, with what lies and forgeries he hath furnished it, what folly and frenzy he hath uttered in it, I am ashamed to report; and therefore being but a twopenny book, I had rather desire you to buy it and so to peruse it than to fill my book with such beastly stuff.

A Miscarriage of Justice

This unbelievably bungled affair was noted by John Waller and recorded in Ralph Holinshed's *Chronicles of England, Scotlande, and Irelande* (London, 1587) Vol. III, p. 1560, with the sad marginal comment 'The jury meant well.' Joan Cason was condemned because she had a guilty conscience about something quite apart from witchcraft, which made her believe that the 'little vermin' in her house spoke to remind her of unfulfilled obligations. Because she admitted that the creature was 'unnatural', even a sympathetic jury was bound to feel the same way and to consider some kind of punishment necessary; interestingly, the jury in its ignorance assumes that invocation of spirits must be a much less serious crime than something causing injury to others.[1] This healthy legal instinct was several centuries too early, and cost Joan her life.

At a great session holden in a town of Kent called Faversham, being a town incorporate and a limb or member of Dover,[2] upon the nine-

---

[1] George Gifford makes the same assumption in his *Dialogue Concerning Witches and Witchcraftes* (1593), K3, *M.B.* 'If they find them guilty to have dealt with devils, and cannot say they have murdered men, the law doth not put them to death.'

'*Dan.* It were to be wished that the law were more perfect in that respect.'

Filmer says in 1653 'ordinarily they condemn none for witches unless they be charged with the murdering of some person.' (*Advertisement to Jurymen*, Bᵛ.) The letter of the law was applied in one or two cases (Edmund Hartley was hanged in 1596/7 for making a magic circle; making a whole family sick by witchcraft rated only imprisonment and this new charge was added at the last moment so that a death sentence could legally be imposed. One or two witches were hanged merely for possessing familiars, but in nearly every case it had to be shown that these demons had killed someone). It seems that 'invocation and conjuration of spirits' did *not* include the feeding of an animal familiar; the precedent thus established survived even the law of James, which made it a technical felony to 'entertain, employ feed or reward any evil and wicked spirit' as well as to invoke or conjure a spirit.

It seems, then, that the Faversham lawyer was strong on law but weak on current interpretation.

[2] Faversham, as a subsidiary of Dover, did not come under the Assize system but had its own independent court, with the power to try felonies. The lack of an experienced judge able to direct the court towards a legal reversal of its mistaken judgment, displays the great weakness of the independent courts.

teenth day of April, in the year one thousand five hundred fourscore and six, before Thomas Barming, then mayor of the same town, and others; Joan Cason, late the wife of one Freeman, was accused, attached, indicted, and arraigned for witchcraft, but condemned and adjudged to die, and executed, for invocation of wicked spirits, according to a statute made in 5. Eliz. c. 2: for that she, the statute aforesaid not at all regarding, upon the first of April, in the seven and twentieth year of Queen Elizabeth, and at divers days and times since, the art of witchcraft and enchantment had used, and upon wicked spirits had invocated and called, contrary to the peace of our sovereign lady the queen; and namely, that she, the second of February in the eight and twentieth year of Queen Elizabeth, had bewitched Jane Cook, of the age of three years, who by her enchantment languished and died. Hereupon seven women and one man gave evidence against her, who though they were all very poor people, yet were they the rather admitted to accuse her, for that they were her near neighbours, and her offence very odious.

The first and principal deposition was made by Sara Cook, mother to the bewitched child in these words following—that is to say, that after her said child had been sick, languishing by the space of thirteen days, a traveller came into her house, to the end to drink a pot of ale (for she kept an alehouse); who, seeing the lamentable case and piteous grief of the child, called her unto him, saying, 'Hostess, I take it that your child is bewitched.' Whereunto she answered, that she for her part knew of no such matter. 'Well,' said the guest, 'if you think it to be so, do no more but take a tile from over the lodging of the party suspected, and lay it in a hot fire; and if she have bewitched the child, the tile will sparkle and fly round about the cradle where the child lieth.'

Now she, conceiving that travellers have good experience in such matters, did steal (as she deposed) a tile from the house of the said Joan Cason (though not from over her lodging) and laid it in the fire besides the cradle, which soon after sparkled about the house, even according to her said guest's information. And within short space, the said Joan, being the suspected party, came into this deponent's house, to see how the child did; which, soon after her coming, looked full in her face, and had not lifted up her eye, nor looked abroad all the night precedent, but within four hours after died; so as by the circumstance of that evidence, she thought it might plainly appear to the jury that the said Joan had bewitched her child to death. Nevertheless, the prisoner did absolutely deny anything done, or purposed by her to have been done in this behalf.

Howbeit, to pursue this matter to proof, and her to death, the other seven persons were all deposed; by whom it was affirmed constantly and approved manifestly, that to the house of one Freeman (whose wife the said Joan Cason then was) not lately, but divers years since, resorted a little thing like a rat, but more reddish, having a broad tail,[3] which some of them had seen, and some had heard of. Insomuch as one heard it cry in the wall like a cricket, another like a rat, another like a toad, another that it ran under a tub and spake these words, that is to say 'Go to, go to, go to.' And it was further deposed by one goodwife Offield (the substantiallest person of them all) that her cat could not kill it.

All these depositions were made and taken, to prove Joan Cason a witch, and, consequently, that she had through her enchantments, and by the help of this vermin or spirit, killed the said Jane Cook. But she, with great attestations, pleaded not guilty, alleging diverse matters and instances of the malicious dealings of her adversaries against her, reciting also certain controversies betwixt her and them, wherein they had done her open wrong. But although she satisfied the bench and all the jury touching her innocency for the killing of the[4] child, denying also that she had any skill in the art of witchcraft, she then and there confessed that a little vermin, being of colour reddish, of stature less than a rat, and furnished with a broad tail, did divers years since (but not lately) haunt her house, and many other houses in the town; and further, that she, as she imagined, heard it cry sometimes 'Go to, go to, go to,' sometimes 'Sick, sick,' sometimes 'Come, come.'

Whereby she gathered that it charged her to see her master Mason's will performed, which she had not executed according to the confidence he had in her, to the trouble of her conscience and vexation of her mind. And yet she honestly confessed that he had the use of her body very dishonestly, whilst she was wife to her husband Freeman.

Upon these foresaid depositions, and upon this her own confession, the jury was charged, went together, and, being loath to condemn her of witchcraft, which they knew to be felony, they acquitted her thereof, and found her guilty upon the said statute for invocation of wicked spirits; thinking thereby to have procured her punishment by pillory or imprisonment and to have saved her from the gallows. So as when the verdict was given up by the jury to the mayor and his brethren,

[3] Perhaps a red squirrel?   [4] Original has 'her'.

sitting on their judgment seat together with their learned council, the said mayor uttered this speech following, that is to say, 'Joan Cason, for so much as it hath pleased God to show such favour this day unto you, as to put it into the hearts of the jury to acquit you of the felony whereupon you were arraigned, it behoveth you to render most humble thanks to God and the Queen, and hereafter to beware that you give no such occasions of offence again. And so you shall do well henceforwards to serve God better, and to resort to sermons oftener, whereby you may learn your obedience to God, and your duty to your neighbour.'[5]

A gentleman, being a lawyer and of counsel with the town, sitting upon the bench with the mayor to assist, or rather to direct him in the course of law and justice, hearing this mild judgment to proceed out of the mayor's mouth, stepped unto him and told him that, under correction, he thought him to err in the principal point of his sentence—that is to say, that instead of life he should have pronounced death, because invocation of wicked spirits was made felony by the statute whereupon she was arraigned. 'Then,' quoth the mayor, 'goodwife Cason, you must be conveyed from hence to the White House from whence you came, and from thence to the place of execution, where you must be hanged until you be dead, and so God have mercy upon you.'

Then was she carried back to their prison, which they call the White House. And because there was no matter of invocation given in evidence against her, nor proved in or by any accusation, whereby the jury might have any colour to condemn her therefore, her execution was stayed by the space of three days after judgment was given. In the meantime, she was persuaded by sundry preachers and learned men to confess it. But no persuasion could prevail to make her acknowledge any other criminal offence but her lewd life and adulterous conversation with one Mason, whose house she kept whilst he was in health, and whose person she tended whilst he was sick. With whom she was conversant at the hour of his death, maintaining his concupiscence all the days of his life, and in the end abused the trust reposed in her, touching the disposition of certain bequests, which he made her only privy unto. For he died of the plague, for fear of which infection none other durst repair unto him, so as she used that matter according to her wicked conscience.

In which report, she said in her confession upon the gallows (taking her death that she died guiltless herein) that the judgment of God was

5 The prisoner is acquitted, but exhorted not to do it again.

in such measure laid upon her, and therewithal made so godly and penitent an end that many now lamented her death which were before her utter enemies. Yea, some wished her alive after she was hanged, that cried out for the hangman when she was alive; but she should have been more beholding unto them that had kept her from the gallows, than to such as would have cut the rope when she was strangled.

IV   Thick-coming Fancies

Cautionary Tales

Reginald Scot's *The Discovery of Witchcraft* (London, 1584) presents the curious case of a work so reasonable as to be almost unreadable in its own day. He admits the existence of good and evil spirits, and the possibility of witchcraft, but devotes his fervour to a Philistine destruction of all *examples* of witchcraft, past and present, and a remorseless explanation of the fallacies of all points of view but his own. Side by side with this Scot displays his own emotional prejudices in coarse and insensitive jeers at Catholic belief and ritual (often equated by him with witch-belief and practice), to an extent distasteful even in the context of Elizabethan polemics.

Though the book was written out of outraged compassion for the victims of folly and superstition, it is not itself compassionate or wide in sympathy; immensely learned and industrious in its gathering of material, it is not scholarly. The things about it which we find refreshing—scepticism concerning supernatural evidence, disrespect for authorities of the past, non-academic style and approach—would have seemed to an educated Elizabethan exciting but insensitive, underbred, unsophisticated and, in a word, bourgeois. Yet by sheer scope and size and weight of critical apparatus, the book took itself out of the popular market and lost the pamphlet audience.

From all that we can gather, the book's main influence seems to have been achieved, ironically, by its use as a source book for magical lore; Scot's collection of conjuring rituals and diagrams, of charms and spells and parlour tricks, of quotations and literary references, is unrivalled anywhere. Jonson, Heywood and Shakespeare all used it; King James, slightly misunderstanding the situation as usual, wrote a refutation of the book—and yet, during his reign in England, acted on all its warnings of trickery and concealed disease in his handling of cases of possession.

It is hard to do justice to this vast (and easily available volume) in quotation, but it does provide us with some of our best authenticated stories of witchcraft in the villages, and with some fruitful suggestions of the sources of those beliefs; in Scot's stories we always find the cautionary factors of the situation, the 'before' and 'after' that the pamphlets and the scholar's books leave out. If only this stubborn, sceptical squire had lived in Essex!

The common people have been so assotted* and bewitched with whatsoever poets have feigned of witchcraft, either in earnest, in jest, or else in derision; and with whatsoever loud liars and cozeners for their pleasures herein have invented; and with whatsoever tales they have heard from old doting women, or from their mother's maids; and with whatsoever the grandfool their ghostly father or any other morrow mass-priest had informed them; and finally with whatsoever they have swallowed up through tract of time, or through their own timorous nature or ignorant conceit concerning these matters of hags and witches—as they have so settled their opinion and credit thereupon that they think it heresy to doubt in any part of the matter, specially because they find this word 'witchcraft' expressed in the scriptures; which is as to defend praying to saints because 'Sanctus, Sanctus, Sanctus' is written in *Te Deum*.

And now to come to the definition of witchcraft, which hitherto I did defer and put off purposely, that you might perceive the true nature thereof by the circumstances, and therefore the rather to allow of the same, seeing the variety of other writers. Witchcraft is in truth a cozening art, wherein the name of God is abused, profaned and blasphemed, and His power attributed to a vile creature. In estimation of the vulgar people it is a supernatural work contrived between a corporal old woman and a spiritual devil. The manner thereof is so secret, mystical and strange, that to this day there hath never been any credible witness thereof. It is incomprehensible to the wise, learned or faithful; a probable matter to children, fools, melancholic persons, and papists.

The trade is thought to be impious, the effect and end thereof to be sometimes evil, as when thereby man or beast, grass, trees, or corn etc. is hurt; sometimes good, as whereby sick folks are healed, thieves bewrayed, and true men come to their goods, etc. The matter and instruments wherewith it is accomplished are words, charms, signs, images, characters, etc., the which words, although any other creature do pronounce in manner and form as they do, leaving out no circumstance requisite or usual for that action, yet none is said to have the grace or gift to perform the matter except she be a witch, and so taken either by her own consent, or by other's imputation.[1]

That words, characters, images and such other trinkets, which are thought so necessary instruments for witchcraft as without the which no such thing can be accomplished, are but baubles, devised by cozeners to abuse the people withal, I trust I have sufficiently proved . . .

It is also to be thought that all witches are cozeners, when Mother Bungy, a principal witch, so reputed, tried and condemned of all men, and continuing in that exercise and estimation many years (having cozened and abused the whole realm, insomuch as there came to her

---

[1] Reginald Scot, *The Discovery of Witchcraft*, ed. cit., Bk. 16, Ch. 2.

witchmongers from all the furthest parts of the land, she being in divers books set out with authority, registered and chronicled by the name of 'the great witch of Rochester', and reputed among all men for the chief ringleader of all other witches) by good proof is found to be a mere cozener; confessing in her death-bed freely, without compulsion or enforcement, that her cunning consisted only in deluding and deceiving the people, saying that she had, towards the maintenance of her credit in that cozening trade, some sight* in physic and surgery, and the assistance of a friend of hers called Heron, a professor thereof. And this I know partly of mine own knowledge, and partly by the testimony of her husband and others of credit, to whom, I say, in her death-bed and at sundry other times she protested these things; and also that she never had indeed any material spirit or devil (as the voice went), nor yet knew how to work any supernatural matter, as she in her lifetime made men believe she had and could do. . . .[2]

An old woman that healed all diseases of cattle, for the which she never took any reward but a penny and a loaf, being seriously examined by what words she brought these things to pass, confessed that after she had touched the sick creature, she always departed immediately, saying:[3]

> My loaf in my lap,
>   my penny in my purse;
> Thou are never the better,
>   and I am never the worse. . . .

Not long since, a young maiden dwelling at New Romney here in Kent, being the daughter of one Master L. Stuppeny (late jurat* of the same town, but dead before the execution hereof), and afterward the wife of Thomas Epps, who is at this instant Mayor of Romney, was visited with sickness; whose mother and father-in-law, being abused with credulity concerning witches' supernatural power, repaired to a famous witch called Mother Baker, dwelling not far from thence at a place called Stonestreet, who, according to witches' cozening custom, asked whether they mistrusted not some bad neighbour. To whom they answered that indeed they doubted a woman near unto them, and yet the same woman was (of the honester and wiser sort of her neighbours) reputed a good creature.

Nevertheless, the witch told them that there was great cause of their suspicion; 'for the same' said she 'is the very party that wrought the

---

[2] *Discovery*, Bk. 16, Ch. 3.   [3] *Discovery*, Bk. 12, Ch. 14.

maiden's destruction by making a heart of wax and pricking the same with pins and needles;' affirming also that the same neighbour of hers had bestowed the same in some secret corner of the house. This being believed, the house was searched by credible persons, but nothing could be found. The witch or wise woman being certified hereof, continued her assertion, and would needs go to the house where she herself, as she affirmed, would certainly find it.

When she came thither, she used her cunning, as it chanced, to her own confusion, or at leastwise to her detection; for herein she did as some of the wiser sort mistrusted that she would do, laying down privily such an image as she had before described in a corner which by others had been most diligently searched and looked into, and by that means her cozenage was notably bewrayed. And I would wish that all witchmongers might pay for their lewd repair to enchanters, and consultation with witches and such as have familiar spirits, as some of these did, and that by the order of the high commissioners (which partly for respect of neighbourhood and partly for other considerations I leave unspoken of). . . .[4]

One sort of such as are said to be witches are women which be commonly old, lame, blear-eyed, pale, foul, and full of wrinkles; poor, sullen, superstitious, and papists, or such as know no religion, in whose drowsy minds the Devil hath gotten a fine seat so as, what mischief, mischance, calamity, or slaughter is brought to pass, they are easily persuaded the same is done by themselves, imprinting in their minds an earnest and constant imagination hereof. They are lean and deformed, showing melancholy in their faces to the horror of all that see them. They are doting, scolds, mad, devilish, and not much differing from them that are thought to be possessed with spirits; so firm and steadfast in their opinions as whosoever shall only have respect to the constancy of their words uttered would easily believe they were true indeed.

These miserable wretches are so odious unto all their neighbours, and so feared, as few dare offend them or deny them anything they ask; whereby they take upon them—yea, and sometimes think—that they can do such things as are beyond the ability of human nature. These go from house to house and from door to door for a pot full of milk, yeast, drink, pottage, or some such relief, without the which they could hardly live, neither obtaining for their service and pains, nor by their art, nor yet at the Devil's hands (with whom they are said to

[4] *Discovery*, Bk. 12, Ch. 16.

make a perfect and visible bargain) either beauty, money, promotion, wealth, worship, pleasure, honour, knowledge, learning, or any other benefit whatsoever.

It falleth out many times that neither their necessities nor their expectation is answered or served in those places where they beg or borrow, but rather their lewdness is by their neighbours reproved. And further, in tract of time the witch waxeth odious and tedious to her neighbours, and they again are despised and despited* of her, so as sometimes she curseth one, and sometimes another, and that from the master of the house, his wife, children, cattle, etc. to the little pig that lieth in the stye. Thus in process of time they have all displeased her, and she hath wished evil luck unto them all, perhaps with curses and imprecations made in form.

Doubtless at length some of her neighbours die or fall sick, or some of their children are visited with diseases that vex them strangely, as apoplexies, epilepsies, convulsions, hot fevers, worms, etc., which by ignorant parents are supposed to be the vengeance of witches. Yea, and their opinions and conceits are confirmed and maintained by unskilful physicians, according to the common saying 'Inscitiae pallium maleficium et incantatio'—witchcraft and enchantment is the cloak of ignorance; whereas indeed evil humours and not strange words, witches, or spirits are the causes of such diseases. Also some of their cattle perish, either by disease or mischance; then they upon whom such adversities fall, weighing the fame that goeth upon this woman (her words, displeasure, and curses meeting so justly with their misfortune) do not only conceive but also are resolved that all their mishaps are brought to pass by her only means.

The witch on the other side expecting her neighbours' mischances, and seeing things sometimes come to pass according to her wishes, curses, and incantations (for Bodin himself confesseth that not above two in a hundred of their witchings or wishings take effect), being called before a Justice, by due examination of the circumstances is driven to see her imprecations and desires, and her neighbours' harms and losses to concur, and as it were, to take effect; and so confesseth that she, as a goddess, hath brought such things to pass. Wherein not only she, but the accuser and also the Justice are foully deceived and abused, as being through her confession and other circumstances persuaded, to the injury of God's glory, that she hath done or can do that which is proper only to God himself. . . .[5]

[5] *Discovery*, Bk. 1, Ch. 3. For other descriptions of witches and the growth of

But that it may appear that even voluntary confession (in this case) may be untruly made, though it tend to the destruction of the confessor, and that melancholy may move imaginations to that effect, I will cite a notable instance concerning this matter, the parties themselves being yet alive, and dwelling in the parish of Selling in Kent, and the matter not long since in this sort performed.

One Ada Davie, the wife of Simon Davie, husbandman, being reputed a right honest body and being of good parentage, grew suddenly (as her husband informed me and as it is well known in these parts) to be somewhat pensive and more sad than in times past. Which thing, though it grieved him, yet he was loath to make it so appear, as either his wife might be troubled or discontented therewith, or his neighbours informed thereof; lest ill husbandry* should be laid to his charge, which in these quarters is much abhorred.

But when she grew from pensiveness to some perturbation of mind, so as her accustomed rest began in the night season to be withdrawn from her through sighing and secret lamentation, and that not without tears, he could not but demand the cause of her conceit* and extraordinary mourning.

But although at that time she covered the same, acknowledging nothing to be amiss with her, soon after, notwithstanding, she fell down before him on her knees, desiring him to forgive her for she had grievously offended (as she said) both God and him. Her poor husband, being abashed at this her behaviour, comforted her as he could, asking her the cause of her trouble and grief, who told him that she had, contrary to God's law and to the offence of all good Christians, to the injury of him and specially to the loss of her own soul, bargained and given her soul to the Devil, to be delivered unto him within short space.

Whereunto her husband answered, saying, 'Wife, be of good cheer, this thy bargain is void and of none effect, for thou hast sold that which is none of thine to sell; since it belongeth to Christ who hath bought it and dearly paid for it, even with His blood which He shed upon the cross, so as the Devil hath no interest in thee.' After this, with like submission, tears and penitence, she said unto him, 'Oh husband, I have yet committed another fault and done you more injury, for I have bewitched you and your children.' 'Be content', quoth he, 'by the grace

---

suspicion, see Gifford (who follows Scot closely) and Harsnett. George Gifford, *A Discourse of the subtill Practises of Devilles by Witches* (London, 1587), G4–G4ᵛ. Samuel Harsnett, *A Declaration of egregious Popish Impostures* (London, 1605), pp. 136–8.

of God, Jesus Christ shall unwitch us; for none evil can happen to them that fear God.' And as truly as the Lord liveth, this was the tenor of his words unto me, which I know is true, as proceeding from unfeigned lips and from one that feareth God.

Now when the time approached that the Devil should come and take possession of the woman according to his bargain, he watched and prayed earnestly, and caused his wife to read psalms and prayers for mercy at God's hands. And suddenly, about midnight, there was a great rumbling below under his chamber window, which amazed them exceedingly, for they conceived that the Devil was below, though he had no power to come up, because of their fervent prayers.

He that noteth this woman's first and second confession, freely and voluntarily made, how everything concurred that might serve to add credit thereunto and yield matter for her condemnation would not think but that if Bodin were foreman of her inquest he would cry 'Guilty!' and would hasten execution upon her, who would have said as much before any judge in the world if she had been arraigned thereupon.

But God knoweth she was innocent of any these crimes, howbeit she was brought low and pressed down with the weight of this humour, so as both her rest and sleep were taken away from her, and her fancies troubled and disquieted with despair and such other cogitations as grew by occasion thereof.

And yet I believe, if any mishap had ensued to her husband or his children, few witchmongers would have judged otherwise but that she had bewitched them. And she, for her part, so constantly persuaded herself to be a witch that she judged herself worthy of death, insomuch as, being retained in her chamber, she saw not anyone carrying a faggot to the fire but she would say it was to make a fire to burn her for witchery. But God knoweth she had bewitched none, neither ensued there any hurt unto any by her imagination, but unto herself.

And as for the rumbling, it was by occasion of a sheep, which was flayed and hung by the walls so as a dog came and devoured it; whereby grew the noise which I before mentioned. And she being now recovered remaineth a right honest woman, far from such impiety and shamed of her imaginations, which she perceiveth to have grown through melancholy.[6]

At the Assizes holden at Rochester, Anno 1581, one Margaret Simons, the wife of John Simons of Brenchley in Kent was arraigned

[6] *Discovery*, Bk. 3, Ch. 10.

for witchcraft at the instigation and complaint of divers fond and malicious persons, and specially by the means of one John Ferrall, vicar of that parish; with whom I talked about that matter, and found him both fondly* assotted in the cause and enviously bent towards her, and (which is worse) as unable to make a good account of his faith as she whom he accused. That which he, for his part, laid to the poor woman's charge was this:

His son (being an ungracious boy and prentice to one Robert Scotchford, clothier, dwelling in that parish of Brenchley) passed on a day by her house, at whom by chance her little dog barked. Which thing the boy taking in evil part, drew his knife and pursued him therewith even to her door, whom she rebuked with some such words as the boy disdained, and yet nevertheless would not be persuaded to depart in a long time. At the last he returned to his master's house, and within five or six days fell sick. Then was called to mind the fray betwixt the dog and the boy; insomuch as the vicar, who thought himself so privileged as he little mistrusted that God would visit his children with sickness, did so calculate as he found, partly through his own judgment and partly (as he himself told me) by the relation of other witches, that his said son was by her bewitched. Yea, he also told me that this his son, being as it were past all cure, received perfect health at the hands of another witch.

He proceeded yet further against her, affirming that always in his parish church, when he desired to read most plainly, his voice so failed him as he could scant be heard at all, which he could impute, he said, to nothing else but to her enchantment. When I advertised the poor woman hereof, as being desirous to hear what she could say for herself, she told me that in very deed his voice did much fail him, specially when he strained himself to speak loudest. Howbeit, she said that at all times his voice was hoarse and low, which thing I perceived to be true.

'But sir', said she, 'you shall understand that this our vicar is diseased with such a kind of hoarseness as divers of our neighbours in this parish not long since doubted that he had the French pox,* and in that respect utterly refused to communicate with him, until such time as (being thereunto enjoyed by Master D. Lewen the Ordinary)* he had brought from London a certificate under the hands of two physicians that his hoarseness proceeded from a disease in the lungs. Which certificate he published in the church in the presence of the whole congregation, and by this means he was cured, or rather excused, of the shame of his disease.'

And this I know to be true by the relation of divers honest men of that parish. And truly, if one of the jury had not been wiser than the other, she had been condemned thereupon and upon other as ridiculous matters as this. For the name of a witch is so odious and her power so feared among the common people that if the honestest body living chance to be arraigned thereupon, she shall hardly escape condemnation. . . .[7]

But you shall understand that these bugs* specially are spied and feared of sick folk, children, women, and cowards, which through weakness of mind and body are shaken with vain dreams and continual fear. The Scythians, being a stout and warlike nation, as divers writers report, never see any vain sights or spirits; it is a common saying 'A lion feareth no bugs.' But in our childhood our mother's maids have so terrified us with an ugly Devil having horns on his head, fire in his mouth, and a tail in his breech, eyes like a basin, fangs like a dog, claws like a bear, a skin like a Nigger, and a voice roaring like a lion,[8] whereby we start and are afraid when we hear one cry 'Boo!'; and they have so frayed* us with bullbeggars, spirits, witches, urchins, elves, hags, fairies, satyrs, Pans, fauns, Silenes, Kit with the canstick,* tritons, centaurs, dwarfs, giants, imps, calcars,* conjurors, nymphs, changelings, Incubus, Robin Goodfellow, the spoorn,* the mare, the man in the oak, the hellwain, the firedrake, the Puckle, Tom Thumb, Hobgoblin, Tom Tumbler, Boneless, and such other bugs, that we are afraid of our own shadows, insomuch as some never fear the Devil but in a dark night, and then a polled* sheep is a perilous beast, and many times is taken for our father's soul, specially in a churchyard, where a right hardy man heretofore scant* durst pass by night but his hair would stand upright. . . . Well, thanks be to God, this wretched and cowardly infidelity, since the preaching of the gospel, is in part forgotten, and doubtless, the rest of those illusions will in short time, by God's grace, be detected and vanish away.[9]

But some affirm that popish miracles are vanished and gone away, howbeit, witches' miracles remain in full force. So as St. Loy is out of credit for a horse-leach, Master T. and Mother Bungy remain in

---

[7] *Discovery*, Bk. 1, Ch. 2.

[8] Mingled with the classical names for the minor spirits of the countryside is an anthology of English superstitions, many now quite vanished or remaining only as names. See the notes of Brinsley Nicholson to this passage, in his edition of the *Discovery*.

[9] *Discovery*, Bk. 7, Ch. 15.

estimation for prophets; nay, Hobgoblin and Robin Goodfellow are contemned* among young children, and Mother Alice and Mother Bungy are feared among old fools. The estimation of these continue, because the matter hath not been called in question; the credit of the other decayeth because the matter hath been looked into.[10]

I thought good here to insert two most miraculous matters; of the one I am 'Testis oculatus', an eye-witness, of the other I am so credible and certainly informed that I dare and do believe it to be very true. When Master T. Randolph returned out of Russia, after his ambassage* despatched, a gentleman of his train brought home a monument of great accompt, in nature and in property very wonderful. And because I am loth to be long in the description of circumstances, I will first describe the thing itself, which was a piece of earth of a good quantity and most excellently proportioned in nature, having these qualities and virtues following:

If one had taken a piece of perfect steel, forked and sharpened at the end, and heated it red hot, offering therewith to have touched it, it would have fled with great celerity; and on the other side, it would have pursued gold, either in coin or bullion, with as great violence and speed as it shunned the other. No bird in the air durst approach near it; no beast of the field but feared it and naturally fled from the sight thereof. It would be here today and tomorrow twenty miles off, and the next day after in the very place it was the first day, and that without the help of any other creature.

Johannes Fernelius writeth of a strange stone lately brought out of India which hath in it such a marvellous brightness, purity, and shining, that therewith the air round about is so lightened and cleared that one may see to read thereby in the darkness of night. It will not be contained in a close room but requireth an open and free place. It would not willingly rest or stay here below on the earth, but always laboureth to ascend up into the air. If one press it down with his hand, it resisteth and striketh very sharply. It is beautiful to behold, without either spot or blemish, and yet very unpleasant to taste or feel. If any part thereof be taken away, it is never a whit diminished, the form thereof being inconstant and at every moment mutable.

These two things last rehearsed are strange, and so long wondered at as the mystery and morality thereof remaineth undiscovered; but when I have disclosed the matter, and told you that by the lump of earth *a man* is meant, and some of his qualities described, and that that

[10] *Discovery*, Bk. 8, Ch. 1.

which was contained in the far fetched stone was *fire*, or rather flame, the doubt is resolved and the miracle ended. And yet, I confess, there is in these two creatures contained more miraculous matter than in all the loadstones and diamonds in the world.[11]

[11] *Discovery*, Bk. 13, Ch. 11.

More Executions at Chelmsford

The Apprehension and confession of three notorious Witches. Arreigned and by Justice condemned and executed at Chelmes-forde, in the Countye of Essex, the 5. day of Julye, last past. 1589.

This is an unusually clear and literate account, with a fiction-writer's organisation behind it, and a style which allows the emergence of all kinds of ironies inimical to the writer's conscious purpose. When we turn to the records printed by Ewen, we realise that the pamphlet is a very stringent selection of material; it deals only with three of the four who were hanged at the assizes, and omits the others accused for witchcraft.

Joan Cunny's daughter was reprieved for pregnancy and hanged in 1590, after the birth; a man and two women were found not guilty, one woman was reprieved, one bailed and the other Cunny daughter was jailed for a year. Those found not guilty had not been accused of felonious witchcraft. The author, in his address to the reader, states that he has published the manner of the accusations 'according to the copies both of the offenders' confession by examination, and their accusations registered', which confirms the use of court documents by trial reporters.

The shocking vagueness of Joan Upney's confession (she seems to have been a trifle feeble-minded) contrasts oddly with the examination of Joan Prentice, where extremely detailed and accurate observation of the behaviour of ferrets co-exists with senile fantasy. Once again, some of those accused are unchaste, and most indigent; children are encouraged to give damning evidence against their mothers and complimented when this brings about conviction. It is worth remembering this when we are shocked by the little frauds who persist in actions that bring old women to the gallows; very similar behaviour often won the highest social approval.

For the judges in this trial were unusually distinguished; Robert Clarke, Baron of the Exchequer, and John Puckering, Queen's Serjeant, and the commendations to the children are theirs.

The arraignment and execution of Joan Cunny of Stisted in the county of Essex, widow, of the age of fourscore years or thereabouts, who was brought before Anthony Mildmay, esquire, the last day of March 1589.[1]

---

[1] The Preface to the pamphlet is omitted, and the extract begins on A3.

Punishments for witchcraft: hanging
The Apprehension and confession of three notorious Witches . . . at Chelmesforde 1589

Imprimis, this examinate saith and confesseth that she hath knowledge and can do the most detestable art of witchcraft, and that she learned this her knowledge in the same of one Mother Humphrey of Maplestead, who told her that she must kneel down upon her knees and make a circle on the ground, and pray unto Satan the chief of the devils (the form of which prayer that she then taught her this examinate hath now forgotten), and that then the spirits would come unto her.

The which she put in practice about twenty years since, in the field

This witch had nine spirits; 2 of them were like unto a black dog, having the faces of a toad.

These spirits belonging to this witch did suck commonly upon a sore leg which his Mother Cunny had.

She had four principal spirits. The first was Jack. The second was Jill. The third was Nicholas. The fourth was Ned.

Jack killed mankind. Jill womenkind. Nicholas killed horses. Ned killed cattle.

Note how God's Spirit confoundeth the imps of wickedness.[2]

of John Wiseman of Stisted, gentleman, called Cowfen Field; and there making a circle as she was taught, and kneeling on her knees, said the prayer now forgotten; and invocating upon Satan, two spirits did appear unto her within the said circle, in the similitude and likeness of two black frogs, and there demanded of her what she would have, being ready to do for her what she would desire, so that she would promise to give them her soul for their travail, for otherwise they would do nothing for her.

Whereupon she did promise them her soul, and then they concluded with her so to do for her what she would require, and gave themselves several names—that is to say, the one Jack and the other Jill, by the which names she did always after call them. And then taking them up, she carried them home in her lap and put them in a box, and gave them white bread and milk.

And within one month after, she sent them to milk Hurrell's beasts, which they did, and they would bring milk for their own eating and not for her. And further, she saith that her spirits never changed their colour since they first came unto her, and that they would familiarly talk with her when she had anything to say or do with them, in her own language.

And likewise she confesseth that she sent her said spirits to hurt the wife of John Sparrow the elder of Stisted, which they did, and also that where Master John Glascock of Stisted aforesaid had a great stack of logs in his yard, she by her said spirits did overthrow them.

And further saith that she hath hurt divers persons within this sixteen or twenty years, but how many she now knowth not. Furthermore, she confesseth that she sent her spirits unto William Unglee of Stisted, miller, and because they could not hurt him, she sent them to hurt one Barnaby Griffin his man, which they did.

Likewise, she confesseth that she sent her said spirits to hurt Master Kitchin, minister of the said town, and also unto one George Coe of the said town, shoemaker, to hurt him likewise. But they could not, and the cause why they could not, as the said spirits told her, was because they had at their coming a strong faith in God, and had invocated and called upon Him, that they could do them no harm.[3]

And further, she saith that Margaret Cunny her daughter did fall out

[2] This note is misplaced about a page earlier in the original.

[3] Joan is behind the times. This comforting theory has already given way to the idea that the Devil can afflict *anyone* in body or goods (see introduction to the account of the Chelmsford trials in 1579), and the exorcists are preparing to see possession itself as a trial from which even the godly are not spared.

with Father Hurrell and gave him cursed speeches, and thereupon she thinketh she sent her spirits to her.

Also she doth utterly deny that she sent her said spirits to Finch's wife, Devenish's wife, and Reynold Ferrer, or any of them to hurt them. And being further examined, she confesseth that although her said spirits at some time can have no power to hurt men, yet they may have power to hurt their cattle.

This Joan Cunny living very lewdly, had[4] two lewd daughters no better than naughty packs,* [who] had two bastard children: being both boys, these two children were chief witnesses and gave in great evidence against their grandam and mothers, the eldest being about 10 or 12 years of age.

Against this Mother Cunny the elder boy gave in this evidence, which she herself after confessed: that she going to Braintree market came to one Harry Finch's house to demand some drink; his wife being busy and a-brewing told her she had no leisure to give her any. Then Joan Cunny went away discontented, and at night Finch's wife was grievously taken in her head, and the next day in her side, and so continued in most horrible pain for the space of a week, and then died. Mother Cunny confessed that she sent her spirit Jill to torment her.

The same boy confessed that he was commanded by his grandmother to fetch a burden of wood, which he gathered, but another boy stole it from him, and he came home without and told his grandam; and she commanded her spirit to prick the same boy in the foot, which was done, and the same boy came to the bar lame, and gave evidence against her.

Again the same boy confessed that his grandam, when he had lost his wood, said she would have wood enough, and bade him go into Sir Edward Huddlestone's ground (being High Sheriff of the shire) and to take with him Jack the spirit; and so he did, who went unseen to anybody but to the boy, and when they came to a mighty oak tree, the spirit went about it, and presently the tree blew up by the roots and no wind at all stirring at this time; which Master High Sheriff acknowledged to be blown down in a great calm.

The confession of Joan Upney of Dagenham in the county of Essex, who was brought before Sir Henry Gray, knight, the third of May 1589.

This examinate saith that one Fustian Kirtle, otherwise called Whitecoat, a witch of Barking,[5] came to her house about seven or eight years

---

[4] Original 'having'. [5] See *Witches at St. Osyth*, note 31.

ago and gave her a thing like a mole, and told her if she owed anybody any ill will, if she did bid it, it would go clap* them.

She saith that mole tarried not above a year with her but it consumed away, and then she gave her another mole and a toad, which she kept a great while, and was never without some toads since, till her last going away from her house, when she confesseth she ran away because she heard John Harrold and Richard Foster say she was a witch, and such[6] other words.

She saith that one day she left a toad under the groundsill at Harrold's house, and it pinched his wife and sucked her till she died, but it never came to her the said Joan Upney again.[7]

She saith that one day another toad went over her threshold as Richard Foster's wife was coming that way, and it went and pinched her and never returned again. Other two toads she left at home when she ran away, but they consumed away.

She saith that her eldest daughter would never abide to meddle with her toads, but her youngest daughter would handle them and use them as well as herself.

The examination of Joan Prentice, one of the women of the almshouse of Sible Hedingham within the said county, being taken the 29 of March, in the 31 year of the reign of our sovereign lady Elizabeth.

Imprimis, this said examinate saith and confesseth, that about six years last past, between the feasts of All Saints and the birth of our Lord God, the Devil appeared unto her in the almshouse aforesaid about ten of the clock in the night time, being in the shape and proportion of a dunnish coloured ferret, having fiery eyes; and the said examinate being alone in her chamber, and sitting upon a low stool preparing herself to bedward, the ferret standing with his hinder legs upon the ground and his forelegs settled upon her lap, and settling his fiery eyes upon her eyes, spake and pronounced unto her these words following, namely: 'Joan Prentice, give me thy soul.'

To whom this examinate, being greatly amazed, answered and said 'In the name of God, what art thou?' The ferret answered 'I am Satan;

---

[6] Original has 'urch'.

[7] These peculiar toads seem to have taken on the attributes of fairies, who punished by pinching, and hedgehogs, which were said to suck milk from cows (see *ante*). Poor muddled Joan also seems to think that the sucking done by familiars is not a bond with the witch, but vampirism towards her enemy.

fear me not, my coming unto thee is to do thee no hurt but to obtain thy soul, which I must and will have before I depart from thee.' To whom the said examinate answered and said that he demanded that of her which is none of hers to give, saying that her soul appertained only unto Jesus Christ by whose precious blood-shedding it was bought and purchased.

To whom the said ferret replied and said, 'I must then have some of thy blood', which she willingly granting, offered him the forefinger of her left hand; the which the ferret took into his mouth and, setting his former feet upon that hand, sucked blood thereout, insomuch that her finger did smart exceedingly. And the said examinate demanding again of the ferret what his name was, it answered 'Bid'; and then presently the said ferret vanished out of her sight suddenly.

Item, the said examinate saith further that about one month after, the said ferret came again unto her in the night time as she was sitting upon a little stool, preparing herself to bedward, as is above said.'Joan, wilt thou go to bed?' to whom she answered 'Yea, that I will by God's grace'; then presently the ferret leapt up upon her lap, and from thence up to her bosom, and laying his former feet upon her left shoulder, sucked blood out of her left cheek, and then he said unto her, 'Joan, if thou wilt have me do anything for thee, I am and will be always ready at thy commandment.' And thereupon she, being a little before fallen out with William Adams his wife of Sible Hedingham aforesaid, willed the ferret to spoil her drink which was then in brewing, which he did accordingly.

Item, the said examinate furthermore saith and confesseth that the said ferret divers times after appeared unto her, always at the time when she was going to bed; and the last time he appeared unto her was about seven weeks last past, at which time she going to bed, the ferret leaped upon her left shoulder and sucked blood out of her left cheek and, that done, he demanded of her what she had for him to do? To whom she answered, 'Go unto Master Glascock's house, and nip one of his children a little, named Sara, but hurt it not.'

And the next night he resorted unto her again and told her that he had done as she willed him, namely, that he had nipped Sara Glascock and that she should die thereof. To whom she answered and said 'Thou villain! What has thou done? I bid thee to nip it but a little and not to hurt it, and hast thou killed the child?' Which speech being uttered, the ferret vanished away suddenly, and never came to her since.

Item, she affirmeth that the occasion why she did will her ferret to nip the said child was for that she being the day before at the house of the said Master Glascock to beg his alms, answer was made to her by one of his maiden servants that both her master and mistress were from home, and therefore desired her to be contented for that time, and thereupon the examinate departed greatly discontented, and that night sent her ferret to nip the child as is aforesaid.

Item, she saith and affirmeth that at what time soever she would have her ferret do anything for her, she used the words 'Bid, Bid, Bid, come Bid, come Bid, come Bid, come suck, come suck, come suck,' and that presently he would appear as is aforesaid and sucked blood out of her left cheek, and then performed any mischief she willed or wished him to do for her unto or against any of her neighbours.

Lastly, the said examinate saith and confesseth that one Elizabeth Whale, the wife of Michael Whale of Sible Hedingham aforesaid, labourer, and Elizabeth Mott, the wife of John Mott of the said town, cobbler, are as well acquainted with her Bid as herself is, but knoweth not what hurt they or any of them have done to any of their neighbours.

When their inditements were read, and their examinations also, they stood upon their terms to prolong life. Yet to make the matters more apparent, sundry witnesses were produced to give evidence against them; and first the judge of the circuit very wisely with a great foresight called in the two bastard children before mentioned, and commended them greatly for telling the truth of that which he should ask them concerning their grandam and their mothers (which they did). And having said what they could, together with the depositions of sundry other witnesses, they having confessed sufficient matter to prove the inditements, the jury found these bad women guilty, and that they had slain men, women and children, and committed very wicked and horrible actions, divers and sundry times, and thereupon the judge proceeded and pronounced the sentence of death against them, as worthily they had deserved.

After they had received their judgments, they were conveyed from the bar back again to prison, where they had not stayed above two hours but the officers prepared themselves to conduct them to the place of execution. To which place they led them, and being come thither, one Master Ward, a learned divine, being desired by the justices did exhort these wicked women to repentance, and persuaded them that they would show unto the people the truth of their wickedness, and to call upon God for mercy with penitent hearts, and to ask pardon at His hands for the same. Some few prayers they said after the preacher, but little else more than this, that they had deserved to die in committing those wicked sins, and so took their deaths patiently.

Note that Mother Upney being inwardly pricked, and having some inward feeling in conscience, cried out saying that she had grievously sinned, that 'the Devil had deceived her, the Devil had deceived her', and that she had twice given her soul to the Devil; yet by the means of God's spirit working in her, and the pains which Master Ward took with her, she seemed very sorry for the same, and died very penitent, asking God and the world forgiveness even to the last gasp, for her wicked and detestable life.

Finis

Witches' Sabbath

Newes from Scotland, Declaring the Damnable life and death of Doctor Fian, a notable Sorcerer, who was burned at Edenbrough in January last. 1591. Which Doctor was regester to the Divell that sundry times preached at North Barrick Kirke, to a number of notorious Witches. With the true examinations of the saide Doctor and Witches, as they uttered them in the presence of the Scottish King . . . London [1591]

This truly horrible case, printed in England 'according to the Scottish Coppie', gives us the first pamphlet account of the Witches' Sabbath as it was said to occur on the Continent. It is possible that this idea had been disseminated in Scotland because of that country's close links with France, and the constant passing to and fro of nobles and their servants; it is also possible that the whole tale resulted from the Inquisitorial situation of a scholarly examiner (in this case the king himself for part of the time) and brutal, unrestricted torture.

Legal records of the trial exist almost complete, and have been reprinted by Robert Pitcairn in his *Criminal Trials* (Edinburgh, 1833). These show that there was a good deal more political content to the affair than appears here, and that James's great enemy, Francis, Earl of Bothwell, was accused of planning and directing the witches' attempt on the king's life.

Remarkably, no contemporary English trial reflects these proceedings, and there is no serious attempt to use the Scottish findings about witches as sensational 'filler' for English witch-pamphlets, even after James became king of England. The Sabbaths of the Samlesbury witches in 1612 and the later Lancashire witches in 1634 turned out to be pure invention by a single witness; in English courts and English superstition, the English witch remained stubbornly independent and anti-social—one might almost say, irreligious.

To the Reader

The manifold untruths which is spread abroad concerning the detestable actions and apprehension of those witches whereof this history following truly entreateth hath caused me to publish the same in print; and the rather for that sundry written copies are lately dispersed thereof, containing:—that the said witches were first discovered by means of a poor pedlar travelling to the town of Tranent, and that by a wonderful manner he was in a moment conveyed at midnight from Scotland to Bordeaux in France (being places of no small distance

The Devil, a wizard and witches
Newes from Scotland 1591-2

between) into a Merchant's cellar there; and after, being sent from Bordeaux into Scotland by certain Scottish merchants to the King's Majesty, that he discovered those witches and was the case of their apprehension; with a number of matters miraculous and incredible, all which in truth are most false.[1]

Nevertheless, to satisfy a number of honest minds who are desirous to be informed of the verity and truth of their confessions (which for certainty is more stranger than the common report runneth, and yet with more truth) I have undertaken to publish this short treatise, which declareth the true discourse of all that hath happened, and as well what was pretended by those wicked and detestable witches against the King's Majesty, as also by what means they wrought the same.

All which examinations, gentle Reader, I have here truly published as they were taken and uttered in the presence of the King's Majesty, praying thee to accept it for verity, the same being so true as cannot be reproved.

[1] See *A Most Wicked work of a wretched Witch* . . .

A true discourse of the apprehension of sundry witches lately taken in Scotland: whereof some are executed, and some are yet imprisoned. With a particular recital of their examinations, taken in the presence of the King's Majesty.

God, by His omnipotent power, hath at all times and daily doth take such care, and is so vigilant, for the weal and preservation of His own, that thereby he disappointeth the wicked practices and evil intents of all such as, by any means whatsoever, seek indirectly to conspire anything contrary to His holy will; yea, and by the same power He hath lately overthrown and hindered the intentions and wicked dealings of a great number of ungodly creatures, no better than devils, who, suffering themselves to be allured and enticed by the Devil whom they served, and to whom they were privately sworn, entered into the detestable art of witchcraft.

[This]² they studied and practised so long time that in the end they had seduced by their sorcery a number of other to be as bad as themselves; dwelling in the bounds of Lothian, which is a principal shire or part of Scotland where the King's Majesty useth to make his chiefest residence or abode. And to the end that their detestable wickedness which they privily had pretended against the King's Majesty, the commonweal of that country, with the nobility and subjects of the same, should come to light: God of His unspeakable goodness did reveal and lay it open in very strange sort, thereby to make known unto the world that their actions were contrary to the law of God, and the natural affection which we ought generally to bear one to another; the manner of the revealing whereof was as followeth.

Within the town of Tranent in the kingdom of Scotland there dwelleth one David Seaton who, being deputy bailiff in the said town, had a maidservant called Gillis Duncan who used secretly to be absent, and to lie forth of her master's house every other night. This Gillis Duncan took in hand to help all such as were troubled or grieved with any kind of sickness or infirmity, and in short space did perform many matters most miraculous.

Which things forasmuch as she began to do them upon a sudden, having never done the like before, made her master and others to be in great admiration,* and wondered thereat; by means whereof the said David Seaton had his maid in some great suspicion that she did not those things by natural and lawful ways, but rather supposed it to be done by some extraordinary and unlawful means.

---

² [This] substituted for 'which'.

Whereupon her master began to grow very inquisitive, and examined her which way and by what means she were able to perform matters of so great importance, whereat she gave him no answer. Nevertheless, her master, to the intent that he might the better try and find out the truth of the same, did with the help of others torment her with the torture of the pilliewinks[3] upon her fingers, which is a grievous torture, and binding or wrenching her head with a cord or rope, which is a most cruel torment also, yet would she not confess anything.

Whereupon they suspecting that she had been marked by the Devil (as commonly witches are) made diligent search about her, and found the enemy's mark to be in her fore-crag,* or fore-part of her throat; which being found, she confessed that all her doings was done by the wicked allurements and enticements of the Devil, and that she did them by witchcraft.

After this her confession, she was committed to prison, where she continued for a season; where immediately she accused these persons following to be notorious witches, and caused them forthwith to be apprehended one after another, viz. Agnes Sampson the eldest witch of them all, dwelling in Haddington, Agnes Tompson of Edinburgh, Doctor Fian alias John Cunningham, master of the school at Saltpans in Lothian, of whose life and strange acts you shall near more largely in the end of this discourse.

These were by the said Gillis Duncan accused, as also George Mott's wife dwelling in Saltpans, Robert Grierson, skipper, and Janet Bandilands, with the porter's wife of Seaton, the smith at the Bridge Halls,[4] with innumerable others in that parts, and dwelling in those bounds aforesaid; of whom some are already executed, the rest remain in prison to receive the doom of judgment at the King's Majesty's will and pleasure.

The said Gillis Duncan also caused Euphemia McCalzean to be apprehended, who conspired and performed the death of her godfather, and who used her art upon a gentleman being one of the lords and justices of the Session, for bearing good will to her daughter; she also caused to be apprehended one Barbara Napier for bewitching to death Archibald, last Earl of Angus, who languished to death by witchcraft

---

[3] pilliewinks: a kind of thumbscrew. George Black tried it on himself, and warns readers not to underestimate the extreme pain caused by even a moderate application. (*A Calendar of Cases of Witchcraft in Scotland*, New York Public Library (New York, 1938), p. 16.)

[4] Halls: covered market in Edinburgh.

and yet the same was not suspected, but that he died of so strange a disease as the physician knew not how to cure or remedy the same. But of all other the said witches, these two last before recited were reputed for as civil honest women as any that dwelled within the city of Edinburgh, before they were apprehended.

Many other besides were taken dwelling in Leith who are detained in prison until his Majesty's further will and pleasure be known, of whose wicked doings you shall particularly hear, which was as followeth.

This aforesaid Agnes Sampson, which was the elder witch, was taken and brought to Holyrood House before the King's Majesty and sundry other of the nobility of Scotland, where she was straitly examined; but all the persuasions which the King's Majesty used to her with the rest of his Council might not provoke or induce her to confess anything, but stood stiffly in the denial of all that was laid to her charge. Whereupon they caused her to be conveyed away to prison, there to receive such torture as hath been lately provided for witches in that country.

And forasmuch as by due examination of witchcraft and witches in Scotland it hath lately been found that the Devil doth generally mark them with a privy mark, by reason the witches have confessed themselves that the Devil doth lick them with his tongue in some privy part of their body before he doth receive them to be his servants; which mark commonly is given them under the hair in some part of their body whereby it may not easily be found out or seen, though they be searched; and generally so long as the mark is not seen to those which search them, so long the parties that hath the mark will never confess anything—therefore by special commandment this Agnes Sampson had all her hair shaven off in each part of her body, and her head thrawen* with a rope according to the custom of that country, being a pain most grievous which she continued almost an hour, during which time she would not confess anything until the Devil's mark was found upon her privities; then she immediately confessed whatsoever was demanded of her, and justifying those persons aforesaid to be notorious witches.

Item, the said Agnes Tompson was after brought again before the King's Majesty and his Council, and being examined of the meetings and detestable dealings of those witches, she confessed that upon the night of All Hallow's Even⁵ last, she was accompanied as well with the

⁵ All Hallow's Eve, or Halloween: the evening of Oct. 31.

persons aforesaid as also with a great many other witches to the number of two hundred; and that all they together went by sea, each one in a riddle or sieve, and went in the same very substantially with flagons of wine, making merry and drinking by the way in the same riddles or sieves, to the kirk* of North Berwick in Lothian; and that after they had landed, took hands on the land and danced this reel or short dance, singing all with one voice:—

> Commer* go ye before, commer go ye;
> If ye will not go before, commer let me.

At which time she confessed that this Gillis Duncan did go before them playing this reel or dance upon a small trump, called a Jew's trump,[6] until they entered into the kirk of North Berwick.

These confessions made the king in a wonderful admiration, and sent for the said Gillis Duncan, who upon the like trump did play the said dance before the King's Majesty, who, in respect of the strangeness of these matters took great delight to be present at their examinations.

Item, the said Agnes Tompson confessed that the Devil being then at North Berwick kirk attending their coming in the habit or likeness of a man, and seeing that they tarried over long, he at their coming enjoined them all to a penance, which was that they should kiss his buttocks in sign of duty to him; which being put over the pulpit bar, everyone did as he had enjoined them.[7] And having made his ungodly exhortations, wherein he did greatly inveigh against the King of Scotland, he received their oaths for their good and true service towards him, and departed; which done, they returned to sea, and so home again.

(At which time the witches demanded of the Devil why he did bear such hatred to the King, who answered 'by reason the King is the greatest enemy he hath in the world'; all which their [c]onfessions and depositions are still extant upon record.)

Item, the said Agnes Sampson confessed before the King's Majesty sundry things which were so miraculous and strange as that his Majesty said they were all extreme liars; whereat she answered 'she

---

[6] Jew's harp?

[7] The 'obscene kiss' was regarded by Inquisitors as a form of worship, a parody of Christian adoration; here it retains the traditional meaning of punishment or humiliation inflicted as a crude joke. As Chaucer (*The Miller's Tale*) knew better than the theologians, this idea is the primary material for school-and-country jests; it occurs as perversity but is simply untenable as blasphemy.

would not wish his Majesty to suppose her words to be false, but rather to believe them, in that she would discover such matter unto him as his Majesty should not any way doubt of.'

And thereupon taking his Majesty a little aside, she declared unto him the very words which passed between the King's Majesty and his Queen at Oslo in Norway the first night of their marriage, with their answer each to other; whereat the King's Majesty wondered greatly, and swore by the living God that he believed that all the devils in hell could not have discovered the same, acknowledging her words to be most true; and therefore gave the more credit to the rest which is before declared.[8]

Touching this Agnes Tompson, she is the only woman who by the Devil's persuasion should have intended and put in execution the King's Majesty's death, in this manner:

She confessed that she took a black toad and did hang the same up by the heels three days, and collected and gathered the venom as it dropped and fell from it in an oyster shell, and kept the same venom close covered until she should obtain any part or piece of foul linen cloth that had appertained to the King's Majesty, as shirt, handkercher,[9] napkin, or any other thing; which she practised to obtain by means of one John Kerrs, who being attendant in his Majesty's chamber, [she] desired him for old acquaintance between them to help her to one, or a piece of, such a cloth as is aforesaid, which thing the said John Kerrs denied to help her to, saying he could not help her to it.

And the said Agnes Tompson by her depositions since her apprehension saith, that if she had obtained any one piece of linen cloth which the King had worn and fouled, she had bewitched him to death, and put him to such extraordinary pains as if he had been lying upon sharp thorns and ends of needles.

Moreover, she confessed that at the time when His Majesty was in Denmark she, being accompanied with the parties before specially named, took a cat and christened it, and afterward bound to each part of that cat the chiefest parts of a dead man, and several joints of his

[8] In her very next statement Agnes admits to 'old acquaintance' with an attendant in the King's chamber, who may well have accompanied the king on his journey to Oslo. Since privacy in a mediaeval castle was only a relative term and depended mainly on the curtains of a four-poster bed, James's surprise is a trifle naive.

[9] Hair, nail clippings or soiled clothes had all been in contact with their owner long enough to have acquired 'sympathy' with his essential being; therefore what was done symbolically to them would be transferred to him.

body; and that in the night following, the said cat was conveyed into the midst of the sea by all these witches sailing in their riddles or sieves[10] as is aforesaid, and so left the said cat right before the town of Leith in Scotland.

This done, there did arise such a tempest in the sea as a greater hath not been seen; which tempest was the cause of the perishing of a boat or vessel coming over from the town of Burnt Island to the town of Leith, wherein was sundry jewels and rich gifts which should have been presented to the now Queen of Scotland, at Her Majesty's coming to Leith.

Again it is confessed, that the said christened cat was the cause that the King's Majesty's ship, at his coming forth of Denmark, had a contrary wind to the rest of his ships then being in his company, which thing was most strange and true, as the King's Majesty acknowledgeth; for when the rest of the ships had a fair and good wind, then was the wind contrary, and altogether against his Majesty. And further, the said witch declared, that his Majesty had never come safely from the sea, if his faith had not prevailed above their intentions.

Moreover, the said witches being demanded how the Devil would use them when he was in their company, they confessed that, when the Devil did receive them for his servants, and that they had vowed themselves unto him, then he would carnally use them, albeit to their little pleasure, in respect of his cold nature; and would do the like at sundry other times.

As touching the aforesaid Doctor Fian, alias John Cunningham, the examination of his acts since his apprehension declareth the great subtlety of the Devil and therefore maketh things to appear the more miraculous. For being apprehended by the accusation of the said Gillis Duncan aforesaid, who confessed he was their Register, and that there was not one man suffered to come to the Devil's readings but only he, the said Doctor was taken and imprisoned and used with the accustomed pain provided for those offences, inflicted upon the rest as is aforesaid.

First by thrawing of his head with a rope, whereat he would confess nothing.

[10] The idea of sailing in a sieve seems to originate in folk-tales dealing with 'an impossible task' accomplished by cunning, i.e. water was carried in a sieve by plastering the mesh with mud. Witch-stories take such themes and spoil their point by substituting charms for brains, witchcraft for wit. The sieve, like the broom, could be regarded as a female 'badge' or symbol of office.

Secondly, he was persuaded by fair means to confess his follies, but that would prevail as little.

Lastly, he was put to the most severe and cruel pain in the world, called 'the boots';[11] who after he had received three strokes, being inquired if he would confess his damnable acts and wicked life, his tongue would not serve him to speak. In respect whereof the rest of the witches willed to search his tongue, under which was found two pins thrust up into the head;[12] whereupon the witches did say 'Now is the charm stinted' and showed that those charmed pins were the cause he could not confess anything. Then was he immediately released of the boots, brought before the King, his confession was taken, and his own hand willingly set thereunto, which contained as followeth:—

First, that at the general meetings of those witches he was always present: that he was clerk to all those that were in subjection to the Devil's service bearing the name of witches, that alway he did take their oaths for their true service to the Devil, and that he wrote for them such matters as the Devil still pleased to command him.

Item, he confessed that by his witchcraft he did bewitch a gentleman dwelling near to the Saltpans, where the said doctor kept school, only for being enamoured of a gentlewoman whom he loved himself; by means of which his sorcery, witchcraft and devilish practices he caused the said gentleman that once in 24 hours he fell into a lunacy and madness, and so continued one whole hour together.

And for the verity of the same, he caused the gentleman to be brought before the King's Majesty, which was upon the 24 day of December last; and being in his Majesty's chamber, suddenly he gave a great screech and fell into a madness, sometime bending himself, and sometime capering so directly up that his head did touch the ceiling of the chamber, to the great admiration of his Majesty and others then present; so that all the gentlemen in the chamber were not able to hold him until they called in more help, who together bound him hand and foot and, suffering the said gentleman to lie still until his fury were past, he within an hour came again to himself when, being demanded of the King's Majesty what he saw or did all that while, answered that he had been in a sound sleep.

[11] the boots: the prisoner's legs were held in iron tubes, and wedges hammered in between flesh and metal.

[12] Probably a rather childish form of sympathetic magic to prevent confession, like biting the tongue. It is unnecessarily complicated to assume with Dr. Robbins that the jailers stuck in the pins themselves as an additional torture.

Item, the said doctor did also confess that he had used means sundry times to obtain his purpose and wicked intent of the same gentlewoman, and, seeing himself disappointed of his intention, he determined by all ways he might to obtain the same, trusting by conjuring, witchcraft and sorcery to obtain it in this manner:

It happened this gentlewoman, being unmarried, had a brother who went to school with the said doctor; and [he] calling his scholar to him, demanded if he did lie with his sister, who answered 'he did.' By means whereof he thought to obtain his purpose, and therefore secretly promised to teach him without stripes, so he would obtain for him three hairs of his sister's privities at such time as he should spy best occasion for it; which the youth promised faithfully to perform, and vowed speedily to put it in practice, taking a piece of conjured paper of his master to lap* them in when he had gotten them. And thereupon the boy practised nightly to obtain his master's purpose, especially when his sister was asleep.

But God, who knoweth the secrets of all hearts and revealeth all wicked and ungodly practices, would not suffer the intents of this devilish doctor to come to that purpose which he supposed it would; and therefore, to declare that He was heavily offended with his wicked intent, did so work by the gentlewoman's own means that in the end the same was discovered and brought to light.

For she being one night asleep, and her brother in bed with her, suddenly cried out to her mother, declaring that her brother would not suffer her to sleep; whereupon her mother, having a quick capacity, did vehemently suspect Doctor Fian's intention, by reason she was a witch of herself, and therefore presently arose and was very inquisitive of the boy to understand his intent, and the better to know the same, did beat him with sundry stripes; whereby he discovered the truth unto her.

The mother, therefore, being well practised in witchcraft, did think it most convenient to meet with the doctor in his own art; and thereupon took the paper from the boy, wherein he should have put the same hairs, and went to a young heifer which never had born calf nor gone to the bull, and with a pair of shears clipped off three hairs from the udder of the cow, and wrapped them in the same paper, which she again delivered to the boy, then willing him to give the same to his said master; which he immediately did.

The schoolmaster, so soon as he had received them, thinking them indeed to be the maid's hairs, went straight and wrought his art upon them. But the doctor had no sooner done his intent to them but presently the heifer or cow whose hairs they were indeed, came unto the door of the church wherein the schoolmaster was,[13] into the which the heifer went, and made towards the schoolmaster, leaping and dancing upon him and following him forth of the church and to what place soever he went, to the great admiration of all the townsmen of Saltpans, and many other who did behold the same.

The report whereof made all men imagine that he did work it by the Devil, without whom it could never have been so sufficiently effected; and thereupon the name of the said Doctor Fian (who was but a very young man) began to grow so common among the people of Scotland that he was secretly nominated for a notable conjurer.

All which although in the beginning he denied, and would not confess, yet having felt the pain of the boots (and the charm stinted,* as aforesaid) he confessed all the aforesaid to be most true, without producing any witnesses to justify the same; and thereupon, before the King's Majesty he subscribed the said confessions with his own hand which for truth remaineth upon record in Scotland.

After that the depositions and examinations of the said Doctor Fian alias Cunningham was taken, as already is declared, with his own hand willingly set thereunto, he was by the master of the prison committed to ward and appointed to a chamber by himself, where, forsaking his wicked ways, acknowledging his most ungodly life, showing that he had too much followed the allurements and enticements of Satan and fondly practised his conclusions by conjuring, witchcraft, enchantment, sorcery and such like, he renounced the Devil and all his wicked works, vowed to lead the life of a Christian, and seemed newly connected towards God.

The morrow after, upon conference had with him, he granted that the Devil had appeared unto him in the night before, apparelled all in black, with a white wand in his hand,[14] and that the Devil demanded of him if he would continue his faithful service according to his first oath and promise made to that effect. Whom (as he then said) he utterly renounced to his face, and said unto him in this manner: 'Avoid, Satan, avoid, for I have listened too much unto thee, and by the same thou hast undone me, in respect whereof I utterly forsake

---

[13] School was taught in the church porch, often extended into a kind of annexe.

[14] A rod or wand was often carried as a mark of office. Spirits, fairies and magicians all used it as the symbolic instrument of power, to blast or heal.

thee.' To whom the Devil answered 'That once ere thou die thou shalt be mine.' And with that (as he said) the Devil brake the white wand, and immediately vanished forth of his sight.

Thus all the day this Doctor Fian continued very solitary, and seemed to have care of his own soul, and would call upon God, showing himself penitent for his wicked life; nevertheless the same night he found such means that he stole the key of the prison door and chamber in the which he was, which in the night he opened and fled away to the Saltpans, where he was always resident, and first apprehended.

Of whose sudden departure when the King's Majesty had intelligence, he presently commanded diligent enquiry to be made for his apprehension, and for the better effecting thereof, he sent public proclamations into all parts of his land to the same effect. By means of whose hot and hard pursuit, he was again taken and brought to prison; and then being called before the King's Highness, he was re-examined as well touching his departure as also touching all that had before happened.

But this doctor, notwithstanding that his own confession appeareth remaining in record under his own handwriting, and the same thereunto fixed in the presence of the King's Majesty and sundry of his Council, yet did he utterly deny the same.

Whereupon, the King's Majesty, perceiving his stubborn wilfulness, conceived and imagined that in the time of his absence he had entered into new conference and league with the Devil his master, and that he had been again newly marked, for the which he was narrowly searched, but it could not in any wise be found. Yet for more trial of him to make him confess, he was commanded to have a most strange torment, which was done in this manner following:—

His nails upon all his fingers were riven and pulled off with an instrument called in Scottish a *Turkas*,* which in England we call a pair of pincers, and under every nail there was thrust in two needles over even up to the heads. At all which torments notwithstanding the doctor never shrunk any whit, neither would he then confess it the sooner for all the tortures inflicted upon him.

Then was he with all convenient speed, by commandment conveyed again to the torment of the boots, wherein he continued a long time, and did abide so many blows in them, that his legs were crushed and beaten together as small as might be, and the bones and flesh so bruised that the blood and marrow spouted forth in great abundance, whereby they were made unserviceable forever.

And notwithstanding all these grievous pains and cruel torments he would not confess anything; so deeply had the Devil entered into his heart, that he utterly denied all that which he had before avouched, and would say nothing thereunto but this—that what he had done and said before was only done and said for fear of pains which he had endured.

Upon great consideration therefore taken by the King's Majesty and his Council, as well for the due execution of justice upon such detestable malefactors, as also for example sake to remain a terror to all others hereafter that shall attempt to deal in the like wicked and ungodly actions as witchcraft, sorcery, conjuration and such like, the said Doctor Fian was soon after arraigned, condemned and adjudged by the law to die, and then to be burned, according to the law of that land provided in that behalf.

Whereupon he was put into a cart, and, being first strangled, he was immediately put into a great fire being ready provided for that purpose, and there burnt in the Castle Hill of Edinburgh on a Saturday in the end of January last past, 1591.

The rest of the witches which are not yet executed, remain in prison till further trial, and knowledge of His Majesty's pleasure.[15]

This strange discourse before recited may perhaps give some occasion of doubt to such as shall happen to read the same, and thereby conjecture that the King's Majesty would not hazard himself in the presence of such notorious witches lest thereby might have ensued great danger to his person and the general state of the land; which thing in truth might well have been feared. But to answer generally to such, let this suffice:—that first, it is well known that the King is the child and servant of God and they but servants to the Devil; he is the Lord's anointed and they but vessels of God's wrath; he is a true Christian and trusteth in God, they worse than infidels, for they only trust in the Devil, who daily serve[s] them till he have brought them to utter destruction.

But hereby it seemeth that his Highness carried a magnanimous and undaunted mind, not feared with their enchantments, but resolute in this—that so long as God is with him, he feareth not who is against

---

[15] Agnes Sampson and several others were strangled and burned; Euphemia McCalzean was burned alive; Barbara Napier was reprieved because of pregnancy, then acquitted—'nobody insisting in the pursuit of her, she was set at liberty'. James was extremely angry at this, and attempted proceedings against the jurors.

him. And truly the whole scope of this treatise doth so plainly lay open the wonderful providence of the Almighty that if he had not been defended by His omnipotency and power, his Highness had never returned alive in his voyage from Denmark; so that there is no doubt but God would as well defend him on the land as on the sea, where they pretended* their damnable practice.

Aerial Adventures of Richard Burt

*A Most Wicked worke of a wretched Witch (the like whereof none can record
these manie yeeres in England. Wrought on the Person of one Richard Burt,
servant to Maister Edling of Woodhall in the Parrish of Pinner in the Countie
of Myddlesex, a myle beyond Harrow. Latelie committed in March last, An.
1592 and newly recognised according to the truth, by G. B. maister of Artes.*
[*London, 1592/3*]

There is no record to confirm this case, and one may feel that the extreme
circumstantiality of the title protests a little too much. There is, besides, a
violent contrast between the pious introduction and the rather racy account
of Richard's misadventures which seems to suggest a selection or re-hash
of older material.

The introduction to the London edition of *Newes from Scotland* (1591
or 1592) mentions many false rumours connected with that case, among
them one of a pedlar aerially transported by witches from Scotland to
France; and Johann Spies' *Faustbuch*, with its aerial voyages, was translated
into English and published in 1592. Since witches have not hitherto been
accused of this form of transportation in England, this pamphlet seems likely
to have been derived from the forementioned sources rather than from fact.

However, it is not impossible that Richard, rather than G.B., was influenced by them; there are odd undertones of the sinister other-world of the
fairies and its deceptive time-scheme in his tale, and it is possible that we have
an account in good faith of country gossip concerning a farm-hand's four-
day absence, and his explanation of it. A notable drinking spree, or an
epileptic fit with hallucinations could have produced both absence and the
disorder in which Richard returned. All the other stories concerning Mother
Atkins are quite simple and usual.

Hexasticon.*

Of wrathful witches this same pamphlet tells,
How most of all on simple folk they work.
What wonders too they may achieve by spells,
God weed them out in every cell they lurk;
God weeds them out, but Satan still doth hatch
Fresh imps, whereby of all sorts he may catch.

Levit. 20: 6.

If any turn after such as work with spirits, and after soothsayers, to go a-whoring after them, then will I set my face against that person, and will cut him off from among his people.

A most wicked work of a wretched witch, wrought on the person of one Richard Burt.

So long, right gentle and courteous reader, as we live here in this wretched vale of misery, and miserable estate of our probationership, we are all, even the best of us all, to account no better of ourselves than that we live in a perpetual warfare, and most dangerous and deadly combat.

Our enemies that we are to fight against are in number three: the world, the flesh and the Devil; two whereof notwithstanding (such is our blind perseverance) the most part esteem their entire friends, whereas indeed they are the hand-ministers of our Archenemy, all under colourable friendship deceiving their familiars and seeking their death both of body and soul.

Our grand foeman Satan, architect of all mischief, in scripture hath many proper names to explain his malicious nature. Of his cruelty he is called Abaddon, a destroyer, because that not like a common enemy he is contented with the death and downfall of our bodies, but imagineth utter destruction of the soul also, and intolerable torments jointly to them both. Of his craft he is termed a thief, because he inventeth by what means he may slily and unwittingly set upon the godly. Of his malice he is called Diabolus, an accuser, because evermore day and night he is busy, accusing the consciences of the righteous.

He is named a dragon of his policy, because that since the time of Adam, among so many thousands, in so many years, there hath been found none so wise or wary that could withstand his stratagems, but he hath wounded and poisoned them well nigh unto death. He hight* a lion also of his power, because that as the solid body of the lion is powerful, so especially consisteth great strength and power in his tail.

We doubt not but this adversary or Apollyon of ours of himself is mighty, puissant and strong enough against such fainty cowards and wilful flow-backs as we are, yet to make his victory more sure and not to fail of his purpose, he useth also the force of his tail—that is, his enthralled bondslaves whom he hath sealed to execute his will and pleasure upon the harmless, which is performed many times divers and sundry ways. Neither doth he so usually show his policy, puissance* and power by any his officers as he doth by subtle seedmen[1] of false

---

[1] Probably Catholics in this context.

doctrine, and enchanting sorcerers; the one instead of instruments to inveigle the mind and soul, the other to assail the mortal body, and beguile and entrap the senses.

I speak nothing of those pseudo-seedmen, but I purpose, God willing, to treat of damnable witches, of their spite and spells, odious in the sight of God, detested of the good and most hurtful to themselves, manifesting what power and prominence[2] through God's permission the father of sin, Satan, hath over sinful worldlings.

About Shrovetide last, one Richard Burt, servant to a gentleman named Master Edling, dwelling at Woodhall in the parish of Pinner in Middlesex, a mile beyond Harrow-on-the-hill, going to his master's barn standing at the town's end, accompanied with a great mastiff dog, suddenly espied an hare start before him and, thinking to have set his dog at her, missed of his purpose. For the dog not only refused to follow, but instead of following began to faint and run round about his master, and to whine pitifully as who should say that kind of game was not for them. The man taking hearty grace himself, followed so nigh that he saw her take in at one Mother Atkins' house, whom before that time he knew to be a notorious witch; whereupon, blessing himself and mindful of the name of God, he boldly said 'Avaunt, witch.'[3]

This was the first occasion (namely the terming of her a witch) of all poor Richard Burt's future tragedy—but to go forward. It happened the said Richard Burt a month after, meeting her near to his master's barn, and giving her the time of the day, like a perverse woman, like a perilous wasp, like a pestiferous witch, incensed with hate at the sight of him, held down her head, not deigning to speak.

The next day, which was on Wednesday the 8 of March, going again to his master's barn to thresh, and serve certain beasts—because he would not trudge to and fro for letting his work, [he] carried his dinner with him, which was bread, butter, cheese and applepie, and a bottle of the best beer; being come to the barn he laid his provision and settled close to his business, labouring hard till twelve of the clock, at which time hunger assailing and custom prevailing, he went to dinner; wherein he had not long continued, but there was opposite to his view a monstrous black cat among the straw, which began to shake the straw and to make a wad thereof.

[2] Original has 'preminence', which may be 'pre-eminence' or 'prominence'.

[3] Here the suggestion appears to be that Mother Atkins is herself the hare—unusual at this time.

The fellow being aghast start up with his applepie in his hand (for it had been pity a poor hungry thresher should have lost so good a repast) suddenly hearing a voice that commanded him 'Come away!' 'Away,' quoth he, 'whither shall I come?' The spirit answering again said 'Come, and leave thy vittles behind thee and thy knife also.'

Poor Simplicity, keeping his applepie still in his hand, came to the barn door, where suddenly he was hoist up into the air, and carried over many fields, by the way espying his master's plough a-ploughing, but not able to call unto them, although he seemed to have his memory most perfect; thence passing over to Harrow, where on the side of the hill there is a great pond, [he] was drawn through it (and there left his hat, which was a token of that torture) because he could stay in no place but was violently rapt up the hill, and over the tops of the trees at Harrow Church. So far he absolutely remembereth, but being haled further he was taken, as he seemeth, into a place which was all fire, where was heard such lamentable howling and doleful crying as if all the damned fiends of hell had been tortured and tormented in that Limbo.[4]

You hear into how strange and passionate a place this Richard Burt was translated; now it remaineth to show with what symptoms* the place was furnished.

First therefore, he affirmeth, it was exceeding hot, replenished with more than Cimmerian darkness,[5] plentiful in filthy odours and stenches, full of noise and clamours, in so much that he seemed to hear infinite millions of discrepant* noises, but saw nothing save only the fire which caused such an unquenchable drouth in his stomach that, presently minding a penny he had in his purse, [he] looked round about for an alehouse where he might spend it.

Hearing therefore these foresaid voices, and thinking some of them had spake unto him, he answered, saying, 'Here is no work for me to do.' Immediately it was re-answered 'Coast away with him; but with this proviso thou passest, that thou be secret, and say nothing when thou comest home.' But he replied and said 'My master will ask me where I have been.'

With that, he was not suffered to speak any further, but his tongue was doubled in his mouth, his legs burnt, hands and arms scorched, his coat pinched off his back and thrown into the fire, [and he] immediately

[4] Figurative; Limbo is technically the abode of those not saved through no fault of their own, i.e. unbaptised infants. It is a Catholic concept.

[5] In Homer, the land of the Cimmerians was a place of frost and darkness.

soaring over hedges and ditches, soused in mire and dirt, scratched with thorns and briars, so singed and disfigured that it is both lamentable and terrible to behold him.[6]

Being brought again to Pinner, where his master doth dwell, he first repaired to a ditch to drink, and afterwards in this pickle visited one of his acquaintance who sometime served Master Edling also; but whether he sorted* thither for that his friend's house was nighest, or would not go home for shame that he had been absent four whole days together, I cannot show you.

Only this, being Sunday morning his master chanced, as his custom was, to pass by that way to church at the same instant who, not knowing poor Richard Burt his lost sheep, demanded of his quondam* servant if he had gotten him a man. 'A man, sir,' quoth he, 'why, it is your man Richard.' 'My man', quoth the gentleman, 'that cannot be;' and therewithal being half amazed made a pause and earnestly beheld him. At length, willing him in the name of God to tell where he had been, though he could not speak, yet having memory made signs, and evermore pointed toward the house where Mother Atkins did dwell, looking so grisly and fiercely that way that he tore and rent all that came in his hands.

In the meanwhile it was thought requisite that the parson of the town, named Master Smith, and Master Burbridge of Pinner Park, gentleman, should be sent for who, coming to the dumb man and pitying his plight, the parson charitably and like himself laboured about him, wrenched open his teeth, got open his mouth, indented his finger under his tongue, and with much ado got it unfolded. The first words he spake were these: 'Woe worth Mother Atkins, woe worth Mother Atkins, for she hath bewitched me.' Whereupon he would not be quiet, but ever requested that he might speak with her.

Master Burbridge and Master Smith caused her to be sent for who, being present, he never ceased till he had scratched and drawn blood on her, persuading himself that was a remedy sufficient under God that would make him well. Neither was it or is it any capital error, experience testifies; for since that he hath mended reasonably, and now goeth to the church.

Thus have you heard briefly the cares and crosses that poor Richard Burt sustained as they say 'in summo gradu',[7] the eighth, the ninth, tenth and eleventh days of March last past, what time he was absent

---

[6] This gives a suggestion of *report* rather than invention.
[7] 'in summo gradu'—in the highest degree.

from his master the foresaid whole days and used, as ye have heard, after the foresaid manner.

Thus then leave we Richard Burt, but with Mother Atkins we must prosecute a little further. It is credibly reported in Pinner that the said Mother Atkins on a time resorting to the house of Master Burbridge for milk, at what time the maids were busy at the dairy, and not obtaining her desire—immediately upon her departure out of doors, the cream began to swell and rise in the churn, that it burst open the top of the churn and run about the kitchen and forth at the sink-hole; and all their huswifery for that day went to wrack, that all was quite lost and nothing could possibly be well ordered.

O rebels towards God! enemies to mankind! caterpillars of a commonwealth, the fire is too good to consume them! Many and sundry like actions of extreme rage and cruelty are imputed to her, only we will conclude and shut up these clauses with this that followeth.

Not long since, the forenamed witch entering the ground of one Gregory Coulson to crave some relief (for she liveth of alms and good people's charity) she found him busily employed about some country affairs—raddling* his lambs, I think it was; and framing her petition to him, because he did not straight way leave all and accomplish it, she flung forth in a fume. But it was not long after her departure but he had finished his labour also, and letting forth two lambs into a yard, suddenly they began so nimbly to skip to and fro that they never ceased after till they died.

Finis.

V Changing Times: The Tricksters

The Fairy Queen in Hampshire

Almost exactly in 1590, there is a marked change in the prose literature of English witchcraft which may reflect a change in the type of author as much as a change in the temper of the times. Reporters of straight news had already begun to drift to those forms which foreshadow the first real newspapers. (No printing of domestic news was allowed till the abolition of the Star Chamber in 1641, but a weekly account of foreign news appeared as early as 1622, and chronicles, newsletters (see Jonson's play *The Staple of News*) and translations of foreign periodicals like *Mercurius Gallobelgicus* (1594–1635) were plentiful after 1600.)

Witchcraft reporting fell into the hands of amateurs, or professionals writing reports on commission. Ministers justify their beliefs; rich families protect their local reputations by 'authentic versions' of events; doctors defend their professional competency; judges display their own models of procedure. Witchcraft itself begins to disappear behind a haze of social and theological considerations, so that Jacobean records often seem less convincing, more difficult to decipher than the early Elizabethan pamphlets.

Attention shifts from the witch's actions and the witch's trial to concern with the behaviour of those about her; the reader is now expected to feel himself involved with the sufferers. Out of this change in emphasis rose first a scholarly, educational type of literature which purported to tell the reader what he should believe about witches as a Christian, and what he should do about them as a juror.

The most humane and down-to-earth example of this class was printed in 1593 by George Gifford, minister of Maldon in Essex 'in waye of a Dialogue, to make the fitter for the capacity of the simpler sort'.[1] It is full of excellent stories and vivid conversations and, though Gifford believes that white witchcraft is as worthy of death as black, he demands the most stringent legal proofs for conviction of a witch; his main contention is that witches only have power because people fear them and consult them instead of putting their faith in God. Unfortunately this sturdy theology of the possible was already old-fashioned, as we see from the most notable example of the second type of pamphlet—*The most strange and admirable discoverie of the three Witches of Warboys*, also printed in 1593.

This book marks the beginning of the tendentious, deadly serious literature of possession which swamps the market for years to come. Most of the reporting here is by people caught up in the theological controversy over exorcism; most of it is propagandist in intent, and there are complicated cases

[1] George Gifford, *A Dialogue concerning Witches and Witchcraftes* (London, 1593), A3.

of fraud and false confession. Those involved are no longer the poor but, overwhelmingly, the middle classes and the minor nobility; their anxieties are not for brewings and bakings and cattle, but for the safety of their heirs and the preservation of their souls—for family security in this world and the next.

Finally, the neglected element of popular entertainment, of delight in a wonderful story, is represented by cheerful tales of notable swindles and deceptions of people who are too superstitious and so end up as figures of fun. (Onstage, the same withdrawal from the serious element in magic is served by a long line of plays about folk-magicians who are clever enough to do wonders by their art and yet to cheat the Devil in the end.) These are often true incidents, but they are written as stories rather than reportage; instead of information or edification, they provide popular reassurance that witchcraft is mostly a matter of swindling after all. These publications become part of the flood of new or reprinted exposés of cheats and gulls by Harman, Awdeley, Dekker and Greene—the fascinating hackwork of creative writers that might collectively be titled *The Real Dope*.

The perfectly amazing case that follows is confirmed by records[2] and by a separate, earlier account in *Kind-Harts Dreame* (1592?), H-H2. Court cases dealing with people swindled by a promise of introduction to the Fairy Queen exist for 1609/10 and 1612, so we must assume that the predilection for treasure-seeking by magic was as strong as ever, and the tricksters (like some magicians) had simply changed the names of the spirits involved to avoid falling foul of the law. Fairies were still powerful agents of superstition among countryfolk and the simpler townsmen, but they were beneath the dignity of lawyers and judges.

The Brideling, Sadling and Ryding, of a rich Churle in Hampshire, by the subtill practise of one Judeth Philips, a professed cunning woman, or Fortune teller. With a true discourse of her unwomanly using of a Trype wife,[3] a widow, lately dwelling on the back side of S. Nicholas shambles in

---

[2] Historical MSS. Commission. Hatfield House, vol. V (1894), pp. 81–3.

[3] This section of the pamphlet is omitted, as it has little new to say about the 'supernatural swindle'. The tripe-wife was a rich and much-wooed widow whom Judith persuaded into ceremonies supposed to locate hidden treasure in her house; one of these ceremonies included the clipping of pubic hair. Swindled out of money and jewels, she was finally made drunk and married to one of Judith's fortune-hunting accomplices; the whole story emerged when she had Judith arrested for theft, and the ballad-makers turned her and her husband into the laughing-stocks of London.

See *A Quest of Inquirie* . . . (London, 1595) printed by A. B. Grosart in *Elizabethan England in Gentle and Simple Life*, Occasional Issues, Vol. XV (1881). G. B. Harrison discusses the case in *The Library*, Series IV, Vol. II, June 1930, pp. 97–101. C. J. Sisson traced an exactly similar case in 1624 which led to lawsuits over the play of *Keep the Widow Waking*. (*The Library*, Series IV, Vol. 8, 39–57, 233–59.)

Judith Philips, fortune-teller and swindler
The Brideling, Sadling and Ryding, of a rich Churle in Hampshire 1595

London, whom she with her conferates,* likewise cosoned. For which fact, shee was at the Sessions house without New-gate arraigned, where she confessed the same, and had judgement for her offence, to be whipped through the Citie, the 14 of February, 1594 [1594/5] (London, 1595)

. . . This[4] is to let you understand that in the month of January last past, in the famous city of London, one Judith Philips, the wife of John Philips (by occupation a gun-maker, now dwelling in Crown Alley in Bishopsgate Street), was brought before her Majesty's Justices of peace at the Sessions house in Old Bailey and there was indited upon cozenage, where she confessed the truth of all her practices before the honourable Lords of the bench.

But know, gentle reader, before I undertake to explain the truth of all her practices done here in London, I will first in most ample manner set forth to the view of the world a notable villainy committed by this cunning and fine-witted woman in the village of Upsborne[5] in Hampshire, in distance seven miles or thereabouts from Winchester.

This Judith Philips before-times having another husband named Pope (being an honest poor man of a good conversation and well

---

[4] Extract runs from A3 to B.   [5] Perhaps modern Upham or Upper Samborne.

beloved amongst his neighbours, but this his wife not contented with his poor estate of living) upon a certain time took on occasion to go away from him and purposed to seek some other course for maintenance of her living;[6] so travelling along the west parts of England, it was her chance to remain for a certain space in the parish of Upsborne, a town situate and being in Hampshire, and there practised many cozening sleights and devices to deceive the simpler sort of people in the country.

Only she betook herself to the profession of a cunning woman, a fortune-teller, and those which she knew did abound in wealth she daily sought means to bring into a fool's paradise, and by one device or other, cozen them of some store of crowns.

Not far from this town there was dwelling a wealthy churl (whose name I here omit) that was somewhat fanatastical, and given to believe every tale he heard, which churl's wealth whetted so the desire of this woman, that she devised a subtle practice to have a share out of his coffers.

First, to bring her purpose to effect, she enquired secretly of his neighbours of what condition and conversation this miser and his wife were of, and in what state the manner of his living lay; likewise she understood that this churl was in suit of law about a piece of ground with one Sir William Kingsman, a worshipful knight in Hampshire. Which being done, this Judith Philips one evening very late went into the back side of this man's house, where under a hollow holly tree she buried an angel of gold and sixpence in white money, and then returned home to her lodging again for the night.

But the next day after, she walked by the churl's house, and it fortuned that his wife sat at her door to take the fresh air, and so when this cunning-witted woman saw her time, [she] stood still and looked very wishly* upon her; which made the churl's wife to marvel much, that a strange woman whom she never saw before should look upon her so steadfastly, which caused her to demand wherefore she looked so earnestly in her face?

'O mistress', said this Judith Philips, 'you are the fortunates[t] woman I saw this many a day, for in your brows I see good fortune sit. Have you not' said she, 'a hollow holly tree standing near unto your house, with certain weeds growing about the root?' 'We have',

---

[6] According to the Hatfield House papers she had lived for some time with the 'Egyptians' or Gypsies, who were then (as they are now) the object of superstitious awe.

answered the miser's wife, 'and what of that?' 'O mistress', said this woman then, 'if I might speak with your husband, and if he be like you in the face, you will come to be exceeding rich; for under that hollow tree there is great store of treasure hid.' 'Come in' then said she, 'and thou shalt see my husband.'

But when this woman came into the place where her husband was, she likewise looked him strangely in the face, and told him that she knew by certain signs in his forehead that he was in suit of law with some great man of that country, and how he should prevail in his suit. Also she told him, if he would be at some charge, she would bring him to great sums of gold and silver that was hidden about his grounds; to whom the man, being somewhat covetous, said, 'If I might first see something of thy skill, I will be at any charge thou wilt; but first tell me what thou art and from where thou camest.'

'I am' said this Judith, 'an Englishwoman born, but come now from the Pope and know more of his mind than any woman in the world.' To confirm her words for truth, she took her oath upon the Bible how that she came from the Pope—which was true, for her husband's name as then was Pope; which being done, she took him by the hand and led him to the root of the hollow tree, where she caused him to dig till he found some gold (which was the angel) and the sixpence which the night before she closely hid.

This brought the covetous churl into such a conceit that he promised to give her whatsoever she desired, so that her promise might be performed. Then she demanded of him for her pains fourteen pounds, whereat he grumbled to lose so great a gub* at one time, yet at last the hope of the treasure hidden under the tree made him to consent; and so with speed [he] gave this woman fourteen pounds in ready gold and silver. Then said this woman, 'Now must I have the largest chamber in your house behung with the finest linen you can get, so that nothing about your chamber but white linen cloth be seen; then must you set five candlesticks in five several places in your chamber, and under every candlestick you must put an angel of gold'—all which was done as she required. 'And likewise' said she, 'you must also get a saddle and a bridle with two new girths thereunto,' all which the covetous churl performed in hope to attain to great wealth.

Then this Judith caused him and his wife to go into the yard, where she set the saddle on his back, and thereon girteth it fast with two new girths, and also put a bridle upon his head; all which being done, she got upon his back in the saddle, and so rid him three times betwixt the chamber and the holly tree. Then said this cozening quean, 'You must lie three hours one by another grovelling on your bellies under this tree, and stir not, I charge you, until I come back again; for I must go into the chamber to meet the Queen of Fairies and welcome her to that holy and unspotted place.'

So this churl and his wife were left quaking in the cold, casting many a long look for the coming of this woman. But she in the meantime took down all the fine linen cloths from the walls of the chamber and wrapped them up close in a bundle, and all the gold from under the candlesticks and put them into her purse; then putting herself into a fair white smock, somewhat disguised with a thing on her head all white, and a stick in her hand, she appeared unto him and his wife. Using some dalliance, as old wives say spirits with night-spells do, she vanished away, and again entered the chamber where her pack lay ready and so roundly went away, leaving the churl and his wife in their cold lodging.

But when the poor fool saw the time expired and his expected woman did not return, he got him up and cast off his saddle and bridle [and] being half dead with cold, retired into the chamber where he supposed to have found this cunning woman talking with the Queen of Fairies. But when he entered his chamber and saw both his linen and his gold conveyed away, [he] fell into such a perplexity of mind as though he had been distraught of his wits, one while grieving for the loss of his fourteen pounds, another while for the abuse of his good name; likewise for the penance and disgrace she put him and his wife unto, the base and ridiculous manner of his saddling, his cold lodging and weary time spent under the tree to his utter infamy and shame, and lastly, the loss of his pure and fine linen.

But yet he dissembled his grief in such order that his neighbours had no suspicion thereof; so in all haste he took horse and road to Winchester, being in distance seven miles from the town where he dwelt, and there certified a kinsman of his of all the actions before happened. So betwixt this churl and his kinsman they made hue and cry after her, by which this deceitful woman was taken and conveyed to prison, where she remained until the great Assizes came, and for the same was arraigned before the right honourable my Lord Anderson, the Lord Chief Justice of the Common Pleas[7] under her Majesty by his office; before whom she confessed herself guilty of all these aforesaid practices and there received such deserved punishment as the law would permit.

[7] Pleas: original has 'place'.

A Country Gentleman

Henry Chettle tells the above story in *Kind-Harts Dreame*, but has a much wittier punch-line. When Judith was asked in court why she had bridled and saddled her dupe—'Faith', said she, 'only to see how like an ass he looked!' Chettle also recounts a form of swindling used by those who deliberately cultivated a reputation for supernatural skill in their own villages.

. . . Now[1] I will draw to an end, concluding with a master-juggler that he may be well known if he be got into any obscure corner of the country. This shifter forsooth carried no less countenance than a gentleman's ability, with his two men in blue coats that served for shares, not wages. He being properly seated in a shire of this realm, and by the report of his men bruited* for a cunning man, grew into credit by this practice.

His house being in a village through which was no thoroughfare, his men (and sometime his mastership in their company) at midnight would go into their neighbours' several grounds, being far distant from their dwelling houses, and oftentimes drive from thence horses, mares, oxen, kine, calves or sheep, whatever came next to hand, a mile perchance or more out of the place wherein they were left.

Home would they return and leave the cattle straying. In the morning, sometime the milkmaids miss their kine, another day the plough-hinds their oxen, their horses another time, somewhat of some worth once a week lightly. Whither can these poor people go but to the wise man's worship?

Perchance in a morning two or three come to complain and seek remedy who, welcomed by one of his men, are severally demanded of their losses. If one come for sheep, another for other cattle, they are all at first told that his mastership is asleep, and till he himself call, they dare not trouble him. But very kindly he takes them into the hall, and, when his worship stirs, promises them they shall speak with him at liberty.

Now sir, behind a curtain in the hall stands a shelf garnished with

[1] Henry Chettle, *Kind-Harts Dreame* [1592?] G2–G2ᵛ.

books, to which my mate goes under to take one down. And as he takes it down, pulleth certain strings which are fastened to several small bells in his master's chamber, and as the bells strike, he knows what cattle his neighbours come to seek, one bell being for oxen, another for kine, another for swine, etc.

A while after he stamps and makes a noise above, the servingman entreats the suitors to go up, and he, hearing them coming, himself kindly opens them the door, and, ere ever they speak, salutes them protesting for their loss great sorrow, as if he knew their griefs by revelation, comforts them with hope of recovery and such like words.

They cry out, 'Jesu bless your mastership, what a gift have you to tell our minds and never hears us speak!' 'Aye, neighbours', saith he, 'ye may thank God, I trust, I am come among ye to do ye all good.' Then, knowing which way they were driven, he bids them go either eastward or southward, to seek near such an oak or row of elms, or water, or such like mark near the place where the cattle were left; and he assures them that by his skill the thieves had no power to carry them farther than that place.

They run and seek their cattle which, when they find—'Oh, admirable wise man! the price of a cow we will not stick with him for! Happy is the shire where such a one dwells!'

Thus do the poor cozened people proclaim, and so our shifter is sought to far and near.[2]

[2] Reginald Scot's *Discovery of Witchcraft* (Bk. 13, Ch. 30) has a similar story of one Pope, who had an arrangement with Stephen Tailor who 'would hide away his neighbours' horses, etc. and send them [the neighbours] to Pope, (whom he before had told where they [the cattle] were) promising to send the parties unto him whom he described and made known by divers signs, so as this Pope would tell them at their first entrance unto the door. . . . This Pope is said of some to be a witch, of others he is accompted a conjuror, but commonly called a wise man, which is all one with a soothsayer or witch.'

Success Story

There are several literary references to a 'wise woman' who lived at Hoxton (Hogsdon) in London, and Thomas Heywood wrote a play, *The Wise Woman of Hogsdon*[1] which shows how such a person gained her reputation for skill.

Act the Second.

Scene I.   Before the Wise-Woman's House.

Enter the Wise-Woman, a Countryman with a urinal, two Citizens' Wives, Taber, and a Kitchen-maid.

Wise-wo.   Fie, fie! what a toil and a moil it is
For a woman to be wiser than all her neighbours!
I pray, good people, press not too fast upon me;
Though I have two ears, I can hear but one at once.
You with the urine.

Enter 2nd Luce in Boy's clothes; she stands aside.

Coun.   Here, forsooth, mistress.
Wise-wo.   And who distilled this water?
Coun.   My wife's limbeck,* if it please you.
Wise-wo.   And where doth the pain hold her most?
Coun.   Marry, at her heart, forsooth.
Wise-wo.   Ay, at her heart, she hath a griping at her heart?
Coun.   You have hit it right.
Wise-wo.   Nay, I can see so much in the urine.
2nd Luce.   Just so much as is told her.   (*Aside.*
Wise-wo.   She hath no pain in her head, hath she?
Coun.   No, indeed, I never heard her complain of her head.
Wise-wo.   I told you so, her pain lies all at her heart;
Alas, good heart! but how feels she her stomach?
Coun.   Oh, queasy and sick at stomach.

---

[1] *Thomas Heywood*, Mermaid series (London, n.d.). The play is conjecturally dated 1604, though first printed in 1638.

Wise-wo.   Ay, I warrant you, I think I can see as far into a millstone as another. . . . Hark you, my friend, you shall take—

(*She whispers.*

2nd Luce.   'Tis strange the ignorant should be thus fooled!
What can this witch, this wizard, or old trot,
Do by enchantment, or by magic spell?
Such as profess that art should be deep scholars.
What reading can this simple woman have?
'Tis palpable gross foolery. . . .

Wise-wo.   You are welcome, gentlewoman.

1st Cit. Wife.   I would not have it known to my neighbours that I come to a wise-woman for any thing, by my truly.

Wise-wo.   For should your husband come and find you here—

1st Cit. Wife.   My husband, woman! I am a widow.

Wise-wo.   Where are my brains? 'Tis true, you are a widow; and you dwell—let me see, I can never remember that place.

1st Cit. Wife.   In Kent-street.

Wise-wo.   Kent-street, Kent-street! and I can tell you wherefore you come.

1st Cit. Wife.   Why, and say true?

Wise-wo.   You are a wag, you are a wag: why, what do you think now I would say?

1st Cit. Wife.   Perhaps to know how many husbands I should have.

Wise-wo.   And if I should say so, should I say amiss?

1st Cit. Wife.   I think you are a witch.

Wise-wo.   In, in: I'll but read a little of Ptolemy and Erra Pater;[2] and when I have cast a figure,[3] I'll come to you presently. . . .

(*Act the Third, Scene Two.*)

2nd Luce.   . . . But, mistress, what mean all these women's pictures, hanged here in your withdrawing room?

Wise-wo.   I'll tell thee, boy—marry, thou must be secret. When any citizens or young gentlemen come hither, under a colour to know their fortunes, they look upon these pictures, and which of them they

---

[2] Ptolemy: Claudius Ptolemaus, astronomer, geographer and mathematician in the 2nd century A.D. Probably put into her head by the full title of Erra Pater, which is: *The pronostycacion for ever of Erra Pater, a Jewe borne in Jewery, a doctour in Astronomye and physicke. Profytable to kepe the bodye in helth. And also Ptholomeus sayth the same.* [London, 1535? and often reprinted till 1700.]

[3] cast a figure, i.e. drawn a horoscope.

best like, she is ready with a wet finger.[4] Here they have all the furniture belonging to a private-chamber—bed, bed-fellow and all. But mum! thou knowest my meaning, Jack.

2nd Luce.　　But I see coming and going, maids, or such as go for maids, some of them as if they were ready to lie down, sometimes two or three delivered in one night; then suddenly leave their brats behind them, and convey themselves into the city again:—what becomes of their children ?

Wise-wo.　　Those be kitchen-maids, and chamber-maids, and some-times good men's daughters, who, having catched a clap,[5] and growing near their time, get leave to see their friends in the country, for a week or so: then hither they come, and for a matter of money here they are delivered. I have a midwife or two belonging to the house, and one Sir Boniface, a deacon, that makes a shift to christen the infants; we have poor, honest, and secret neighbours, that stand for common gossips.* But dost not thou know this ?

2nd Luce.　　Yes, now I do; but what after becomes of the poor infants ?

Wise-wo.　　Why, in the night we send them abroad, and lay one at this man's door, and another at that, such as are able to keep them; and what after becomes of them, we inquire not. And this is another string to my bow. . . .

2nd Luce.　　. . . But, mistress, are you so cunning as you make yourself ? you can neither write nor read: what do you with those books you so often turn over?

Wise-wo.　　Why, tell* the leaves; for to be ignorant, and seem ignorant, what greater folly!

2nd Luce. (*Aside*)　　Believe me, this is a cunning woman; neither hath she her name for nothing, who out of her ignorance can fool so many that think themselves wise.—But wherefore have you built this little closet[6] close to the door, where sitting, you may hear every word spoken by all such as ask for you?

---

⁴ with a wet finger, i.e. instantly, without trouble.

⁵ catched a clap, i.e. become pregnant outside marriage.

⁶ *The severall Notorious and lewd Cousnages of John West and Alice West, falsely called the King and Queene of Fayries.* . . . (London, 1613/14) adds to the account of the Wests' cozening of Thomas Moore a whole grab-bag of stories about Alice as a wise-woman. (One story is identical with that of Judith Philips' swindling of the tripe-wife, and mentions the fact, which seems a little suspicious.) Alice 'had by the porch and door to her house a little closet where she might hear every word spoken at her door'. When there were visitors 'she

Wise-wo.   True, and therefore I built it. If any knock, you must to the door and question them, to find what they come about,—if to this purpose, or to that. Now, they ignorantly telling thee their errand, which I, sitting in my closet, overhear, presently come forth, and tell them the cause of their coming, with every word that hath passed betwixt you in private; which they admiring, and thinking it to be miraculous, by their report I become thus famous. . . .

Wise-wo.   . . . Let me see how many trades have I to live by; first, I am a wise-woman, and a fortune-teller, and under that I deal in physic and fore-speaking,[7] in palmistry, and recovering of things lost; next, I undertake to cure mad folks; then I keep gentlewomen lodgers, to furnish such chambers as I let out by the night; then I am provided for bringing young wenches to bed;[8] and, for a need, you see I can play the match-maker.

She that is but one, and professeth so many,
May well be termed a wise-woman, if there be any.

(*Exit.*

---

would send one to the door by sundry interrogatories to understand their business; as whether they had lost a spoon, or come to use her advice in physic, or if a maid came to know who should be her husband, or a bachelor whether he should have such a maid, or such a widow. Which no sooner in her closet she heard, but she would straight come to the door, give them entertainment, bid them welcome, and tell them that the Queen of Fairies had told her their business . . .' (C).

    [7] fore-speaking, i.e. bewitching (probably here means 'unwitching').

    [8] Robert Greene tells of an 'old Witch' of Hogsdon who prostituted her beautiful daughter to a succession of gallants, turning each one away when his money was gone. When the girl became pregnant, her mother saved her reputation by pretending to give birth herself. (*A Disputation betweene a Hee Conny-catcher, and a Shee Conny-catcher* (London, 1592); reprinted in Bodley Head Quartos (London, 1923) ref. pp. 28–9).

VI Possession

The Devil in the Nursery

The question of possession by evil spirits is a very vexed one, yet it is crucial to the history of witchcraft in England. The term 'possession' covers a group of symptoms which can be considered theologically, medically or psycho-analytically, and attached to different theories and explanations in each case. For the present we shall use the term to cover the symptoms rather than any one interpretation of them.

Signs of possession are of several kinds; physical convulsions like those of epilepsy and the exercise of unusual strength, alternating with apparent paralysis and collapse: mental disturbances, including hallucinations and variations in personality, sometimes accompanied by poltergeist activity or apparent extra-sensory perceptions: violent reactions against the patient's usual religious beliefs, and equally violent repentance.

The patient may feel himself tormented by evil beings outside his body but in control of it: he may be *obsessed*, a state in which the original person-ality seems to co-exist with another being which compels him to thoughts, ideas and actions repugnant to him: or he may be truly *possessed*, a state in which the intrusive personality completely displaces the original for long periods, so that the sufferer seems to have no knowledge or recollection of what happened during these episodes. Most English cases are of the first two kinds, but all are loosely referred to as 'possession'.

Possession by the God one serves, which produces many of the same symptoms in an approved setting, has usually been regarded as a desired goal; hundreds of nominally Christian sects in Africa (and in remote parts of America) still regard trance, reached through convulsions, as 'the descent of the Holy Spirit'[1] and structure their worship towards the attainment of this state. At the same time, those mental illnesses which cause uncontrolled outbreaks of similar behaviour outside this approved setting, or involve

[1] On 6 April 1967 (Channel 1, 9.40 p.m.) British television carried a pro-gramme on *The Witch-doctor*, by Dr. Stephen Black, in which he showed trance taking place in pagan and Christian services in Africa; this trance was specifically ascribed by one girl to possession by the Holy Ghost. The convulsive cries of those in this state could not be better described than by the phrase in John Darrell's *A True Narration of the strange and grevous Vexation by the Devil, of 7. persons in Lancashire, and William Somers of Nottingham* (1600), B1: 'a strang and supernatural loud whupping'.

Dr. Black stated that there was two or three times as much psychosomatic illness in Africa as in Britain because Africa is in a transitional phase of society, which renders people more susceptible to the physical ills and hardships of their surroundings. This would certainly apply to Elizabethan England.

expressions of unorthodoxy, are ascribed to spontaneous possession by evil spirits, as they have been since the beginning of history.

Secular medicine has always attempted to expel the demon by a variety of devices aimed at making the patient's body uncomfortable and so un-inhabitable (unfortunately these sometimes killed the patient); religious treatment prescribed the spiritual violence of prayer and exorcism. This tradition descended into Christian civilisation and was perpetuated by dogmas which in effect proclaimed that a child was born subject to the power of the Evil One and could only be delivered by a form of exorcism and baptism into the true faith. The rites of exorcism, and baptismal exorcism are still printed in many Catholic manuals.[2]

During the reign of Elizabeth, one of the deepest sources of controversy between Protestants, Catholics and Anglicans focused on the Church's power of exorcism. As part of the opposition to relics and saint-worship Protestants and Anglicans insisted that physical miracles involving the direct partici-pation of supernatural beings, however necessary to the establishment of the faith in the days of Christ, were now ceased. Furthermore, 'extra' rituals depending on the specialty of the priestly role as an intermediary between man and spirit were no longer valid; the power of priest or minister resided in his faith and dedication and was in effect little greater than that of a godly layman. Baptismal exorcism was dropped in 1552, and exorcism itself, dis-couraged in the Anglican church throughout the reign of Elizabeth, was finally forbidden in 1603, unless special permission had been obtained from the bishop. Such permission was given very rarely indeed.

Shrewdly, the Catholic missionary priests in England stressed their ability to exorcise by the special Catholic rite, though they suggested that possession occurred as a consequence of incorrect faith, and kept clear of public accusations of witchcraft. This tactic was sufficiently effective in winning converts for Bishop Bancroft to hold a full-scale investigation and publish the results in a coarse, unfair but zestful discrediting of the priests' good faith—Samuel Harsnett's *Declaration of Egregious Popish Impostures* (London, 1603).

On the other hand, the Puritanically-inclined Protestants (Lutheran rather than Calvinist) attempted to prove the efficacy of Puritan faith and prayer by their own non-ritual exorcisms. They began harmlessly, with gatherings of neighbours and friends to pray for the afflicted;[3] if 'the spirit' could not bear holy words, they were repeated continually until 'he' was driven into a rage and finally expelled, and the patient returned to his natural virtue.[4]

[2] *Rituale Romanum*, New York, 1947.

[3] An interesting early example of spontaneous possession without accusations of witchcraft occurs in *A Booke Declaringe the Fearfull Vexasion, of one Alexander Nyndge . . .* (London, [1573/4]).

[4] Pierre Janet was able to cure a 'possessed' patient by addressing himself to the devil rather than the patient and tricking 'him' into hypnotising the patient so that the source of his trouble could be discovered! *Un Cas de possession et d'exorcisme moderne*, from *Névroses et idées fixes*, Paris, 1898, Vol. i, pp. 375–

There is the zest of a game about the early contests with the Devil, a kind of re-enactment of the riddling ballads in which the Devil is outwitted by a quick-thinking girl or little boy; this comes across clearly in the first of the following pamphlets *The disclosing of a late counterfeyted possession . . .* (London, [1574]). But there is always a leader in such a group, and this man soon begins to think of himself as a professional, a man with a gift. The man becomes an exorcist, acquiring a public following; the exorcist, extending his skills, forcing the unwilling spirit to disclosures of hidden matters, becomes a witch-finder like John Darrell (see pp. 298–302).

At this point the Church of England always stepped in, as it did against the Catholics, and attempted to discredit the 'miracles' of the Puritans by ascribing all so-called possessions to fraud or to natural disease. (This did not help witches much, as they were still supposed to be capable of inflicting physical disease by means of their familiars.) Thus much of the pamphlet literature which deals with cases of possession and exorcism is vitiated by the desperate need to prove a case for or against the genuineness of the phenomena in question, and by theological positions which warped observation and records. (See selections from Harsnett in following pages.) The witch and her trial recede into the background and become of much less importance than the fate of the exorcist and the spiritual state of the possessed.

For these reasons, the Warboys case has been selected for re-printing (almost complete) in preference to accounts of William Somers,[5] Thomas Darling,[6] or the Starkey children.[7] Most of the Warboys records were made by parents or relatives who had great curiosity but no preconceptions as to the course of the disease or its final outcome. Ministers of religion played throughout a minor role, and were at first most hesitant to intervene; exorcism was not attempted (even sustained prayer was mostly abandoned when it caused violent fits) and the children were finally freed only by the deaths of the witches. Despite occasional fears by one of the children, the children were not considered to be occupied by the spirits (as were other demoniacs) but spoke to spirits beside them, listened, and repeated the answer they had 'heard' in a normal voice. It was the witch who felt the spirits within her belly.

Thus, in this case the fate of the witch was considered to be more important than techniques for expelling the spirits; since the spirits acted from the outside and under the particular instruction of the witch, her execution left them powerless and without access to the children.

---

406. For partial translation, see T. K. Oesterreich, *Possession, Demoniacal and Other*; trans. by D. Ibberson (University Books, Inc., New York, 1966) from Tubingen edition of 1921.

[5] See note 1. Notestein lists several contemporary accounts in *History of Witchcraft in England, 1558–1718*, ed. cit., pp. 352–56. See also below, *The Devil at Large*, for summaries.

[6] *The most wonderfull and true storie, of a certaine Witch named Alse Gooderige. . . . As also a true Report of the strange Torments of Thomas Darling . . .* (London, 1597).

[7] See note 1, and note 5.

However, the symptoms displayed by the children were highly influential in determining the manifestations of illness in later hysterics who were considered to be occupied by spirits, for the case was widely known and considered to be unshakably authentic. (Darrell jeered at Harsnett for refusing to attack the credibility of the account because 'it was so generally receaved for truth' and also 'they were the children of an Esquier'.)[8] In mental illness as in sheer fraud, the expectations of others often determine the precise form taken by manifestations of illness. For instance, the useful trick of being deaf to all except one's playmate occurs in Darrell's cases, but I have not found it before the Warboys book was written.

It is hard to decide on the 'reality' of the children's afflictions, since all theories have drawbacks. Some of the symptoms such as skin eruptions, muscular pain and weakness, suggest a physical disorder, perhaps connected with faulty diet. (Severe vitamin deficiency, lack of calcium or ergotism could all produce at least some of the reported ailments. Warboys was on the edge of the wettest fenland, then undrained and ague-ridden.) But Lady Cromwell and the children continued to suffer during quite long absences from the house, though the servants were cured as soon as they left; and the children were cured suddenly and completely in their own home when the witches were executed. Both parents and a small son were apparently unaffected throughout.

It is hard to suggest that all the adults affected were shamming, since one of them died; if the affliction spread so easily among adults (seven at least suffered severely), it would be arbitrary to say that adults were really ill but the children were only pretending. We must, I think, postulate a situation like that of the Blackburn school,[9] in which elements of pretence could bring about and co-exist with a kind of collective hysteria, about which there was no pretence at all.

Between the original haphazard accusation of witchcraft and the illness of two other sisters a month elapsed—a month filled with messages to eminent doctors, two verdicts of bewitchment, and the giving up of physic as useless; these events and family discussion of them must have sustained and developed the idea in the minds of the children. Within a few weeks, the illness of the other sisters caused the parents to suspect witchcraft very seriously, and to begin that series of 'experiments' and 'tests of the spirit' which were enough in themselves to render retreat from pretence impossible, and to deepen any half-belief into terror and conviction.

The continuous crowding of the house with visiting relatives and their concentration on the children's illness made the house a perfect centre for confirming and spreading the hysterical affliction. After all, the fits went on for three and a half years, which seems incredible unless we see them as an emotional illness tied to surroundings and environment which reinforced the hysteria.

This kind of seizure, born of parental repression, religious guilt and super-

---

[8] *A Detection of that sinnful, shamful, lying, and ridiculous discours of Samuel Harshnet* (1600), pp. 39, 21.

[9] See Introduction, pp. 45–6.

stition, is not fashionable in middle-class society today, except in schools; our different pressures explode outwardly in violence, or inwardly to aliena-tion and true madness. Yet, apart from the behaviour seen in asylums, if we consider the trances and manifestations of a spiritualist seance, the uncontrollable antics of a teenage crowd listening to pop singers, the mental convulsions of a Southern revivalist meeting, the contagious communal obsessions and rituals of the McCarthy era or the Hitler era, the actions of the Throckmorton children begin to seem less bizarre and unfamiliar.

We rather feebly accept the modern manifestations as natural to our picture of man, without much consideration of what this means; to the Throckmortons, with a strict and limited sense of what man was and could do, the theory of witchcraft seemed the only alternative to an unthinkable breakdown of the natural order of the universe. Nothing is more human than the dogged refusal to accept an unlabelled mystery; yet nothing is more limiting to later sympathy or understanding than an outmoded explanation with a price-tag written in blood.

a) *The disclosing of a late counterfeyted possession by the devyl in two maydens within the Citie of London.* [1574]

The Preface.

To declare or discourse the late dissimulation of certain maidens which were possessed with the Devil (as was commonly reported) may be thought of some men mere vanity, and too superfluous, for that the handling of that matter may sufficiently disclose to wise men what was done and meant thereby; and yet to detect the wilful and indurate* ignorance of such as had the matter in handling, being (as they pro-fessed themselves) godly men, plentifully adorned with faith, and sent of God to disturb the devil of possession—as they were very exorcists by office, to adjure the devil—may be thought not vain but necessary, for the instruction of the people hereafter in like cases.

And although this realm is known by common experience, and of late, to be troubled with witches, sorcerers, and other such 'wise men and women' as they call them, yet that the Devil should so possess actually men and women in such manner as was avouched and, to make thereof a plain matter, so constantly reported and spread by their printed books (not publicly licensed) is mere vanity and falsehood; as the parties, throughly examined and favourably used, have confessed the same as hereafter shall ensue. . . . And for that such pamphlets of Rachel Pinder be already spread abroad, not able to be called in again, this is therefore published to countervail the same in the hearts of God's people; wherein shall be truly set out some part of the speeches of this maid Rachel Pinder, and also her confession of that hypocrisy whereof she seemeth to be very sorry and repentant. With confession also of Agnes Briggs; which both of them on Sunday the 15 day of August 1574 did acknowledge their counterfeitings at Paul's Cross, with repentant behaviour, and their examinations and confessions openly there read by the preacher.

And although the vanity of this matter might seem sufficient to instruct men from the like hereafter, yet there is added a part of an Homily, written by that learned man John Chrysostom,[1] sometime Archbishop of Constantinople, which may sufficiently instruct us all to beware, not only of witchcrafts, but also inveigheth specially against Jews and witches which seem to do good, and to heal such as be hurt by others. Farewell.

The very copie in wordes and orthographie, subscribed by their handes the 16 of July 1574.[2]

William Long spake thes woordes folowying. 'I command the Sathane in the blode of Jhesus Christe, speake and tell me wherfor camest thou heayther?' And sathane spake, but we cowlld not understand what he sayde, but he mad a mowmlyng. But after he sayde, 'O Jone, Jone, leatt Jone alone.'

Then William Turner spake, and sayde, 'I command the sathane in the blowd of Jesus Christ, speake out, that al this peopell may heare the.' Then he sayd he colld not speake.

Then William Turner, and William long, sayd he leayd, and commandid him in the blowd of Jhesus Christ, and by his meyghtey powre for to specke lowd-/dowre. Then we al upon owr knees lyfted up our hartes unto almighteye God, and mad our prayers altogether, as our saviour Jhesus Christe haithe taught us in the sixt of Mathewes Gospel.

Then we commandid him in the blowde of Jesus Christ, to tel us whom seant hym heyther. He sayd, 'olld Jone.' 'Wherfore did she send the heayther?' 'For her [Rachel's] body and soulle.' We sayde, 'thow shalt not have it, Jhesus Christe hath bought it with his preasseyos blowd.' Then he sayd, 'thow leayest,' dyvers tymes.

[1] St. John Chrysostom *c.* 345–407. This is omitted.
[2] This original is a unique example of near-illiterate Elizabethan prose which was printed as written, for the sake of authenticity. The absolutely phonetic spelling, read aloud, preserves the sound of four-hundred-year-old Cockney.

Devil appearing as a headless bear
A Miracle of Miracles . . . 1614

Then William Turner said, 'Jesus Christ saythe in his holy gospel, that saythan was a leayer from the beginning, & therfor I beleave Jesus Christ, I wyll not beleave the, thow art a leayer.' Then Saythan sayd, 'she haithe sinned against the holy gost,' and hur sinnes weare before hur fayse, and he wollde have hur.

Then we said he showlld not have hur, 'Jesus Christe haithe bowght hur with his preasseyows blowd, & through faythe in the same, hath forgeyven hur hur sinnes, and thow shalt not have hur.' Then saythane sayd he wolld have us all.

Then we sayd, 'thou shalt have none of us.' Then Saythan sayde, 'Al the worlde is myne. Heare me, heare me: Dyd not I take Christe from the crosse?' Then we said, 'thow art a leayer from the begynnyng, howe darest thow be so bowllde to leaye in the presence of the Lord Jesus?'

Then we commandid him in the blowd of Jhesus Christ, and in the meyghtey power of his kyngdome, to tel us 'What is they name.'

Saythan sayde, 'I cowlde not tell.' We Sayd, 'thou leayest, thou shalt tell us,' and he sayde unto us divers times, 'thou leayest.'

Then we commandid hym 'In the blowd of Jhesus Christ, and by his meyghtey powre, tell us what they name is, and defrawd the teyme no longer.' Then he said 'lelygion, lelygion'[3] divers tymes. Then we asked hym how maney ther was in numbar. Saythan sayd. '5000 lelygons'.

Then we commanded hym 'In the blowd of Jhesus Christ, and by his meyghtey powre, come out of the Sarvant of Jhesus Christ, and bey and bye with owt hurtyng of aneything.' Then saythan sayde he wold tare us all in pesses. Then we defeyed hym, and sayd, 'the lord god shal defend us.' Then saythan said, 'how can you cast out. 5. thowsand legyons of deallves.'

Then we commandid sathane In the blowd of christ, and by his meyghtey powre to come out, and do no hurt. Then he sayd, 'geve me somewhat'. Then we sayd, 'thou shalt have nothing Sathan.' Then saythan sayd, 'I wyll not go.'

Then we sayd, 'thou shalt goo to the etternall pytt of heall, which is prepared for the before the creaseyone of the world.' Then sathan sayd he wold tare hur in pesses, and dyd torment hur presently. And Sathan sayd he wolld bryng 3. deathes, one for hur, and one for Uemphre whom Foxe[4] had beged att gods hand, and one for the mayde In lothberre, 'and I will tare Fox In peasses.' Then sathen creyed, 'O deathe, deathe' verre terrabelleye.

Then we all to geather mayed owr prayers for hur and theam, that the Lorde God wolld release hur. And when we had endid our praiers to God for hur, we commandid Sathan by the meyghtey powre and

[3] An ignorant or stammering attempt at the name 'Legion', often considered to be a name of the Devil because of *Mark* 5: 9; 'My name is Legion: for we are many.'

[4] Almost certainly John Foxe (1516–87) author of the *Acts and Monuments*, better known as *Foxe's Book of Martyrs*. At this time he was settled in London, in the parish of St. Giles in Cripplegate, and preached frequently at St. Paul's; in 1572 he had edited *Reformatio Legum Ecclesiasticarum* for Archbishop Parker, who examined Rachel Pinder two years later. A gentle, learned and honest man, he was much in demand as a spiritual counsellor, and his unsuspicious nature apparently accepted the girls' trickery at face value. John Darrell, the singularly unlovable Puritan exorcist, complained of the harsh treatment accorded to him when he was accused of encouraging frauds in the '90s. 'Was that good man of reverend memory (M. Fox), deceived by Anne Briggs and Rachel Pinder, called into question for the same? He was not.' (Trial of Olive Barthram, appended to *The Triall of Master Dorrell* (London, 1599), F2.)

blowd of Jesus, to departe out of hur bey & bye with out aney more wordes. Then saythan sayd, 'you have not written ytt.'[5] Then John Boush sayd, sarvant unto William Long, 'if we have not writtine ytt, the Lord God hath writtine ytt in our hartes.' Then we commandid sathan with al owr myght and poore, that God had gyven us, that 'thow shalte depart out of the sarvaunt of Jhesus Christ.'

Then Sathan sayd, 'gyve me a cherre and I will go.' And we sayd, 'thou shalt have nothinge'. Then we commandid sathan In the name of Jhesus Christe to depart without hurtinge of aney thynge, and sathan sayde, 'gyve me anappell'. We sayd, 'thou shallt have no-thinge.' Then we commandid sathane for to depart.

Then sathan sayd, 'gyve me a thred band.'* We sayd, 'thow shalt have nothinge'. Then we commandid sathane to depart. He said, 'gyve me a lyttle hare.' We sayd, 'thow shallt have nothing.'

Then sathan sayd, 'shall I have nothing? I had of olld Jone a drop of blowd to com heayther, & shall I depart awaye with nothinge?' Then we sayd to sathane, 'depart, thow shallt have nothinge.'

Then sathane sayd, 'wage your fynger, and I will depart.' Then we sayd to sathan, 'we wil not, thow shalt not have so muche.' Then sathan sayd, 'gyve me the paring of your nalle.' Then we sayd, 'thou shallt not have so much to laye to owr charge att the day of judgment.'[6]

Then sathan Sayd, 'say but "I praye yowe," and I will go.' Then we sayd, 'we will not pray the, but will commande the blowd of Jhesus Christ, and by his meyghtey pore to depart bey and beye with owt hurtinge of aney thinge.'[7] Then Sayd sathan, I will tarre fore skore yeare and teane, if you will gyve me nothinge.'

Then we mad a prayer to the almeightey god with earnest hartes, cravinge ayd and comfort att his almeightey handes for hur comfort

---

[5] To write it would be to present the 'Devil' with a sample of one's writing, and so to give him power over the writer.

[6] Compare Shakespeare:

> Some devils ask but the parings of one's nail,
> A rush, a hair, a drop of blood, a pin,
> A nut, a cherry-stone;
> But she, more covetous, would have a chain.

(*Works of Shakespeare, ed. cit. The Comedy of Errors*, IV. iii. 72–5.)

[7] The distinction between *praying* and *commanding* the spirit was crucial. The first attributed to him independent sovereignty; the second recognised that he had power only in human weakness and 'the permission of God', and made no concessions to him.

and deliverie. Then we commandid sathane in the blowd of Jesus to depart. Then sathan creyd with a lowd voyse, & perfet speach that al meight heare, 'Heare me, heare me,' diverse tymes, afore we wolld gyve eare to him.

Then saythan said to us in al owr hearring, 'leat me tarre tyll to morrow that my ladey comes, & I wil tel you more of my mynd.' Then we sayd unto hym, 'thou shallt not tarre for nothinge,' and so commandid sathane steyll by the meytey pore and kyngdome of Jhesus Christe, to depart out of hur, and so he departed.

[Here there is a list of 16 witnesses]

William Long asked Satan, 'Who commanded thee hither? In the name of Jesus Christ I command thee tell us'. Satan answered, 'Old Joan, old Joan'. 'Which Joan?' said Master Debbett. He answered, 'Joan Thornton, dwelling upon the quay'.

'After what sort did she command it to go?' Satan answered, 'She said the Pater noster 3 times, and then I did come'. Then said William Edwards, 'Thou liest'. Satan answered 'Na'.

Master Long said then, '4 times', and Satan said, '5 times'; William Long said, '6 times', and Satan said, '7 times', and Master Long said, '8 times'; Satan said, '9 times', and Master Long said, '10 times'; Satan said, '11 times', and then Master Long said, 'Then, Satan, thou liest'.

And Satan being asked what was his name, he answered, 'Ark, Ark'. And being asked of whom she learned it [witchcraft] 'Of Denholm'. 'And where did Denholm learn* it thee?' 'In the uppermost room of Thornton's house'. 'How long ago?' 'Three years'. 'What did she give thee, Satan?' 'One drop of her blood'. 'Where haddest thou it, Satan?' 'On the fore-finger on the inside of her left hand'. 'Where did she keep that, that she works by?' 'In her bosom next to her skin'. 'What is it, Satan?' 'Sometimes like a dog, and sometime like a toad'.

And then William Long charged him in the blood of Jesus Christ to depart into the bottomless pit of hell. Satan answered, 'What wilt thou give me?' He said, 'Nothing; and I charge thee depart and never enter any more'. And Satan answered, he would. Then said the said Long, 'In token thou wilt come no more here, blow out the candle'; but he blew not out the candle,[8] but said, 'Give me a thread'. And

---

[8] Once confronted with an impossible request, the child brings her performance to a conclusion.

immediately the child rose up, and held up her hands, and said, 'He is gone, he will come no more'.

The manner of the voice out of the child: the lips moved with none such moving as could pronounce the words uttered, the eyelids moved, but not open; she had great swelling in her throat and about the jaws,[9] and the voice was somewhat bigger than the child's voice. And speaking with a loud voice, being commanded in the name of Jesus Christ to speak louder, the voice then spake louder, that all might hear.

[Here is a list of 7 witnesses]

The examination and confession of, etc.

Agnes Briggs, daughter to William Briggs of London, clothworker, examined, saith that she hath been afflicted ever since Lent last past. And the first time that she fell into any trance was about midsummer last. And she saith that upon Monday next shall be six weeks, she was at Master Foxe his house (the preacher), where at that time came in one Mistress Pinder, dwelling at Galley Quay, and a maid child of her own with her, about 11 year old.

And there the said Mistress Pinder demanded of this examinant how she was troubled. And she answered that she was much troubled in mind. And she this examinant saith that the said Pinder's wife then declared unto the said Master Foxe and others there present, that her daughter had been possessed of a devil, and said that when she had any trance, she would swell and heave with her body marvellously, and that she did avoid* at her mouth in her trances hair, a black silk thread, and a feather; which this examinant hearing, determined to practise the like.

And the same night after, the said Agnes came home, and of purpose she fell into a trance. And afore that time she had pulled some of her hair from her head, which she had put in her mouth; and in her trance she cast the same out of her mouth. And the next time that she feigned her sickness, she voided out of her mouth a little piece of lace, which she had pulled off her sleeve, and a crooked pin which afore that she had put in her mouth.

And the next fit after that, she cast out at her mouth one crooked pin, which afore she herself had bowed and put in her mouth. And the next fit after that, she voided out of her mouth one tenterhook,* which she saith she took out of a corner of a window in the chamber where she lay, and afore had put the same in her mouth. And the next

[9] Presumably from the effort of speaking without use of the normal muscles.

fit, she cast out at her mouth two nails, which afore she had pulled from the valance of her bed, and had put the same in her mouth.

And she saith that many and sundry times she did cast out at her mouth crooked pins, which afore she had bowed and put in her mouth, but to what number she doth not remember. And in this time, in those fits, she divers times of purpose disfigured herself with divers strange countenances, feigning divers strange voices and noises, by her counterfeit in monstrous manner, to the great displeasure of Almighty God, a slander to His word, a very evil example, and a great deceit of the Queen's Majesty's people; for the which she is heartily sorry and repentant, desiring God to forgive her, with intent never to do so again.

And she saith that all that she did was feigned and counterfeit, and no truth therein; and she saith that nobody was privy to her doings but herself.

Examined by me Robert Hodgson, by the commandment of Sir John Rivers, knight, Lord Mayor of London, in the presence of me James Style, minister and parson of St. Margaret's-in-Lothbury, of John Taylor, and John Kent, mercer.

The examination and confession of, etc.

Rachel Pinder, examined, saith she had divers times trances, and in one trance or fit, she voided out at her mouth certain hair which she had pulled off from the coverlet that lay upon her, and had put the same into her mouth, which she did divers times; and sometime she filled her mouth so full that it would stop in her throat, so as she was fain to drink after the same, and this hair did her mother keep together.

At another time in a fit she voided a feather which she had taken upon the bed; and in another fit she voided at her mouth a little short end of silk, which she pulled off the bed covering and put it in her mouth. Another time, she took a woollen thread which she pulled from the side of the covering, and voided it at her mouth. And furthermore, in her trance she feigned divers strange and hollow speeches within her throat; and she saith that all she did and said in her trances were counterfeited, feigned, false, and untrue.

And when they commanded the devil to speak, and asked what was his name, she answered, 'Lilegion'. And they asked who sent him thither; then the said Rachel answered 'Old Joan'. 'Which Joan?' said they. 'Joan of London', said she. 'Where dwelleth she?' said they. And she answered that she dwelled upon the quay. And where there was one that spake to her in Latin, she answered that she would speak no Latin. And one there was that spake Dutch to her;[10] and she answered, 'I will spreaken no Dutch.'

Item, in a trance which she had betwixt Easter and Whit Sunday, she said that Old Joan had bewitched her, which she saith was also but feigned. And further, where she said that Denholm had taught the said Joan, she saith the same is untrue, and was as the other, feigned; for which she is now very sorry, and desirous to ask the said Joan Thornton forgiveness, the which she hath done.

Also she saith that her mother only willed her before the fit came what she should like the devil to, as sometimes to a man with a gray beard, sometimes like five cats, sometimes to ravens and crows, etc. And she saith she is heartily sorry for her said offences, praying God and the world to forgive her, whom she hath mocked and deluded by her subtle and foolish practices, never intending to do so again.

All this she confessed and avouched before the most Reverend Father Matthew, L. Archbishop of Canterbury; Sir Roland Hayward, knight, alderman of the City of London; and William Fleetwood, esquire, Recorder of the same city; and others; the 11 day of August in the year of our Lord 1574, and of the reign of our sovereign Lady Queen Elizabeth the 16.

b) *The most strange and admirable discoverie of the three Witches of Warboys, arraigned, convicted, and executed at the last Assizes at Huntington, for the bewitching of the five daughters of Robert Throckmorton Esquire, and divers other persons, with sundrie Divellish and grievous torments: And also for the bewitching to death of the Lady Crumwell, the like hath not been heard of in this age.* (London, 1593)[1]

To the right worshipful Master Edward Fenner, one of the Justices of the Court of Her Majesty's Bench.

In these times, right worshipful, wherein every idle wit seeks to blaze abroad their vain-ness, there ought to be no small care for the

---

[10] One of the first cases of false possession in Elizabeth's reign occurred in the Dutch church at Maidstone; Scot gives the name of a pamphlet concerning the matter. (*Discovery of Witchcraft*, ed. cit., Bk. 7, Ch. 3.)

[1] The edition used as the basis of this modernisation is in the British Musum. A copy in the Bodleian has a different title and pagination but the same text; its title is the inside heading of this copy—*A True and Particular Observation of a notable Piece of Witchcraft* . . . (For bibliography, See *Notes and Queries*, Series 12 (I), 8 April 1916, pp. 283, 304.)

restraining of trivial pamphlets, as well to exercise the readers in matter necessary as to cut off the writing of things needless.

Among other, your Worship's care as well for the furthering of the truth of this arraignment (being judge at the trial of the malefactors) as also the crossing of whatsoever pamphlets should have been preferred respecting either the matter partly or confusedly—emboldens me to prefer the patronage hereof to your Worship; not doubting but as you have been careful as well for the trial and judgment of such heinous offenders, and withal taken extraordinary pains in perfecting this work to others' example, you will likewise vouchsafe to pardon our boldness.[2]

To the Reader

At length, though long first, gentle reader, this notable arraignment and examinations of Samuel, his wife and daughter for their sundry witchcrafts in Huntingdonshire are come to view. It hath for special cause been so long deferred, as well that nothing might escape untouched which they had done, as that everything might be throughly sifted, lest it should pass any way corruptly.

These cares having perfected the work, it is now passed the press to your presence, wherein I presume ye shall find matter as admirable as ever this age afforded.

A true and particular observation of a notable piece of witchcraft practised by John Samuel the father, Alice Samuel the mother, and Agnes Samuel their daughter, of Warboys in the county of Huntingdon upon five daughters of Robert Throckmorton of the same town and county, esquire, and certain other maidservants[3] to the number of twelve in the whole, all of them being in one house: November, 1589.

[2] Variations of style within the book appear to suggest that it is a patchwork —that notes taken at the time of certain events were written up, then linked together by the 'author' without comprehensive re-writing. We know that Gilbert Pickering and Robert Throckmorton both took notes; a section after the arrests is ascribed to Doctor Dorington, and someone at the trial recorded procedure there. It is possible that Edward Fenner's 'extraordinary pains in perfecting this work' indicate that he wrote or checked the account of the trial; he might even have seen the book through the press, as he was influential enough to 'cross' or prevent publication of other accounts of the case.

[3] We hear nothing of these servants, and nothing of Robert, the youngest child and only son in the family. Taken for granted by the adults to the point

About the tenth of November which was in the year 1589, Mistress Jane, one of the daughters of the said Master Throckmorton, being near the age of ten years, fell upon the sudden into a strange kind of sickness and distemperature of body, the manner whereof was as followeth:

Sometimes she would sneeze[4] very loud and thick for the space of half an hour together, and presently as one in a great trance and swoon lay quietly as long; soon after she would begin to swell and heave up her belly so as none was able to bend her or keep her down; sometime she would shake one leg and no other part of her as if the palsy had been in it; sometimes the other; presently she would shake one of her arms and then the other, and soon after her head, as if she had been infected with the running palsy.

Continuing in this case two or three days, amongst other neighbours in the town there came into the house of Master Throckmorton the foresaid Alice Samuel to visit this sick child, who dwelt in the next house on the north side of the said Master Throckmorton. The child when the old woman came into the parlour was held in another woman's arms by the fire-side, so she went into the chimney corner and sat down hard by the child; the grandmother of the child and the mother being also present, she had not been there long but the child grew something worse than she was at her coming, and on the sudden cried, saying, 'Grandmother, look where the old witch sitteth'— pointing to the said Mother Samuel. 'Did you ever see' said the child, 'one more like a witch than she is? Take off her black thrummed* cap, for I cannot abide to look on her.'

The mother of the child, little then suspecting any such matter as afterwards fell out, was very angry with her child, and rebuked her for saying so; and thinking that it might proceed of some lightness in the child's brain, by reason of her great sneezing and want of sleep, took her and laid her down upon a bed, and hanged curtains against the windows, thereby hoping to bring her into a sleep; but much ado they

---

of being invisible, these 'blank' characters in the drama could well have provided by their gossip much of the information which the girls acquired 'supernaturally' from the spirits. At the beginning of their affliction the children were aged as follows: Joan, 15 or just under; Elizabeth 13; Mary 12; Jane, just under 10 or 11; Grace, 9 or just under; Robert, 6. Nobody was very interested in the precise ages of the children and there are contradictions.

[4] Here and throughout the obsolete 'neese' or 'neeze' is used.

had to pacify and quiet the child. The old woman, hearing this, sat still and gave never a word, yet looked very ruefully, as afterwards was remembered by them that saw her.

The child still continuing her manner of sickness, rather worse than better, within two days after her parents sent the child's urine to Cambridge to Doctor Barrow, a man well known to be excellent skilful in physic, who returned this answer: namely, that he did perceive no kind of distemperature, save only that he thought she might be troubled with worms, and therefore sent his medicine accordingly; but the child was no whit the better.

So within two days after they sent again to the same man, declaring unto him the manner of her fits more at large; he said that the urine which they then again brought to him showed no such kind of disquietness to be in her body, and as for the falling sickness,* which the parents did suspect to be in the child, he would warrant her clear from that disease. Then he sent other prescripts as he thought good to purge her body, which took no place nor prevailed anything in the child as he looked for.

Then the parents sent to him the third time, as his desire was to understand how his physic wrought, declaring that it wrought nothing at all as he looked for, neither that the child was any way amended. Then Master Doctor, looking again in the urine, and perceiving the child's body to be in good temper, as he then said, for anything that he saw, demanded whether there was no sorcery or witchcraft suspected in the child; answer was made 'no'.

Then said he, 'All surely cannot be well'; for it is not possible that the child's body should be distempered by any natural cause as was then declared to him, and no sign thereof at all to appear in the urine; notwithstanding, for their better assurance, if the messenger would go to any other skilful man in the town to take further advice, he said he would be very well contented.

Whereupon the messenger went to Master Butler who, considering of the urine and hearing the manner of the child's trouble, said that he thought it might be the worms, which yet he did not perceive to be by the urine, and if it were the worms, than then it was a very strange kind of grief to be caused by them in that sort; and appointed the same medicine and physic for the remedy which before Doctor Barrow had prescribed.

Which being known, was not applied to the child because Master Doctor Barrow had said that if Master Throckmorton (to whom he wished very well, as he then said, by reason of ancient acquaintance with him) would follow his advice, he should not strive any more therewith by physic, nor spend any more money about it; for he himself said that he had some experience of the malice of some witches, and he verily thought that there was some kind of sorcery and witchcraft wrought towards his child.

After which answer from Master Doctor Barrow, Master Throckmorton resolved himself to rest upon God's pleasure, not striving any further by physic to help his daughter; yet both himself and his wife were free from any such conceit of witchcraft which Master Doctor Barrow did suspect until, within one just month after (the very day and hour almost observed) two more of his daughters, elder than the other by two or three years fell into the same like extremeties as the other sister before them was in, and cried out upon Mother Samuel, saying, 'Take her away, look where she standeth here before us in a black thrummed cap' (which kind of cap indeed she did usually wear, but she was not then present); 'It is she' said they, 'that hath bewitched us and she will kill us if you do not take her away'.[5]

This thing did something move the parents, and strike into their mind a suspicion of witchcraft, yet devising with themselves for what cause it should be wrought upon them or their children, they could not imagine; for they were but newly come to the town to inhabit, which was but at Michaelmas before, neither had they given any occasion (to their knowledge) either to her or any other to practise any such malice against them.

Within less than a month after that, another sister younger than any of the rest, about the age of nine years, fell into the like case, and cried out of Mother Samuel as the other did. Soon after, Mistress Joan, the eldest sister of them all, about the age of fifteen years, was in the same case and worse handled indeed than any of the other sisters were; for she having more strength than they, and striving more with the spirit than the rest, not being able to overcome it was the more grievously tormented. For it forced her to sneeze, screech and groan very fearfully; sometime it would heave up her belly, and bounce up her body

[5] Thomas Darling (*The most wonderfull and true storie, of a certaine Witch named Alse Gooderige* . . . (London, 1597), A4ᵛ, first suspected that he was bewitched because he heard his aunt and a neighbour discussing the possibility; doubtless such discussion kept alive Jane's original whim in the others. Most parents unconsciously assume that children hear only what is said directly to them.

with such violence that, had she not been kept upon her bed, it could not but have greatly bruised her body. And many times sitting in a chair, having her fit, she would with her often starting and heaving almost break the chair she sat in.

Yet was there no striving with them in this case, for the more they laboured to help them and to keep them down, the more violently they were handled; being deprived of all use of their senses during their fits, for they could neither see, hear, nor feel anybody, only crying out of Mother Samuel, desiring to have her taken away from them, who never more came after she perceived herself to be suspected.

These kind of fits would hold them, sometimes longer, sometimes shorter, either an hour or two, sometimes half the day, yea, the whole day; and many times they had six or seven fits in an hour. Yet when it pleased God to deliver them of their fits, they neither knew what they had said, neither yet in what sort they had been dealt withal, as hereafter shall be declared in particular.

After that Mistress Joan had been thus handled a while, the spirit as it should seem would sound in her ears something which she would declare in her fit; and amongst the rest, it showed unto her one time that there should be twelve of them which should be bewitched in that house, in one sort or other, and named them all unto her, being all womenkind and servants in the house, herself and her sisters being five of the number. All which proved afterwards very true, for they had all their several griefs and most of them afflicted in the same sort and manner as these five sisters were; of whom and the manner of their faith, if it should be written in particular how they were dealt withal, there would be no end of this book.

And this may suffice to be known concerning the servants, that when they first fell into their fits, they all cried out of Mother Samuel as the children did, saying 'Take her away, Mistress, for God's sake take her away and burn her, for she will kill us all if you let her alone!'—having the same miseries and extremities that the children had; and when they were out of their fits they knew no more than the children did, what either they had done or said.

And presently upon their departure from Mistress Throckmorton's house they were all very well, as at any time before, and so have continued ever since, without suspicion of any such kind of vexations; and those servants that came in their places, for the most part of them they were afflicted in the like sort as the other, for the space of two years together.

Upon Friday, being Saint Valentine's Even the thirteenth of February, in the two-and-thirtieth year of Her Majesty's reign, Gilbert Pickering of Titchmarsh Grove in the county of Northampton, esquire, being uncle to the said child, and hearing how strangely they were vexed and troubled, went to Warboys as well to visit and see them and also to comfort their parents. Coming to the house where they were, [he] found them all at that present very well as any children could be; and about one half hour after, the said Master Pickering was informed that one Mistress Andley, and Master Whittle of St. Ives,[6] and others, were gone to the house of Mother Samuel to persuade her to come to see and to visit the said children.

And because they tarried long, it seemed to the said Master Pickering that they could not bring her, although that the said Mother Samuel had often said she would come to the said children whensoever it pleased their parents to send for her, and she would venture her life in water up to the chin, and lose some part of her best blood to do them any good; but now as it seemed, her mind was clean altered.

The cause was, as it was suspected, for that all the said children (as it is said before) in their fits cried out of her, saying that she had bewitched them, and that she also feared the common practice of scratching would be used on her; which nothing less at that present was intended, for both the parents and the said Master Pickering had taken advice of good divines of the unlawfulness thereof. Wherefore the said Master Pickering went to Mother Samuel's house as well to see her as also to persuade her that if she were any cause of the children's trouble, that it might be amended; who coming to the said house found there the foresaid Master Whittle, Mistress Andley, and others persuading her to visit the said children, but she with loud speeches utterly refused the same. Whereupon the said Master Pickering told Mother Samuel that he had authority to bring her, and if she would not go with him willingly and of her own accord, he would force and compel her whether she would or no; which he then did, together with her daughter Agnes Samuel and one Cicely Burder, who were all suspected to be witches, or at the least in the confederacy with Mother Samuel.

And as they were going to the said Master Throckmorton's house, Master Whittle, Mistress Andley, and others going before Mother Samuel, Agnes Samuel and the said Cicely Burder in the middle part, and the said Master Pickering behind them—the said Master Pickering

[6] St. Ives in Huntingdonshire.

perceived[7] that old Mother Samuel would have willingly talked with her daughter Agnes, but the said Master Pickering followed so near behind them that they could not confer; and when they came at the door of Master Throckmorton's house, Mother Samuel used courtesy to the said Master Pickering, offering him to go into the house before her, which he refused, and in the entry of that same house (for either then or not at all) she thought that she should have had time to speak to her daughter: the said Mother Samuel did thrust her head as near as she could to her daughter's head and said these words 'I charge thee, do not confess anything!' Which the said Master Pickering being behind them perceiving, thrust his head as near as he could between their heads whilst the words were spoken, and, hearing them, presently replied to old Mother Samuel, 'Thou naughty woman, dost thou charge thy daughter not to confess anything?' 'Nay', saith she, 'I said not so, but I charged her to hasten herself home to get her father his dinner.'

In the meantime, whilst these words were in speaking, Master Whittle, Mistress Andley, and others went into the house, and three of the children [were] then standing in the hall by the fire perfect well. But no sooner had Mother Samuel entered the hall but at one moment the said three children fell down upon the ground strangely tormented, so that if they had been let lie still on the ground they would have leaped and sprung like a quick pickerel* newly taken out of the water, their bellies heaving up, their head and their heels still touching the ground as though they had been tumblers; and would have drawn their heads and their heels together backwards, throwing out their arms with great groans most strangely to be heard, to the great grief of the beholders.

But not long after they were thus fallen to the ground, the said Master Whittle took up one of the said children, which was Jane Throckmorton, and carried her into an inward chamber, laying her upon a bed; and being a man of as great strength as most be this day in England, and the child not above nine years old, yet he could not hold her down to the bed, but that she would heave up her belly far bigger and in higher measure for her proportion than any woman with child ready to be delivered, her belly being as hard as though there had been for the present time a great loaf in the same; and in such manner it would rise and fall an hundred times in the space of an hour, her eyes being closed as though she had been blind and her arms spread abroad

7 Original has 'perceiving'.

so stiff and strong that the strength of a man was not able to bring them to her body.

Then the said Master Pickering went into the parlour where the said child was and, standing on the farther side of the bed from the child, viewing the order of her, presently the said child stretched forth her right arm to that side of the bed next to the said Master Pickering, and there scratching the covering of the bed, said these words very often, 'Oh, that I had her! oh, that I had her!' whereupon the said Master Pickering was in great admiration what the meaning of the said words should tend unto, and the rather for that the said Master Gilbert Pickering was of that opinion that scratching was merely unlawful.

Yet the said Master Pickering put his own hand to the child's hand whilst she was speaking the words, but the child feeling his hand would not scratch it, but forsook his hand and scratched still on the bed, her face being turned on the contrary side from the said Master Pickering, her eyes being closed, and Master Whittle lying in a manner with his whole body and weight over her to hold down her belly, fearing that she would have burst her back.

Notwithstanding, the occasion being thus offered by the child, or rather by the spirit in the child, to disclose some secret whereby the witches might be by some means or token made manifest and known, the said Master Pickering went into the hall and took Mother Samuel by the hand (who went as willingly as a bear to the stake) and brought her to the further side of the bed from the child, who lay scraping with her nails on the bed covering, saying 'Oh, that I had her!'

Then the said Master Pickering in very soft speeches, so that the child could not hear, said to Mother Samuel, 'Put your hand to the child's hand', but she would not. Then the said Master Pickering for example's sake put his hand to the child's hand, so did also Mistress Andley and others at the same instant, but the child would scarce touch, much less scratch, any of their hands. Then the said Master Pickering, without either malice to the woman, confidence or opinion in scratching (only to taste by this experiment whereto the child's words would tend) took Mother Samuel's hand and thrust it to the child's hand; who no sooner felt the same, but presently the child scratched her with such vehemency that her nails brake into spills with the force and earnest desire that she had to revenge.

Whilst the child was thus scratching, the said Master Pickering did cover Mother Samuel's hand with his own hand, to try what the child would do in this extraordinary passion; but the child would not scratch his hand, but felt to and fro upon the bed for that which she missed, and if by any means she could come with her hand or but with one of her fingers to touch Mother Samuel's hand, she would scratch that hand only and no other. Yea, sometimes whiles the said Master Pickering with his hand did cover Mother Samuel's hand the said child would put one of her fingers between the fingers of the said Master Pickering and scratch Mother Samuel's hand that lay nethermost with that one finger, all her other fingers lying on the hand of the said Master Pickering without moving.

And in this passion, if at any time Mother Samuel's hand had been hidden or withdrawn from the child, she would have mourned and showed apparent tokens of dislike, as though there had been some great discourtesy offered. And this is to be noted for a most certain truth, for so it was by the said Master Pickering at the Assizes in Huntingdon given in evidence, that the child's eyes were closed so that she could not see any person, for so was the order of their fits; and though she at that present could have seen, yet the child's head and neck were so turned backward into Master Whittle's bosom, who covered (as before is said) both her head, face and body with his body, in such sort and so close, that it was unpossible for the child to see the company which stood on the further side of the bed.

This being done, the said Master Pickering departed out of that place into another parlour where there was a woman holding one of the other children, which child, as the said Master Pickering passed by, scraped the woman's apron that held her, saying, 'Oh, that I had her! oh, that I had her!' Then the said Master Pickering went into the hall and did bring Cicely Burder to the said child, and (for brevity sake) as the said Master Pickering did with Mother Samuel to the first child, so did he to Cicely Burder, and as the first child did to Mother Samuel, so this second child did to Cicely Burder in all respects.

There was a third child also at that present in the hall, which spake the same words, but the father of the children and Master Doctor Dorington, parson of the same parish, came then into the house, not allowing that which was done, by reason whereof the third was not put in proof.

The same night after supper, the children being all very well and out of their fits, Master Doctor Dorington made motion to have some prayers before the company departed; the company then kneeling down, Doctor Dorington began to pray. But no sooner had he uttered the first word, but even at one instant of time all the children fell into their fits, with such terrible screeches and strange sneezings, so wonderfully tormented as though they should have been torn in pieces; which caused Doctor Dorington to stay in the midst of his prayers, and said these words, or the like in effect 'Were we best to go any further?'

But he had no sooner made stay, and his breath stayed from praying, but the children were quiet (but still in their fits); then he began to pray again, and then the children, or rather the wicked spirit in the children forced them as before. This was proved often in the time of prayer, for when he had made an end of any one prayer the children ceased and were quiet; when he began to pray, they began to shriek; when he ended, they ended.

The next day, being St. Valentine's Day, the said Master Pickering brought home to his house at Titchmarsh Grove aforesaid one of the said children called Elizabeth Throckmorton, being in her fit; who no sooner was[8] on horseback and out of Warboys town but she was well, and so continued till she came into the said Master Pickering's house.

But no sooner had she entered into the house but that the fit took her suddenly; gasping, being not able to speak, only thus 'It cometh!' she pitched herself backwards, all the joints of her backbone being as it were drawn together, thrusting out her belly so strongly that none could bend her back again, being very strong and heavy, shaking her limbs and oftentimes her head (when it riseth so high), but specially her arms, like to those which struggle and plunge betwixt life and death; being both dumb, deaf and blind, her eyes closed up. Now this held her not a quarter of an hour, but with a gasp she came again to herself, stroking her eyes as though she had been but asleep.

Sometimes, being taken in her fit she is but deaf only, when she can speak, or rather (as we think) the spirit in her, but very vainly; and she can see also but with a small glimmering, when if you look upon her, ye would deem her to have no sight at all. Sometimes also she can hear only, and not everybody, but someone whom she liketh and chooseth out from the rest; sometimes she seeth only, and as plainly as any other, but neither heareth nor speaketh anything, her teeth being set in her head; sometimes both hearing and seeing very well, and yet not able to speak.

Above all things she delighteth in play; she will pick out some one body to play with her at cards, and but one only, not hearing, seeing or speaking to any other; but being awake she remembereth nothing

[8] Original has 'being'.

that she did, heard, or spake, affirming that she was not sick, but only slept.

She continued well until night, and before supper in time of thanksgiving it vexed her very strangely, taking her at the very name of grace, and holding her no longer than grace was in saying. She sat very well at the table, but no sooner had she put up her knife but it pitched her backwards; then being taken from the table she was well until thanksgiving, all which time she was most grievously vexed and no longer.

Afterwards she was very quiet and well until motion was made of prayers, all which time it seemed as though it would have rent her in pieces, with such screeching and outcries and vehement sneezing as that it terrified the whole company; but prayers being ended she was quieted, but still in her fit.

Then Master Pickering and others that were acquainted with the manner of it said that if any should read the Bible or any other godly book before her, it would rage as before so long as they read; but because it was a thing very strange and therefore hardly believed, one did take a Bible and read the first chapter of Saint John,[9] the first verse. At the hearing whereof she was as one besides her mind; when he that read held his peace she was quiet. When he read again it tormented her; when he ceased, it ceased; this divers did prove many times.[10]

Nay, at the motion of any good word (as if any that stood by chanced to name God, or prayed God to bless her, or named any word that

[9] The conviction that it was wrong to do anything that the Devil wanted led the parents and friends of possessed children not to *avoid* but to *stress* the actions which brought on fits. A favourite reading to vex the Devil was the first chapter of St. John—a passage which had been worn in amulets or repeated as a charm since the earliest days of the Catholic Church, and was still powerful as such. After tormenting the child to the utmost, the Devil would depart in a final paroxysm, and the child would be able to engage in holy exercises unhindered. (Oddly, a modern psychiatric treatment for obsessive fears consists of confronting the patient with the feared object till he cracks and is then receptive to new suggestions.)

[10] Naturally, a good deal of mere curiosity was mixed up in this, and the exorcist Darrell warned against the idle wish to produce a fit (*Alse Gooderige* ... D^v). Nonetheless, the parents of an afflicted child had much to do '. . . attending on such as came to see him, whereof many were of very good account' (*Alse Gooderige* ... A4^v). The Elizabethans regarded personal fortune or misfortune as 'exempla' to benefit all; neither unhappiness, illness nor childbirth carried any right of privacy, and to turn away even curious strangers would apparently have been regarded as an unthinkable breach of hospitality.

tended to God or godliness) it raged all one as if any had read or prayed by her, and thus she was carried to bed still continuing in her fit.

In the morning, being the Sabbath day, she came down into the hall towards prayer time, and being asked whether she would tarry the time of prayers or not, she answered that she would do as they would have her. Then was she asked whether she could read; she said that she could once, but she had almost forgotten now. Then being asked further whether she had prayed that day, she made answer 'it would not suffer her'; then whether she used to pray at home, she answered that it would not give her so much time.

Then one said to her 'Since it will not suffer you to pray, nor any other (seeming to have ears), pray to yourself secretly in your heart and spirit'; and beginning to tell her that God understood the inward sighs and groans of the heart as well as the loudest cries of the mouth, she suddenly fell into her fit, being more strongly and strangely tormented that ever she was before.[11] And being carried away, her fit continued and increased all prayer time, albeit she was out of the hearing, with such vehement cries, screeching, and continual sneezing that many times prayers were constrained to be ceased for the time, so much it amazed the whole company. Prayers being ended, she came to herself with a gasp, wiping her eyes, being presently as well as anybody as though it had never been she.

She came down to dinner, and during the time of grace, it held her again, which was usual; yet will it suffer better another to say grace than herself, but nobody well. At dinner time it played with her, (for sometimes she hath merry fits) putting her hand besides her meat, and her meat besides her mouth, mocking her and making her miss her mouth, whereat she would sometimes smile and sometimes laugh exceedingly; and amongst many other things this is worthy to be noted, that being in her fit, she looked far more sweetly and cheerfully than when she is awake, and although being tormented most pitifully, that

---

[11] The children's fits seemed to be based on two contradictory desires—the desire to *get* attention and the desire to avoid *paying* attention. The silent fits allowed them to ignore anything they did not wish to hear (mainly adult instruction and edification); the violent fits allowed them to express blasphemous feelings through unbecoming actions and to produce, not disapproval, but awe and sympathy. Thus parents were compelled to devote all their thought and care to the frightening plight of their offspring, but were unable to rule or discipline children so frequently 'deaf' to them. (This is not to say that the fits were fully deliberate or controllable—only that they had distinct psychic advantages.)

it would have grieved any to see it, yet being once awake and out of her fit, she is as well as anybody.

At length Master Gilbert Pickering called to mind an experiment which was made at Warboys which was, that if one took any of those children in their fits and carried them into the churchyard which is adjoining to the house, they presently awaked, but bring them in again—they were as before; carry them forth and they came to themselves: go into the house and immediately their fit took them, and this was as often found true as proved. Hereupon we proved the like with this child, and carried her out of the house, and she presently recovered; but within the house it took her again.

But the certainty of this failed us soon (as Satan is most uncertain); yet for three days' space, if she were carried abroad in her fit, it would leave her and not take her again until she was brought into the house.

[The account of this child's seizures and obsessions continues for many pages.[12] The adults, in their strange scientific desire to 'test' the spirit and find rules for its behaviour are put through an extraordinary series of performances, carrying the girl indoors and out, feeding her in the fields a mile from the house, checking up on her statements about the activities of sisters in other places; Elizabeth is always one jump ahead, changing the rules as fast as they discover them.

Mother Samuel is not forgotten, however; she appears to the child in a white sheet with a black child on her shoulders, and on another occasion forces a mouse (i.e. spirit) into the girl's mouth. These visions seem to cause very genuine terror. Finally Elizabeth is taken home.]

Now that you have heard the particular manner of the fits of this child Mistress Elizabeth, you may imagine and aim at the manner of handling of the rest of her sisters (during this time remaining in other places) who were no less strangely dealt withal than she was; of whom it should particularly be observed, as is done in her—as strange wonders (if anything hitherto seem strange) befell every one of them severally as are these which you have already heard. And by some of them were showed matters of far greater admiration; but this may suffice, lest in entering into the rest no end could be found, so infinite is the matter.

It pleased the providence of God that, not long after Master Gilbert Pickering had carried away this child to his house (about a month or such a thing) the Lady Cromwell, wife of Sir Henry Cromwell, knight, who then lay in Ramsey, a town two miles distant from Warboys, came to Master Throckmorton's house together with her

12 Sigs. B4^v–D3^v are here omitted.

daughter-in-law Mistress Cromwell, to visit these children and to comfort their parents, with whom she was well acquainted.

She had not long stayed in the house but the children which were there fell all into their fits, and were so grievously tormented for the time that it pitied the good lady's heart to see them, insomuch that she could not abstain from tears. Whereupon she caused the old woman Mother Samuel to be sent for, who durst not deny to come, because her husband was tenant to Sir Henry Cromwell; who after she was come, the children grew to be worse than they were before, which caused the greater sorrow.

Then the Lady Cromwell took Mother Samuel aside, and charged her deeply with this witchcraft, using also some hard speeches to her; but she stiffly denied them all, saying that Master Throckmorton and his wife did her great wrong so to blame her without cause. The Lady answered her that neither Master Throckmorton nor his wife accused her, but the children themselves in their fits did it, or rather the spirit by them.

One of them, Mistress Joan by name, being then in her fit, hearing the old woman thus clearing herself (for she heard not the Lady, nor any other) said that it was she that caused all this, 'and something there is', saith she 'that doth now tell me so'; asking if nobody heard it but she, affirming that it squealed very loud in her ears, and marvelled that nobody could hear it, wishing the old woman to listen to it.

But Mother Samuel still continued her denial. Then the Lady Cromwell would have taken her up into a chamber to have examined her more narrowly, Master Doctor Hall, a doctor of divinity, being present, but she by no means would go with them but rather fained many excuses to go home.

In the end, when the lady perceived that by no good speeches neither she nor any other could prevail with her, and that fain she would have been gone, she suddenly pulled off her kercher* and taking a pair of shears, clipped off a lock of her hair, and gave it privily* to Mistress Throckmorton, mother of the children, together with her hair-lace, willing her to burn them.[13]

---

[13] A later witch-pamphlet suggests that the hair of a witch cannot be cut but will turn the edge of a pair of scissors (*The Trial of Master Dorell* (London, 1599), G2–G4). Here the cutting of the hair seems connected with the idea of scratching—any breach in the witch's physical invulnerability not only signifies but *causes* loss of power, because the devil whose dwelling she is will be offended and depart.

Mother Samuel, perceiving herself thus dealt withal, spake to the lady thus: 'Madam, why do you use me thus? I never did you any harm as yet.' These words were afterwards remembered, and were not at that present time taken hold of by any. Towards night, the Lady departing left the children much what as she found them.

The same night, after the Lady Cromwell departed from Warboys, she suffered many thing in her dream concerning Mother Samuel, and was very strangely tormented in her sleep by a cat (as she imagined) which Mother Samuel had sent unto her, which cat offered to pluck off all the skin and flesh from her arms and body; but such was the struggling and striving of the Lady that night in her bed, and mournful noise which she made speaking to the cat and to Mother Samuel, that she wakened her bedfellow,[14] who was Mistress Cromwell before named, wife to the worshipful Master Oliver Cromwell, son and heir to Sir Henry Cromwell, who that night was from home.

Mistress Cromwell being awakened, and perceiving the Lady thus disquieted, awakened her also, who greatly thanked her for it; declaring how she had been troubled in her dream with Mother Samuel and her cat, with many other circumstances which she did very well remember, neither could she take any quiet rest or sleep all that night after for fear thereof. Not long after, the Lady fell very strangely sick and so continued unto her dying day, which was some year and quarter after her being at Warboys.

The manner of her fits was much like to the children's, save only that she had always her perfect senses; for sometime her pain would be in one arm, sometime in the other, now in the one leg, by and by in the other, many times in her head. Yea, sometimes it would take her but in one several finger or toe, and always shake the grieved part as if it had been the palsy. And that saying of Mother Samuel which she used to her at Warboys, which was, 'Madam, I never hurt you *as yet*' would never out of her mind. And thus leaving this good Lady in Heaven with God, we will return to these children.

About Christmas after, Anno 1590 (for there was nothing noted all that time although there befell 100 wonders), Master Henry Pickering,

[14] People of the Middle Ages and Renaissance seem to have suffered severely and frequently from nightmare. By this they meant, not just a frightening dream, but that specific variety in which there is a sense of suffocation and weight on the chest, accompanied by extreme terror and often by erotic feelings as well. Theologically, nightmare was attributed to an incubus or succubus (male and female demons of unchastity); medically, it was associated with melancholy.

uncle to these children, being then a scholar of Cambridge, went to Master Throckmorton's house and continued there some three or four days. [He] was desirous to speak with Mother Samuel and taking a convenient time, he requested two other scholars of his acquaintance (then being in the town) to go with him; to whom they granted, and presently went without the knowledge of any in Master Throckmorton's house.

As they were going, she came out of her own house and crossed the street before them; when they saw her they determined rather to follow her whither she went than stay her return, because her husband was a froward* man and would not suffer her to talk with any if he might know it. She went to a neighbour's house for some barm,* and carried a little wooden tankard in her hand, and a little barley in her lap to exchange for the barm.

When she came to the house whither she purposed to go, the scholars followed her immediately and heard her tell her errand to the wife of the house, who had not that for which she came. Being ready to depart, the scholars desired to speak with her but she seemed loth to stay; yet they entering into questions with her stayed her a little.

But she was very loud in her answers and impatient, not suffering any to speak but herself. One of them desired her to keep the woman's virtue and be more silent; she answered that she was 'born in a mill, begot in a kill,* she must have her will', she could speak no softlier.

The greatest part of her speech was railing words against Master Throckmorton and his children, saying that he did misuse her in suffering his children so to play the wantons in accusing of her and bringing her name into question; often repeating that the children's fits was nothing but wantonness in them and, if they were her children, she would not suffer them so to escape without punishment one after the other.

The scholars enquired about her service of God and profession of her faith, but all that they could get of her was that 'her God would deliver her, her God would defend her and revenge her of her enemy' —alway using the phrase of 'my God will do this and that for me'. Which being noted by one of them, he asked her if she had a God alone, or if she did not serve the same God that others did? She answered 'Yes, she did'; yet much ado they had to bring her from the phrase of 'my God' to say 'the God of heaven and earth'.

In the end she would needs be gone, saying that her husband would beat her for her long tarrying. Then the uncle of those children, being somewhat more moved than the rest, at the parting said that if she were the woman that had wrought this wickedness upon these children, the vengeance of God would surely wait upon her unto death and, howsoever she might deceive herself and the world for a time, yet there was no way to prevent the judgements of God but by her confession and repentance; which if she did not in time, he hoped one day to see her burned at a stake, and he himself would bring fire and wood, and the children should blow the coals. Her answer to him was this (for they were then in the street hard by a pond) 'I had rather' said she 'see you doused over head and ears in this pond!' and so they parted.

Now to come to the point; the eldest of Master Throckmorton's daughters was then in her fit, sitting at home in a parlour, her father and grandmother with some other of her sisters in their fits being present with her. On the sudden said she, 'Now is my uncle (naming him) and the two other (whom she also named) going to Mother Samuel: we shall hear some news by and by.'

Presently she said 'Look where Mother Samuel goeth trotting in the streets before them, with a wooden tankard in her hand and her apron is tucked up before her—I believe' saith she, 'there is somewhat in it. She is gone into such a man's house that keepeth an alehouse.' The man's name she could not hit of, but described him by his red head.

'Hark!' said she to her sisters, 'Mother Samuel is very loud, and my uncle bids her speak softly, but she saith she cannot'—repeating to her father and the rest the same words (*viz.* that she was born in a mill, etc.) after the same manner that Mother Samuel spake them to her uncle and the other scholars.

To be short, she declared particularly every word that passed between Mother Samuel and those scholars at that time. And at the parting she said 'There, Mother Samuel, my uncle did touch you, I think;' repeating again the very same words that her uncle had done, wishing that that day were once come, 'for I myself' said she 'would blow the coals. But he had been as good he had said nothing to her,' said she, 'for she wished him over head and ears in the pond for it.'

Master Throckmorton standing by and hearing all this, after that the child had said that now Mother Samuel and the scholars were parted, enquired for his brother the child's uncle, asking if any knew whither he was gone. Answer was made that he came not home from the church since evening prayer (for it was on a Saturday) but where he was, nobody knew.

'It may be' said Master Throckmorton, 'that he is with Mother Samuel', and went immediately out of his own house to see if he could perceive where they were. As he went, he met them in the church-yard coming from Mother Samuel's. 'Where have you been?' said he. They told him. 'I could have told you so much myself,' said he, and repeated to them the whole matter as his daughter before had showed.

When they were come into the parlour where she was, there was also another of her sisters in her fit sitting by; and this her other sister could hear her said uncle speak unto her and nobody else, and so by her mouth (for they could for the most part hear one another in their fits) he enquired of her sister all those matters over again which she did in his own hearing repeat—'but' said she, 'the wind was so great that I had much ado to hear them'—whereas indeed there was then no wind stirring.

After this the spirit (or 'the thing' as the children called it) would many times appear unto them in their fits in some kind of shape or other, but most commonly in the likeness of a dun chicken, and would talk familiarly with them, saying that they came from Mother Samuel (whom they called their dame) and were sent by her to the children to torment and vex them in that sort.

It would declare to the children many things concerning Mother Samuel, insomuch that she could do nothing almost at home for a great time but the spirit would disclose it, if it were required by the children in their fits: viz. as to know what she was then in doing at home or in what place of her house or elsewhere she was, the spirit would tell; which by a messenger presently sent of purpose, was proved true.

Now did the spirits manifestly begin to accuse Mother Samuel to the children in their fits, saying it was she that had bewitched them and all those servants which were bewitched in the house; and told them that whensoever they were in their fits and were either carried to Mother Samuel's house, or she caused to come to them, they should be presently well.

This many times was proved true, and never failed once, so that if the children at any time being in their fits had been carried to Mother Samuel's house (for it was a very hard thing to get Mother Samuel to Master Throckmorton's house) although they were in such a case as that a strong man could scarcely hold them, they would so struggle, start and sprawl in his arms, yet if they came but once to the threshold of Mother Samuel's door, they would wipe their eyes and say 'I am well—why do you carry me? set me down!' as though some shame had been offered them in that they were carried in the streets, not knowing anything in what case they had been.

While they continued in the house they were very well, but determining once to come away, and offering to come out of the door, they fell presently down on the ground and were brought from thence in the same case that they were carried thither. Contrariwise, whensoever Mother Samuel came to Master Throckmorton's house, in what kind of extremity soever these children were in (as it was most wonderful strange to see them many times), so soon as ever she had set foot into the parlour or hall where they were, they would all presently start up upon their feet and be as well as any in the house, and so continue while she was present.

But when she offered to depart, they would all sink down as a stone upon the ground; if she turned but her face again and came towards them, they would be well as before, which was tried twenty times in one hour. And when she departed from the house, she left them in the same estate wherein she found them, so long as their fit continued upon them.

After this Master Throckmorton thought good to disperse his children, and sent them abroad, some to one friend's house, some to another for a time, to see how they should be dealt withal, yet always keeping some one of them at home with him. If it should be declared how these were all severally handled for the time they were abroad, it would ask a long discourse, and longer indeed than is thought meet at this time, although very strange things, and such as may seem worth the noting befell every one of them, as this for one:—

They could tell being in their fits in what case or estate their other sisters were at that instant, being separated some of them eight, ten, or twelve miles asunder, and have said, 'Now is my sister (naming her and the place where she was in her fit) very sore handled', as she herself was at that instant. It was proved to be most true by the just computation of times, with many such like things.

But this may suffice concerning them being abroad—that they were never altogether clear and free from their fit, although it be true that some of them, whether at home or abroad, had not their fits above once in a month, sometimes once in half a year; and one of them was clear a whole year together. And this also is verified and true in some other of these five sisters, that they were never clear nor free from some kind of fit or other three weeks together—I think scarcely three days since the first day it took them, except now since these last Assizes in Kent whereat these witches were executed.

To pass over all that which might be spoken of them for a year and almost an half, we will come nearer unto these latter times wherein the spirits, whether moved by their own malice (as it passeth the reach of man to sound the depth of the Devil's malice to mankind) or moved by the malice of the senders and setters-on, or both, it is not known; or whether for the conclusion and consummation of their parents' patience in this point it pleased the wisdom of God, who in His providence had determined their end, to grant them therefore more liberty for the time to exercise their malice against these children, we leave it to God; but truth it is that they were more strangely vexed and more grievously tormented in their body now of late, and take them generally altogether, than at any time almost from the beginning.

And to begin this time at Michaelmas[15] last past, or thereabouts, four of these children were all together at Warboys in their father's house, and the fifth, which was the eldest of them, was at her uncle's house, Gilbert Pickering, esquire, dwelling at Titchmarsh Grove.

About this time, which was Michaelmas 1592, one of these four children, the youngest save one, near upon the age of fourteen[16] years, was in a very strange kind of fit, the manner whereof was as followeth: every day for the space of three weeks or more she had a senseless fit, some one time of the day or other, and sometimes many fits in one day. In which fit she could neither hear, see, nor speak to anybody, besides her inward griefs, that she would heave, and start, and swell up her body, which was very troublesome to her for the time.

When she was out of these fits, she would go up and down the house very well, she would eat and drink and sometimes be very pleasant in outward gesture with her sisters; she would do anything which by any sign she did understand should be done, she would make a reverence as she passed by unto those where she saw it was due, insomuch that any man ignorant of her estate could perceive nothing to be amiss in her, yet would she never speak to any in particular, neither could she hear any that spake to her during that time; except sometimes she would prattle a little to an infant which was newly born in the house, wherein she took great delight.

[15] Michaelmas: Sept. 29, one of four quarter days in England.
[16] If this was Jane, she was said to be nearly 10 in November 1589, which would make her nearly 13 now.

It pleased God, about the beginning of these kind of fits in her, an aunt of hers being then in the house was delivered of a child, upon which occasion many of her uncles and aunts and other kindred and friends resorted to the house, and some of them stayed a week or ten days altogether, all which time the child was in these kind of fits; and, as it happened, Mother Samuel amongst the rest came to the house and was brought up into the gentlewoman's chamber, where commonly the greatest company was.

So soon as she came in, this child in question being there, espied her and presently spake to her, bidding her welcome and, saying that she was a great stranger there, she fetched her up both meat and drink, and would do anything readily that she willed her to do. In the end, she asked Mother Samuel whose that little child was which she herself had in her arms; the old woman told her, and likewise the name of it, which thing she also demanded.

The child marvelled, saying, 'Is my aunt brought to bed? I am very glad of it. Why then,' saith she, 'such and such of mine uncles and aunts promised to be here'—who were then indeed in the house, and some of them in that company. Then Mother Samuel told her that such and such whom she asked for were in presence. The child said that she saw nobody but her and that little child which she had in her arms, although she looked full in their faces. Many such like strange things then fell out, which is too long to speak of. When the old woman departed, the child lost the use of all her senses, and continued in the same case wherein she was when the old woman came into the house.

When she had continued thus three weeks or more, she came one day out of her aunt's chamber into the hall, and she had not long stayed there but she fell into a most troublesome fit for the time, but it continued not long. Presently she spake and said, 'I am glad, and very glad', repeating it often; on the sudden she wiped her eyes and came out of her fit. Her mother being in the hall, she asked her blessing, and enquired of many things, and amongst others asked how her aunt did, from whom a little before she came, and knew of nothing that was done, neither that any company had been there for the space of three weeks before.

It followeth to speak of the rest of her sisters together with herself, who all of them, as the year grew towards an end, so their grief and extremity of troubles increased, insomuch that every day brought with it increase of pain and strangeness in their manner of fits.

Towards All Hallowstide[17] the spirits grew very familiar with the children, and commonly towards the end of their fits (when the greatest trouble was over) would talk with them half an hour together, and sometimes longer. The greatest matter of their talk was about their manner of fits which they should have, and concerning Mother Samuel, whose pleasure it was that they should be so used; but the spirits said many times that they would bring her to shame for it in the end. If in this time (being in their fits) they had enquired of their spirit when they should come out of that fit wherein then they were, and when they should have another, it would have told them and not missed any whit at all.

If they had asked how many fits they should have the next day following, and the third day, or any day that week, and how many fits they should have in one day, and what manner of fits they should be, whether more grievous or less, how long every fit should continue, and in what part of the day they should begin and when they should end, it hath told them and not failed in one point, for it hath been presently set down in writing as the children have spoken it (for it was not possible to remember the times for them all) and proved wholly true.

The times and signs which the spirits did appoint unto them for the beginning or ending of their fits were usually these: in the morning so soon as they did offer to arise out of their beds; so soon as they were up or ready; so soon as they asked their father b[l]essing, or their mother, or their grandmother; so soon as they took a book in hand to pray, or when they had ended their prayers; so soon as they went to breakfast, so soon as dinner was set upon the board, or so soon as they did offer to say grace either before or after dinner; so soon as they themselves were set down to dinner, or at the first bit of meat they put in their mouths; or so soon as dinner was ended or they had put up their knife after dinner, the same circumstances at supper also observed.

Or if it had been upon the Sabbath day, or any day wherein the bells ought to be rung, so soon as the first, second or third peal ringeth, or have done ringing, with many such like signs which would be too long to speak of, appointed by the spirit for the children to fall in or out of their fits, which they duly observed and failed not a minute, as may be thought.

After they had continued in this case about a month together or such a thing, whether the spirits were weary (as they oftentimes said unto

[17] Original has 'All Hollantide', i.e. Feast of Allhallows, or All Saints' Day: October 31.

the children in their fits, that they now waxed weary of their dame Mother Samuel), or whether that through the power of God's goodness and special protection of the children the spirits perceived that their own malice and the malice of their dame to the children was restrained and kept under in such sort that they could not kill the children, as they desired—for we may not think that it agreeth with the nature of the evil spirit to sport and play with man as these spirits oftentimes did with these little children: they said to them that now ere long they would bring their dame either to her confession or confusion.

And this was the greatest stay of comfort and prop of patience which the parents of these children, and friends, always had; namely, that when these children were in their greatest torment and miseries as might be devised, in such sort as that it made the heart of the beholders many times to melt in their bodies, being without all hope ever in this world to see them alive again—yet, whensoever it pleased God to deliver them out of their fits, they would wipe their eyes and be presently well, as if it had never been they, not knowing anything that had befallen them; so that now it would seem that God Himself would take the matter into His own hands and, having in His council determined an end thereof, so He would also appoint the means to bring it to pass, which was even by the spirits themselves, the instruments of this wickedness.

For now they began to accuse Mother Samuel openly to her face, and say that 'they shall not be well in any place except they continue in her house, or she be brought to continue with them; and besides that, they shall have more troublesome fits than ever they had, except one of these two be brought to pass'.

Master Throckmorton, still thinking that the spirits might lie, was contented to try the uttermost for three weeks together, all which time his children had very many most grievous and troublesome fits; insomuch that when night came, there was never a one of them able to go to their beds alone, their legs were so full of pain and sores, besides many other griefs they had in their bodies, being out of their fits, which was not usual with them. And one of them also for all that time of three weeks never had use of her legs, except it were an hour or two in one day while Mother Samuel was in the house; and then she was able to go and was very well, as the rest also were; otherwise her legs were thrust up to her body as if they had been tied with strings, and where you set her down, there you should find her, except she crept away.

Master Throckmorton, perceiving that by no means he could get leave of old John Samuel for the old woman to come to his house, although he offered very largely for it; which was to allow him (if it came to ten pounds in the year) for the board and wages of the best servant in Huntingdonshire to do his business, if he would, in her stead, besides his promise and bond, if he would require it, for the well using of his wife while she was with him: he could find no other remedy for the health of his children but to carry them thither, which he did, who as soon as they came into the house were all presently well.

Which he perceiving, said that his children should dwell there, and out of the house they should not go—he would provide for their necessities. The man seeing this, that there was no striving with the company, quenched out the fire (and it was a cold season) saying that he would starve* them, besides very many evil words which came from him and his daughter at that time.

All that day they continued there very well, and did both eat and drink and read in their book, and were very merry. At night when the man John Samuel perceived that they should lodge there, he thought that they would be very troublesome to him, and therefore gave his faithful promise that his wife should come to Master Throckmorton's house the next morning and continue with him; whereupon Master Throckmorton took home his children, and they were in their fits so soon as they came out of his doors, and so continued all that night.

The next morning Master Throckmorton went for the old woman, but she was gone nobody knew whither, so he sent again for his children who, so soon as they came into the house, were well. Towards night, came in the old woman, who said that she had been 2 or 3 miles out of the town, and her husband knew of her going because she should not come to Master Throckmorton's; which when he understood that she had spoken (for she spake it privately, desiring them to whom she spake it not to tell her husband), he utterly forswore the matter, and presently fell upon his wife and beat her very sore with a cudgel—many being present—before she could be rescued by them.

In the end, when the man perceived Master Throckmorton still to continue in the same mind aforesaid, he was contented to let his wife go home with them that night, who went all to Master Throckmorton's house very well together, and so continued the space of nine or ten days following, without any manner of soreness, lameness, or any manner grudging* of fits, and in better case than they had been (as it was well known), all of them together, for the space of three whole years before.

This made the parents right glad, and to use the woman as a welcome guest. At the ten days' end, the old woman entreated Mistress Throckmorton—for her husband was gone forth that morning—that she might go home, making her excuse to fetch something that she wanted. Mistress Throckmorton was very loath to grant it, promising that she herself would rather fetch what she would have than that she should go out of her house; yet the old woman saying that nobody could come by that thing that she would have but herself (which haply was true) and promising her present return, she yielded to her request.

Soon after she was gone, some of the children fell into their fits again as before times, and the spirit then talking with them said that now Mother Samuel was feeding of her spirits and making a new league and composition with them; which was, that although now she came again to the house, they shall be no whit the better, but rather the worse for her being there, because she would not remain any longer there.

Which thing seemed to be true that the child spake, for so soon as she came again (which was not before she was sent for, four or five hours after she went) the children which were in their fits at their coming so continued, and they that were not, after her coming fell into their fits, all of them crying out that now Mother Samuel had made a new composition with her spirits, and now they should be no whit better for her presence but rather the worse.

Master Throckmorton, when he came home, and perceiving the case otherwise with his children than he left it, and the cause why, could not be but heartily sorry; yet referred all to the good pleasure of God, and would not suffer the old woman to depart his house, for this cause chiefly—because his children, being in their fits, could neither hear, see, nor speak to anybody but to her, and some of the children could take nothing but that which she either gave them or touched with her hands.

Mother Samuel remaining thus with the children, she could not be in any place of the house alone, neither doing anything about the house, but the children in their fits would reveal it; specially when she was feeding of her spirits, for then the children would say, 'Now is Mother Samuel in such a place of the house feeding of her spirits.' When they went and looked, there they should find her, but whether doing any such thing or not, God and her conscience are the best witnesses.

Many times also as she sat talking with these children, being in their fits by the fire-side, they would say unto her, 'Look you here, Mother Samuel, do you not see this thing that sitteth here by us?' She would answer 'No, not she.' 'Why,' they would say again, 'I marvel that you do not see it—look how it leapeth, skippeth, and playeth up and down!' pointing at it with their fingers here and there as it leaped. Sometimes also they would say, 'Hark, Mother Samuel, do you not hear it? hark how loud it is! I marvel you do not hear it—nay, you cannot but hear it!' She would deny it, and bid them ask their father, or some other whom she saw to stand by whether they heard it or not. The children would answer that they saw nobody, although they stood hard by them. Then would they tell Mother Samuel that it telleth them that she both heareth it, seeth it, and sent it.

The father of these children, Master Throckmorton, to make a kind of experience of this matter, one night willed Mother Samuel (as he might have done to any other then being present) to name how many fits those three children that were then in their fits should have the next day following, and what kind of fits they should have, when they should begin and how long they should continue.

Mother Samuel was very loath to be brought unto it; yet in the end, their father saying that she should do it, she said, 'One of them shall have three fits (naming the child) such and such for the manner (namely, easy fits, appointing the time for their beginnings and endings); the other shall have two in like sort (the time appointed by her); and the third shall have none but be well all the day.' All which fits proved very justly in every one of them the next day as she had spoken.

At another time not long after, Mother Samuel sitting by these children being in their fits as before, Master Throckmorton their father, and some other also being with him, demanded of Mother Samuel, saying that he had heard that those that were acquainted with these spirits (as the children say that she is) and had retained them in their service to do for them as they commanded, that they did feed them and reward them with something from them, but most usually with their blood, and that every day; 'now therefore,' said he, 'make open confession and shame the Devil in telling the truth, whether you do any such thing or not.'

She most vehemently denied it with many bitter words and curses upon herself, desiring the Lord to show some present token from Heaven upon her that all the world might know that she was such a kind of woman as they suspected her for, if she used any such thing, or rewarded them any such way, or had any spirits, or knew what they were.

Presently* after, Master Throckmorton and Master Henry Pickering, uncle to the said children, who was then with him, hearing her use such protestations [and] being half terrified in their hearts (because they alway vehemently suspected her guiltiness) that she should thus violently with her own hands, as it were, pull down the judgments of God upon her head—went out of the doors; and before they were gone ten paces from the house, another young gentleman, Master John Lawrence (cousin to the said children) that stayed behind in the parlour, came to Master Throckmorton and Master Henry Pickering and said that Mother Samuel's chin did bleed.

Whereupon they returned into the parlour again where she was, and saw the napkin wherewith she had wiped away the blood from her chin to be bloody to the quantity of eight or ten drops. Then Master Throckmorton, with the rest, looked upon her chin and there was no more to be seen than upon the back of a clean hand, only there appeared some few little red spots, as if they had been flea-bitings. Then Master Throckmorton demanded of her whether her chin used to bleed so or not? She said that it did, very often. He asked her who could witness it but herself? She said 'nobody', for it did always bleed when she was alone, and she never told anybody of it.

This her bleeding at the chin, she did confess to the said Master Henry Pickering after she was condemned, that the spirits were then sucking at her chin when she made that protestation to Master Throckmorton and him; and that when she wiped them off with her hand, her chin bled, which sometimes it had done before after their sucking, but not often, and never so much as then—nay, scarcely the quantity of one drop at any time before.

And this by the way, as a general note throughout the book: where there is one of these strange things set down (if they be so accounted as strange) there are ten omitted which may as well be put in and, in the judgment of them that hear of them, are no less strange than these. And for that which this book doth contain, it is set down upon the sudden[18] and as it cometh to present memory, at the request of divers right worshipful, and especially for the motion sake of the right worshipful Master Justice Fenner, one of the patrons hereof.

[18] This is the conventional disclaimer of a well-born author, and appears to be contradicted by the careful dating and the several references to notes taken at the time of certain incidents (see note 2).

And for the truth of the most of these things herein contained: they were given in evidence, and ready to be given against the parties accused if either need should have required or time served, upon the oath of divers gentlemen on the Assizes day at Huntingdon, before the said parties. And for the rest which were not then alleged, if any shall make doubt thereof, there are divers gentlemen of honest report ready to confirm the same upon their oaths, if need should so require, that were present, some at one time, and some at another, at all these several tragedies (as they may be termed).

At another time soon after, the spirits told the children (then being in their fits, the old woman also standing by them) that if their father, Master Throckmorton would then presently go to John Samuel's house, his daughter Agnes Samuel, who then dwelt at home with her father and is not yet brought into question about any of these matters, would hide herself and not be seen of him. Master Throckmorton, hearing them, said that he would go presently and make trial thereof. When he came to the house Agnes Samuel, whether perceiving Master Throckmorton or any of his company, or whatsoever else it was it is not known—but she went up into the chamber (there being but one in the house) the stairs whereof stood in the same parlour below where her father was, and the door thereof was a trap-door, whereupon she set sacks of corn and tubs with some such like things to keep it down.

Master Throckmorton hearing a noise in the house thought there was some such matter in hand, and continued still knocking at the door. Presently John Samuel asked who was there and what he would, with some such like questions, and in the end, knowing what he was, said he should not come in.

Then Master Throckmorton went on the other side of the house and, finding the back door open, went in; and when he came into the parlour where the man was in his bed, being about eight of the clock or something before, he asked for Agnes Samuel his daughter, and where she was. John Samuel had not his oath to seek, but presently swore as God judge his soul (which was his common oath, and used also divers times before the Bench at his arraignment, yea, and until the very time of his execution) that he knew not where she was.

Master Throckmorton asked when he saw her. He answered 'that since the evening she was in the house, but where now she is, he could not tell'. He asked if she was not in the chamber over them; he swore he could not tell, which thing he could not indeed but know, for it was a very low chamber, and she could not stir her foot in it but he must

needs hear her; besides her going up into it, for the stairs stood hard
at his bed's feet, and the noise also she made in the hearing of Master
Throckmorton and the rest coming into the house.

Master Throckmorton verily suspecting that she was there, called
to her three or four times, and willed her to answer if she were there,
for it was all that he desired, to know where she was; but she would
not answer. Then Master Throckmorton took the candle and said he
would go up and see, but when he came to the top of the stairs the
trap door was so fast that he could not stir it; which he perceiving, said
that surely he would break open the door or break up the plancher* of
the chamber, for he would go into it before he went out of the house,
and willed one of the company to fetch him a bar of iron or some such
like thing, for he would do it indeed.

The maid hearing Master Throckmorton thus resolute, answered
that she was there; then Master Throckmorton willed her to come
down, which she did, removing those things that before she had set
upon the door. So he departed home to his house, challenging the
man for his naughty lie, which yet he stiffly stood in.

But to let an hundred of these things pass with their fellows, and to
come nearer the old woman's confession and the manner of it: you
shall understand that Mother Samuel grew now to be marvellous weary
of Master Throckmorton's house, both because she could do nothing
in the house but the children in their fits would reveal it, and especially
because the children in their fits likewise had told her twenty times to
her face that she should confess this matter before the Tuesday after
Twelfth day,[19] and that the spirits had told them that they would
enforce her to confess it in despite of her, and she had often experienced
that whatsoever the spirits foretold proved most true.

Now this Tuesday which the children so often named was not then
thought upon of any that heard it to be the Sessions[20] day at Huntingdon, as it is generally in most places of England—no, not within a
week or more after the children had spoken of it. Yet were they often
whispering with themselves (always in their fits, as you must understand it) about that Tuesday, wishing oftentimes that it were once
come, for that was some happy day, they would say, belike for them,
for after that day the spirits had told them they should never have
more fits. So that all their joy in their fits was for that day, yet they
would say to themselves that the spirits doth tell them that it may

[19] Twelfth Day: Epiphany or January 6.
[20] Quarter Sessions, presided over by local Justices of the Peace.

happily be before that Tuesday, but on the Tuesday at the farthest she must confess it and they must be well; but if she would confess it before, they should be well presently whensoever she did confess it.

For this cause the children in their fits continually would exhort her to confess it that they might be well, which yet she always would deny to do, saying that she would not confess that which she never did know of, nor consented unto. The children would answer that they would not wish her to accuse herself for anything, and therefore willed her to look to that in any respect; yet they said that they enforced no more upon her than what the spirits had told them.

Yet to speak the truth of these children and no more, if anything herein written of them be strange, this for strangeness goeth beyond all other, and for truth equal to the rest: such were the heavenly and divine speeches of these children in their fits to this old woman, some at one time, some at another, concerning her confession of this fact, as that if a man had heard it he would not have thought himself better edified at ten sermons.

The matter of their speech was this: concerning chiefly the joys of heaven which she should lose and the torments of hell which she should endure if she being guilty would not yet confess, and the eschewing of the one and enjoying of the other if she would confess and be sorry for that she had done. They rehearsed likewise unto her her naughty manner of living, her usual cursing and banning of all that displeased her, and especially of their parents and of them (which she could not deny), her negligent coming to church and slackness in God's service; all which she confessed to them 'but she would now begin to amend', she said.

Her lewd bringing up of her daughter, in suffering her to be her dame, both in controlling of her and beating of her, which before had been proved to her face, and she herself had also confessed. They remembered also unto her that which they had heard some speak of when they were out of their fits—namely, that she had said that their fits were but wantonness in them; they asked her now whether she was still of that mind or not? She answered 'No'—with many such like speeches, and in the end concluded with their hearty prayer to God for her, saying that they would forgive her from the bottom of their heart if she would confess it that they might be well—besides that, that they would entreat their parents and their friends, so much as in them lay, clearly to forgive and forget all that was past.

Their manner of behaviour in this their exhortation to her was that, as for the most part they began with tears, so they continued, and always ended with tears; insomuch that there was not any that heard them could abstain from weeping; only the old woman was little or nothing moved.

This kind of behaviour in the children passed on until nearer Christmas, yet without any touch or stirring of the old woman. In the mean season every day almost this old woman had a fit of bleeding at the nose, and bled very much at a time, which is not usual in old age; so that now she waxed faint and looked very pale, insomuch that Master Throckmorton and his wife were very careful for her, fearing some harm should come unto her in his house, and comforted her by all the means they could, not suffering her to want anything that she desired if possibly they could come by it. So that she did confess to all that came to her that she was marvellous well used of Master Throckmorton, and thought herself greatly bound to him—as truly she had no other cause.

For as for her business, she did nothing but her own work, and for her diet she sat at his own board, or with his children if they were in their fits and could not sit down; and for her lodging she lay continually in his own chamber, and for the most part with one of his children.

And to tell you one thing more of her before her confession, one of these children, Mistress Elizabeth Throckmorton, was one day not well at ease and could not eat any meat; yet when night came and supper was ready she thought to make herself amends. But when she was ready to sit at the table, she fell presently into her fit, and yet that was not all the punishment she had, but her mouth was locked up that she could neither eat, drink, nor speak (as it was an usual thing with them all to have their mouths shut up, especially at mealtimes, and other whiles shut and open half a dozen times in a dinner, so would the spirits sport with them).

But she went so to bed, very sorrowful and weeping—what her grief was, none can tell because she was not able to utter it. When the next day came, she was sick and ill as the day before, yet out of her fit and ate very little or nothing at all; when night came, she said she felt herself well amended and very hungry, not knowing for her part but that she had eaten her supper the night before.

Then was she counselled by them that feared the worst to eat something, but she said she would not, purposing to eat her part at supper. When the time came and meat was set upon the board, she fell into the same case as she had been in the night before; which Master Throckmorton perceiving, he said to the old woman that stood by her, 'I think, Mother Samuel, you are disposed to pine* that wench.' She made him answer 'no, she was rather sorry to see it.' 'Well,' said he, 'surely you shall neither eat nor drink until she can do both, and therefore', said Master Throckmorton, 'whilst she fasteth, you shall fast, and when she can eat, you shall eat—but not before, use the matter as you will.' And thus they continued both fasting until supper was almost ended, and the company ready to arise; the one fasting upon necessity, because she could not eat, and the other for Master Throckmorton's pleasure, because she might not.

The old woman perceiving that Master Throckmorton was in good earnest with her, and that the meat was carried out of the parlour—on the sudden, upon what motion God He knoweth, the child fetched a great sigh (for she had been weeping all supper-time) and spake, saying, 'If I had some meat now I could eat it.'

Mistress Throckmorton, the child's mother, hearing her speak (as did also all the rest that were in the parlour) commanded presently that meat should be given to them both, the company not giving notice to Mother Samuel of the matter; so they both fell to their meat very heartily, but especially the old woman who, as it should seem, was then very hungry, as she had always a good stomach.

And from that time forwards, during the old woman's continuing in the house, neither that child nor any of her sisters had their mouths shut up at any time when they should eat their meat or, if they were, they did not long continue so; although it was a common custom with them before time to have gone supperless to bed upon that very occasion many a time.

After all these matters were passed over, and as it waxed nearer and nearer to the time appointed, Mother Samuel every day complained of a new grief to befall her. Sometimes she would cry out of her back, that it was so full of pain that she was not able to stir herself in her bed all the day long, nor take any rest at night, sometimes she would in like sort cry out of her head, otherwhiles of her stomach; yet she would eat her meat, saying that she had a gnawing at her heart, and the next day after it would be in her knee or lower, so that she would go halting up and down the house.

And to speak the truth of her, it should seem that something there was that troubled her, whatsoever it was, for she would so grieve and moan herself in the night-time, one while complaining of this part of her body, another while of that, that indeed she rested but little in the night-time herself, and greatly disquieted those also that lay in the chamber by her.

And one night amongst all the rest, she cried out very pitifully of her belly, insomuch that she disturbed and awakened both Master Throckmorton and his wife that lay by her. Saith Master Throckmorton, 'In God's name, Mother Samuel, what aileth you and why do you groan so?' Said she, 'I have a marvellous great pain in my belly on the sudden, and I know not how it should be caused.' 'Why,' said he, 'what is the matter in your belly?' She answered that there was something in it which, as she thought, stirred, and it was as big as a penny loaf, and put her to marvellous pain.

Whereupon Mistress Throckmorton arose out of her bed, and went and felt upon her belly, and there was indeed a marvellous swelling to the quantity before likened, but she felt it not stir, not staying long with her, the weather was so cold. And (be it spoken without offence to women) it may be that she bred then that child wherewithal she said she was when she was asked what she could say by my Lord the Judge, why sentence of death should not be given against her, as hereafter you shall hear.

But whatsoever it was, she cried out to Master Throckmorton of her belly and said she was full of pain; and further she said that she had often told him that she thought there was some evil spirits haunted his house which did thus torment his children, which thing he told her that he did easily believe was true—'and now,' saith she, 'I verily believe that one of them is gotten into my belly.' Master Throckmorton said that all this might very well be true.

So she said that it was an evil house, and haunted with spirits, and wished that she had never come into it; he told her that if there were any evil spirits haunted the house, they were of her sending, and so he would grant all that she said. In the end she passed away that night with groaning and moaning, and the next morning she was very ill at ease, she said, but her swelling in her belly was gone; and where her greatest pain was she could not tell, it was in so many places, but her stomach was the best of any part. And after this she continually complained of one part of her body or other so long as she stayed in the house.

Within a very short time after, one of the children fell into a most terrible fit, Mother Samuel standing by, and it was so grievous upon her for the time as that neither she nor any of her sisters had the like for the space of a year or two before, and especially her sneezing fit was so terrible and strong upon her as if it would have caused her eyes to start out of her head. This fit did greatly quail* Mother Samuel, for she herself did then think that she should have seen the child dead at that present, and this wrung out of Mother [Samuel] prayers, so that she desired the Lord then to help her and to preserve her in that danger and she hoped never to see her in the like again.

But the more earnest Mother Samuel was in her prayers, the greater was the child's trouble and torment, and the oftener she named GOD or Jesus Christ, the stronger the child's fit was upon her. And at that very instant (as hereafter you shall hear of the rest) when she had thus continued some two hours or more, the spirit spake unto the child and said that there was a worse fit than this to come yet, wherein she must be worse handled than thus. The child answered that she cared neither for him nor his dame, but willed them to do their worst they could to her for, she said, she hoped God would deliver her; and soon after she came out of her fit and was very well. But the sight of this fit was so terrible to Mother Samuel as she would many times pray that she might never see the like again in any of them.

The children continued still all of them calling upon Mother Samuel to make confession of this matter, saying that she must do it before it be long, and as good at first as at last, but if she would now do it, that they might be well before Christmas, they would then think themselves beholding to her. They told her further that now Christmas was at hand, and if she would now confess it, they should be presently well and keep (by the grace of God) a merry Christmas.

She answered that she would do for them all the good she could but, for confession of this matter, she would not, for it was a thing she never knew of nor consented unto. Their father Master Throckmorton, hearing his children and the old woman thus talk together, stepped in and said, 'Mother Samuel, you hear what these children say, which is that if you would confess this fact, they should be presently well; and they say that you must confess it before it be long, and you know that they have not used to tell lies in their fits. Now therefore, in the name of God, if there be any such matter, confess it; it is never too late to repent and to ask for mercy.' But she made to him the like answer that she had done to the children before.

Then said he, 'But what say you to that grievous fit which the spirit of late threatened to my daughter Jane? I would fain know when that should be.' 'Oh,' saith she (remembering the terror of it), 'I trust in God I shall never see her in such a case again, nor any of them all.'

'Yes,' saith Master Throckmorton, 'I verily think she shall have it, and that shortly, for the spirit, you know, useth not to fail them in anything he promiseth.' 'Oh,' saith she, 'I trust in God she shall never have it'—speaking marvellous confidently. 'Why,' saith Master Throckmorton, 'charge the spirit in the name of God that she may escape this fit which is threatened.'

She presently said, 'I charge thee, spirit, in the name of God, that Mistress Jane never have this fit.' The child sitting by said, 'Truly, "the thing" saith (I thank God) that I shall never have this fit that he hath foretold me of.' Saith Master Throckmorton, 'Why, that is well, thanks be to God; go on, Mother Samuel, and charge the spirit in the name of God, and speak from your heart, that neither she nor any of them all have their fits any more.'

So she said as Master Throckmorton willed her, speaking marvellous heartily. The same child again said, 'Truly, "the thing" saith (I thank God) that I shall never have it more after the Tuesday after Twelfth day.' Saith Master Throckmorton, 'It is well, thanks be to God; charge the spirit again in the name of God—and speak from your heart and be not afraid—that he depart from them all now at this present and that he never return to them again'; which words she uttered very loud and very boldly.

So soon as she had ended, then those three children that were then in their fits, and had so continued for the space of three weeks, wiped their eyes, and at that instant thrust back the stools whereon they sat, and stood upon their legs, being as well as ever they were in their lives.

Master Throckmorton had his face now towards the children and his back to the old woman, and seeing them so to start up suddenly said, 'Thanks be to God!' While he was thus speaking (little knowing or thinking indeed of any such matter) the old woman fell down behind him on her knees and said, 'Good master, forgive me!' He turned him about and, seeing her down said, 'Why Mother Samuel, what is the matter?'

'Oh sir,' said she, 'I have been the cause of all this trouble to your children.' 'Have you, Mother Samuel?' said he, 'and why so? What cause did I ever give you thus to use me and my children?' 'None at all,' said she. Then said Master Throckmorton, 'You have done me the more wrong.' 'Good master,' said she, 'forgive me.' 'God forgive you,' said he, 'and I do. But tell me, how came you to be such a kind of woman?' 'Master,' said she, 'I have forsaken my maker and given my soul to the Devil' (these were her very words).

And old Mistress Throckmorton their grandmother and Mistress Throckmorton their mother being now in the hall (for this was done in the parlour), hearing them very loud, not understanding the matter perfectly, came into the parlour; of whom, when Mother Samuel saw her, she asked likewise forgiveness. Mistress Throckmorton their mother presently without any questions forgave her with all her heart, yet she could not well tell what the matter was. Mother Samuel asked those three children that were there forgiveness, and afterwards the rest, kissing all of them; the children easily forgave her, for they knew not that she had offended any of them in their own persons, except what they saw in their sisters, when they themselves were out of their fits.

Master Throckmorton and his wife, perceiving the old woman thus penitent and so greatly cast down (for she did nothing but weep and lament all this time) comforted her by all the good means they could, and said that they would freely forgive her from their hearts, so be it their children might never be more troubled. She answered that she trusted in God they should never have their fits again, yet would she not be comforted for anything that they could say.

Then Master Throckmorton did send for Master Doctor Dorington, the minister of that town, and told him all the matter with the circumstances, desiring him to comfort her, which they all joining together did so well as they could at that present; yet could she not forbear weeping, and so continued all the night. The next day, which was the Sabbath day and Christmas Even, Master Doctor Dorington chose his text of repentance out of the Psalmist[21] on set purpose to comfort her, and there declared in the open assembly all the matter of Mother Samuel's late confession, applying his speech directly to the comforting of a penitent heart, and so by consequence of her.

All this sermon time, Mother Samuel did nothing but weep and lament, and many times was so very loud with sundry passions that she caused all the church to look on her. And thus much farther you shall know for this point: Master Throckmorton, the same day after prayers were ended, very wisely remembering himself and the old woman's unconstancy heretofore, called to mind that there was none present at her confession but himself and Master Doctor, with his own household, who might be all thought partial in this matter [and] willed therefore Mother Samuel to come into the body of the church and there demanded of her before his neighbours whether that confession

[21] Original has 'Psal.' which could be 'Psalms' or 'Psalmist'.

which she over night had made to him and Master Doctor was wrested and wrung out of her, or whether it proceeded frankly and freely of and from herself. She answered before them all that it came of herself, and desired all her neighbours to pray to God for her and to forgive her.

Towards night, Master Doctor Dorington understanding the old woman still to continue in this heavy case, came to Master Throckmorton's house (who is his brother-in-law by marriage) and entreated him upon simplicity of good will, tendering the old woman's comfort, to give her leave to go home to her husband, and he would be a means that her husband should receive her, and to reconcile them together; wherein the old woman was marvellous dutiful. To this motion Master Throckmorton did easily grant at the first, being as willing to comfort the old woman as any, and indeed used the means himself also that her husband might receive her, little suspecting that anything should fall out thereby otherwise than well. The man, when he understood of it, spake bluntly as his manner was, saying that she might come home if she would.

Now that you have heard this old woman's confession, it may haply seem strange in some points to some, but for the truth of it, it is as certainly true as is any part of this book, both the matter and the manner and the words also observed in all points, so near as possibly could be remembered. Mother Samuel is now upon Christmas Even at night gone home to her husband and her daughter, where we doubt she hath a cold welcome for her entertainment, and the rather because she hath confessed this matter; for it should seem that they both set upon her (as she herself after confessed) and so far forth prevailed with her as that the next morning, which was Christmas Day, she denied all that she had said before, and it was no such matter with her.

Before night it came to Master Throckmorton's hearing that this new convert had revolted again, and had denied all that she had spoken to him; the best comfort he had therein was the open confession she made in the church, and thereupon did hardly believe that which was reported of her.

The same day in the evening, Master Doctor Dorington and Master Throckmorton went to her house to know the truth; and when they came at the door, it pleased God that John Samuel, his wife and his daughter were talking of this matter (for it should seem that it was all their talk), which they understanding, stayed awhile and heard the daughter say these words, 'Believe them not, believe them not for all their fair speeches.' Hereupon they went both presently into the house and charged the daughter with these words, which she utterly denied, as did also the father and the mother.

Then did Master Throckmorton demand of her concerning the matter which before she had confessed in his house and in the church, telling her that he had heard that she had denied it again. She answered that she would deny that she was a witch, or any cause of the troubling of his children. 'Why,' said he, 'did not you confess so much unto me?' 'I said so,' saith she, 'indeed, but it is nothing so.' 'Why then,' said he, 'I must not show you that favour which I promised; I will surely have you before the Justices; but,' said he, 'why did you confess it to be so to me if it be not so?' She answered, 'For joy.'

'For joy,' said he (smiling to himself, marvelling what she could make of it), 'and why for joy?' 'Because,' said she, 'I did see your children so presently well after your good prayers and mine.' Then said Master Throckmorton unto her, 'I pray God so continue them; notwithstanding, howsoever it be I will not let pass this matter thus; for seeing it is published, either you or I will bear the shame of it in the end'. And so they departed for that night.

The next morning betimes, Master Throckmorton went to Master Doctor Dorington's house and told him that he would not suffer this matter thus to die in his hand, lest the worser sort of the people should imagine that this was but some device of theirs to bring the old woman into further danger. So they agreed to approve her once again in this matter, and sending for her to the church, they found her farther off from confessing anything that she had said or done than ever she was before.

Then Master Throckmorton took her by the hand and said that both she and her daughter should that day (by God's grace) go with him to my Lord the Bishop of Lincoln's. So he presently sent for the constables and charged them with the mother and daughter, and willed them to provide for the journey.

When the old woman perceived preparation for the journey, and the constables in readiness, Master Throckmorton also putting on of his boots, she came to him and said, 'Master, if you will go with me into the parlour, I will confess all to you alone.' Said he, 'I will go.' So they went together, and there she confessed the whole matter again unto him which before she had done. 'Why then,' said he, 'tell me why have you denied it all this time?' 'Oh,' said she, 'I would never have denied it but for my husband and my daughter, who said that I was a fool in confessing of it, and that it had been better for me to have died in the same estate I was in than to confess myself a witch; for now everybody will call me "old witch' whilst I live.'[22]

Master Throckmorton told her, if she would persist in confessing the truth, he would show her all the favour he could. In this meanwhile cometh in unto them Master Doctor Dorington, and he fell into questioning with her, but she seemed something coldly to confess that unto him which before she had done; so he drew her aside, and Master Throckmorton went from them. Then did Master Doctor Dorington call for pen, ink and paper, and wrote down that confession which she made.

In the meantime Master Throckmorton sent to the church which is adjoining to his house and, there being divers of his neighbours, for it was about prayers time, he desired them to come to him and, telling them the matter, placed them hard underneath the parlour window where Master Doctor and this old woman were talking together. Whereof, when notice was given to Master Doctor, he spake very loud, and willed the old woman to lift up her voice also, faining something, so that the neighbours which were without might easily hear all the words that passed between them.

When they had done, Master Throckmorton went unto them into the parlour, and desired them to come forth into the hall; when they came, there stood all the neighbours that had heard this matter. Then began Master Doctor to read in their presence that which the woman had confessed, but she would fain have denied all again. 'Nay,' said the neighbours to her, 'it is too late to deny anything now, for we heard all this with our ears'—telling to her the place where they were.

When she perceived herself thus catched in a trap, she would have made the best of it, but it would not prevail. As they were thus in the

---

[22] The fate of a convicted but unexecuted witch could be very hard indeed in a small town, tenacious of memory and unforgiving. Sir George Mackenzie speaks of one who stands for many:

'I went when I was a Justice-depute to examine some Women, who had confest judicially, and one of them, who was a silly creature, told me under secresie that she had not confest because she was guilty, but being a poor creature, who wrought for her meat, and being defam'd for a Witch, she knew she would starve, for no person thereafter would either give her meat or lodging, and that all men would beat her, and hound Dogs at her, therefore she desired to be out of the World; whereupon she wept bitterly, and upon her knees call'd God to witness what she said.' (*Laws and customes of Scotland in matters criminal* (Edinburgh, 1678), p. 87.)

house together, came in John Samuel the old woman's husband, who had understood that there was something to do in the house concerning his wife. When he was come, Master Throckmorton told him that which his wife had again confessed, and with the rest he said that his wife would never have denied that which she did but for him and his daughter.

'Hast thou said so?' said he to his wife, giving her a foul term—and with that would have stricken her, had not others stood betwixt them. The old woman perceiving her husband thus fiercely coming towards her, fell down presently in a counterfeit swoon before them all. Mistress Throckmorton standing by, was on the sudden marvellously amazed thereat, and called for *aqua vitae** for her. When they took her up, they perceived her countenance nothing altered, but that she looked cheerful enough.

One of her neighbours standing by, peradventure better acquainted with her fashions than the rest, said, if they would let her alone, he would be their warrant that she would do well enough; so presently after, she came to herself again and all was well.

These circumstances about her confession are therefore the more expressly set down, although they be not so pertinent to the matter, neither indeed should have been declared at all, had it not been reported by some in the country (and those that thought themselves wise) that this Mother Samuel now in question was an old simple woman, and that one might make her by fair words confess what they would. But to leave that to the judgment of them that knew her well enough, Master Throckmorton continued on his journey, purposing to discharge himself of the matter, and caused the old woman with her daughter to be carried the same day to my Lord the Bishop of Lincoln; and there he examined her and her daughter.

The Examination of Alice Samuel of Warboys, in the county of Huntingdon, taken at Buckden before the right reverend Father in God, William, by God's permission Bishop of Lincoln, the 26 of December 1592.

Being asked whether a dun chicken did ever suck on her chin, and how often, the said examinate saith that it sucked twice and no more since Christmas Evens even last. Being asked whether it was a natural chicken, she saith it was not; she knoweth it was no natural chicken because when it came to her chin she did scarce feel it, but when she wiped it off with her hand, her chin did bleed. She saith further, that the said dun chicken did first come unto her and suck on her chin before it came to Master Throckmorton's house, and that the ill and the trouble that hath come to Master Throckmorton's children hath come by means of the said dun chicken; the which chicken she knoweth is now both gone from them and from her. And further she saith, that Master Throckmorton and Master Doctor Dorington shall bring further information of such things as yet she hath not declared.

The Examination of Alice Samuel of Warboys in the County of Huntingdon, taken at Buckden the 29 day of December 1592, before the reverend Father in God, William, by God's permission Bishop of Lincoln, Francis Cromwell, and Richard Tryce, esquires, Justices of Her Majesty's peace within the county aforesaid.

She saith, she never did hurt to any, saving to the children in question. Being demanded how she knoweth the said dun chicken is gone from the said children, she saith, because the said dun chicken with the rest are now come into her, and are now in the bottom of her belly, and make her so full that she is like to burst. And this morning they caused her to be so full that she could scant lace her coat; and that on the way as she came, they weighed so heavy that the horse she rid on did fall down and was not able to carry her.

And further she saith, that the upright man* of whom she hath confessed to Master Throckmorton told her that Master Throckmorton was a hard man and would trouble her much, wherefore he would give her six spirits that should vex and torment his children, and so he did. Which spirits had reward of her by sucking of her blood oftentimes when they were without her body, and that the said spirits did suck of her blood before she sent them forth any whither.

She saith further, that whatsoever the children of Master Throckmorton did speak in their fits proved true, and was true; as for example, whensoever the said children said they did see the said spirits, then were the spirits there, and she did also see them. And she saith that oftentimes she did give a privy beck or nod with her finger or head, and then the spirits did presently stop the children's mouth that they could not speak until they came out again; and then would the children wipe their eyes and be well again.

Further she saith that it was taught her of a man that did come unto her house (but where he did dwell, or what his name was, she cannot tell) who told her that if she would call the said six[23] spirits they would

[23] Joan mentioned 9; Mother Samuel in her final confession could remember only 3.

come, and she called them and they appeared in the likeness of dun chickens; their names were as followeth: first, Pluck; second, Catch; the third White, and the other three she called with her mouth with three smacks. And two of them she (this examinate) sent to Master Robert Throckmorton of Warboys and his wife, and they returned again and told her that God would not suffer them to prevail.

Whereupon she (this examinate) sent the said spirits to the children of the said Master Throckmorton, by means whereof they have been so strangely tormented as to the neighbours and country hath been seen. She said further, that what they children did speak in their fits in her hearing, that it was true, and so it fell out.

Being asked further what the upright man's name was that gave her the devils, she said she could not tell; whereupon she was moved to go into another chamber and demand of her spirits what his name was, which she presently did; and there with a loud voice said these words as followeth: 'Oh thou devil, I charge thee in the name of the Father, the Son and the Holy Ghost that thou tell me the name of the upright man which gave me the devils'; which thing she did three times and then returned saying that her spirits had told her that his name was Langland. And being demanded where the said Langland dwelled, she said she could not tell.

Then was she moved to go into the said chamber again and demand of her spirits where the said Langland dwelt; which also she presently did, and there with a loud voice three times said: 'O devil, I charge thee in the name of the Father, the Son and the Holy Ghost, tell me where the said Langland dwelleth.' Then she returned and said that he had no dwelling. Then was she further moved to go again and demand where the said Langland was at that present, which also she did, and demanded as before, and returned with this answer 'That her spirits told her that he went the last voyage beyond the seas.' After these confessions thus made, Mother Samuel and her daughter were committed to the gaol of Huntingdon.

Now that we have brought Mother Samuel to the gaol, we will let her there rest in God's peace and the Queen's until the next general assizes day holden at Huntingdon; and although many things fell out unhappily concerning her during her continuance in the gaol, whereof she was greatly suspected, as the death of one of the gaoler's servants whom she threatened, the extreme sickness of one of his children, with his present amending after the scratching of her, and divers other things which are shrewd pieces of evidence against her, if there had been nothing else laid to her charge—yet, because they do not concern the trouble of these children, neither is a matter so perfectly known to the authors of this book, it is therefore but touched by the way.

And to come unto the daughter Agnes Samuel, who now cometh upon the stage with her part in this tragedy, you shall understand that she was left with her mother in the gaol until the sessions day held at Huntingdon the ninth of January following, which day was the Tuesday that the children so often had spoken of to the old woman.

At dinner time Master Throckmorton made his request to the high Sheriff and the Justices to bail this maid, and to have her home to his house to see if it might please God whether any such evidences of guiltiness would appear against her as had before appeared in the children against the mother. This suit was not easily granted, for it was a demur amongst the Justices whether the maid was bailable by law in this case or no. In the end Master Throckmorton continuing his suit, they being resolved of the doubt granted it, but it was almost three of the clock in the afternoon before, as everybody can witness that were then present; which time is therefore here mentioned because it hath relation to the next point that hereafter followeth, as you shall hear.

The report of Master Doctor Dorington of that which happened at Warboys on Tuesday, which was the Sessions day at Huntingdon, the ninth of January. [*1593*]

About twelve of the clock, a little before dinner, Mary, Joan, and Grace, the daughters of Robert Throckmorton of Warboys aforesaid, esquire, fell into their accustomed fits of lameness, blindness, deafness and want of feeling; only their youngest brother Robert, of the age of nine years, might speak unto Jane with her understanding, and she only might speak in the like manner to Mary and Grace. . . .

Mary and Jane, whispering secretly one in the other's ear, spake thus much in our hearing oftentimes: 'I marvel how she should know that thing; I am sure none of this house told her, and therefore it cannot be but that the spirits told her'. . . .

[The children foretell the coming of Agnes Samuel and forecast their behaviour in their fits when she arrives.]

. . . After Agnes Samuel was brought to Master Throckmorton's house the children continued for three or four days without any fits at all, so that their parents were put in great comfort that their children should then have been clean delivered from their torments; but it should seem that the matter was not yet brought to an end, for the children fell all of them afresh into their fits again, and were as grievously afflicted as ever they were in the old woman's time. And then the spirits did begin as plainly to accuse the daughter as ever they did the mother and do tell the children that the old woman hath set* over her spirits to her daughter, and that she hath bewitched them all over again, and that she will deal worse with them than ever her mother did . . .[24]

[Joan, the eldest child, comes home from Titchmarsh Grove where she had been staying, and immediately makes herself the centre of attention. She talks 'very familiarly' with the spirit, which announces that she will have worse fits than any of her sisters, and soon invents an amazing low-comedy team of spirits who quarrel and beat each other like Mr. Punch and his friends.]

. . . The next day which was Saturday the tenth of February . . . she fell suddenly into bleeding at the nose and bled very much, whereat she marvelled (for she did perceive it) saying, 'I pray God send me good news after this, for it is strange with me to bleed—I bled not so much this seven years before.' When she had much bloodied her handkerchief she said that it was a good deed to throw the handkerchief into the fire and burn the witch, for she knew, she said, that this bleeding came of no good cause.

After she had talked thus to herself a little, it should seem the spirit came to her, for she said thus, smiling to herself and casting her eyes about her, 'What is this in God's name that cometh thus tumbling to me? It tumbleth like a football; I think it be some puppet-player, it is much like his dame's old thrummed cap. What is your name, I pray you?' said she. 'The thing' answered, as it should seem, that his name was Blue; for presently upon the question demanded of his name, she made answer again herself, saying, 'Master Blue, you are welcome; I never saw you before—I thought' said she, 'that my nose bled not for nothing. What news have you brought?'

It told her as before. 'What, dost thou say' saith she, 'that I shall be worse handled than ever I was? Ha,' saith she, 'what doest thou say?' (for she would ever repeat the spirit's words after him, as they all would do when they were talking with them, bending their heads to the ground)—'that I shall now have my fits when I shall both hear, see and know everybody? That is a new trick indeed! I think never any of my sisters were so used! But I care not for you,' said she, 'do your

[24] H3v.

worst; and when you have done you will make an end.' These were her very words.[25]

. . . when night came and supper was ended, she first fell into her sensible fit and after that was ended, she fell into her senseless fit. Anon, fetching a great sigh, she said, 'Who sent for you, Master Smack?' He made answer that he was come according to his promise which he made unto her on Sunday at night. 'Belike' said she, 'you will keep promise, but I had rather you would keep you away and come when I send for you; but what news have you brought?' 'I told you' said he, 'that I had been a-fighting the last Sunday night, but I have had many battles since.' 'Yea, so it seemeth,' saith she, 'for here was both Pluck, Catch and Blue, and they all came maimed unto me.' 'Yea,' said he, 'I have met with them all.' 'But I marvel' said she, 'that you could beat them; they are very great and you are but a little one.' Said he, 'I am good enough for two of the best of them together.'

'But' said she, 'I can tell you news.' 'What is that?' said he. 'They will all at one time fall upon you and beat you.' He said he cared not for that, he would beat two of the best of them. 'And who shall beat the other two?' said she, 'for there is one that hath been many times spoken of, and he carrieth the name of Hardname; for his name standeth upon eight letters, and every letter standeth for a word, but what his name is we know not; only Hardname.'

The spirit answered that his cousin Smacks would help him to beat the other two. (There are also two other Smacks as you may read in the old woman's confession.) 'What!' said she, 'Shall your cousins Smacks help you? What, is there kindred amongst devils? I never heard of that thing before, that the devils were cousins—God keep me from that kindred!' Such like foolish talk they had together at that time . . . [26]

[One of the children evolved a formula (told by the spirit, of course) which would bring them out of their fits. This was used to convince company; Joan's spirit once advanced the time of a promised fit because 'strangers were come, and now she must have her fit to prove Agnes Samuel a witch!'[27]]

. . . So the child's father called for Agnes Samuel and willed her to say to the child [Elizabeth] these words, 'I charge thee, devil, in the name of the God of heaven and earth, as I hate thee and am no witch, nor guilty of this matter, that thou depart from this child and suffer her to come forth of her fit.' This said by the maid, the child moved

[25] H4^v.   [26] I-3^v.   [27] K.

not. Then the child's father willed her to say thus, 'I charge thee, thou devil, as I love thee and have authority over thee, and am a witch and guilty of this matter, that thou suffer this child to be well at this present.' These words were no sooner ended but the child wiped her eyes and was as well as any in the parlour. . . .[28] [This formula was later amended by Joan to 'As I am a witch and consenting to the death of the Lady Cromwell, so I charge thee to depart and to let her come forth of her fit,'[29] with the same success; later she added the bewitching of Mistress Pickering of Ellington 'most grievously tormented with pain and breaking out in her legs,'[30] of her sisters, and of herself 'to death' and lameness.[31]

Joan suffered a good deal of physical pain, particularly in the legs and head; her 'fits' were often convulsive, but she had also a trance-like variety when it seemed that she had ceased to breathe, and it was noticed that this held her 'always the longer when any of her friends or other company stood by and comforted her'.[32] Despite this, the girls were apparently even more convincing than they had been earlier, even to Agnes Samuel. 'And being asked of the matter, what she thought of it and whether it was wantonness or not, as she had often-times said before she came to the house, as well as her mother had done; but now she could not deny but that it was some supernatural work in the patient.'[33]

On February 23, Joan's spirit announced that she should be free of fits for a week (except when there were visitors) if she got up early the next morning; but he also told her that she should shortly have a very 'sick week'. Towards the end of the 'free week' Mary, apparently the most lightly afflicted, fell into a fit of shuddering, and then an insensible fit, at the end of which she said to the spirit, 'Is it true? do you say this is the day wherein I must scratch the young witch?' Her uncles Edward and Henry Pickering decided to bring Agnes to the child 'to see what would be the issue of it, knowing very well that the maid was able to keep herself from scratching if three such as the child was should set upon her at once'.][34]

. . . So soon as the maid came into the chamber where the child was, the child said, 'Art thou come, thou young witch, who hast done all this mischief?' The maid seemed to stand amazed at those words, for she was not accustomed to hear any such hard speeches from the child.

[28] I–2.   [29] I–4[v].   [30] L4.
[31] L4[v]–M[v].   [32] L3.   [33] I–2[v].
[34] K2.

So one in the company willed the maid to take up the child and carry her down (for her legs were taken from her).

Mistress Mary suffered herself very quietly to be taken up in her arms and clasped her hands about her neck; but even as the maid began to lift her up she fell on scratching of her so eagerly and so fiercely as that it was a wonder to all that saw it, saying, 'I will scratch you, you young witch, and pay you home for this punishing of me and my sisters! "The thing" telleth me that I had been well and never should have had my fits any more but for you!'

The maid stood still holding down her head (for the child kneeled upon her knees) and cried very pitifully, yet either would not or could not once pluck away her head. 'Nay,' said the child, 'I know you cry, but the spirit said that I should not hear you, because I should not pity you, and he it is that holdeth you now that you cannot get away from me.' So the child scratched her face until the skin came off the breadth of a shilling, but there came no blood at all, but water. In the end the maid brought her down into the parlour, where the child sitting awhile in her stool seemed to be wonderful sorry for that she had done and said, 'I would not have scratched Nan Samuel, but "the thing" told me that I should do it, and forced me thereunto, stretching forth mine arms and straining my fingers whether I would or not, and made me to scratch her.' And truly they that saw the manner of it and knew the mild disposition of the child might easily see that she was overruled in the action; for she was carried with such vehemency and cruelty for the time against the maid as that it appeared to be altogether besides her nature.[35]

[Next day, March 2, Mary was told by the spirit that she would have no more fits because she had scratched Agnes, and so it proved; she was the only child to be so cured, though all the others scratched Agnes.[36] Joan, even more jealous of her sisters than they of her, promptly took up the challenge, and on the same day (the text erroneously says February 2) she foretold her 'sick week' to begin on Monday March 5.

[35] K2–K2v.

[36] On March 21 even Grace the youngest, who had suffered only from silent fits 'groaning and weeping most lamentable to see' fell on Agnes 'but such was the child's short nails and want of strength that she could not once ripple the skin of the back of her hands' (L4v).

These scratching incidents are curious because they do not cure anyone but Mary, yet they seem to cause both genuine excitement and genuine distress to the children. It is almost as though they were punishing themselves in this other disobedient and uncontrollable daughter.

This was duly carried out, and she had violent pains in head, stomach and legs, as well as two kinds of fits—a screeching and twitching that went on for hours, and a breath-holding trance. The most violent manifestations occurred on Saturday March 10.

Predictably, Elizabeth was also very ill all week, and on Saturday March 10 surpassed herself with a horrible episode in which she flew at Agnes] . . . and scratched one of her hands most fiercely to see with both her hands, and saying that it was she that had bewitched her and all her sisters, and she had been well long since but for her—'Oh thou young witch, oh thou young witch, fie upon thee, fie upon thee— whoever heard of a young witch before?' And thus she cried with such vehemency of speech and eagerness of scratching as that both her breath and strength failed her . . . then she rubbed her hand upon the maid's hand that bled a little and wiped the blood upon her own hands, and this the child did oftentimes while she talked with her. Presently upon the scratching ended the child began to weep. . . .

When this weeping fit was something assuaged, she began to exhort her, lifting up her voice with such vehemency and desire for her amend-ment as that we may verily think the like was never heard to come forth of a child's mouth.[37]

[As she preached, she demanded the presence of John Samuel so that she might scratch him too; he arrived at that moment, but her courage failed before his grim looks and she contented herself with lecturing him for an hour and a half.]

. . . The man was so rude in his behaviour and so loud in his speeches that the child could not be heard for him. His answers to the child were, that she lied and so did all the company in saying he was a witch; and he said she had been taught her lessons well enough, and that she was above seven years old[38] (though indeed she was not twice seven),[39] with many such like speeches, and would not be silent nor suffer the child to speak for anything until he was almost forced unto it by the child's father. Although he might perceive very well, as also did all the company that the child could not hear him nor answer to any of his speeches, neither yet stayed her words at his talking in anything she intended to speak to him, although he greatly interrupted the same (if she could have heard him); but she neither heard him nor any other in the company, yet she saw him and his daughter and not any other.[40]

[37] K4–L.   [38] The age of reason, or understanding.
[39] The age at which a child could legally be a witness, or a criminal.
[40] L2.

[He was tested with the command to the spirit devised by Joan, and of course Elizabeth came out of her fit; he was allowed to go home for the time being.

Jane, who had started the whole business when she first called Mother Samuel a witch in her first strange illness, now took up the cue and on March 15 declared John Samuel a witch: ' "I did think . . he was as bad as the worst, he looked so ill favouredly!" '41 She said that her fit would last till he charged the spirit to depart, but he refused to come to the house, and her fit lasted till the day of the Assizes, when he pronounced the formula in court (under threat of being held guilty if he did not) and she was cured.

Jane's fits had from the beginning taken the attention-getting form of attempted suicide; she would fling away her knife in horror, or attempt to thrust her head into the fire.] . . . Yet this hath been observed continually in all these temptations, that she was never tempted to any of these dangers (that ever was known) being alone, but always when there were some company and assistance by to help her; which thing thus considered, whether it hath proceeded of the gracious providence and goodness of GOD, which cannot be denied but that it hath showed itself most strange and most wonderful both in the preservation of her, as also in the rest of her sisters in these their troublesome extremities—or whether it hath been some secret illusion and mockery of the Devil to deceive the standersby, it resteth doubtful and cannot be determined amongst men. But whether one or the other, or whatsoever, God deserveth the glory.42

[On the same fifteenth of March Jane scratched Agnes, clawing her hand till she was 'weary and windless'.43 Doctor Dorington, who seems to have overcome his objections to this exercise, was present, and improved the occasion with a sermon to the weeping Agnes.]

. . . Then Doctor Dorington began to instruct the maid and to exhort her with many good speeches, saying that God would surely not suffer her to be thus cried out upon by these wicked spirits, and afflicted in this sort by these innocent children contrary to their wills, if she were not consenting, or at the least concealing, and of some knowledge of these wicked practices which her mother had confessed. The maid very stiffly denied all that could be said, and desired God to show some present token upon her that they all might know that she was guilty of these matters.

Presently after these words her nose began to bleed and she bled

41 N2v.   42 M4v–N.   43 N2.

very much; which thing, whether it were a sign of God's sending at that time in token of her guiltiness or not, that He knoweth only, and man, I think, may without offence greatly suspect. Yet this she could say, being charged withal, that she had bled four times that day before, which thing was very true; bleeding very much every time, always saying that she had not bled so much to her remembrance in seven years before, wishing that this often bleeding would foreshow no evil towards her.[44]

[But it was indeed an ill omen for her. Assizes day was April 4; on Sunday March 25 Joan staged a marathon conversation with the spirit Smack, laying down all kinds of new conditions for her fits and charges for ending them.]

... Then Master Throckmorton, with others that were then in company, perceiving the spirit to be willing to declare so many things of the maid, willed her to charge the spirit in the name of God to answer her to certain questions which she should ask it, and not to lie; the maid gave that charge to the spirit [and] the spirit said to Mistress Joan, 'The young witch (for so he in all this talk and speech hath called her) chargeth me to tell the truth in certain questions which she shall ask me ...'[45]

['The spirit' also implicated the whole Samuel family in the death of Lady Cromwell, foretold the end of Joan's fits on Assizes day, listed Mother Samuel's nine spirits, and told of two neighbours who had been bewitched by John Samuel.

For at least six weeks Joan had been gloating over the prospect of scratching Agnes; this time Agnes was forced by the family to ask 'the spirit' where Joan should scratch her, and 'the spirit' relayed both question and answer to Joan, who spoke them aloud to the company she 'could not' hear!

On April 2, as predicted on March 19, Joan acted out this big moment]. ... Mistress Joan fell into her fit a little before supper, and so continued all supper time, not being able to stand on her legs. So soon as thanksgiving after supper was beginning to be said, she start up upon her feet and came to the table side, and stood with her sisters that were saying of grace; and presently when grace was ended she fell upon the maid Nan Samuel and took her head under her arms and first scratched the right side of her cheek and, when she had done that 'Now,' said she, 'I must scratch the left side for mine Aunt Pickering', and scratched that also until blood came forth of both sides very abundantly. The

[44] N2.   [45] M.

maid stood stone still and never once moved to go from her, yet cried very pitifully, desiring the Lord to be merciful unto her.

When she had done scratching, Mistress Joan set herself upon a stool and fared as though she had been out of breath, for she took her wind marvellous thick (yet the maid never struggled with her) and was able to hold never a joint of her but trembled as it had been a leaf; and [she] called for a pair of shears to pare her nails, but when she had them she was not able to hold them in her hands, so she desired somebody to do it for her.

Then Master Doctor Dorington's wife (who was her aunt) standing by her took the shears and pared her nails, but Mistress Joan herself saved the nails as her fingers were pared, and when she had done threw them into the fire and called for some water to wash her hands; which, after she had done, she threw the water also into the fire.

When this was done, this Mistress Joan fell upon her knees and willed the maid to come and kneel down by her and to pray with her. They said the Lord's prayer together and likewise the Creed, but it should seem that Mistress Joan could not hear the maid, for she would say amiss many times, and then the company would help her out; but Mistress Joan did not stay for her, so that she had ended her prayers before the maid had half done hers.

After this Master Doctor Dorington took a prayer book and read certain prayers which he thought good; and when he had done, then Mistress Joan fell to exhorting of the maid, and gave her many good exhortations. And as she was thus in speaking to her she fell into a marvellous weeping and sobbed so greatly that she could not well utter her words, saying that she would not have scratched her, but that she was forced unto it by the spirit.[46]

[Elizabeth then came up and repeated the whole series of actions.]

On Wednesday April 4, the day of the Assizes, Joan was taken to Huntingdon and lodged at the Crown Inn with Agnes. During the day 'five hundred men' at least visited to stare at her fits and to try experiments in bringing them on or alleviating them. In the evening Master Justice Fenner the Judge came 'with a great assembly of Justices and gentlemen' and proved to the satisfaction of all that the fits could only be ended by a charge from Agnes Samuel—a charge which was a confession: ' "As I am a witch and a worse witch than my mother, and did consent to the death of the Lady Cromwell, so I charge the devil to let Mistress Joan Throckmorton come out of her fit at this present." '[47]

[46] M3^v–M4.   [47] N4.

After other confessions of this nature 'presently the said Mistress Joan was well as ever she was in her life, and so hath continued without any grief or fits till this day.'[48]

Sister Jane had been cured even more spectacularly in court the same day, when John Samuel was finally forced on pain of immediate sentence of death to utter the charge she had demanded on March 16:

' "As I am a witch and did consent to the death of the Lady Cromwell, so I charge the devil to suffer Mistress Jane to come out of her fit at this present." Which words being no sooner spoken by the old witch but the said Mistress Jane, as her accustomed order was, wiped her eyes and came out of her fit, and then, seeing her father, kneeled down and asked him blessing; and made reverence to her uncles that stood near her (which before she took no show of knowledge) and wondering said, "O Lord, father, where am I?" '[49]]

... The next day, being Thursday in the morning, there were three several inditements made and delivered to the great inquest, whereof the one was against old Father Samuel, old Mother Samuel and Agnes their daughter for bewitching unto death the Lady Cromwell, late wife of Sir Henry Cromwell of Hinchingbrook in the county of Huntingdon, knight, contrary to God's laws and the statute made in the 15 year of the Queen's Majesty's reign that now is, etc.

The other two inditements were framed upon the said statute for bewitching Mistress Joan Throckmorton, Mistress Jane Throckmorton and others, contrary to the said statute.

The inditements being delivered to the grand jury, the evidence was given them privately by Master Dorington, doctor of divinity and parson of the town of Warboys aforesaid, by Gilbert Pickering of Titchmarsh in the county of Northampton, esquire, by Robert Throckmorton, esquire, father of the said children, by Robert Throckmorton of Brampton in the said county of Huntingdon, esquire, by John Pickering and Henry Pickering, gentlemen, and by Thomas Nut, master of art and vicar of Ellington. The grand jury made no great delay but found them all guilty.

And about eight of the clock, the evidence of the forenamed gentlemen was openly at large delivered in the court to the jury of life and death, and with great patience of the Judge, it was continued till one of the clock in the afternoon. So many of these proofs, presumptions, circumstances and reasons contained in this book was at large delivered as that time would afford, which was 5 hours without intermission or

[48] N4ᵛ.   [49] Oᵛ.

interruption, until both the Judge, Justices and jury said openly that the cause was most apparent; their consciences were well satisfied that the said witches were guilty and had deserved death. And therewithal the gentlemen ceased to give any further evidence . . .[50]

Then the confession of old Mother Samuel before specified, made the 26 day of December 1592 last past at Buckden before the reverend father in God William, Bishop of Lincoln, was openly read. So also was read the confession of the said Mother Samuel made at Buckden aforesaid the 29 day of December 1592, before the said reverend father in God William, Bishop of Lincoln, Frances Cromwell and Richard Tryce, esquires, Justices of her Majesty's peace within the county of Huntingdon, which also is before specified.

After these confessions read and delivered to the jury, it pleased God for the further proof and overthrow of these wicked persons to rear up more witnesses (at that time unexpected) who spake some things of their own knowledge and some of report. The first was Robert Poulter, vicar and curate of Brampton aforesaid, who said openly that one of his parishioners called John Langley, at that instant being very sick in his bed, had told him that one day he, being at Huntingdon at the sign of the Crown, did in the hearing of old Mother Samuel forbid Master Knowles of Brampton aforesaid to give her any meat, for that she was an old witch.

And thereupon in the afternoon as he went from Huntingdon to Brampton, having a good horse under him, he presently died in the field; and within two days after, by the providence of God he did escape death twice or thrice very dangerously. And though it pleased God not to suffer the Devil to have the mastery of his body at that time, yet presently after he lost as many good and sound cattle (to all men's judgments) as were worth twenty marks,* himself not long after in body extraordinarily handled. And the same night of the day of Assizes, as after it proved true, the same John Langley died.

Also the forenamed Master Robert Throckmorton of Brampton which before had given some evidence against the said witches in the children's behalf, now[51] spake for himself: that he likewise at Huntingdon and in other places having dealt very roughly in speeches with the said Mother Samuel, on Friday the tenth day following had one of his two-year-old beasts died; and on Sunday next after, another beast

---

[50] Nearly 2 pages (O–O^v) concerning Jane's cure in court on Wednesday April 4 are here inserted in the original, confusing the apparent sequence of events.

[51] Original has 'now he'.

of the same company and like age died also. The next week after on Friday he had a yearling calf died, and the next Sunday following he had another calf of the same company and like age died also. The next week after on Friday, he had an hog died, and the next Sunday after he had a sow having ten pigs sucking on her died also.

Whereupon advice was given him that whatsoever thing next died, to make a hole in the ground and burn the same. Likewise the fourth week on Friday he had a very fair cow worth four marks died, and his servants made a hole in the ground and buried the same cow in it, and threw faggots and fire on her and burnt her, and after that all his cattle did well. Of this last matter Mother Samuel being examined the night before her execution, she confessed the bewitching of the said cattle in manner and form as is declared.[52]

[Another piece of evidence from neighbours had been recounted by Joan in her fit on March 25, and probably figured in the evidence read by Robert Throckmorton.]

... The spirit told Mistress Joan that it was Chappel and his wife, which two parties were the old man's next neighbours and were at some variance and contention with him, and did greatly suspect themselves of such a matter; for they were both of them a little before that time marvellously troubled with bleach,* the woman not able to stir herself and the man was for a fit or two in the same case that these children were in. Yet said 'the thing', 'If Chappel will beat the old witch well he may peradventure never be more troubled with him.' 'The old witch,' said the spirit, 'would once have broken his neck by giving him a fall upon the causeway in the street as he met him, for he caused on the sudden both his pattens* to be broken, and if he had fallen on the stones as he fell in the mire, he had been maimed!'

This last point of Chappel's fall was not known to any in the house at that time, and Mistress Joan being asked of the same when she came forth of her fit said that she never heard of any such thing. But when it was inquired of Chappel, he confessed that he had once such a fall as he met with old Samuel in the streets, and both his pattens were broken at one instant; and because he would not fall upon the causeway on the stones he cast himself in the falling besides the causeway (for it was but narrow) into the mire, wherein he was marvellously soiled, and if another neighbour had not been with him he had been in greater danger.[53]

[52] Ov–O2v.   [53] M2v.

... Then[54] the jailer of Huntingdon gave this evidence: that a man of his, finding Mother Samuel very unruly whilst she was prisoner, at a time chained her to a bedpost; wherefore not long after his man fell sick and in all respects was handled as the forenamed children were, with heaving up and down of his body, shaking his arms, legs and head, having more strength in him in his fits than any two men had, crying out of Mother Samuel, saying that she did bewitch him. And thus remaining in this extraordinary course of sickness, about five or six days after died.

The said jailer said also that not long after the death of his servant, he had one of his sons fell sick and was for the most part handled as his servant beforenamed was, so that it was most apparent that he was bewitched. Therefore the said jailer went into the prison and brought Mother Samuel to his son's bedside and there held her until his son had scratched her, and so presently his son amended.

And to draw to some end, the jury of life and death in the afternoon found all the inditements *Billa vera*; which when old Father Samuel heard, he said to his wife in the hearing of many, 'A plague of God light upon thee, for thou art she that hath brought us all to this, and we may thank thee for it'.

Then the Judge grew to sentence and asked old Father Samuel what he had to say for himself why judgment of death should not be pronounced on him; whereat he answered that he had nothing to say but 'the Lord have mercy on him'.

Then the Judge asked old Mother Samuel what she had to say for herself to stay judgment; whereat she answered that she was with child, which set all the company on a great laughing and she herself more than any other because (as she thought) there should for that cause no judgment have been given.[55] Her age was near fourscore, therefore the Judge moved her to leave that answer, but in no case she would be driven from it till at length a jury of women were empanelled and sworn to search her, who gave up their verdict that she was not with child unless (as some said) it was with the Devil. And no marvel; for after she was found guilty there went the forenamed Master

---

[54] Continuing from point reached at note 52; reprint now continues without a break till end of book.

[55] A plea of 'pregnant' meant delay of sentence, usually for a year, if the jury of women empanelled to search the prisoner declared her to be pregnant in truth. Since early pregnancy is not always easy to diagnose, the plea itself (in women of child-bearing age) sometimes seems to have won a measure of delay.

Henry Pickering unto her where she stood amongst the prisoners to persuade her to confess the truth, and amongst other things she confessed that the forenamed William Langland[56] who gave unto her the spirits had carnal knowledge of her body when she received them. Some are of opinion that it was the Devil in man's likeness.

After all this the Judge asked Agnes Samuel the daughter what she had to say why judgment of death should not be given her; at which time there was one (being a prisoner) standing by her that willed her to say that she was also with child. 'Nay,' said she, 'that will I not do; it shall never be said that I was both a witch and a whore.'

And so the Judge, after very sound and divine council given severally to them all, proceeded to judgment, which was unto death. The next day certain godly men went to the prison to persuade the condemned parties to repentance, and to confess their sins to the world and crave pardon at God's merciful hands; at which time Mother Samuel, being asked by Master John Dorington, esquire, one of her Majesty's Justices of the county of Huntingdon, whether she did not bewitch the Lady Cromwell, she said 'No, forsooth, I did not.' Then her husband, old Father Samuel standing behind and hearing her deny the same, said 'Deny it not but confess the truth; for thou didst it one way or other.'

The confession of the old woman Alice Samuel unto certain questions that were demanded of her by Master Doctor Chamberlain at the time and place of her execution; being upon the ladder.

First, being demanded what the names of those spirits wherewith she bewitched were called, she said they were called Pluck, Catch and White, the which names she often repeated. Being asked whether she had bewitched the Lady Cromwell to death or not, she answered that she had. Being asked with which of her spirits she did bewitch the said Lady to death, she said, 'With Catch'; and being demanded for what cause she did it, she answered, for that the said Lady had caused some of her hair and her hair-lace to be burned; and that, she said, Catch willed her to be revenged of the said Lady; and that thereupon the said Mother Samuel bid him go and do what he would. And being asked what Catch said to her when he came back again, she confessed that he said that he had been revenged of her. Moreover she confessed,

---

[56] Original has 'Langley' here, perhaps by confusion with the bewitched John Langley.

and upon her death did say for truth that she was guilty of the death of the Lady Cromwell.

Being demanded whether she had bewitched Master Throckmorton's children, she confessed that she had done it. Being asked with which of her spirits, she said that it was Pluck. Being asked what she said to him when she sent him about that matter, she confessed that she willed him go torment them but not hurt them. Being asked how long they should be in that case, she said, she could not tell, and that she did not see Pluck since Christmas last.

Being asked what she did with White, she said that she never did hurt with him, and that she had sent him to the sea, and that he had sucked upon her chin, but the other two had not any reward. And likewise she confessed that she had those spirits of one whose name, she said was Langland;[57] where he dwelleth she knew not. And for that her husband would not confess anything of the witchcraft at the time of his death, nor of the privity of himself or his daughter as accessories to the same, it was demanded of her whether her husband was privy to the death of the Lady Cromwell or not; she answered, 'He was'.

Being demanded whether her husband was a witch, or had any skill in witchcraft, she said, he had, and could both bewitch and unwitch; but touching her daughter she would in no sort confess anything, but sought by all means to clear her. And for her daughter herself, she confessed nothing at all touching the witchcraft, but, being willed by Master Doctor Chamberlain to say the Lord's prayer and the Creed when as she stood upon the ladder ready to be executed, she said the Lord's prayer until she came to say 'But deliver us from evil,' the which by no means she could pronounce,[58] and in the Creed she missed very much, and could not say that she believed the Catholic Church.

After the execution was ended and that these three persons were thoroughly dead, the jailer (whose office it is to see them buried) stripped off their clothes and, being naked, he found upon the body of the old woman Alice Samuel a little lump of flesh, in manner sticking out as if it had been a teat to the length of half an inch; which both he and his wife perceiving, at the first sight thereof meant not to disclose because it was adjoining to so secret a place which was not decent to be seen. Yet in the end, not willing to conceal so strange a matter, and decently

---

[57] See note 56.

[58] Agnes had a very poor memory, as the Throckmortons found when they tried to teach her a simple grace (K2). See also K^v and M4.

covering that privy place a little above which it grew, they made open show thereof unto divers that stood by.

After this the jailer's wife took the same teat in her hand and, seeming to strain it, there issued out at the first as if it had been 'beesenings' (to use the jailer's word) which is a mixture of yellow milk and water; at the second turn there came out in similitude as clear milk, and in the end very blood itself. For the truth of this matter, it is not to be doubted of any, for it is not only the jailer's report unto all that require of him, but there are forty others also in Huntingdonshire of honest conversation that are ready to confirm the same upon their own sight.

And thus ye have the story of these three witches of Warboys, so plainly and briefly as may be delivered unto you. If any be desirous to know the present estate of these children, how they are and have been since the death of these parties, you shall understand that since their day of execution not any one of them have had any fit at all, neither yet grudging or complaining of any such thing, but have all of them been in as good estate and as perfect health as ever from their birth. God's blessed name be evermore praised for the same. Amen.[59]

Finis

[59] Sir Henry Cromwell, husband of the dead Lady Cromwell, as lord of the manor received in forfeit the goods and chattels of the executed family. He used the money to found an annual sermon at Huntingdon, to be delivered by a fellow of Queen's College, Cambridge, who was to preach against the detestable sin of witchcraft. This sermon (though finally used to denounce belief in witchcraft) was given annually till 1812.

Sir Henry's two sons, Oliver and Henry, who had direct experience of the Warboys case besides the death of their mother, sat in the House of Commons when it helped to pass James' Witchcraft law of 1604.

The Devil at Large

John Darrell, a Puritan minister, began his career by expelling an evil spirit from a Nottingham girl in 1586 with the aid of prayer. In addition to this temporary success (she was re-possessed later), he forced the spirit to name the witch who sent him; but on denouncing the woman to a justice of the peace, he was threatened with arrest and she was discharged.

Ten years later he tried again; Thomas Darling of Burton-on-Trent suffered from fits, accompanied by weird visions and violent reactions against his usual piety. After it had been suggested that he was bewitched, he told of meeting and unintentionally offending an old woman, who cursed him; local opinion pointed to Alse Goodridge or Elizabeth Wright, her mother.

The two were searched, and on Alse the women found a sore where it seemed that an excrescence had been cut off. She was jailed and interrogated without success. Then a 'cunning man' procured an offer of confession by putting her near a fire in new leather shoes—a simple but effective torture when her feet swelled and the leather contracted. The ordeal over, she refused to confess.

Finally she did break down and told of sending the Devil in the form of a dog to vex the boy. She was finally tried and sentenced before Lord Chief Justice Anderson (see p. 313) but died in prison before execution. Darrell was called in just before the trial and succeeded in expelling possessing spirits from the boy by prayer and fasting (though the first day of school produced a temporary relapse, met by a somewhat less sympathetic attitude on the part of his family).

Darrell was then called upon to wind up the case of a whole household of children and servants, afflicted in ways suspiciously reminiscent of the Throckmorton household. The strange behaviour of the Starkey children had originally been met by the father's retaining of a conjuror, who seemed to have the power to keep the children well. However, Edmund Hartley's high-handedness and increasing demands for money and property alienated his employer, and he was finally suspected of bewitching the children himself by kissing them.

He was arrested and charged with bewitching (not a felony), but executed because the father suddenly remembered having seen him make a magic circle (conjuration). His death did *not* free the children; Darrell arrived hot foot and succeeded in throwing them into convulsions and finally expelling the spirits.

Immediately after this, he took up the case of William Somers, possessed because of the malice of a witch he had offended. Somers conveniently fell into fits at the very sight of a witch, and Darrell was soon able to accuse 13, as well as to induce strange feats of playacting in the boy. However, there were local sceptics who thought Somers' abilities a little too good to be true; he was himself arrested on a charge of bewitching to death, and placed in a house of correction, where he confessed to imposture. Lord Chief Justice Anderson acquitted the one (well-born) witch put on trial, and referred Somers and Darrell to Archbishop Whitgift. After much ado, Somers was finally branded as a counterfeit, and Darrell and his assistant George More were deposed from the ministry and committed to jail.

Darrell and his supporters carried on a pamphlet war with the Anglican establishment for several years; but as an exorcist he was finished. The following extracts are taken from Samuel Harsnett's book exposing the trickery practised by John Darrell, the collusion of those declared by him to be possessed, the unreliability of the witnesses, and the misrepresentations of the printed records of his cases. It is undeniable that Harsnett bullied witnesses, some of whom were unstable and suggestible, and Darrell protests as much; but Darrell seems to have made no effort to protest Harsnett's account of the vicissitudes to which written evidence was subjected before publication. It is a sobering account of honesty struggling in the grip of preconception, and may serve to remind us that, though there was fraud and pretence in supernatural matters (as well as a substratum of genuine but not yet explicable phenomena), the strangest events described arise from honest but distorted perception, and honest but misleading description.

A Discovery of the fraudulent practises of John Darrel, Bacheler of Artes, concerning the pretended Possession and Dispossession of William Somers of Nottingham (London, 1599)

a) *What the witness saw.*[1]

Furthermore, one Richard Mee did depose before the said commissioners 'That he had seen William Somers stand and turn his face directly backward, not moving his body, and that his eyes were as great as beast's eyes, and that his tongue would be thrust out of his head to the bigness of a calf's tongue.'

The several parts of this deposition are pretermitted by Master Darrell in his *Apologie*, saving that of turning his face backwards, which he doth somewhat alter, terming it 'the setting of his face against his back'. But let us see what the said Mee hath deposed upon his re-examination.

'Whereas I have been conceived to say and swear, as is before expressed, my meaning was and is' saith he, 'that he the said Somers turned his face a good way towards his shoulder, and not otherwise;

[1] Samuel Harsnett, *A Discovery of the fraudulent practises of John Darrell . . .* (London, 1599), p. 216.

and likewise my meaning was and is, that his eyes were somewhat goggling out, but otherwise no more than ordinary. And thirdly, my meaning was and is, that by reason it was candle-light when I saw his tongue thrust out, and by reason of my conceit of the strangeness of Somers' troubles before I saw him, his tongue being thrust out, it seemed somewhat bigger than if Somers had been well I should have thought it to have been. . . .'

b) What the witnesses wrote.
[In speaking of *The most wonderfull and true storie, of a certaine Witch named Alse Gooderige* . . . (London, 1597), which told of the torments and dispossession of Thomas Darling, bewitched by Alse, Darrell said 'I account that history to be true in substance, but I will not justify it in every circumstance.' Harsnett seizes on this admission with glee and describes the construction of the book as follows.[2]]

Concerning therefore the credit of this book, it was penned by one Jesse Bee, a sadler of Burton, allied by marriage unto the said Darling, in this sort: 'Darling having had many fits in my absence, sometimes I was informed of them by word of mouth from those two that kept him, and sometimes I received some short notes. But for the most part such informations as I had were by word of mouth, both from the said keepers and divers others.

'And when I was present myself at his fits, I took the notes of his speeches and other things which happened, which notes (when I came home) I joined together as my memory would serve me, always studying rather to write them in better order than the boy spake them than in worse, and rather binding myself to the sense of the boy's words than to the words themselves.

'I also confess that the boy's speeches were oftentimes delivered so fast one upon another as I, not being able to write the brief notes of them, one man would tell me one piece and another some other piece which, when I came home, I did still join together as is before expressed. But I am not sure that either they told me the truth directly, or that I have therefore written everything as I should have done.'

And again 'I do confess that in penning the said book, I did of purpose set down many points to favour and give credit unto Thomas Darling's pretended torments, and that in all my speeches and dealings

[2] Samuel Harsnett, *A Discovery of the fraudulent practices of John Darrell* . . . (London, 1599), p. 266. The original has marginal page-references to the examinations of Bee and Denison before the Archbishop.

I used to countenance and make likely the boy's pretended possession; wherein I confess myself to have been greatly overseen'.

Besides, the said Jesse Bee being absent from Darling by the space of a month and at London, one Thomas Saunders procured the latter part of this book to be penned, and that in this order. He the said Saunders did take short notes in his tables* and, when he came home, he did cause one Edward Wightman upon his report to set them down.

Also, upon the said Jesse Bee's return from London, the schoolmaster of Burton told him something which he likewise thrust into the latter end of the book 'so as' saith he, 'all these points touching my treatise considered, there may be for aught I know very many untruths in it'.

This book being penned thus faithfully by Jesse Bee and others was afterward abridged by one Master Denison, a minister, at the request of Master Walkden, Thomas Darling's grandfather. 'In doing whereof,' saith Master Denison, 'after I had read two or three leaves together of the said treatise, I did set down the sum of them as my memory would serve me, leaving out many things, and adding sometimes of mine own according to the general sense, as I imagined.

'Furthermore, being fully persuaded by the constant reports which I had heard that those things which were written by* the boy were in substance true, I did in the contracting of the said book very willingly amplify the boy's commendation, as well in respect of his own words as also those speeches which sometimes the beholders used of him, and I did bend myself to make many things appear more probable than they were in the written copy.

'As when I found such points as I thought might seem absurd or repugnant one to another, I did of purpose leave them out, or else amended them as well as I could. For example—where it was in the written copy at large, the boy's torments and afflictions in his fits were all of them no doubt mere illusions, I, judging those words to cross the whole intent and meaning of the book, did of purpose leave them out of my abstract. Again, where it is in the said written copy of the boy's fits which he had the ninth of May, viz. "Wilt thou give me whatsoever I will desire of thee if I will give thee leave to enter into me again? Avoid, Satan, thou wert in me late enough"—all these words I purposedly omitted (as I think) for that they could not agree with the rest of the discourse of the boy's fits before the supposed dispossession.

'Moreover, by reason I did so much trust my memory in the contracting of this book, I perceive by comparing it with the written copy that I have disordered some of the fits, and likewise the circumstance belonging unto them, ascribing that to one fit which did belong to another; as also some points of the boy's supposed speeches to Satan are mistaken by me, and some displaced, altering the sense from the written copy.'

Besides these omissions, alterations and mistakings confessed by Master Denison himself, it further appeareth that his abstract, falling afterwards into some huckster's hands received some new additions. [P. 15 and p. 39. He suggests that Darrell is responsible. Harsnett tells us after this that the abridged book was sent by Walkden to be printed in London; Darrell and Hildersham, a local vicar, asked for the MS. back in order to check it. The copy was returned, checked through (and perhaps altered) by them, and sent again to the London printer.]

VII   Deaths and Sentences

Death of an Earl

The following account of the death of Ferdinando, Earl of Derby in 1595, is recorded in the *Annals of England* by John Stow.[1] Several people were arrested on suspicion of witchcraft or poisoning, but the final outcome remains obscure. The extract is remarkable for its detailed description of the Draconian measures thought appropriate for serious illnesses of the affluent; dying under the care of Elizabethan doctors obviously required a very strong constitution.

The 16th of April, Ferdinando Earl of Derby[2] deceased at Lathom, whose strange sickness and death (gathered by those who were present with him at the time thereof) was such as followeth: his diseases apparent were, vomiting of sour or rusty matter with blood, the yellow jaundice, melting of his fat, swelling and hardness of his spleen, a vehement hiccock,* and four days before he died, stopping of his water. The cause of all his diseases were thought by the physicians to be partly a surfeit, and partly a most violent distempering himself with vehement exercise, taken four days together in the Easter week.

[1] John Stow, *Annales* (London, 1600), pp. 1275–7. To make for ease of reading, the many dates in this extract have been modernised by the addition of 'th'.

[2] This enigmatic young man was involved in some curious episodes of Elizabethan history. Ferdinando Stanley, Lord Strange, became Earl of Derby by the death of his father on 25 September 1593. Two months later he was approached by Richard Hesketh, a Jesuit, on behalf of the turncoat and exile Sir William Stanley; he was offered unlimited support from Catholics at home and abroad if he would rebel, seize the crown from Elizabeth, and rule as a Catholic king. Ferdinando denounced the man, who was arrested and condemned. His own death 5 months later led inevitably to official suspicion that he had been poisoned (or bewitched) by Catholics in revenge. (Historical MSS. Commission, Salisbury Papers, Vol. IV, pp. 423, 461, 515, 517).

Ferdinando had also been patron of 'Strange's Men' (later 'the Earl of Derby's Men'), one of the first companies to perform plays by Shakespeare. When Ferdinando died, the company reorganised, most of its members becoming 'Chamberlain's Men'; this was the company that secured all Shakespeare's existing play-scripts, and the company for which he wrote all his succeeding plays. It is, then, quite possible that the unusual use of the cauldron in the witch scenes of *Macbeth* is based on events connected with the Earl's death rather than on Ovid's tales of Tisiphone and Medea.

The 5th of April, about six of the clock at night, he fell sick at Knowsley, where he vomited thrice.

The 6th, he returned to Lathom and, feeling his health to sink more and more, sent to Chester for a doctor of physic.

The 7th, before the coming of the doctor he had cast* 7 times; the colour of his vomits was like to sooty or rusty iron, the substance very gross and fatty, the quantity above seven pints, the smell not without offence; his waters were in colour, smell and substance not unlike his vomits. The same night he took a glister* to draw the course of the humours downward, which wrought five times and gave some ease.

The 8th, he took a gentle infusion of rhubarb and manna in a draught of chicken broth, which wrought very well nine times.

The 9th, because of his continual bleeding by mouth with his vomits, he was instantly entreated to be let blood, to divert and stay the course thereof, but by no means he could be persuaded thereunto; wherefore that day only fomentations, oils and plasters were outwardly applied to stay and comfort his stomach.

The 10th, he took one other glister, which wrought well six times.

The 11th, he took one other purge, which wrought with great ease 9 times upon the humours. The same night he took a little diascordium[3] with the syrup of lemons and scabious water, which somewhat stayed his stomach and gave him some rest.

The 12th, because his vomiting continued still, he was moved to take a vomit, that thereby the bottom of his stomach might be scoured and cleansed from so vile and loathsome matter wherewith he was troubled; but by no persuasion he would yield thereunto. Notwithstanding, the same day he took a medicine to procure sweat, but prevailed not; the very same night his water stayed upon a sudden, to the astonishment of all.

The 13th, all means were offered to provoke water, as glister drinks, fomentations, oils, poultices, plasters, and stirrings, but nothing happily succeeded.

The 14th and 15th was used an instrument called a catheter, which, being conveyed into his bladder, was strongly sucked by the chirugeon,[4] but no water followed.

[3] diascordium: medicine made from dried leaves of water-germander (*Teucrium Scordium*) and other herbs.

[4] chirugeon, i.e. surgeon; responsible mainly for manual operations under the direction of a physician.

The 16th day, about five of the clock at night, he most devoutly yielded his soul to God.

In all the time of his sickness, he often took bezar's stone and unicorn's horn;[5] his pulse was ever good, his strength indifferent. The number of his vomits were 52 and of his stools 29; his physicians were Doctor Canon, Doctor Joiner, Doctor Bate, Doctor Case.

A true report of such reasons and conjectures as caused many learned men to suppose him to be bewitched.[6]

The first of April, being the Monday before his Honour fell sick, a woman offered unto him a supplication of petition, wherein her request was that if it would please him to give or assign her a dwelling place near unto himself, that she might from time to time reveal unto him such things with speed which God revealed unto her for his good. This petition was thought vain, and therefore refused.

On the fourth of April, he dreamed that his lady was most dangerously sick to death, and in his sleep being sore troubled therewith, he wept, suddenly cried out, started from his bed, called for help, sought about the chamber betwixt sleep and waking but, being fully awaked, was comforted because he found her well. Here we omit strange dreams, or divinations of divers grave men, which happened before or about the time of his sickness.

On the fifth of April, in his chamber at Knowsley about six of the

[5] bezar's stone: bezoar stone, a stone formed in the intestines of an animal by accumulation of matter round a foreign object.

unicorn's horn (so-called) was usually narwhal horn. Both substances were regarded as universal antidotes, and it is obvious that the doctors suspected poisoning, despite their initial reassuring diagnosis. Apart from the strong pulse, which they remark upon with surprise, the Earl's symptoms are consonant with those of poisoning by arsenic, though a similar picture might have been presented by the European form of cholera still prevalent at this time.

[6] Poison and witchcraft—crimes which could be carried out while the criminal was elsewhere—were strongly connected in the popular mind, and produced the same hunt for dreams, portents and forebodings as clues. A wise-woman's herb lore was bound to include knowledge of England's poisonous plants, and conjurors often had some primitive understanding of chemicals; disreputable practicioners sold this knowledge. (Some who suffered for it were employed by Frances Howard, who first tried to kill her husband, then rendered him impotent by a combination of philtres and sheer malice, won a nullity suit by poisoning Overbury (an inconvenient witness) and triumphantly married Carr, the king's favourite, in 1613.)

clock at night, there appeared suddenly a tall man with a ghastly and threatening countenance, who twice or thrice seemed to cross him as he was passing through the chamber; and when he came unto the same part of the chamber where this shadow appeared, he presently fell sick and there vomited thrice. After, Goborne, one of his secretaries attending then upon him, saw nothing, which more amazed him. The same night he dreamed that he was in fighting, and twice or thrice stabbed to the heart, and also wounded in many other places of his body.

The 10th of April about midnight, was found in his bedchamber by one Master Halsall an image of wax with hair like unto the hair of his Honour's head twisted through the belly thereof from the navel to the secrets. This image was spotted, as the same Master Halsall reported unto Master Smith, one of his secretaries, a day before any pain grew, and spots appeared upon his sides and belly. This image was hastily cast into the fire by Master Halsall before it was viewed, because he thought by burning thereof (as he said) he should relieve his lord from witchcraft and burn the witch who so much tormented his lord; but it fell out contrary to his love and affection for, after the melting thereof, he more and more declined.[7]

The 12th of April one Jane, a witch, demanded of Master Goborne whether his Honour felt no pain in the lower parts, and whether he made water as yet or no; and at that very time, notwithstanding all helps, his water utterly stopped and so remained till he died.

Sir Edward Filton, who with other justices examined certain witches, reporteth that one of them, being bidden to say the Lord's Prayer, said it well; but being conjured in the name of Jesus that if she had bewitched his Honour she should not be able to say the same, she could never repeat that petition 'Forgive us our trespasses'—no, not although it was repeated unto her.[8]

A homely woman about the age of fifty years was found mumbling in a corner of his Honour's chamber, but what, God knoweth. This wise woman (as they termed her) seemed often to ease his Honour both of his vomiting and hiccock; but so it fell out, which was strange, that when so long as he was eased, the woman herself was troubled

[7] To burn something belonging to a witch, or an animal she had bewitched, would torment her; the destruction of an image containing hair or nails would affect the person to whom the charmed hair or nails belonged, unless the charm had first been broken.

[8] This test seems to be becoming more frequent as an indication of guilt.

most vehemently in the same manner, the matter which she vomited being like also unto that which passed from him.

But at the last, when this woman was espied by one of the doctors tempering and blessing (after her manner) the juice of certain herbs, her pot whereinto she strained the juice was tumbled down by the said doctor and she rated out of the chamber; nothwithstanding she did still say that she would not cease to ease him, although she could not perfectly help him because he was so strongly bewitched.

All physic wrought very well, yet had he none or little ease thereby; his diseases were many and his vomits, with stopping of his water, grievous; yet ever his pulse remained as good and perfect as ever it did in time of his best health till one quarter of an hour before he died.

He himself in all the time of his sickness cried out that the doctors laboured in vain, because he was certainly bewitched. He fell twice into a trance, not able to move hand, head or foot, when he would have taken physic to do him good. In the end, he cried out often against all witches and witchcraft, reposing his only hope of salvation upon the merits of Christ Jesus his Saviour.

One excellent speech cannot be omitted amongst many in the time of his sickness, especially the day before he departed, at which time he desired one of his doctors whom he especially loved to persuade him no longer to live, 'because', saith he, 'although out of thy love thou wouldest stir up hope of life, and dost employ all thy wit, art and travail to that end yet, knowing for a certainty that I must now die, I pray thee cease, for I am resolved presently to die, and to take away with me only one part of my arms[9]—I mean the eagle's wings; so will I fly swiftly into the bosom of Christ my only saviour'.

And with that he sent for his Lady, and gave her his last 'Vale' or farewell, desiring her to take away and love his doctor, and also to give him some jewels with his arms and name, that he might be remembered, the which thing immediately after his death was most honourably performed. His spiritual physicians were the Bishop of Chester and Master Lee his chaplain.

[9] The Earl's family crest shows an eagle alighting on a swaddled infant. He seems to be thinking, rather pathetically, of Isaiah 40: 28–31, which ends (A.V.): 'But they that wait upon the Lord shall renew their strength; they shall mount up with wings as eagles; they shall run and not be weary; and they shall walk and not faint.'

W—L

Death of a Queen

This extract is taken by Nichols from a manuscript source in the British Museum. That it is not an isolated story is confirmed by other MS. sources, also reprinted by Nichols in his *Progresses of Queen Elizabeth*.[1] Sir Robert Cary's very vivid account of Elizabeth's death says, 'This that I heard with my ears and did see with my eyes, I thought it my duty to set down, and to affirm it for a truth, upon the faith of a Christian, because I know there have been many false lies reported of the end and death of that good lady.' John Chamberlain writes to Dudley Carleton '. . . no doubt but you shall hear her Majesty's sickness and manner of death diversely related; for even here the Papists do tell strange stories, as utterly void of truth as of all civil honesty or humanity.'

Her Majesty being in good health one day, a Privy Councillor presented her with a piece of gold of the bigness of an angel,[2] dimly marked with some small characters, which he said an old woman of Wales bequeathed her on her death-bed; and thereupon he discoursed how the said old woman by virtue of the same lived to the age of an hundred and odd years and, in that age having all her body withered and consumed, and wanting nature to nourish (she said), commanded the said piece of gold to be carefully sent her Majesty, alleging further that as long as the said old woman wore it upon her body, she could not die.

The Queen, upon the confidence she had thereof, took the said gold and wore it upon her ruff. Now, though she fell not suddenly sick, yet daily decreased her rest and feeding, and within a few days [she] fell sick indeed; and the cause being wondered at by a lady with whom she was very private and confident, her Majesty told her (commanding her to conceal the same) that she saw one night in her bed her body

---

[1] *Ex Personii Jesuitae maledictâ discussione*, p. 217, from Cotton MS. Julius, F. VI, fol. 121; in J. Nichols' *Progresses of Queen Elizabeth* (London, 1823, repr. New York, 1964), pp. 603–13 etc. The same account of Elizabeth's death is found in Lady Southwell's MS. at Stonyhurst College.

[2] angel: gold coin worth about 10/– at this time. It was presented to those who were touched for the King's Evil (scrofula) and many of them continued to wear it thereafter as a charm.

exceeding lean and fearful in a light of fire. This sight was at Whitehall, a little before she departed from thence to Richmond, and may be testified by another lady who was one of the nearest about her person, of whom the Queen demanded whether she was not wont to see sights in the night, telling her of the bright flame she had seen.

Afterward, in the melancholy of her sickness, she desired to see a true looking-glass, which in twenty years she had not seen, but only such a one as was made of purpose to deceive her sight; which glass being brought her, she fell presently into exclaiming against [those] which had so much commended her, and took it so offensively that some which before had flattered her durst not come into her sight.

Now falling into extremity, she sat two days and three nights upon her stool ready dressed, and could never be brought by any of her Council to go to bed, or to eat or drink; only my Lord Admiral one time persuaded her to drink some broth. For that any of the rest, she would not answer them to any question, but said softly to my Lord Admiral's persuasions that if he knew what she had seen in her bed, he would not persuade her as he did; and commanding the rest of the lords to depart her chamber, willed my Lord Admiral to stay, to whom she shook her head, and with a pitiful voice said unto him, 'My Lord, I am tied with a chain of iron about my feet'; he alleging her wonted courage, she replied, 'I am tied, tied, and the case is altered with me.'

About the same time, two ladies waiting on her in her chamber discovered in the bottom of her chair the Queen of Hearts with a nail of iron knocked through the forehead of it, and which the ladies durst not then pull out, remembering that the like thing was reported to be used to others for witchcraft. Another lady waiting in these times on the Queen, and leaving her after in her privy chamber at Richmond at the very first distemper of her sickness, met her, as she thought, three or four chambers off, and fearing that she would have been displeased that she left her alone, came toward her to excuse herself, but she vanished away; and when the lady returned into the same chamber where she left the Queen, she found her asleep as before.

So in time growing past recovery, having kept her bed nine days, the Council sent unto her the Bishop of Canterbury and other of the prelates, upon sight of whom she was much offended, cholerically rating them, bidding them be packing, and afterwards exclaiming to my Lord Admiral that she had the greatest indignity offered her by the Archbishop that a prince could have, to pronounce sentence of death against her as if she had lived an atheist. And some lords mentioning to have other prelates to come unto her, she answered that she would have none of those hedge priests, and so none of them came to her till after she was past sense and at the last gasp, at which time some prayers were said not far from her.

The Queen being departed this life, the Lords of the Council went to London to proclaim His Majesty, leaving her body with charge not to be opened, such being her desire; but some for some reasons having given a secret warrant to the surgeons, they opened her, which the rest of the Council did not contradict. Now the body being cered* up was brought to Whitehall, where it was watched every night by six several ladies; who being all about the same, which was fast nailed up within a board³ coffin with leaves of lead covered with velvet, it happened that her body brake the coffin with such a crack that it splitted the wood, lead and cere-cloth,* to the terror and astonishment of all that were present. Whereupon the next day she was fain to be new trimmed up, insomuch as all were of the opinion that if she had not been opened, the breath of her body would have been much worse.⁴

Divers other particularities, for that they concern special personages, I have thought good for some causes to conceal.

³ Original has 'brod'.

⁴ This extract uses some of the same events and speeches recorded by Sir Robert Cary and others, but manages to interpret them in a completely different light.

Opinions of a Judge

This extract is taken from Sloane MS. 831 in the British Museum, from Dr. Stephen Bradwell's unprinted work *Marie Glovers[1] late woefull case, together with her joyfull deliverance written upon occasion of Doctor Jordens discourse of the Mother.[2] ... A defence of the truthe against D.J. his scandalous Impugnations.* Doctor Jordan's book was written in 1603 and deals with a curious episode at the very end of Queen Elizabeth's reign.

Mary Glover, aged 14, suffered from recurrent fits which caused her friends to declare her possessed, and Elizabeth Jackson was tried and condemned to prison and pillory (the act of 1604 would have prescribed death) for bewitching her, despite medical testimony that Mary's disease was 'natural'. Bishop Bancroft declared the girl a fraud and asked the Recorder of London to examine and test her; he was convinced that her fits were not feigned. Puritan ministers and neighbours of the Glovers (in a gathering reminiscent of Rachel Pinder's dispossession in 1574) conducted a day-long exorcism of prayer which cured the girl.

These three points of view are represented in three books published in 1603, at least two of which were presented to King James when he came to London. Samuel Harsnett jeered at the fraud in *A Declaration of Egregious Popish Impostures* (p. 166); John Swan, a divinity student, gave a zealous account of the exorcism in *A True and Briefe Report, of Mary Glovers Vexation ...*, and Dr. Edward Jordan supported his position in court by *A brief discourse of a disease called the Suffocation of the Mother, written upon occasion which hath beene of late taken thereby, to suspect possessions of an evill spirit, or some such like supernaturall power. Wherein is declared that divers strange actions and passions of the body of man, which in the common opinion, are imputed to the devill, have their true naturall causes, and do accompanie this Disease.*

Dr. Jordan remained in favour with King James and supervised the Queen's treatments at Bath; Elizabeth Jackson appears to have been released.

[1] An interesting account of the case is given by Henry N. Paul in *The Royal Play of Macbeth* (New York, 1950), pp. 90–112.

[2] Mother: literally 'the womb', once thought to cause hysteria by rising or swelling in the body and disturbing the action of other organs. Later used figuratively to describe the disease 'hysterica passio' or hysteria, which affected men also. (See *King Lear*, ed. cit., II. iv. 56–7.) Symptoms most often noted by Elizabethan doctors were gaseous distension, a sense of choking, overbreathing, convulsions and general emotional disarray.

Punishments for witchcraft: sinners cast into hell-mouth
A Booke Declaringe the Fearfull Vexasion, of one Alexander Nyndge 1573–4

The Lord Anderson, hearing Doctor Jordan so often insinuate some feigning or dissembling fashions in the maid, and withal so much to beat upon these words 'For these causes, I think it may be natural', and 'These accidents and symptoms for aught I see be natural'—pressed him to answer directly, whether it were natural or supernatural. He said that, in his conscience, he thought it was altogether natural.

'What do you call it?' quoth the judge. 'Passio Hysterica'[3], said the doctor. 'Can you cure it?' 'I cannot tell; I will not undertake it, but I think fit trial should be made thereof.' Lord Anderson: 'Do you think she counterfeiteth?' Dr. Jordan: 'No, in my conscience, I think she doth not counterfeit.' Lord Anderson: 'Then, in *my* conscience, it is not natural; for if you tell me neither a natural cause of it, nor a natural remedy, I will tell you that it is not natural.'

After this, pausing awhile, the Lord Anderson spake to the jury in effect as followeth: 'The land is full of witches; they abound in all places. I have hanged five or six and twenty of them; there is no man here can speak more of them than myself. Few of them would confess it; some of them did, against whom the proofs were nothing so manifest as against those that denied it. They have on their bodies divers

[3] A diagnosis of hysteria had been made by a different physician in a Norfolk case of possession in 1600. The witch had been released, but died after being repeatedly scratched by the patient. (British Museum Additional MSS. 28223, f. 15, transcribed by C. H. L'Estrange Ewen, *Witchcraft and Demonianism*, ed. cit., pp. 190–3.)

strange marks at which (as some of them have confessed) the Devil sucks their blood;[4] for they have forsaken God, renounced their baptism, and vowed their service to the Devil, and so the sacrifice which they offer him is their blood. This woman hath the like marks on sundry places of her body as you see testified under the hands of the women that were appointed to search her.

The Devil is a spirit of darkness, he deals closely and cunningly; you shall hardly find any direct proofs in such a case, but by many presumptions and circumstances you may gather it. When they are full of cursing, use their tongue to speak mischievously, and it falls out accordingly, what greater presumption can you have of a witch? This woman hath that property; she is full of cursing, she threatens and prophesies and still it takes effect; she must of necessity be a prophet or a witch.

Their malice is great, their practices devilish, and if we shall not convince* them without their own confession, or direct proofs, where the presumptions are so great, and the circumstances so apparent, they will in short time over-run the whole land. The maid now affected I have seen, and you have beheld.'

Then he repeated the trial himself had made, as above written, saying further to the physicians: 'You talk of the mother; I pray you, have you ever seen or heard of the mother that kept it course unchangeably every second day and never missed, and yet that changeth his course upon the presence of some one person, as this doth at the presence of this woman? Divines, physicians—I know they are learned and wise, but to say this is natural and tell me neither the cause nor the cure of it—I care not for your judgment; give me a natural reason and a natural remedy, or a rush for your physic!'

---

[4] Devil's mark and the teat at which the familiar sucked are here assumed to be one and the same thing.

Witches Abroad

A Strange Report of Sixe most notorious Witches, who by their divelish practises murdred above the number of foure hundred small Children: besides the great hurtes they committed upon divers other people: Who for the same, and many other like offences, were executed in the princely Cittie of Manchen in high Germanie the .29. of July. 1600. Printed at Nuremberge by Lucas Mayr Ingraver, dwelling in Kramergesle: and now translated out of Dutch, according to the same Coppy there imprinted. (London, 1601)

Although printed for Thomas Pavier, this pamphlet appears to be exactly what it states. H. C. Lea cites records of a case which matches in place, date, and many details of punishment.[1] Despite Elizabethan interest in bloodthirsty murders, martyrdoms and famous last words, there are very few translations of foreign works dealing with the mass killings attributed to Continental witches, or the elaborate tortures often inflicted on the condemned. The flat nastiness of the present account is unique, and displays better than any explanation the elements foreign to the English witch persecutions and alien to the tastes of those involved.

There is not any Christian (I am sure) but in heart will relent, and with great admiration lift up his eyes toward heaven, and stand amazed at the wicked practices of six of the most notorious wicked witches that ever they heard of; who (giving both bodies and souls to eternal damnation) committed so many inhuman murders, so many strange robberies, pillages and riots; spoiling both corn and cattle; causing strange hail and tempest and such like annoyances to the inhabitants of Germany,[2] that I think it a matter worthy to be kept in memory, whereby the shameful end of such malefactors may serve as a notable example to our eyes, a grief to the godly, and a terror to the wicked and reprobate people. The names of these vile offenders, and of their wicked dealings, hereafter followeth.

[1] H. C. Lea, *Materials towards a History of Witchcraft*, ed. cit., Vol. III, p. 1126; quotation from Sigmund Riesler, *Geschichte der Hexenprozesse in Bayern* (Stuttgart, 1896), pp. 198–9.

[2] The conventional lists of deeds with which Continental witches were charged. English witches did not often meddle with the weather, though storms were ascribed to the Devil and (sometimes) to conjurors' ritual.

First, Paul Gamperle, alias Poppenhamor.
Second, Anne Gamperle, wife to the said Paul.
Third, Simon Gamperle ⎱
Fourth, Jacob Gamperle ⎰ their two sons.
Fifth, Ullrich Sehelltibaum, Armourer.
Sixth, George Smallts, Tailor.

These six persons, being many years before this held in great suspicion
for practising witchcraft, yet not any sufficient proof thereof, were now
taken all together near to the town of Dettingen, in a cave or vault

Witches, wizard and priest in hell
The most wonderfull and true Storie, of a certaine
Witch named Alse Gooderige 1597

deep in the ground, where many times before they had likewise met;
and (as they thought), there to remain still secure from the knowledge
of their neighbours, fell to their accustomed practices, and by their
witchcrafts raised so great a storm or tempest that all the towns and
villages were greatly endamaged thereby.

But God, not suffering these vile offenders to remain any longer undiscovered, brought all their actions to light; and by the howling of a dog strucken mad with the fearfulness of that tempest, certain of their neighbours were brought to the said cave or vault, where they were all six attached and the next day, being the 24 of July, were brought before the governor of Munich who, finding them guilty by their examinations, commanded them to prison.

But now mark what happened: the governor's clerk or secretary, when he took paper in his hand to make a warrant, suddenly both his feet were taken from him, by reason whereof he had such a fall that the hucklebone* of his thigh was strucken out of joint, whereof within three days after he died.

Hereupon the governor commanded them to be searched by his officers, where they found hidden under every one of their clothes next to their skins a bag of swine's dung;[3] which being taken away, stunk so filthily that no man could endure the smell. And in Paul Gamperle's bosom (being their principal or ring-leader) they found a devilish book of conjuration and the picture of a man made in tin, holding in his hand a scroll or writing containing these three words 'Magoll, Cumath, Hellbeza'.

By the same were so plainly manifested their wicked practices that they immediately confessed (without any further trouble) all their murders and execrable feats that ever they had committed in their life times, as it doth well appear hereafter.

The confession of Paul Gamperle.

Paul Gamperle, alias Poppenhamor, of the age of eight and fifty years, confessed that he had used the practice of witchcraft from his childhood, and that he had been trained up in the same by his old grandmother, a woman dead many years ago.

In like manner he confessed, that he had murdered in his time by witchcraft and sorcery about the number of a hundred small children.

In like manner he confessed, that he had made lame and crooked ten of the richest citizens of Munich, because they would not forgive him certain debts he owed them.

In like manner he confessed, that by witchcraft he had made away two of his uncles, to come by their goods.

In like manner he confessed ten church-robberies, fifteen murders by

[3] Reginald Scot mentions several charms which incorporate this unlovely substance; Ursula Kemp used it at St. Osyth in 1582.

the highway's side, robberies by night in merchants' cellars, by himself done four and twenty several times; and that no lock nor door could withstand him but by witchcraft he could make fly open.[4]

Finally, he confessed that in his life time he had by night fired eight of his neighbours' houses, whereby were burnt in their beds both men, women and children to the number of sixteen; besides divers other mischiefs by him committed to the great annoyances of the whole country.

The confession of Anne Gamperle.

Anne Gamperle his wife, of the age of threescore years, confessed that in her life time she had murdered likewise by witchcraft to the number of a hundred small children.

In like manner she confessed, that she had deformed and made crooked and withal murdered by witchcraft, to the number of nineteen old people.

In like manner she confessed, that by witchcraft she had caused an innkeeper's wife to run into a hot burning oven, where she burned herself to death; and likewise caused the same woman's husband to be so miserably vexed that he thrust his head into a swilling tub full of swine's meat and there smothered himself.

In like manner she confessed, that she had spoiled cattle in great abundance, with corn upon the ground oftentimes; and that she had set fire upon two haystacks which had fired a whole village, had not help of people prevented it. From the like, God of His mercy deliver us all!

The confession of Simon Gamperle.

Simon Gamperle their natural son, of the age of two and twenty years, confessed that he had murdered by witchcraft to the number of thirty small children, beside six old folks which he likewise made crooked and lame and after killed.

Moreover he confessed, that he had committed nine church-robberies, four robberies by the highway side, twelve robberies done in merchants' ware-houses; riot and pillage committed by night six times; spoiled with hail and tempests cattle and grounds oftentimes.

[4] Criminal skills, or crimes with overtones of blasphemy or unnatural disregard for life (church-robbing, fire-raising or poisoning) were often identified with witchcraft in the minds of law-abiding citizens because they were not 'natural'.

Moreover he confessed, that by witchcraft he had made himself invincible,[5] by which means he alone set upon six persons at a time, and robbed them, and after killed them every one; without many other practices of theft and murder, which here I omit.

The confession of Jacob Gamperle.

Jacob Gamperle their other son, of the age of one and twenty years, confessed that he had murdered to the number of three score and five small children, beside five old folks that he had made lame and crooked and after murdered.

Moreover, he confessed five church-robberies, ten robberies in merchants' houses, four robberies committed by the highway; five houses set on fire, riots and thefts by night in the streets, committed twelve several times.

Moreover he confessed, that by witchcraft he had caused a herd of cattle in a tempest to be blown into a river, and there drowned; and the said tempest or storm to be so violent, that travellers could hardly travel by the highway; with many other like wicked practices.

The confession of Ullrich Sehelltibaum.

Ullrich Sehelltibaum of Dettingen, of the age of three score and eight years, confessed that in his life time he had murdered by witchcraft to the number of three score and ten small children, and had made crooked and killed thirty old folks.

Moreover, he confessed robberies in churches and merchants' cellars, thefts and murders by night, cattle and grounds spoiled, in such abundance and so oftentimes that he could not well reckon them.

The confession of George Smaltes.

George Smaltes, Taylor of Peon, of the age of fifty years, confessed in his life time he had murdered to the number of thirty six small children, beside old people made crooked and killed the number of fifteen. Murders by the high way, robberies in villages, firing of houses, robbing of churches, I think it needs not to number down. But to conclude, it was his custom above the rest to ransack by night dead

---

[5] invincible; possibly a variant spelling for 'invisible'.

men's graves, and to make pillage of what he there found, whether it were linen or otherwise; for badder livers than these six were, I think are not now remaining upon the earth.

Therefore let all Christians pray that God in His mercy may bless us and all others from the like practices; and to weed from the face of the earth all such like offenders, as He did these, and with the like shame and punishment reward them, O God, I beseech Thee!

These aforesaid confessions being taken before the Governor and other Burgesses of the city of Munich, they were arraigned, convicted, and condemned; and upon the nine and twenty of July were executed in this manner and form following:—

First, they were all six brought before the town house of Munich, where the woman, being placed betwixt her two sons, had both her breasts cut off; with the which breasts the executioner struck her three times about the face, and in like manner her two sons, who sat on each side of her, were likewise beaten about the face with their mother's breasts three times apiece. This being done in the presence of many people, the woman had six stripes given her with a whip of twisted wire; and after had both her arms broken with a wheel, and [was] then set in a settle made of purpose:[6] her body was immediately burnt.

After this, the other five men-witches had also six stripes apiece, and both their arms likewise broken with a wheel, and four of them tied unto a stake in the same place and burnt. But Paul Gamperle, the father and master-witch of them all, was spitted alive and so roasted to death, and after had his body likewise burnt into cinders.[7]

Thus, gentle reader, hast thou heard the life and death of these six most notorious and wicked witches. For the truth whereof let no man make doubt, for it is not only reported of by many men of good sufficiency, but translated out of the Dutch copy as it was there first imprinted.

Therefore let us all in general fall down upon our knees, and with contrite hearts desire of His Majesty, by Whose sufferance all their wicked practices were committed, that he will abate the pride and malice

---

[6] This settle might have been one of the witch-chairs used in Germany; some had a seat studded with spikes, and some an iron seat which could, slowly or quickly, be made red-hot by a fire underneath.

[7] There was a widespread belief that the witch's body (like that of the vampire with whom she was sometimes confused) must be burned to ashes in order to banish her spirit completely.

of Satan, now reigning amongst mankind, and to put in our hearts such strong faith that the like assaults never assail us; but that we may serve Him in perfect love and godliness, Who is the mighty King of all Kings; to Whom be all praise, glory and dominion for ever. Amen.

Finis

The Witch in the Alehouse

The most cruell and bloody murther committed by an Inkeepers Wife, called Annis Dell, and her Sonne George Dell. . . . With the severall Witch-crafts, and most damnable practises of one Johane Harrison and her Daughter upon severall persons, men and women at Royston, who were all executed at Hartford the 4 of August last past. 1606. (*London 1606*)

The bizarre and terrible murder recorded in the first part of the pamphlet is confirmed by the execution of the two Dells after Hertford Summer Sessions, 1 August 1606. Public records show the execution of Alice Stokes and Christiana Stokes for witchcraft at the same time,[1] but no trace of Harrisons, so it is likely that the author of the pamphlet has recorded the story of the Stokes under a mistaken or substituted name.

The writing and printing bear traces of great haste and carelessness, particularly in the middle section; if the work is a fabrication, the impression of hearsay reporting has been developed with unusual skill for such a rushed job. It seems most likely that the 'literary' style which has cast doubt on the authenticity of the pamphlet is simply a result of the trend towards entertainment in such works which we noted earlier.

The several practices of Joan Harrison and her daughter, condemned and executed at Hertford for witchcraft the 4 of August last, 1606.

At the Assizes held in the beginning of August last in the county of Hertford in the King's Majesty's behalf, for gaol delivery, there were by the verdict of the country four only offenders found worthy to have deserved death; of which 2 as have been spoken of, the mother and the son for murder, and one Joan Harrison and her daughter for damnable witchcraft, wrayed time[2] that offences should come thus prodigious— that the offspring born to be a comfort to the parents and the parents as much to be delighted in the children, should be cause of one another's untimely death and fatal overthrow.

This J. H. dwelling at Royston in the said county of Hertford, of long time having been suspected for witchcraft, now upon just cause was apprehended; and her house, according to the true course of justice, being searched, there was found in a chest of hers such sufficient

[1] C. H. L'Estrange Ewen, *Witch Hunting and Witch Trials*, ed. cit., p. 197.
[2] wrayed (i.e. betrayed) time: exposed the nature of the age.

instruments (which she after confessed were helps to her in her practices) that could there have been no other proof for evidence against her, they only had been sufficient to judge her unworthy of long life.

This chest being opened, there was first taken out by the officer all the bones[3] due to the anatomy of man and woman, and under them hair of all colours that is customarily worn; in the bottom was found a parchment lapt* up in a compass no bigger than a groat,* but being open, was in breadth every way 2 spans.[4] In the midst of this parchment was coloured in the purest colours a heart proportionable to the heart of a man; and round about, fitting even to the very brim of the parchment, were coloured in several colours very curiously, divided branches, on which hung dangling things like ashen keys, and at the ends of them in some places figured, and others proportioned, a mouth[5]—in brief, the whole joints and arteries of a man.

This J.H. being upon her examination, and finding such apparent witness induct* against her of her several felonies and murders, neglected not to confess her utmost secret therein; that she had power (by the help of that parchment, man and woman's bones, and man and woman's hair) to inflict (by the help of her spirits which she reported to have 2 attending on her, one for men, another for cattle) in any joint, sinew or place of the body by only but pricking the point of a needle in that place of the parchment where in his or her body she would have them tortured.

Which torture of hers once begun in them, their pain should continue so restless that a present death had been more happier than so lingering a calamity; and those whom she intended to kill had the same in effect, if she gave a prick in the middle of the parchment where she had placed the heart: which relation of her may certainly be believed by the several consequents that she was condemned upon.

First a good country yeoman (a neighbour of hers) and she falling at some words together, he calling her 'old hag' or some such like name

[3] Under the law of 1604 it became a felony to take up a corpse, skin or bone for purposes of witchcraft.

[4] Possibly one of the manuscripts surviving from the wreck and spoliation of the monastic libraries; these were used to bind books, to clean guns, to stop draughts, to wrap fish. 'In my grandFather's dayes' says Aubrey sadly, 'the Manuscripts flew about like Butterflies.'

[5] It is hard to make sense of this passage, but it sounds like an illiterate description which includes the labelling devices (the mouths? the keys?) as part of the basic anatomical scheme.

of reproof, she made him this answer: 'I will say little to thee, but thou shalt feel more from me hereafter.' The honest man had scarce been departed from her half an hour but he felt himself as if he had been set into your Scotch-boot;[6] or Spanish strappado or your *Morbus Gallicus*[7] was nothing to it—sometimes in a pestiferous heat, at others a chill cold, but at all times in continual aches and racking of his limbs as if the Devil had set him on his tenters[8] to make broadcloth of him.

In this perplexity he continued consuming himself, not being able neither to go nor stand, nor physic could help him, nor no means be had to ease him; when one of his neighbours coming in neighbourly love to visit him, he began to open his mind to him that he persuaded himself by such a one he[9] was bewitched, and he was as faithfully persuaded that if he could but have 2 or 3 good scratches at her face whereby he might draw blood of her, he should recover presently.

His neighbour advised him by some wile to send for her home yet (that between them both held unconvenient, for that either suspecting herself or for not being friends, she would not come) that in the night following his neighbour would have this sick man carried in a chair and lodged in his house, and in the morning his wife (whom he knew she was good friends withal) should by some wile or another draw her thither; when if he of himself were not strong enough to scratch her, he (as he held charily*) would help him.

This the next morning was done accordingly; the witch comes and is well scratched, upon which within 3 or 4 days (as fast as the man could recover strength) he is up and goes abroad. Which this J.H. perceiving, arrests him and by a trial in law for this battery had 5/- damages and her costs of suit given her. The man, according as he was condemned, paid her, which [was] no sooner by her received but that honest man fell into his former passion, languishing a while, and died. In the same manner she served another who, meeting her out of the town in a lane, took the like revenge upon her and recovered.

Both which blown over (only a little murmured against by a neighbour of hers) a young woman [was][10] washing clothes in an outer room

---

[6] Instrument of torture for crushing leg-bones; see *Newes from Scotland*.

[7] Morbus Gallicus: 'the French evil' (known to the French as 'the English disease'); syphilis.

[8] tenters, i.e. wooden frames, set with *tenter-hooks* or bent nails to hold cloth as it is being stretched and dried.

[9] Original has 'she'.

[10] Original has 'being'.

next the street, where in a wainscot cradle[11] her child lay asleep, when this J.H. daughter chanced to come by just in the instant as she was throwing out a little rinsing water and by chance some of which unawares sprinkled upon her—which the wench, seeming moved at, called to her with these words: 'Do you throw your water upon me, gossip? Before it be long I'ld be revenged for it.'

The woman, sorry for the offence, had done, followed her business and thought no further of it, when on a sudden (while she was stepped but into a next room to hang up some clothes) the cradle wherein her child lay was thrown over, shattered all to pieces, the child upon the face whelmed under it and killed.

Thus we see the Devil hath such power on these his damnable servants that neither men nor infants are to be pitied by them.

Not long after, she had all-bewitched a wealthy man's daughter in the town, who having a good substantial yeoman to her brother, in pity of his sister's grief [he] rode to Cambridge; and there acquainting a friend of his with his sister's affliction, the scholar told him she was bewitched yet, in regard they two had been of an ancient friendship and that himself had some acquaintance with his sister, in spite of her incubi,[12] her spirits, and the Devil and all, he'd help. Which according to promise he performed, and by that time her brother was returned, his sister was recovered.

In revenge of [this] (for that her sorcery was crossed and the maid reduced to health by her brother's carefulness) she caused such a plague upon all his cattle that they all immediately perished and consumed, not one of that great store he had being left to be a remembrance of the rest; himself shortly after died.[13]

These and a number more at her trial were inferred against; only one more amongst the rest, though but a homely tale, for that it made all the bench to laugh I'll record of her, and conclude.

How the witch served a fellow in an ale-house.

There was an honest fellow, and as boon a companion, dwelling in Royston, one that loved the pot with the long neck almost as well as his prayers, 'for' quoth he, 'as I know one is medicinable for the soul, I am sure the other's physic for the body.'

[11] Cradle made of solid panels of oak or other wood.

[12] Very rare concept in English trials till a late date; it probably means no more than 'witch's familiar' here.

[13] Original has 'did these' without punctuation.

It was this fuddle-cap's chance (with 3 or 4 as good malt-worms as himself, and as sure, where the best lap[14] was to be found, together as 4 knaves in a pair* of cards) to be drinking where this witch came in, and stood gloating upon them. Now this good-fellow, not enduring to look upon a bad face but his own, especially when he is cup-shot,* called aloud to her, 'Do you hear, witch? look t'other ways, I cannot abide a nose of that fashion! or else turn your face the wrong side outward, it may look like raw flesh for flies to blow maggots in!'

Still as the witch was ready to reply, he would cross her with one scurvy jest, and between every jest drink to her, yet swear 'God damn him, she should starve ere she should have a drop on't; since the pot was sweet he'd keep it so, for should but her lips once look into the lid on't, her breath's so strong, and would so stick in the cup, that all the water that runs by Ware would not wash it out again.'

At last the witch got so much time to call to him; 'Dost thou hear, good friends?' quoth she. 'What sayest thou, ill-face?' quoth he. 'Marry, I say' quoth she, 'that thou throw'st in thy drink apace, but shalt not find it so easy coming out.' 'Nay, as for the coming out', answered the fellow, 'I throwed it in above and it shall come out beneath, and then thou shalt have some of it, if thou wilt, because I am in hope it will poison thee.'

Then with this greeting, away goes the witch in a chafe,* and the fellow sits down to follow his drink. But as the end of all drunkards is either to ming[15] or to sleep, so out goes this fellow and, drawing his gentleman-usher against a pale-side, finds me atop of his nose a red lump as big as a cherry, and in his belly felt such a rumbling as if the Tower of Babel had fallen about his ears. Oh! the sight thereof drave his heart to an ague and his tongue to an alarum, and out he cries, 'The witch! the witch! I am undone! I am undone! Oh God, women of Royston, help! help! The witch, the witch! I am a man spoiled! Help, I am undone!'

At that word 'help, the witch' in comes one of his fellows, runs in haste, and asked him what they should help, the witch? 'Oh', quoth he, 'to the gallows, for I am undone by her.' Well, yet out he runs, where for that night she would not be found; but next morning meeting her in a lane, his pain rather increased than lessened, and there fastening[16]

---

[14] lap: slang phrase as in 'tipple' (the noun).
[15] ming: urinate. 'gentlemen-usher' and 'nose' are appropriate euphemisms.
[16] Original has 'fasts'.

his ten commandments[17] upon her, he almost scratched out her eyes—
nay, left her not till he brought her to the town, where for this and the
rest she was apprehended, and she and her daughter, with George Dell
and his mother, worthily suffered death the 4 of August.

[17] ten commandments: fingers or finger-nails.

VIII Jacobean Style

The Swimming Test

The law of 1604 (q.v.) differed from that of 1563 mainly in its strengthening of already existing penalties for those who caused bodily harm, injured goods and cattle, and sought love or gold by supernatural means. Two new clauses attempted to clarify the section dealing with witchcraft and conjuration as such by making it a felony to dig up dead bodies, skin or bone for use in sorcery, or to 'consult, covenant with, entertain, employ, feed or reward' an evil spirit.

Grave-rifling seems to have taken place in England mainly as a variety of simple theft, and it does not figure in English witch trials without accompanying accusations of death or injury caused by witchcraft (see cases of Joan Harrison, 1606, and Anne Chattox, 1612). However, the keeping of a familiar devil in animal form was the most common popular sign of a witch, and giving it legal recognition as a felony *in itself* might have been expected to result in a great increase in convictions for witchcraft. Michael Dalton, for instance, in the first (1618) edition of his *Countrey Justice* (a legal handbook for the use of the Justices of the Peace who received the first complaints and depositions for cases to be tried at the Assizes) lists the familiar as the first evidence against witches, and the teat sucked by the familiar as the second, referring to the 1612 trial of Lancashire witches as his precedent; confession only is a better 'proof'.[1]

The Authorised Version of the Bible, completed in 1611, did nothing to weaken the identification of 'pythoness' or 'ventriloquist' or 'diviner' with the popular idea of a witch—'a woman that hath a familiar spirit' (I *Samuel* 28: 7); in passages like *Deuteronomy* 18: 10–12 and *Leviticus* 20: 27, it extended the use of that phrase. Theological works concerning witchcraft other than possession appeared in increasing numbers after 1600;[2] though all were Protestant or Puritan, their influence was diffuse, since they disagreed radically about the tests which 'proved' a person to be a witch. However, many attached importance to the familiar, and nearly all believed 'good' witchcraft to be as felonious as 'bad' (the virtuous William Perkins would even have sanctioned torture to extract confessions).

[1] Michael Dalton, *The Countrey Justice* (London, 1618).

[2] George Gifford, *A Dialogue concerning Witches* . . . reprinted 1603. King James I, *Daemonologie* . . . reprinted 1603. William Perkins, *A Discourse of the Damned Art of Witchcraft*, 1608. James Mason, *The Anatomie of Sorcerie* . . . 1612. Alexander Roberts, *A Treatise of Witchcraft* . . . 1616. John Cotta, *The Triall of Witchcraft* . . . 1616 (medical approach). Thomas Cooper, *The Mystery of Witchcraft* . . . 1617, etc.

Yet in the courts, most judges refused to meddle with the heresy of witch-craft, and continued to demand testimony of legal crimes committed by the witch (however gullible they seem in the testimony they accepted, judges and juries made some distinctions invisible to us which resulted in a great number of acquittals). Since law relied so heavily on precedent, actual court practice could not change rapidly. And curiously, the actions of King James himself reinforced the caution of judges, making even the witch-hunters among them unwilling to be too radical in dealing with the crime of witchcraft.[3] For James, as we see from his *Daemonology*, drew his idea of witchcraft from the theology of the Continent and from the Scottish trials which were brought about under the double influence of France and Geneva. Witchcraft to him meant regicide, the Satanism of the Sabbath, unnatural powers to fly through the air or move across the sea; the antics of possessed children —the typical English form of bewitchment—were to him mostly too frivolous and uncertain an exercise of the Devil's power to be taken seriously, and he intervened in a good many such trials to discountenance the child witnesses and to disgrace judges too quick to give sentence of death on their evidence.[4] Where death or serious injury were involved, the law was allowed to take its course without interference from the royal detective.

Thus an increased popular concern about witchcraft as such, fed by the

[3] Dr. A. D. J. Macfarlane has made an intensive study of the Essex Assize records between 1560 and 1680, and has found 503 indictments of 303 persons under witchcraft statutes during that period. (With a comparable survival of records, Essex has four times as many indictments for witchcraft as Hertfordshire, Kent, Surrey and Sussex combined.) He has most kindly allowed me to quote the following table of accusations from his forthcoming book *Witchcraft in Tudor and Stuart England: a regional study*, to be published by Routledge and Kegan Paul.

	Number of cases	Number of persons involved
Injuring/killing people or property	462	271
Invocation of evil spirits	28	29
Treasure or lost goods sought by witchcraft	9	11
'Intent' to murder or injure	2	2
Using dead bodies for witchcraft	1	1
Fortune telling	1	1
'Consulting' witches	1	1

(Some of the cases and persons overlap from different categories; for instance half those accused of invoking evil spirits were also accused of particular injuries inflicted on people or property. The totals of table 2 are, therefore, larger than the actual totals of persons and cases.)

[4] Notably Sir Humphrey Winch and Sir Randolph Crew at Leicester in 1616; they hanged nine witches on the accusation of one possessed child, and trial of six other women was stopped by James. The many scattered records of the case are listed by Ewen, *Witchcraft and Demonianism*, ed. cit., pp. 228–9. For a summary of interventions by James, see Kittredge, *Witchcraft in Old and New England*, ed. cit., pp. 314–28.

new law and by increasing numbers of theological treatises, was often frustrated in the courts; fortunately so, for the mentality of persecution appears with increasing frequency. In the pamphlets that follow, we catch a new tone of self-righteous condemnation of sin, a Pharisaic jeer at the wretchedness of those who make the bad bargain with evil, which accompanies an increased popular brutality and an increased willingness to take arbitrary and extra-legal measures. The 'prefatory remarks' of the Elizabethan publisher seem to have spread, and blurred the whole scene.

The king himself had said that witches could be discovered by the confessions of other witches and by two physical tests—'the finding of their marke, and the trying the insensiblenes thereof. The other is their fleeting [i.e. skimming or floating] on the water.'[5] The insensible mark was much less common in English superstition at this date than the teat at which the ubiquitous familiar sucked; but the idea of the swimming test (recorded in Scottish witch trials in 1597, and prevalent in the North of England shortly thereafter)[6] linked up with memories of an ancient tradition of ordeal by fire or water, which could be used as a test of guilt in felonies up till 1217. Thus the water ordeal became a common pre-trial exercise, sometimes ordered by Justices of the Peace, but more often initiated by complainants independently.

When regular assizes were suspended during the Civil War, popular tests like pricking, swimming and 'watching' became pre-eminent as legal proofs of guilt or innocence, and the ratio of convictions to accusations, which had declined steadily since 1617, leaped sky-high.[7] With the re-establishment of the assizes and regular legal procedures, the downward trend re-asserted itself, and by 1700 those attacking a supposed witch were themselves in danger of serious trouble from the law.

It is well to remember, as we read the following examples of popular spite and legal credulity that, though Throckmorton in 1593 and Rutland in 1619 were able to get witches executed for deaths and injuries inflicted on their families, the powerful Fairfax[8] was unable to do so in 1622, despite two trials.

Witches Apprehended, Examined and Executed, for notable villanies by them committed both by Land and Water. With a strange and most true triall how to know whether a woman be a Witch or not. (London, 1613).

. . . At[9] a place called Milton, some three miles from Bedford, was lately dwelling one Mother Sutton who, being a widow and of declining years, had her daughter called Mary Sutton (as it was thought by the

---

[5] King James, *Daemonologie, in forme of a Dialogue* (Edinburgh, 1597), p. 80.
[6] See account of swimming test in following pamphlet.
[7] C. H. L'Estrange Ewen, *Witchcraft and Demonianism*, ed. cit., p. 100.
[8] *A Discourse of Witchcraft As it was acted in the Family of Mr. Edward Fairfax of Fuystone in the County of York, in the year 1621*. Edited R. Monckton Milnes, *Miscellanies of the Philobiblon Society* (London, 1858–1859), Vol. V, and elsewhere. A MS. version with illustration is Brit. Mus. Add. MSS. 32496.
[9] Introduction omitted; extract starts on A4.

Test for witchcraft: swimming a witch
Witches Apprehended, Examined and Executed . . . 1613

neighbours thereabouts) resident with her as a stay and comfort to her age, when she kept her but as a furtherer to her devilish practices—nay indeed, to make her a scholar to the Devil himself.

This Widow Sutton having been dwelling a long time in the foresaid town of Milton, and not suspected as then to have been a practicer in this devilish exercise of witchcraft, was by the townsmen (being held but poor) for her better relief chosen to be the hog-herd, or hog-keeper. In which service she continued long, not without commendations for her dutiful care had therein.

And though many cattle oftentimes miscarried, and were taken with staggerings, frenzies and other diseases, to their confusions and impoverishing of the owners, yet she [was] not till of late suspected to be a cause thereof, though since it hath evidently been proved against her.

Continuing thus almost for the space of twenty, or one and twenty years (and in that time had brought her daughter to be as perfect in her devilish charms as herself) there grew some difference between a gentleman of worship called Master Enger dwelling at Milton Mills and this Mother Sutton, on whom she had vowed to take a strange and actual revenge for the discontent she had conceived against him.

Which rancour of hers she thus prosecuted: his horses that were left well in his stable overnight, she caused them to be found dead in the morning, some strangled, some having beaten out their brains, others dead and no cause perceived how. Besides this loss, which for the strangeness bred some amazement in him for that it happened not once but often, this also did second it: when his swine were in the fields at their troughs, eating their meat, some of them would suddenly fall mad, and violently fall to tearing out the guts and bowels of their fellows; others by ten and twenty in a company, as if they had been carried with one desire, would leave their feeding and run headlong into the mill dams and drown themselves.[10]

So that, not by accidental means but the hellish and most damnable witchcrafts of this Mother Sutton and her daughter, many these harmless cattle and oxen made as needful reliefs to the necessity of man, were thus perplexed; and an honest and worshipful gentleman, Master Enger, from who she had oftentimes both food and clothing, damnified by her means to the value of two hundred pounds in less than two years.

In the time of these aforesaid losses happened to Master Enger, one Henry Sutton, the bastard son of Mary Sutton (for it is to be noted that, although she was never married, yet she had three bastards) coming to play himself about the mill-dam, fell to throwing in of stones, dirt and filth, with other such unhappiness incident to children. Of which having been often forewarned by an ancient servant of Master Enger's who was then about the mills, and finding the boy notwithstanding his admonishment rather to persevere than to desist from his knavery, he came to him and, giving him a little blow or two on the ear, the boy went home crying, and the ancient fellow went back to his labour.

This Henry Sutton coming home, began to tell his mother how a

---

[10] Pigs are given to cannibalism (if fed swill containing pork, for instance) and to senseless herd behaviour such as that recorded in *Luke* 8: 26–33. Epidemic diseases of stock were an almost total mystery at the date of this pamphlet, though it was known that certain plants in the pasture would cause poisoning. Deliberate poisoning by the witch is not absolutely out of the question.

man of Master Enger's (naming him) had beaten him, whose venomous nature being soon enkindled, though he had received no hurt, she vowed to take revenge, and thus it followed.

This ancient servant with another of his master's men were on the morrow (being Market day at Bedford) appointed by their master to carry a cartload of corn for the furnishing of the market. Being on their way, at Milton town's end they espied a goodly fair black sow grazing, who as they drove their team still kept pace with them till they came within a mile of Bedford. Where, on a sudden, they perceived her to turn twice or thrice about as readily as a windmill sail at work; and as suddenly their horses fell to starting, and drawing some one way, some another. At last the strongest prevailing, they drew away the cart and corn, and left the wheels and axletree behind them. The horses they ran away with their load as if they had been mad, and the two fellows after the horses, the horses being affrighted half out of their strength and the fellows as much mad to see them.

Down went one sack on this side the cart, and another on that; the horses they ran as if they would have sweltered* themselves, and the fellows after them breathless, and sweating to make the wild jades stay. All which till the Devil and the witch had played their parts would not serve turn.

At last this tragic-comedy drawing to an end, they made a stand; when the servants bringing them back and finding their axletree, pins, and all things unbroken, took up their corn, made fit their cart again, and the horses drew as formally as could be. And they went forthwards towards Bedford, mistrusting nothing, though they saw the sow following and grazing, as they did before.

Being come to Bedford, and having unloaden the cart and made sale of the corn, the one fell to driving the team home again, leaving his ancienter fellow behind him at Bedford; who, happening into a company, fell a-carousing with boon companions like himself, and in the height of their cups, they as desirous to hear as he to tell, he related unto them the manner and form how his cart and wheels were divorced as he was coming to town.

Some wondered; all laughed; the company broke up; and this ancient servant took his horse with purpose to overtake his fellow who was gone before with the cart. Who no sooner was out of Bedford town's end but he might behold the same sow (as near as he could judge) grazing again, as if the Devil and the witch had made her his footman to wait upon him. But the fellow not mistrusting anything, made his nag take a speedy amble, and so to overtake the cart, while the sow side by side ran along by him.

Then[11] he, overtaking his fellow, had[12] scarce spoken to him but the horses as before fell to their old contention, running one from another; only the horses were better furnished than before, for where at first they left both wheels and axletree behind them, they now had the axletree to take their part, leaving the wheels in the highway for the servants to bring after.

The horse in this manner coming home drove all the beholders into amazement, and the servants beginning to have mistrust of the black sow, they watched whither she went, whom they found to go into Mother Sutton's house; of which they told their master, and of all the accidents aforesaid, who made slight of it to them, whatsoever he conceived of it himself, and saying he supposed they were drunk, they departed.

The same old servant of Master Enger's within few days after going to plough, fell into talk of Mother Sutton and of Mary Sutton her daughter, of what pranks he had heard they had played thereabouts in the country, as also what accidents had befallen him and his fellow as they had passed to and from Bedford. In discoursing of which a beetle came and struck the same fellow on the breast; and he presently fell into a trance as he was guiding the plough, the extremity whereof was such as, his senses altogether distract and his body and mind utterly distempered, the beholders deemed him clean hopeless of recovery.

Yea, his other fellow upon this sudden sight was stricken into such amazement as he stood like a lifeless trunk divided from his vital spirits, as far unable to help him as the other was needful to be helped by him. Till at length, being somewhat recovered and awaked from that astonishment, he made haste homeward and carried his master word of what had happened.

Upon delivery of this news (for he was a man highly esteemed by him for his honest and long service) there was much moan made for him in the house, and Master Enger himself had not the least part of grief for his extremity, but with all possible speed hasted into the field and used help to have him brought home. After which he neglected no means, nor spared any cost that might ease his servant, or redeem him from the misery he was in, but all was in vain.

For his ecstasies* were nothing lessened, but continued a long time in as grievous perplexity as at first; yet though they suspected much,

[11] Original has 'When'. [12] Original has 'and had'.

they had no certain proof or knowledge of the cause. Their means were therefore the shorter* to cure the effect. But as a thief, when he entereth into a house to rob, first putteth out the lights according to that 'Qui male agit, odit lucem' (he that doth evil hateth light) so these imps that live in the gunshot of devilish assaults go about to darken and disgrace the light of such as are toward* and virtuous, and make the night the instrument to contrive their wicked purposes.

For these witches, having so long and covertly continued to do much mischief by their practices, were so hardened in their lewd and vile proceeding that the custom of their sin had quite taken away the sense and feeling thereof; and they spared not to continue the perplexity of this old servant both in body and mind, in such sort that his friends were as desirous to see death rid him from his extremity as a woman great with child is ever musing upon the time of her delivery. For where distress is deep and the conscience clear, 'Mors expectatur absque formidine, exoptatur cum dulcedine, excipitur cum devotione' (death is looked for without fear, desired with delight, and accepted with devotion.)

As the acts and enterprises of these wicked persons are dark and devilish, so in the perseverance of this fellow's perplexity he, being in his distraction both of body and mind, yet in bed and awake, espied Mary Sutton (the daughter) in a moonshine night come in at a window in her accustomed and personal habit and shape, with her knitting work in her hands, and sit[13] down at his bed's feet, sometimes working and knitting with her needles, and sometimes gazing and staring him in the face [so] as his grief was thereby redoubled and increased.

Not long after she drew nearer unto him and sat by his bedside (yet all this while he had neither power to stir or speak) and told him if he would consent she should come to bed to him, he should be restored to his former health and prosperity.[14] Thus the Devil strives to enlarge his kingdom, and upon the neck of one wickedness to heap another, so that 'Periculum probat transeuntium raritas, pereuntium multitudo'. (In the dangerous sea of this world, the rareness of those that pass the

---

[13] Original has 'sitting'.

[14] This pathetic old man's vanity marks the first appearance in the witch-pamphlets of the witch as demonic sexual temptress, though there are legends of saints afflicted by similarly explicit incubi and succubi. Earlier incubus-nightmares were more frightening than erotic, and were attributed to the witch's familiar—a cat in the case of Lady Cromwell (*The Witches of Warboys*) and Doll Barthram (*The Triall of Maister Dorrell*). The English witch was frequently unchaste, but in the usual prosaic fashion.

same over safe and the multitude of others that perish in their passage, sufficiently prove the peril we live in.)

In the ocean sea, of four ships not one miscarries; in the sea of this world, of many fours not one escapes his particular cross and calamity. Yet in our greatest weakness and debility, when the devil is most busy to tempt us and seduce us from God, then is God strongest in the hearts of His children and most ready to be auxiliant* and helping to save and uphold them from declining and falling. God's liberality appears more than His rigour, for whom He draws out [of]the Devil's throat by faith, He would have to trample him down by virtue, lest he should only have fled, not foiled his enemy.

This is made shown in His miraculous working with this fellow; for he that before had neither power to move or speak, had then presently by divine assistance free power and liberty to give repulse to her assault, and denial to her filthy and detested motion, and to upbraid her of her abominable life and behaviour, having before had three bastards and never married. She upon this, seeing her suit cold and that God's power was more predominant with him than her devilish practice, vanished, and departed the same way she came.

She was no sooner gone, but as well as he could he called for his master, told him that now he could tell him the cause of this vexation; that Mother Sutton's daughter came in at the window, sat knitting and working by him, and that if he would have consented to her filthiness, he should have been freed from his misery; and related all that had happened.

His master was glad of this news for that, the means found out, the matter and manner of his grief might be the easier helped and redressed; yet was he distrustful of the truth, and rather esteemed it an idleness of his brain than an accident of verity. Nevertheless he resolved to make proof thereof. The next morrow he took company along with him and went into the fields, where he found her working and tending her hogs. There Master Enger, speaking to her [said] 'She was a very good housewife and that she followed her work night and day'. 'No sir,' said she, 'my housewifery is very slender, neither am I so good a follower of my work as you persuade me.' With that, he told her that she was, and that she had been working at his house the night before.

She would confess nothing, but stood in stiff denial upon her purgation, insomuch as the gentleman by fair entreaties persuaded her to go home with him to satisfy his man, and to resolve some doubts that were had of her. She utterly refused, and made answer she would not stir a foot, neither had they authority to compel her to go without a constable; which Master Enger perceiving, and seeing her obstinacy to be so great, fell into a greater dislike and distrust of her than he did before, and made no more ado, but caused her to be set upon an horseback to be brought to his house.

All the company could hardly bring her away, but as fast as they set her up, in despite of them she would swerve down, first on the one side, then the other; till at last they were fain by main force to join together and hold her violently down to the horseback, and so bring her to the place where this perplexed person lay in his bed.

Where being come, and brought by force to his bed-side he (as directions had been given unto him) drew blood of her, and presently began to amend and be well again. But her assiduity and continual exercise in doing mischief did so prevail with her to do this fellow further hurt that, watching but advantage and opportunity to touch his neck again with her finger, it was no sooner done and she departed, but he fell into as great, or far worse vexation than he had before.

The report of this was carried up and down all Bedfordshire, and this Mary Sutton's wicked and lewd courses being rumoured as well abroad as in Master Enger's house, at last it came into the mouth of Master Enger's son, being a little boy of seven years old; who, not long after, espying old Mother Sutton going to the mill to grind corn, and remembering what speeches he had heard passed of her and her daughter, followed the old woman, flinging stones at her and calling her 'Witch!'

Which she observing, conceited a rancour and deadly hatred to this young child, and purposed not to suffer opportunity pass to be revenged. As soon, therefore, as she had despatched at the mill, she hasted homewards and could not be quiet till she had grumbled to her daughter what had happened, and how the child had served her.

Then, conferring how Master Enger had used Mary Sutton the daughter, and how his[15] little son had used the mother, they both resolved and vowed revenge. This conference and consultation of villainy was had and concluded in the presence and hearing of Henry Sutton, the bastard of Mary Sutton, little thinking that his fortune should be to give in evidence to break the neck of his own mother and grandmother.

To effect their devilish purpose to the young child of Master Enger, they called up their two spirits, whom she called Dick and Jude; and

[15] Original has 'her'.

having given them suck at their two teats which they had on their thighs (found out afterwards by enquiry and search of women) they gave them charge to strike the little boy and to turn him to torment. Which was not long in performing, but the child, being distract, was put to such bitter and insupportable misery as by his life his torments were augmented, and by his death they were abridged. For his tender and unripe age was so enfeebled and made weak by that devilish infliction of extremity as in five days, not able longer to endure them, death gave end to his perplexities.

The gentleman did not so much grieve for the loss and hindrance he had in his cattle (which was much) nor for the miserable distress that his servant had endured (which was more) as that the hopeful days of his young son were so untimely cut off (which touched his heart most of all). Yet did his discretion temper his passions with such patience that he referred the remembrance of his wrongs to that heavenly power that permits not such iniquity to pass unrevealed or unrevenged.

As he was thus rapt in a sea of woes, there came a gentleman (a friend of his, forth of the north) that, travelling towards London, sojourned with him all night. He, perceiving Master Enger to be full of grief, was desirous to know the cause thereof; and he was as unwilling by the discourse of his misfortunes to renew his many sorrows, till at last his friend's urgent importunacy* persuaded him not to pass it over with silence.

Upon Master Enger's relation of what had happened, the gentleman demanded if he had none in suspicion that should do these wrongs unto him. 'Yes,' quoth Master Enger, and therewithal he named this Mary Sutton and her mother, and told him the particulars of his losses and miseries. His friend understanding this, advised him to take them, or any one of them, to his mill dam (having first shut up the mill gates that the water might be at highest) and then, binding their arms cross, stripping them into their smocks and leaving their legs at liberty, throw them into the water.

'Yet lest they should not be witches, and that their lives might not be in danger of drowning, let there be a rope tied about their middles, so long that it may reach from one side of your dam to the other, where on each side let one of your men stand, that if she chance to sink they may draw her up and preserve her. Then if she swim, take her up and cause some women to search her, upon which, if they find any extraordinary marks about her, let her the second time be bound, and have her right thumb bound to her left toe and her left thumb to her right toe, and your men with the same rope (if need be) to preserve her, and be thrown into the water when, if she swim, you may build upon it that she is a witch. I have seen it often tried in the north country.'[16]

The morrow after, Master Enger rode into the fields where Mary Sutton (the daughter) was, having some of his men to accompany him; where after some questions made unto her, they assayed to bind her on horseback when, all his men being presently stricken lame, Master Enger himself began to remember that, once rating her about his man, he was on the sudden in the like perplexity; and then, taking courage and desiring God to be his assistance, with a cudgel which he had in his hand he beat her till she was scarce able to stir.

At which his men presently recovered, bound her to their master's horse, and brought her home to his house; and shutting up his mill gates, did as before the gentleman had advised him. When being thrown in the first time, she sunk some two foot into the water with a fall, but rose again and floated upon the water like a plank. Then he commanded her to be taken out, and had women ready that searched her and found under her left thigh a kind of teat which, after, the bastard son confessed her spirits in several shapes—as cats, moles, etc.—used to suck her.

Then was she the second time bound cross her thumbs and toes, according to the former direction, and then she sunk not at all but sitting upon the water, turned round about like a wheel, or as that which commonly we call a whirlpool; notwithstanding Master Enger's men standing on each side of the dam with a rope tossing her up and down to make her sink,[17] but could not.

And then, being taken up, she as boldly as if she had been innocent asked them if they could do any more to her; when Master Enger began to accuse her with the death of his cattle, the languish of his man (who continued in sorrow both of body and mind from Christmas to Shrovetide)[18] as also the death of his son. All which she constantly

[16] Few records exist for the North of England at this date, but the test may have spread from Scotland (see headnote). During the witch-hunt raised after the attack on James in 1590 (*Newes from Scotland*) some witches escaped to England (*Calendar of state papers relating to Scotland* (London, 1858), Vol. II, pp. 587–89).

[17] In 1596 Thomas Darling of Burton-on-Trent had visions of a green cat that tossed him up and down 'in a string'; it is possible he had seen such a test performed.

[18] Shrovetide: Quinquagesima Sunday, Shrove Monday and Tuesday. A period of festival preceding Lent.

denied and stood at defiance with him till, being carried towards a Justice, Master Enger told her it was bootless* to stand so obstinately upon denial of those matters, for her own son Henry had revealed all, both as touching herself and her mother, and of the time and manner of their plotting to torment his little boy.

When she heard that, her heart misgave her, she confessed all, and acknowledged the Devil had now left her to that shame that is reward to such as follow him. Upon which confession the mother also was apprehended and, both being committed to Bedford gaol, many other matters were there produced against them, of long continuance (for they had remained as before about twenty years) in the prosecution of these lewd and wicked practices.

But for this matter of Master Enger at the last Assizes, the evidence of the bastard son, and the confessions severally taken both of old Mother Sutton and her daughter Mary, found them guilty in all former objections. So that, arraigned at Bedford on Monday the thirtieth of March last past, they had a just conviction, and on Tuesday the next day after they were executed.

Finis

Northamptonshire Witches

The Witches of Northamptonshire

Agnes Browne	*Arthur Bill*	*Witches*
Joane Vaughan	*Hellen Jenkenson*	
Mary Barber		

Who were all executed at Northampton the 22. of July last. 1612. (*London 1612*)

The case is confirmed by a manuscript account in the British Museum; *A Brief abstract of the Arraignment of nine Witches at Northampton: July 21, 1612* (Brit. Mus. Sloane 972, f. 7)[1] which mentions five more witches and gives details of Mr. Avery's speeches and visions in his fits of possession. It also records a great deal of pre-trial brutality—beating, scratching, swimming, searching for witch-teats, and repetition of Creed and Lord's Prayer under duress.

It is noteworthy that the swimming test (recorded in the pamphlet) is ordered by the Justices of the Peace, and the author justifies this by a long and unacknowledged quotation from King James' *Daemonology.*

The Arraignment and execution of Agnes Brown, and Joan Vaughan or Varnham her daughter, who were both executed at Northampton the 22 of July last.[2]

This Agnes Brown led her life at Guilsborough in the county of Northampton, of poor parentage and poorer education, one that as she was born to no good, was for want of grace never in the way to receive any; ever noted to be of an ill nature and wicked disposition, spiteful and malicious, and many years before she died both hated and feared among her neighbours, being long suspected in the town where she dwelt of that crime which afterwards proved true. This Agnes Brown had a daughter whose name was Joan Vaughan or Varnham, a maid (or at least unmarried) as gracious as the mother, and both of them as far from grace as heaven from hell.

This Joan was so well brought up under her mother's elbow that she hanged with her for company under her mother's nose. But to the

---

[1] This MS. has been transcribed and modernised by C. H. L'Estrange Ewen, *Witchcraft and Demonianism*, ed. cit., pp. 209–12; I quote from this version below.

[2] Introductory matter is omitted; the extract starts at B2.

Witches visiting a sick friend
The Witches of Northamptonshire 1612

purpose. This Joan one day happening into the company of one Mistress Belcher, a virtuous and godly gentlewoman of the same town of Guilsborough, this Joan Vaughan, whether of purpose to give occasion of anger to the said Mistress Belcher, or but to continue her vile and ordinary custom of behaviour, committed something either in speech or gesture so unfitting and unseeming the nature of womanhood that it displeased the most that were there present.

But especially it touched the modesty of this gentlewoman, who was so much moved with her bold and impudent demeanour that she could not contain herself, but suddenly rose up and struck her—howbeit, hurt her not, but forced her to avoid the company. Which this chicken of her dam's hatching taking disdainfully, and being also enraged (as they that in this kind having power to harm, never have patience to bear) at her going out told the gentlewoman that she would remember this injury and revenge it. To whom Mistress Belcher answered that she neither feared her nor her mother, but bade her do her worst.

This trull* holding herself much disgraced, hies home in all haste to her mother and tells her the wrong which she suggested Mistress

Belcher had done unto her. Now was the fire and the tow met, all was inflamed; nothing but rage and destruction! Had they had an hundred spirits at command, the worst and the most hurtful had been called to this council and employed about this business! Howbeit, upon advice (if such a sin may take or give advice) they stayed three or four days before they practised any thing, to avoid suspicion; whether the mother advised the daughter or the daughter the mother I know not, but I am sure the Devil never gives advice to any man or woman in any act to be wary.

The matter thus sleeping (but rage and revenge do never rest) within a while was awaked, which Mistress Belcher to her intolerable pain too soon felt; for being alone in her house, she was suddenly taken with such a griping and gnawing in her body that she cried out, and could scarce be held by such as came unto her. And being carried to her bed, her face was many times so disfigured by being drawn awry that it bred both fear and astonishment to all the beholders; and ever as she had breath, she cried, 'Here comes Joan Vaughan! Away with Joan Vaughan!'[3]

This gentlewoman being a long time thus strangely handled, to the great grief of her friends, it happened that her brother, one Master Avery, hearing of his sister's sickness and extremity came to see her, and being a sorrowful beholder of that which before he had heard, was much moved in his mind at his sister's pitiful condition, and the rather for that, as he knew not the nature of her disease, so he was utterly ignorant of any direct way to minister cure or help to the same.

He often heard her cry out against Joan Vaughan alias Varnham and her mother, and heard by report of the neighbours that which before had happened betwixt his sister and the said Joan; insomuch as having confirmed his suspicion that it was nothing else but witchcraft that thus tormented his sister, following rage rather than reason, [he] ran suddenly towards the house of the said Agnes Brown with purpose to draw both the mother and the daughter to his sister for her to draw blood on.

But still as he came near the house he was suddenly stopped and

[3] According to the MS. account, her illness 'was generally suspected to be witchcraft, but she would never be so persuaded by any of her friends for almost a year's space, till March 15th last past, when being in her fit, some spectators by nominated sundry suspected parties, which she still disclaimed, and at last, naming Jone Brown, daughter to Agnes Brown, she replied, "hath she done it", then they named her again, and Mrs. Belcher answered again, "did she", and so from that time forth persisted to accuse Jone Brown. . . .'

could not enter; whether it was an astonishment through his fear or that the spirits had power to stay him I cannot judge, but he reported at his coming back that he was forcibly stayed and could not for his life go any further forward—and they report in the country that he is a gentleman of a stout courage. He tried twice or thrice after to go to the house, but in the same place where he was stayed at first, he was still stayed. Belike the Devil stood there sentinel, kept his station well! Upon this, Master Avery being sorry and much aggrieved that he could not help his sister in this tormenting distress, and finding also that no physic could do her any good or easement, took a sorrowful leave and heavily departed home to his own house.

The imp of this dam (and both imps of the Devil) being glad that they were both out of his reach, showed presently that they had longer arms than he. For he felt within a short time after this coming home that he was not out of their reach, being by the devilish practices of these two hell-hounds suddenly and grievously tormented in the like kind and with the like fits of his sister; which continued until these two witches, either by the procurement of Master Avery and his friends (or for some other devilish practice they had committed in the country) were apprehended* and brought to Northampton gaol by Sir William Saunders of Cottesbrooke, knight.

To which place the brother and the sister were brought, still desirous to scratch the witches. Which act, whether it be but superstitiously observed by some, or that experience hath found any power for help in this kind of action by others, I list not to enquire; only this I understand—that many have attempted the practising thereof, how successively* I know not. But this gentleman and his sister being brought to the gaol where these witches were detained, having once gotten sight of them in their fits, the witches being held, by scratching they drew blood of them, and were suddenly delivered of their pain. Howbeit they were no sooner out of sight but they fell again into their old trances and were more violently tormented than before; for when Mischief is once afoot, she grows in short time so headstrong that she is hardly curbed.

Not long after Mastery Avery and his sister having been both in Northampton and having drawn blood of the witches—riding both homewards in one coach, there appeared to their view a man and a woman riding both upon a black horse. Master Avery having spied them afar off, and noting many strange gestures from them, suddenly spake to them that were by and (as it were prophetically) cried out in these words 'that either they or their horses should presently miscarry'. And immediately the horses fell down dead.

Whereupon Master Avery rose up praising the grace and mercies of God, that He had so powerfully delivered them, and had not suffered the foul spirits to work the uttermost of their mischief upon men made after His image, but had turned their fury against beasts. Upon this they both hied them home, still praising God for their escape, and were never troubled after.

I had almost forgotten to tell you before, that Master Avery was by the judges themselves in the Castle yard of Northampton seen in the midst of his fits, and that he strangely continued in them until this Joan Vaughan was brought unto him.

But now to draw near unto their ends; this Agnes Brown and her daughter Joan Vaughan or Varnham, being brought to their arraignment, were there indited for that they had bewitched the bodies of Master Avery and his sister Mistress Belcher in manner and form aforesaid, together with the body of a young child to the death (the true relation whereof came not to my hands).

To all which they pleaded not guilty, and putting themselves upon the country, were found guilty. And when they were asked what they could say for themselves, why the sentence of death should not be pronounced against them, they stood stiffly upon their innocence. Whereupon, judgment being given, they were carried back unto the gaol, where they were never heard to pray or to call upon God, but with bitter curses and execrations spent that little time they had to live until the day of their execution; when never asking pardon for their offences, either of God or the world, in this their dangerous and desperate resolution died.

It was credibly reported that some fortnight before their apprehension, this Agnes Brown, one Katherine Gardiner, and one Joan Lucas, all birds of a wing,[4] and all abiding in the town of Guilsborough, did ride one night to a place not above a mile off called Ravensthorpe, all upon a sow's back, to see one Mother Rhodes, an old witch that dwelt there. But before they came to her house the old witch died, and in her last cast cried out that there were three of her old friends coming to see her but they came too late; howbeit, she would meet with them in another place within a month after. And thus much concerning Agnes Brown, and her daughter Joan Varnham.

[4] birds of a wing, i.e. 'birds of a feather'.

The arraignment, conviction and execution of one Arthur Bill of Raunds in the county of Northampton.

This Arthur Bill, a wretched poor man both in state and mind, remained in a town called Raunds in the county aforesaid, begotten and born of parents that were both witches; and he (like a gracious child) would not degenerate, nor suffer himself to stray from his father's wicked counsels, but carefully trod the steps that he had devilishly taught him.

This Arthur Bill was accused that he should bewitch the body of one Martha Aspine alias Jeames, the daughter of one Edward Aspine of the same town—to death. But this matter remaining doubtful that it could not be clearly tried upon him, he being strongly suspected before by bewitching of divers kinds of cattle to be guilty of that crime; and being also publicly known to be of an evil life and reputation, together with his father and mother; the justices and other offices, thereby purposing to try the said Arthur by an experiment that (many think) never fails, caused them all to be bound, and their thumbs and great toes to be tied across, and so threw the father, mother and son— and none of them sunk, but all floated upon the water.

And here by the way, it is a special thing worthy general noting and observation, that there are two signs or tokens which are tokens as more certain than others to detect and find out witches by. The one is the mark where the spirits suck, and the trying of the insensibleness thereof. The other is their fleeting* on the water.[5]

Concerning which though I dare affirm nothing for certainty, there being for aught I know neither evident proof in nature, nor revelation from heaven to assure us thereof; yet methinks I may say the like of this as is held of the bleeding of a slain body in presence of the murderer.

For as in a secret murder, if the dead carcase be at any time either seen or handled by the murderer, it doth straightway gush out of

---

[5] This is adapted from King James' *Daemonologie* (p. 80) and changes his 'their mark' to the English idea, 'the mark where the spirits suck', though this was *not* normally insensible. The next paragraph expresses hesitancy about the natural or theological basis for these tests, showing that they were not yet legally or even generally accepted, and then James' example of the bleeding of a dead body in the presence of the murderer is quoted almost exactly, as a justifying analogue. But where James is definite as to God's appointment of this sign, the author hedges with 'it may be', 'as may seem', 'as may be thought', indicating how the confused theological position in England prevented the formation of an absolute, official view of these tests as proof of witchcraft.

blood, as if the blood should by issuing forth in such strange manner cry unto heaven for revenge of the murderer; God having as may seem appointed that secret supernatural sign for trial of that secret unnatural crime, that the blood left in the body should thus appear and as it were challenge the murderer for that blood which he before had feloniously stolen from the body.

So it may be that God hath appointed for a supernatural sign of the monstrous impiety of witches that the element of water should refuse to receive them in her bosom that have shaken from them the sacred water of baptism, and wilfully refused the benefit thereof by making that breach and fall from God in participating thus vilely with the spirits of Belial. By whom, and in the exercise of which sin, their hearts are so hardened that not so much as their eyes are able to shed tears, threaten or torture them as you please, God not permitting them, as may be thought, to dissemble their obstinacy in so horrible a crime— no, not the women, though that sex be ready to shed tears upon every light occasion. But to return to our matter.

These three, the father, mother, and son being thus seen floating upon the water, the suspicion that was before not well grounded was now confirmed. Whereupon the said Arthur Bill being the principal or (I think) the only actor in this tragedy, was apprehended and sent to Northampton gaol the nine and twentieth day of May last by Sir Gilbert Pickering, of Titchmarsh alias Tichmase in the same county, knight.[6]

And presently after his commitment fearing that his old father would relent, and so haply confess that which might be prejudicial unto him, [he] sent for his mother to come unto him, to whom bewraying* his mind, they both joined together and bewitched a round ball into the throat of the father, where it continued a great while, his father not being able to speak a word. Howbeit the ball was afterwards had out, and his father proved the principal witness against him.[7]

His mother (for fear of hanging, not any hatred or detestation she bare unto the sin) many times fainted, and would often pitifully complain unto her spirit that the power of the law would be stronger than

---

[6] Apparently the same man who was so busy in the case of his nieces, the bewitched girls of Warboys.

[7] 'Globus hystericus' or the sense of a choking lump in the throat is a common sign of nervous derangement or hysterical fear. Several witches, rather understandably, had their speech stopped in this way.

the power of her art, and that she saw no other likelihood but that she should be hanged as her son was like to be.

To whom her spirit answered, giving this sorry* comfort, that she should not be hanged but to prevent that, she should cut her own throat. She, hearing this sentence and holding it definitive, in great agony and horror of mind and conscience fell a-raving, crying out that the irrevocable judgment of her death was given, and that she was damned perpetually, cursing and banning the time wherein she was born and the hour wherein she was conceived.

Her neighbours, often hearing her bitter execrations, bade her call upon God, and to be sorry for the sins which she had committed, but she could in no case endure to hear it. And having thus for 3 or 4 days tormented herself in this agony, at last she made good the Devil's word and, to prevent the justice of the law and to save the hangman a labour, cut her own throat.

Her son being all this while in prison, and hearing of his mother's death and that his father was become a witness against him, was much perplexed in his mind that his mother was dead, in whom he most trusted, and his father living, whom he most feared. Howbeit he stiffly stood still in the denial of everything, pleading nothing but his innocency: notwithstanding that he had before at unawares confessed that he had certain spirits at command which, being employed, would do any mischief to any man, woman or child that he would appoint.

It is said that he had three spirits to whom he gave three special names (the Devil himself sure was godfather to them all). The first he called Grizel, the other was named Ball, and the last Jack, but in what shapes they appeared unto him I cannot learn. For devils can appear both in a bodily shape and use speech and conference with men.

Our Saviour saith that 'a spirit hath neither flesh nor bones'; a spirit hath a substance, but yet such as is invisible. Whereupon it must needs be granted that devils in their own nature have no bodily shape nor visible form; it is moreover against the truth and against piety to believe that devils can create, or make bodies, or change one body into another, for those things are proper to God.

It followeth therefore that whensoever they appear in a visible form it is no more but an apparition and counterfeit show of a body, unless a body be at any time lent them. And when they make one body to bear the likeness of another, it is but a colour.

Some man will say, 'What reason is there to show they can do so much, being of an essence invisible?' We may not stay here within the limits of our own reason, which is not able to comprehend what way devils should be able to work such operations. We may not, I say, measure their power and subtleties in working for our own capacity and understanding, but we must look what the canon of Scripture doth testify in this behalf.

We have manifest proof that the Devil can take a bodily shape, for when Aaron had cast down his staff and it was turned into a serpent, the enchanters of Egypt cast down their staves and they became serpents; which was indeed but in show and appearance which the Devil made. For he deluded the senses both in hiding the form of the staves, which indeed were not any way changed, as also in making a show of such bodies as were not. This was done openly, otherwise it might be thought to be a mere illusion.

For we see that men in extreme sickness think they hear a voice and see a shape which none other in presence either heareth or seeth—some are so melancholy that they imagine they hear and see that which they do not.[8] For Satan do so delude the fantasy that the party supposeth that his very outward senses do perceive the matter. But here was no such thing. All that were with Pharaoh did think there were very serpents indeed, saving that Moses and Aaron did know it the juggling of the Devil.

But to return to this Arthur Bill. He, miserable man, lying in prison from the 29 day of May to the 22 of July following, many resorted to him, willing him to leave off all colour and dissimulation, and not to suffer his conscience to double with his tongue, but to clear his heart and his thoughts before the Majesty of Him to Whom no secrets are hid; that the world might be witness of his confession and contrition to pray with him and for him. For although he had wandered and gone astray, he might by his true contrition and their hearty prayers be brought unto the fold again.

But his conscience being seared, and his heart steeled, could receive no impression but stood like an image of adamant, more easy to be broken in pieces than be pierced. In this obstinacy of mind and spirit

---

[8] John Cotta, a physician of Northampton who believed in witches, and described cases of bewitchment (real and apparent) which he had treated, advised caution in accepting the evidence of the bewitched for precisely this reason. Yet he believed that bewitched patients might know and relate what was happening at a distance, and instanced the children at 'Warbozyes'. For the (probable) case of Mrs. Belcher, see his *Triall of Witchcraft* (London, 1616), pp. 66-7.

he continued until the Assizes, where being arraigned for several crimes committed, but especially for the murder of the said Martha Aspine, contrary to the peace of our Sovereign Lord the King, his crown and dignity, he pleaded to them all 'Not guilty,' and putting himself upon the country, was by them found guilty.

Upon the verdict whereof, his countenance changed, and he cried out that he had now found the Law to have a power above justice, for that it had condemned an innocent.

It seems to me that these vile spirits which these witches have at command, and by their employment are suffered to have power to hurt the bodies of others, have a greater power over them that set them awork. For they do not only feed upon them, participating with the blood of human flesh, for the redemption whereof Christ shed His own precious blood; but it appears that they have also power even over their souls, leading them into wandering byways, and such erroneous labyrinths that in the wilful obstinacy and perverse sufferance of their own minds to stray in this dangerous desert of obduracy, they are lost for ever.

But to conclude with this Arthur Bill, that so ill concluded with the world: he being brought to the place of execution and standing upon that fatal stage for offenders, pleaded still his innocency, that authority was turned to tyranny and justice into extreme injury; to the great wonder and disdain of all the lookers on.

Thus with a dissembling tongue and a corrupted conscience, he ended his course in this world, with little hope or respect, as it seemed, of the world to come.

The arraignment and execution of Helen Jenkenson.

This Helen Jenkenson, dwelling at a town called Thrapston in the county of Northampton, was noted a long time to be of an evil life and much suspected of this crime before her apprehension, for bewitching of cattle and other mischiefs which before time she had done.

This Helen was apprehended for bewitching of a child to death, and committed to Northampton gaol the 11 of May last by Sir Thomas Brooke of Oakley, knight. A little before whose apprehension one Mistress Moulsho of the same town (after she was so strongly suspected) getting her by a wile into a place convenient would needs have her searched, to see if they could find that insensible mark which commonly all witches have in some privy place or other of their bodies. And this Mistress Moulsho was one of the chief that did search her and found at the last that which they sought for, to their great amazement.

At that time this Mistress Moulsho had a buck* of clothes to be washed out. The next morning the maid, when she came to hang them forth to dry spied the clothes, but especially Mistress Moulsho's smock, to be all bespotted with the pictures of toads, snakes and other ugly creatures. Which making her aghast, she went presently and told her mistress who, looking on them smiled, saying nothing else but this, 'Here are fine hobgoblins indeed!'

And being a gentlewoman of a stout courage, went immediately to the house of the said Helen Jenkenson, and with an angry countenance told her of this matter, threatening her that if her linen were not shortly cleared from those foul spots, she would scratch out both her eyes; and so, not staying for any answer, went home and found her linen as white as it was at first.

This Helen being brought to the bar and being indicted of the murder of the child, pleaded thereunto 'Not guilty'; but the verdict being given up against her, she cried out, 'Woe is me, I now [am] cast away!' but like the rest, did stoutly deny the accusations and said that she was to die an innocent. (I think, as innocent as the rest).

And at the place of execution made no other confession but this, 'that she was guiltless', and never showed sign of contrition for what was past, nor any sorrow at all more than did accompany the fear of death. Thus ended this woman her miserable life, after she had lived many years poor, wretched, scorned and forsaken of the world.

The arraignment and execution of Mary Barber.[9]

This Mary Barber, of Stanwick in the said county of Northampton, was one in whom the licentiousness of her passions grew to be the master of her reason, and did so conquer in her strength and power of all virtue that she fell to the apostasy of goodness, and became diverted and abused unto most vile actions, clothing her desperate soul in the most ugly habiliments that either malice, envy or cruelty could produce from the blindness of her degenerate and devilish desires.

As she was of mean parents, so was she monstrous and hideous both in her life and actions, her education and barbarous nature never

[9] This section makes up for lack of precise information by a particularly unpleasant rhetoric, which seems keyed to the whining, nasal delivery adapted by Puritan preachers and mocked on stage by Jonson and Heywood. Exorcism, however, seems to have been dropped in these circles.

promising to the world anything but what was rude, violent and without any hope of proportion more than only in the square of viciousness.

For out of the oblivion and blindness of her seduced senses, she gave way to all the passionate and earthly faculties of the flesh, and followed all the Phantasma's vanities and Chimera's of her polluted and unreasonable delights, forsaking the society of grace and growing enamoured upon all the evil that malice or frenzy could minister to her vicious desires and intendments.

As appeared by her bewitching a man to death, and doing much other hurt and harm to divers sorts of cattle in the country; for which she was committed to Northampton gaol the 6 day of May last by Sir Thomas Tresham, and the same (and many other matters) being plainly and evidently manifest and proved against her by good evidence, she had the sentence of death worthily pronounced against her. In the time of her imprisonment she was not noted to have any remembrance or feeling of the heinousness of her offences or any remorseful tongue of the dissolute and devilish course of her life.

The prison, which makes men be fellows and chambermates with thieves and murderers (the common guests of such despised inns) and should cause the imprisoned party, like a Christian arithmetician to number and cast up the account of his whole life, never put her in mind of the hateful transgressions she had committed, or to consider the filth and leprosy of her soul, or entreat heaven's mercy for the release thereof.

Prison put her not in mind of her grave, nor the grates and locks put her in remembrance of hell, which deprived her of the joy of liberty which she saw others possess. The jangling of irons did not put her in mind of the chains wherewith she should be bound in eternal torments, unless heaven's mercy unloosed them, nor of the howling terrors and gnashing of teeth which in hell every soul shall receive for the particular offences committed in this life, without unfeigned hearty contrition. She never remembered or thought she must die, or trembled for fear of what should come to her after death.

But as her life was always known to be devilish, so her death was at last found to be desperate, for she (and the rest before named) being brought from the common gaol of Northampton to Northampton Castle, where the Assizes are usually held, were severally arraigned and indited for the offences they had formerly committed but to the inditements they pleaded 'Not guilty.'

Putting therefore their causes to the trial of the country, they were found guilty, and deserved death by the verdict of a credible jury returned. So, without any confession or contrition, like birds of a feather, they all held and hanged together for company at Abington gallows hard by Northampton, the two and twentieth day of July last past; leaving behind them in prison many others tainted with the same corruption, who, without much mercy and repentance, are like to follow them in the same tract* of precedency.*

Finis.

Lancashire Witches

The Wonderfull Discoverie of Witches in the Countie of Lancaster. With the Arraignement and Triall of Nineteen notorious Witches, at the Assizes and generall Gaole deliverie, holden at the Castle of Lancaster, upon Munday, the seventeenth of August last, 1612. Before Sir James Altham, and Sir Edward Bromley. . . . Published and set forth by commandement of his Majesties Justices of Assize in the North Parts. By Thomas Potts, Esq. (London, 1613)

This famous pamphlet is most easily available in the 1929 edition by G. B. Harrison.[1] It is an account by the clerk of the court of a case involving two families in the Forest of Pendle; their enmity to each other and to most of their neighbours culminated in a trial in which one family destroyed the other and then turned suicidally on itself, children betraying siblings and parents.

Since Mr. Potts—and the judge—considered confession and the testimony of relatives of prime importance, most of the evidence appears in one of these two forms; it is thus unrevealing of the charges and circumstances producing such formal statements. There are accounts of two witch-feasts which offer a pale shadow of the Continental Sabbath, obviously elicited by leading questions from people who have never heard of such a thing.[2] There are souls bargained to a devil in human form—the first time English witches have made the formal Faustian pact—and all the small change of village witchcraft: wax images, familiars, curses, charms, spoilt drink, 'unwitching', and theft. We have in fact a complete survey of local superstition seen through distorting glasses; in the tireless zeal of Roger Nowell, JP, we see an up-to-date version of Brian Darcy's labours at St. Osyth thirty years before.

Thirty-five possible witches were 'discovered'; ten were hanged and one died in gaol.

[1] Bodley Head Quartos, London, 1929. There are excellent notes in the edition by James Crossley, *Chetham Society*, Vol. VI, Manchester, 1845.

[2] A really full-blooded account of a Sabbath with orgies, vampirism and baby-killing, turned out to be a story concocted by a Catholic priest and taught to a young girl as evidence against some lapsed Catholics—at least, the evidence against the Samlesbury witches was dropped on these grounds.

The prominence given to this incident in Potts' account (as well as the dedication of the book to Sir Thomas Knyvet, who arrested Fawkes in the discovery of the Gunpowder Plot of 1605) suggests that Potts was writing against Catholics as much as against witches. The manor of Samlesbury was held by the Southworth family, which figures largely in this part of the *Discoverie*; it was a centre of recusancy in a county still notoriously Catholic in sympathy.

[Elizabeth Southerns, alias Demdike] . . . was a very old woman, about the age of fourscore years, and had been a witch for fifty years.[3] She dwelt in the Forest of Pendle, a vast place, fit for her profession; what she committed in her time, no man knows.

Thus lived she securely for many years, brought up her own children, instructed her grandchildren, and took great care and pains to bring them to be witches. She was a general agent for the Devil in all these parts: no man escaped her or her furies that ever gave them any occasion of offence, or denied them anything they stood need of, and certain it is, no man near them was secure or free from danger.

But God, who had in His divine providence provided to cut them off and root them out of the commonwealth, so disposed above that the Justices of those parts, understanding by a general charm and muttering, the great and universal resort to Malkin* Tower, the common opinion, with the report of these suspected people, the complaint of the King's subjects for the loss of their children, friends, goods and cattle—as there could not be so great fire without some smoke—sent for some of the country and took great pains to enquire after their proceedings and courses of life. . . .

The voluntary confession and examination of Elizabeth Southerns alias Demdike, taken at the Fence in the Forest of Pendle in the county of Lancaster, the second day of April. . . .

The said Elizabeth Southerns confesseth and saith, that about twenty years past, as she was coming homeward from begging, there met her this examinate near unto a stonepit in Goldshaw in the said Forest of Pendle, a spirit or devil in the shape of a boy, the one half of his coat black and the other brown, who bade this examinate stay, saying to her that if she would give him her soul, she should have anything that she would request.

Whereupon this examinate demanded his name, and the spirit

[3] Yet she sold her soul to the devil only 20 years before the trial, and sealed the bargain with blood six years later—about the time she persuaded Anne Whittle alias Chattox to make the same bargain. The enmity between the families broke out 11 years before the trial, after the death of Elizabeth Demdike's son-in-law was blamed on Anne Chattox, and after the Demdike family accused the Chattoxes of robbery. This period 11–14 years before the trial may mark the stage at which both families became frightened by developing local hostility; Elizabeth Demdike (correctly or not) mentions a mental collapse at the beginning of this period.

answered, 'his name was Tibb'. And so this examinate in hope of such gain as was promised by the said devil or Tibb was contented to give her soul to the said spirit; and for the space of five or six years next after, the said spirit or devil appeared at sundry times unto her this examinate about daylight-gate,* always bidding her stay, and asking her this examinate what she would have or do.

To whom this examinate replied 'Nay, nothing'; for she this examinate said, she wanted nothing yet. And so about the end of the said six years, upon a Sabbath day in the morning, this examinate having a little child upon her knee and she being in a slumber, the said spirit appeared unto her in the likeness of a brown dog, forcing himself to her knee to get blood under her left arm; and she being without any apparel saving her smock, the said devil did get blood under her left arm.

And this examinate awaking, said 'Jesus save my child'[4], but had no power nor could not say 'Jesus save herself.' Whereupon the brown dog vanished out of this examinate's sight, after which this examinate was almost stark mad for the space of eight weeks.

And upon her examination she further confesseth and saith, that a little before Christmas last, this examinate's daughter having been to help Richard Baldwin's folks at the mill, this examinate's daughter did bid her this examinate go to the said Baldwin's house and ask him something for her helping of his folks at the mill, as aforesaid. And in this examinate's going to the said Baldwin's house, and near to the said house, she met with the said Richard Baldwin, which Baldwin said to this examinate and the said Alison Device (who at that time led this examinate, being blind) 'Get out of my ground, whores and witches—I will burn the one of you and hang the other'.

To whom this examinate answered, 'I care not for thee, hang thyself!' Presently whereupon, at this examinate's going over the next hedge, the said spirit or devil called Tibb appeared unto this examinate and said, 'Revenge thee of him!' To whom this examinate said again to the said spirit, 'Revenge thee either of him or his!' And so the said spirit vanished out of her sight and she never saw him since.[5]

And further this examinate confesseth and saith, that the speediest way to take a man's life away by witchcraft[6] is to make a picture of

---

[4] A grand-child? She is apparently 66 at this date, and this may be a confused recollection of an earlier mental disturbance following childbirth.

[5] Apparently, like the promises of help given by fairies, the devil's assistance can be called upon only once.

[6] John Walsh described the same process in 1566.

clay like unto the shape of the person whom they mean to kill and dry it thoroughly; and when they would have them to be ill in any one place more than another, then take a thorn or pin and prick it in that part of the picture you would so have to be ill. And when you would have any part of the body to consume away, then take that part of the picture and burn it; and when they would have the whole body to consume away, then take the remnant of the said picture and burn it, and so thereupon by that means the body shall die.[7]

... The said Elizabeth Southerns saith upon her examination, that about half a year before Robert Nutter died (as this examinate thinketh) this examinate went to the house of Thomas Redfern, which was about midsummer as this examinate remembereth it. And there within three yards of the east end of the said house, she saw the said Anne Whittle alias Chattox, and Anne Redfern, wife of the said Thomas Redfern and daughter of the said Anne Whittle alias Chattox, the one on the one side of the ditch and the other on the other, and two pictures of clay or marl lying by them; and the third picture the said Anne Whittle alias Chattox was making, and the said Anne Redfern her said daughter wrought her clay or marl to make the third picture withal.

And this examinate passing by them, the said spirit called Tibb, in the shape of a black cat, appeared unto her this examinate and said 'Turn back again and do as they do.' To whom this examinate said, 'What are they doing?' whereunto the said spirit said, 'They are making three pictures.' Whereupon she asked whose pictures they were, whereunto the said spirit said, 'They are the pictures of Christopher Nutter, Robert Nutter and Mary, wife of the said Robert Nutter.'

But this examinate denying to go back to help them to make the pictures aforesaid, the said spirit, seeming to be angry, therefore shove[d] or pushed this examinate into the ditch, and so shed the milk which this examinate had in a can or kit,* and so thereupon the spirit at that time vanished out of this examinate's sight. But presently after that, the said spirit appeared to this examinate again in the shape of a hare, and so went with her about a quarter of a mile, but said nothing to this examinate, nor she to it. ....[8]

---

[7] *The Wonderfull Discoverie* ... pp. 16-20.
[8] *The Wonderfull Discoverie* ... pp. 39-40.

The examination of James Device,[9] son of Elizabeth Device, taken the seven and twentieth day of April. . . .

And further saith, that twelve years ago the said Anne Chattox at a burial at the new church in Pendle did take three scalps* of people which had been buried and then cast out of a grave, as she the said Chattox told this examinate, and took eight teeth out of the said scalps, whereof she kept four to herself and gave other four to the said Demdike, this examinate's grandmother.

Which four teeth now showed to this examinate are the four teeth that the said Chattox gave to his said grandmother as aforesaid, which said teeth have ever since been kept, (until now found by the said Henry Hargreaves and this examinate) at the west end of this examinate's grandmother's house, and there buried in the earth; and a picture of clay there likewise found by them, about half a yard over in the earth where the said teeth lay; which said picture so found was almost withered away, and was the picture of Anne, Anthony Nutter's daughter, as this examinate's grandmother told him.[10]

. . . This Anne Whittle, alias Chattox, was a very old, withered, spent and decrepit creature, her sight almost gone: a dangerous witch, of very long continuance, always opposite to old Demdike, for whom the one favoured, the other hated deadly; and how they envy and accuse one another in their examinations may appear. . . .[11]

The examination of Alison Device, daughter of Elizabeth Device, [grand-daughter of old Demdike] taken . . . the thirtieth day of March. . . .

This examinate saith, that about eleven years ago, this examinate and her mother had their fire-house broken and all, or the most part of their linen clothes, and half a peck of cut oatmeal and a quantity of meal gone, all which was worth twenty shillings or above. And upon a Sunday then next after, this examinate did take a band and coif, parcel of the goods aforesaid, upon the daughter of Anne Whittle alias Chattox, and claimed them to be parcel of the goods stolen as aforesaid.

And this examinate further saith, that her father, called John Device, being afraid that the said Anne Chattox should do him or his goods any hurt by witchcraft, did covenant with the said Anne that if she would hurt neither of them, she should yearly have one aghen-dole* of meal;

---

[9] Elizabeth Southerns, alias Demdike, had a daughter Elizabeth who married John Device, or Davis; the daughter's children were Alison, James and Janet.

[10] *The Wonderfull Discoverie* . . . pp. 44–5.

[11] *The Wonderfull Discoverie* . . . p. 33.

which meal was yearly paid until the year which her father died in, which was about eleven years since, her father upon his then-death-bed taking it that the said Anne Whittle alias Chattox did bewitch him to death because the said meal was not paid the last year.

And she also saith, that about two years agone, this examinate being in the house of Anthony Nutter of Pendle aforesaid and being then in company with Anne Nutter, daughter of the said Anthony—the said Anne Whittle alias Chattox came into the said Anthony Nutter's house, and seeing this examinate and the said Anne Nutter laughing, and saying that they laughed at her the said Chattox—'well said then!' says Anne Chattox; 'I will be meet* with the one of you!' And upon the next day after, she the said Anne Nutter fell sick, and within three weeks after died. . . .[12]

The confession and examination of Anne Whittle alias Chattox, being prisoner at Lancaster, taken the 19 day of May. . . .

First, the said Anne Whittle alias Chattox saith, that about fourteen years past she entered (through the wicked persuasions and counsel of Elizabeth Southerns alias Demdike), and was seduced to condescend and agree to become subject unto, that devilish abominable profession of witchcraft; soon after which the Devil appeared unto her in the likeness of a man, about midnight at the house of the said Demdike, and thereupon the said Demdike and she went forth of the said house unto him.

Whereupon the said wicked spirit moved this examinate that she would become his subject and give her soul unto him; the which at first she refused to assent unto, but after, by the great persuasions made by the said Demdike, she yielded to be at his commandment and appointment. Whereupon the said wicked spirit then said unto her that he must have one part of her body for him to suck upon, the which she denied then to grant unto him, and withal asked him what part of her body he would have for that use; who said he would have a place of her right side near to her ribs for him to suck upon, whereunto she assented.

And she further saith, that at the same time there was a thing in the likeness of a spotted bitch that came with the said spirit unto the said Demdike, which then did speak unto her in this examinate's hearing, and said that she should have gold, silver, and wordly wealth at her will. And at the same time, she saith, there was victuals, viz. flesh, butter, cheese, bread and drink, and [he] bid them eat enough. And

[12] *The Wonderfull Discoverie* . . . pp. 45–6.

after their eating the devil called Fancy and the other spirit calling himself Tibb carried the remnant away.

And she saith, that although they did eat, they were never the fuller nor better for the same; and that at their said banquet the said spirits gave them light to see what they did, although they neither had fire nor candle-light, and that they were both she-spirits[13] and devils. . . .[14]

[Another confession] . . . And this examinate further saith, that Robert Nutter did desire her daughter, one Redfern's wife, to have his pleasure of her, being then in Redfern's house, but the said Redfern's wife denied the said Robert. Whereupon the said Robert, seeming to be greatly displeased therewith, in a great anger took his horse and went away, saying in a great rage that if ever the ground came to him, she should never dwell upon his land.

Whereupon this examinate called Fancy to her, who came to her in the likeness of a man in a parcel of ground called The Laund, asking this examinate what she would have him to do. And this examinate bade him go revenge her of the said Robert Nutter, after which time the said Robert Nutter lived about a quarter of a year and then died . . .[15] [Another examination, on the second of April] . . . She the said examinate saith, that she was sent for by the wife of John Moore to help drink that was forespoken or bewitched, at which time she used this prayer for the amending of it, viz.

A Charm.

Three Biters hast thou bitten,
The Heart, ill Eye, ill Tongue:
Three bitter shall be thy boot,*
Father, Son, and Holy Ghost
a God's name.
Five Pater-nosters, five Ave's,
and a Creed,
In worship of five wounds
of our Lord.[16]

[13] These spirits otherwise appear only as males or animals, and the whole episode sounds rather like a fairy-feast misrepresented by someone looking for a witches' Sabbath. Fairy feasts are common in folk-lore and often incorporate eerie lighting and unsatisfying food.
[14] *The Wonderfull Discoverie* . . . pp. 21–2.
[15] *The Wonderfull Discoverie* . . . p. 36.
[16] This spell is reminiscent of Anglo-saxon charms against 'elf-shot'; Kittredge

After which time that this examinate had used these prayers and amended her drink, the said Moore's wife did chide this examinate, and was grieved at her.

And thereupon this examinate called for her devil Fancy, and bade him go bite a brown cow of the said Moore's by the head, and make the cow go mad; and the devil then in the likeness of a brown dog went to the said cow and bit her, which cow went mad accordingly and died within six weeks next after, or thereabouts. . . .[17]

The Examination and evidence of Janet Device[18] . . . *against Elizabeth Device her mother.* . . .

The said Janet Device, being a young maid about the age of nine years, and commanded to stand up to give evidence against her mother, prisoner at the bar: her mother, according to her accustomed manner, outrageously cursing, cried out against the child in such fearful manner as all the court did not a little wonder at her, and so amazed the child as with weeping tears she cried out unto my Lord the Judge, and told him she was not able to speak in the presence of her mother.

(This odious witch was branded with a preposterous mark in nature even from her birth, which was her left eye standing lower than the other, the one looking down, the other looking up, so strangely deformed as the best that were present in that honourable assembly and great audience did affirm they had not often seen the like).

No entreaty, promise of favour or other respect could put her to silence, thinking by this her outrageous cursing and threatening of the child to enforce her to deny that which she had formerly confessed against her mother before Mr. Nowell; forswearing and denying her own voluntary confession which you have heard given in evidence against her at large, and so for want of further evidence to escape that which the justice of the law had provided as a condign punishment for the innocent blood she had spilt and her wicked and devilish course of life.

In the end, when no means would serve, his Lordship commanded

---

records two versions used in 1538 and several from the seventeenth century or later. *Witchcraft in Old and New England*, ed. cit., p. 39.

[17] *The Wonderfull Discoverie* . . . pp. 42–3.

[18] One Janet Device was condemned for witchcraft, though apparently not executed, in the outrageous Lancashire trials of 1633; the evidence of the chief juvenile witness in that case is based on scraps of legend and gossip surviving from 1612.

the prisoner to be taken away, and the maid to be set upon the table in the presence of the whole court; who delivered her evidence in that honorable assembly to the gentlemen of the jury of life and death,[19] as followeth, viz.

Janet Device, daughter of Elizabeth Device, late wife of John Device, of the Forest of Pendle aforesaid, widow, confesseth and saith, that her said mother is a witch, and that this she knoweth to be true; for that she hath seen her spirit sundry times come unto her said mother in her own house (called Malkin Tower) in the likeness of a brown dog which she called Ball. And at one time amongst others, the said Ball did ask this examinate's mother what she would have him to do, and this examinate's mother answered that she would have the said Ball to help her to kill John Robinson of Barley, alias Swyer, by help of which said Ball, the said Swyer was killed by witchcraft accordingly; and that this examinate's mother hath continued a witch for these three or four years last past.

And further, this examinate confesseth that about a year after, this examinate's mother called for the said Ball, who appeared as aforesaid, asking this examinate's mother what she would have done; who said that she would have him to kill James Robinson, alias Swyer, of Barley aforesaid, brother to the said John. Whereunto Ball answered 'he would do it', and about three weeks after, the said James died.

And this examinate also saith, that one other time she was present when her said mother did call for the said Ball, who appeared in manner as aforesaid, and asked this examinate's mother what she would have him to do; whereunto this examinate's mother then said she would have him to kill one Mitton of the Roughlee, whereupon the said Ball said 'he would do it', and so vanished away, and about three weeks after, the said Mitton likewise died.[20]

[Against her brother] ... The said Janet Device, his sister, in the very end of her examination against the said James Device, confesseth

---

[19] The Grand Jury (mainly minor gentry) examined presentments of evidence and accepted the case as 'true bill' or dismissed it ('ignoramus'). Presentments found 'true bill' became indictments; they were read aloud at the Assizes and the accused pleaded 'Guilty' or 'Not guilty'. Those pleading 'Not guilty' were then tried before the Petty Jurors—mostly artisans and yeoman—who decided on the guilt or innocence of the accused, and so were in a felony case 'the jury of life and death'. (For this brief account I am indebted to Dr. Macfarlane's unpublished work, cited elsewhere.)

[20] *The Wonderfull Discoverie* ... pp. 54–6.

and saith that her mother taught her two prayers: the one to get drink, which was this, viz.

Crucifixus hoc signum vitam Eternam. Amen.[21]

And she further saith, that her brother James Device, the prisoner at the bar, hath confessed to her this examinate that he by this prayer hath gotten drink, and that within an hour after the saying the said prayer, drink hath come into the house after a very strange manner. And the other prayer, the said James Device affirmed, would cure one bewitched, which she recited as followeth, viz.

A Charm.[22]

1. Upon Good Friday I will fast while I may,
   Until I hear them knell
   Our Lord's own bell;
2. Lord in his mass
   With his twelve apostles good,
   What hath he in his hand?
   Ligh in leath wand.[23]
   What hath he in his other hand?
   Heaven's door-key.

[21] Making the sign of the cross was often accompanied by a devotional form of words; this little ritual was frequently corrupted into a rite of protective magic, particularly after Catholic ritual ceased to be the rule in England. 'Crucifixus' was probably once 'crux Christi' or 'cruci Christi' and the phrase would mean something like 'This sign of Christ's cross gives eternal life.' Magical use and original meaning are here totally divorced.

[22] This charm (my numbering) is a mixture of pure spells and orthodox theology as taught to the illiterate. From very early times priests had explained the substance of the Latin catechism and creed in rhymed vernacular versions (see the Early English Text Society publications *The Lay Folks' Mass Book*, p. 21, and *The Lay Folks' Catechism*); sections 1 and 3 here seem to incorporate fragments of such instructional material (see Crossley's note to this passage for a late seventeenth century version). Section 2 is a version of the White Paternoster, a bed-time blessing, and section 4 is a charm of the same pattern as the famous one for toothache 'Peter was sitting on a marble stone . . .' (J. O. Halliwell Phillipps, *Nursery Rhymes and Nursery Tales of England*, n.d., pp. 290–1). See also K. M. Briggs, *Pale Hecate's Team*, ed. cit., Ch. 11, which gives excellent examples of the use of religious material in spells and charms.

[23] 'Leath' probably equates 'lethe'—obsolete word meaning 'supple or flexible'. 'Ligh' has too many possibilities for discussion. A slim white wand or rod was a sign of office and power (carried by magicians, devils and fairies— See *Newes from Scotland*), and such an object would fit the context.

> Open, open, heaven door-keys;
> Stick, stick, hell-door.
> Let crisom child
> Go to it[s] mother mild.

3. What is yonder that casts a light so farrandly?*
   Mine own dear son that's nailed to the tree.
   He is nailed sore by the heart and hand
   And holy brain-pan.[24]
   Well is that man
   That Friday-spell can
   His child to learn.
   A cross of blue and another of red,
   As good Lord was to the rood.

4. Gabriel laid him down to sleep
   Upon the ground of holy weep;
   Good Lord came walking by.
   'Sleep'st thou, wak'st thou, Gabriel?'
   'No, Lord, I am stayed with stick and stake
   That I can neither sleep nor wake'.
   'Rise up, Gabriel and go with me;
   The stick nor the stake shall never dere* thee'.
   Sweet Jesus our Lord, Amen.
                              James Device.[25]

*The examination of James Device . . . taken the seven and twentieth day
of April. . . .*

And being examined, he further saith that upon Sheare-[26]Thursday
last in the evening, he this examinate stole a wether* from John
Robinson of Barley and brought it to his grandmother's house (old
Demdike), and there killed it; and that upon the day following, being
Good Friday, about twelve of the clock in the daytime there dined in
this examinate's mother's house a number of persons, whereof three
were men (with this examinate) and the rest women, and that they
met there for three causes following, as this examinate's said mother
told this examinate.

[24] Harrison transcribes 'barne Panne' Briggs and Crossley 'harne Panne'.
'Harn' is an obsolete word for 'skull' or 'brain'.

[25] *The Wonderfull Discoverie* . . . pp. 79–80.

[26] Sheare-Thursday, i.e. Sheer Thursday. The day before Good Friday, a
day of confession and purification; on this 'Maundy Thursday' the king ritually
washed the feet of poor people.

1. The first was for the naming of the spirit which Alison Device, now prisoner at Lancaster, had, but [they] did not name him because she was not there.

2. The second cause was for the delivery of his said grandmother, this examinate's said sister Alison, the said Anne Chattox and her daughter Redfern: killing the gaoler at Lancaster; and, before the next Assizes, to blow up the castle there,[27] to the end the aforesaid persons might by that means make an escape and get away. All which this examinate then heard them confer of.

3. And the third cause was for that there was a woman dwelling in Gisborne parish who came into this examinate's said grandmother's house, who there came and craved assistance of the rest of them that were then there for the killing of Master Lister of Westby; because (as she then said) he had borne malice unto her and had thought to have put her away at the last Assizes at York, but could not. And this examinate heard the said woman say that her power was not strong enough to do it herself, being now less than before-time it had been.

And also, that the said Janet Preston had a spirit with her like unto a white foal with a black spot in the forehead.

[He lists the names of those present whom he knows.] . . . And this examinate further saith, that all the said witches went out of the said house in their own shapes and likenesses, and they all, by that they were forth of the doors, were gotten on horseback like unto foals, some of one colour, some of another; and Preston's wife was the last, and when she got on horseback they all presently vanished out of this examinate's sight.[28] And before their said parting away, they all appointed to meet at the said Preston's wife's house that day twelve-months, at which time the said Preston's wife promised to make them a great feast. And if they had occasion to meet in the meantime, then should warning be given that they all should meet upon Romilly's Moor.[29]

[27] This improbable idea may derive from the Gunpowder Plot seven years earlier.

[28] The implications of this disingenuous passage are that the witches *could* have changed their shapes (though they did not), the foals *must* have been devils 'like unto foals', and the company *must* have 'vanished' in some sinister and unnatural way. The prosaic evidence actually offered by the witness is given a damning appearance simply by the preconceptions of those who elicited and recorded it.

[29] *The Wonderfull Discoverie* . . . pp. 75–6.

Malice and Maleficium*

The Wonderful Discoverie of the Witchcrafts of Margaret and Phillip Flower, daughters of Joan Flower neere Bever Castle: Executed at Lincolne, March 11, 1618 [/1619]. Who were specially arraigned and condemned before Sir Henry Hobart, and Sir Edward Bromley, Judges of Assise, for confessing themselves actors in the destruction of Henry Lord Rosse, with their damnable practises against others the Children of the Right Honourable Francis Earle of Rutland. Together with the severall Examinations and Confessions of Anne Baker, Joan Willimot, and Ellen Greene, Witches in Leicestershire. (London, 1619).
References to this case are found in the *Calendar of State Papers Domestic,* 1619–23, p. 129, and the *Historical MSS. Reports Commission,* Rutland Papers Vol. IV, p. 514. The Earl of Rutland was head of one of the richest families in England (and Catholic, though this seems to have no bearing on the case); King James was a visitor at Belvoir Castle and picked the Earl's only daughter as a fit match for his favourite Buckingham in 1620, despite her recent 'extreme maladies and unusual fits'.

The confessions of the witches show how astonishingly little the practice of country witchcraft had changed since 1566; it is still as confused, unsystematic and idiosyncratic as John Walsh described it, rooted deep in local customs and fairy superstitions, a mixture of good and bad and a matter of daily use. It is fear of the witch that has spread, and now carries a heavy weight of complex and neurotic fears that have little to do with witchcraft itself. In the passions aroused by the social vicissitudes of the Flowers we may see with unusual clarity one source of the anger, guilt and fear that waited behind the law for a scapegoat.

... After[1] the right honourable Sir Francis Manners succeeded his brother in the earldom of Rutland, and so not only took possession of Belvoir Castle, but of all other his domains, lordships, towns, manors, lands and revenues appropriate to the same earldom, he proceeded so honourably in the course of his life—as neither displacing tenants, discharging servants, denying the access of the poor, welcoming of strangers, and performing all the duties of a noble lord—that he fastened as it were unto himself the love and good opinion of the country: wherein he walked the more cheerfully and remarkable

---

[1] This extract begins on C2, omitting a long and pious introduction which, for proof of the reality of witchcraft lists 'infinite treatises'—many of them pamphlets reprinted in the present volume.

Witches with familiars
The Wonderful Discoverie of the Witchcrafts of Margaret and Phillip Flower 1619

because his honourable Countess marched arm in arm with him in the same race, so that Belvoir Castle was a continual palace of entertainment and a daily receptacle for all sorts, both rich and poor, especially such ancient people as neighboured the same.

Amongst whom one Joan Flower, with her daughters Margaret and Philippa were not only relieved at the first from thence, but quickly entertained as charwomen,* and Margaret admitted as a continual dweller in the Castle, looking both to the poultry abroad and the washhouse within doors; in which life they continued with equal corresponddency* till something was discovered to the noble Lady which concerned the misdemeanour of these women.

And although such honourable persons shall not want of all sorts of people either to bring them news, tales, reports, or to serve their turn in all offices whatsoever, so that it may well be said of them, as it is of great kings and princes, that they have large hands, wide ears, and piercing sights to discover the unswept corners of their remotest confines, to reach even to their furthest borders and to understand the secrets of their meanest subjects; yet in this matter, neither were they busybodies, flatterers, malicious politicians, underminers nor supplanters one of another's good fortune, but went simply to work as regarding the honour of the Earl and his Lady, and so by degrees gave light to their understanding to apprehend their complaints.

First, that Joan Flower the mother was a monstrous malicious woman, full of oaths, curses, and imprecations irreligious and, for anything they saw by her, a plain atheist. Besides, of late days her very countenance was estranged; her eyes were fiery and hollow, her speech fell* and envious, her demeanour strange and exotic,* and her conversation* sequestered,* so that the whole course of her life gave great suspicion that she was a notorious witch.[2] Yea, some of her neighbours dared to affirm that she dealt with familiar spirits and terrified them all with curses and threatening of revenge if there was never so little cause of displeasure and unkindness.

Concerning Margaret, that she often resorted from the Castle to her mother, bringing such provision as they thought was unbefitting for a servant to purloin, and coming at such unseasonable hours that they could not but conjecture some mischief between them; and that their extraordinary riot and expenses tended both to rob the Lady and to maintain certain debauched and base company which frequented this Joan Flower's house (the mother) and especially her youngest daughter.

Concerning Philippa, that she was lewdly transported with the love of one Thomas Simpson, who presumed to say that she had bewitched him; for he had no power to leave her, and was, as he supposed, marvellously altered both in mind and body since her acquainted company.

These complaints began many years before either their conviction or public apprehension. Notwithstanding, such was the honour of this Earl and his Lady; such was the cunning of this monstrous woman in observation towards them; such was the subtlety of the Devil to bring his purposes to pass; such was the pleasure of God to make trial of his servants; and such was the effect of a damnable woman's wit and malicious envy that all things were carried away in the smooth channel of liking and good entertainment on every side.

Until the Earl by degrees conceived some mislike against her, and so peradventure estranged himself from that familiarity and accustomed conferences he was wont to have with her; until one Peak[3] offered her some wrong, against whom she complained, but found that

---

[2] The mental aberrations of age are well known; it is possible that mental and temperamental changes occurring in middle life (like these) are a result of menopausal difficulties.

[3] Original varies between 'Peat' and 'Peak'.

my Lord did not affect her clamours and malicious information; until one Mr. Vavasour abandoned her company, as either suspicious of her lewd life, or distasted with his own misliking of such base and poor creatures, whom nobody loved but the Earl's household; until the Countess, misconceiving of her daughter Margaret, and discovering some undecencies both in her life and neglect of her business, discharged her from lying any more in the Castle, yet gave her 40 shillings, a bolster and a mattress of wool, commanding her to go home;[4] until the slackness of her repairing to the Castle, as she was wont, did turn her love and liking toward this honourable Earl and his family into hate and rancour. Whereupon, despited to be so neglected, and exprobated* by her neighbours for her daughter's casting out of doors, and other conceived displeasures, she grew past all shame and womanhood and many times cursed them all that were the cause of this discontentment and made her so loathsome to her former familiar friends and beneficial acquaintance.

When the Devil perceived the inficious* disposition of this wretch, and that she and her daughters might easily be made instruments to enlarge his kingdom, and be as it were the executioners of his vengeance, not caring whether it lighted upon innocents or no, he came more nearer unto them, and in plain terms (to come quickly to the purpose) offered them his service and that in such a manner as they might easily command what they pleased; for he would attend you in such pretty forms of dog, cat, or rat, that they should neither be terrified nor anybody else suspicious of the matter.

Upon this they agree and (as it should seem) give away their souls for the service of such spirits as he had promised them; which filthy conditions were ratified with abominable kisses and an odious sacrifice of blood, not leaving out certain charms and conjurations with which the Devil deceived them, as though nothing could be done without ceremony and a solemnity of orderly ratification.

By this time doth Satan triumph, and goeth away satisfied to have caught such fish in the net of his illusions; by this time are these women devils incarnate and grow proud again in their cunning and artificial power to do what mischief they listed; by this time they have learned the manner of incantations, spells and charms; by this time they kill what cattle they list and, under the covert of flattery and familiar enter-

---

[4] This unusually large severance pay suggests that Margaret's real fault may have been to become a little too popular with male members of the household.

tainment, keep hidden the stinging serpent of malice and a venomous inclination to mischief; by this time is the Earl and his family threatened, and must feel the burden of a terrible tempest which from these women's devilish devices fell upon him, he neither suspecting nor understanding the same; by this time both himself and his honourable Countess are many times subject to sickness and extraordinary convulsions, which they taking as gentle corrections from the hand of God, submit with quietness to His mercy, and study nothing more than to glorify their Creator in heaven and bear His crosses on earth.

At last, as malice increased in these damnable women, so his family felt the smart of their revenge and inficious disposition, for his eldest son Henry Lord Roos,[5] sickened very strangely and after a while died. His next, named Francis, Lord Roos accordingly, was severely tormented by them and most barbarously and inhumanly tortured by a strange sickness;[6] not long after, the Lady Katherine[7] was set upon by their dangerous and devilish practices and many times in great danger of life through extreme maladies and unusual fits; nay (as it should seem and they afterwards confessed) both the Earl and his Countess were brought into their snares as they imagined, and indeed [they] determined to keep them from having any more children. Oh unheard-of wickedness and mischievous damnation!

Notwithstanding all this did the noble Earl attend his Majesty both at Newmarket before Christmas and at Christmas at Whitehall, bearing the loss of his children most nobly, and little suspecting that they had miscarried by witchcraft or such like inventions of the Devil; until it pleased God to discover the villainous practices of these women and to command the Devil from executing any further vengeance on innocents but leave them [the women] to their shames and the hands of justice, that they might not only be confounded for their villainous practices but remain as a notorious example to all ages of His judgment and fury.

Thus were they apprehended about Christmas and carried to Lincoln jail, after due examination before sufficient Justices of the Peace and discreet magistrates, who wondered at their audacious wickedness. But Joan Flower the mother, before conviction (as they say) called for bread and butter and wished it might never go through her if she were

---

[5] Henry was buried on 16 September 1613.

[6] Francis died on 5 March 1619/20.

[7] Katherine survived to marry Buckingham, the king's favourite, in 1620, and to have children of her own.

guilty of that whereupon she was examined;[8] so mumbling it in her mouth, never spake more words after, but fell down and died as she was carried to Lincoln jail, with a horrible excruciation* of soul and body, and was buried at Ancaster.

When the Earl heard of their apprehension he hastened down with his brother Sir George and, sometimes examining them himself, and sometimes sending them to others, at last left them to the trial of law before the Judges of Assize at Lincoln; and so they were convicted of murder and executed accordingly about the 11 of March, to the terror of all the beholders and example of such dissolute and abominable creatures.

And because you shall have both cause to glorify God for this discovery and occasion to apprehend the strangeness of their lives and truth of their proceedings, I thought it both meet and convenient to lay open their own examinations and evidences against one another, with such apparent circumstances as do not only show the cause of their misliking and distasting against the Earl and his family, but the manner of their proceedings and revenges, with other particulars belonging to the true and plain discovery of their villainy and witchcraft.

The examination of Anne Baker of Bottesford in the county of Leicester, spinster, taken March 1, 1618, by the right honourable Francis, Earl of Rutland, Sir George Manners,[9] knight, two of his Majesty's Justices of the Peace for the county of Lincoln, and Samuel Fleming, doctor of divinity, one of his Majesty's Justices of the Peace for the county of Leicester aforesaid.

She saith that there are four colours of planets, black, yellow, green and blue, and that black is always death, and that she saw the blue planet strike Thomas Fairbarn, the eldest son unto William Fairbarn of Bottesford aforesaid by the pinfold* there; within the which time the said William Fairbarn did beat her and break her head, whereupon the said Thomas Fairbarn did mend. And being asked who did send that planet? answered, 'It was not I.'

Further she saith, that she saw a hand[10] appear unto her, and that she heard a voice in the air said unto her, 'Anne Baker, save thyself,

---

[8] This was a very ancient form of ordeal in England, and it is interesting that folk-memory of it apparently survived till this date.

[9] Brother to the Earl of Rutland.

[10] Church windows sometimes represented God the Father by a shining hand appearing from a cloud to ordain a miracle. (Archbishop Laud in his diary for

for tomorrow thou and thy master must be slain.' And the next day her master and she were in a cart together and suddenly she saw a flash of fire, and said her prayers and the fire went away; and shortly after a crow came and picked* upon her clothes and she said her prayers again and bade the crow go to whom he was sent. And the crow went unto her master and did beat him to death, and she with her prayers recovered him to life, but he was sick a fortnight after; and saith, that if she had not had more knowledge than her master, both he and she and all the cattle had been slain.[11]

Being examined concerning a child of Anne Stannidge which she was suspected to have bewitched to death, saith, the said Anne Stannidge did deliver her child into her hands and that she did lay it upon her skirt but did no harm unto it. And being charged by the mother of the child that upon the burning of the hair and paring of the nails of the said child the said Anne Baker came in and set her down and for one hour's space could speak nothing; confesseth she came into the house of the said Anne Stannidge in great pain, but did not know of the burning of the hair and nails of the said child, but said she was so sick that she did not know whither she went.

Being charged that she bewitched Elizabeth Hough, the wife of William Hough, to death for that she angered her in giving her alms of her second bread,[12] confesseth that she was angry with her and said she might have given her of her better bread, for she had gone too often on her errands; but more she saith not.

This examinate confesseth that she came to Joan Gill's house, her child being sick, and that she entreated this examinate to look on the child and to tell her whether it was forespoken or no, and this examinate said it was forespoken;[13] but when the said child died she cannot tell.

---

11 August 1634, mentions one Robert Seal who had visions in which 'a hand appeared unto him, and death'.) Such pictures, seen time after time, must have influenced the forms of hallucination.

[11] This pathetic creature appears to have suffered from epilepsy or migraine (odd visual disturbances are common to the onset of attacks in both) and to have been mentally disturbed as well. The idea that planets of various colours (governing the four humours?) 'strike' to cause illness is degenerate medical lore of the middle ages, confused with folk-ideas of coloured fairies which can 'take' (afflict) people. John Walsh (q.v.) said that there were black, green and white fairies, and the black were 'the worst'. Joan Willimot (see below) has a fairy for a familiar and says that the Earl's son is 'stricken with a white spirit'.

[12] Second-day—i.e. stale—bread?

[13] forespoken: bewitched, or 'taken by a fairy'.

And being asked concerning Nortley carrying of his child home unto his own house, where the said Anne Baker was; she asked him who gave the said child that loaf, he told her 'Anthony Gill', to whom this examinate said 'He might have had a child of his own if he would have sought in time for it'; which words she confessed she did speak.

[She was][14] blamed by Henry Mills in this sort: 'A fire set on you, I have had two or three ill nights,' to whom she made answer, 'You should have let me alone then,' which she confesseth.

The said Anne Baker, March 2, 1618, confessed before Samuel Fleming, doctor of divinity, that about 3 years ago she went into Northamptonshire and that at her coming back again, one Peak's wife and Dennis his wife of Belvoir told her that my young Lord Henry was dead, and that there was a glove of the said Lord buried in the ground, and as that glove did rot and waste, so did the liver of the said Lord rot and waste.

Further, she said March 3, 1618, before Sir George Manners, knight, and Samuel Fleming, doctor of divinity, that she hath a spirit which hath the shape of a white dog, which she calleth 'her good spirit'.

Samuel Fleming   test.*

The examination of Joan Willimot, taken the 28 of February in the 16 year of the reign of our Sovereign Lord James, over England King, etc., and over Scotland the 52, before Alexander Amcotts, esquire, one of his Majesty's Justices of the Peace of the said parts and county.

This examinate saith, that Joan Flower told her that my Lord of Rutland had dealt badly with her and that they had put away her daughter, and that although she could not have her will of my Lord himself, yet she had spied my Lord's son, and had stricken him to the heart. And she saith that my Lord's son was stricken with a white spirit, and that she can cure some that send unto her, and some reward her for her pains, and of some she taketh nothing.

She further saith, that upon Friday night last her spirit came to her and told her that there was a bad woman at Deeping who had given her soul to the Devil; and that her said spirit did then appear unto her in a more ugly form that it had formerly done, and that it urged her much to give it something, although it were but a piece of her girdle, and told her that it had taken great pains for her; but she saith that she would give it nothing, and told it that she had sent it to no place

[14] Original has 'Being'.

but only to see how [Francis] my Lord Roos did, and that her spirit told her that he should do well.

The examination of the said Joan Willimot, taken the second day of March in the year abovesaid before the said Alexander Amcotts.

This examinate saith, that she hath a spirit which she calleth 'Pretty', which was given unto her by William Berry of Langham in Rutland-shire, whom she served three years, and that her master when he gave it unto her willed her to open her mouth and he would blow into her a fairy which should do her good. And that she opened her mouth, and he did blow into her mouth, and that presently after his blowing, there came out of her mouth a spirit which stood upon the ground in the shape and form of a woman, which spirit did ask of her her soul, which she then promised unto it, being willed thereunto by her master.

She further confesseth, that she never hurt anybody but did help divers that sent for her which were stricken or forespoken, and that her spirit came weekly to her and would tell her of divers persons that were stricken and forespoken. And she saith, that the use which she had of the spirit was to know how those did which she had undertaken to amend, and that she did help them by certain prayers which she used, and not by her own spirit; neither did she employ her spirit in anything but only to bring word how those did which she had under-taken to cure.

And she further saith, that her spirit came unto her this last night (as she thought) in the form of a woman, mumbling, but she could not understand what it said. And being asked whether she were not in a dream or slumber when she thought she saw it, she said 'No', and that she was as waking as at this present.

Alexander Amcotts.
Thomas Robinson　test.

The examination of Joan Willimot of Goadby in the county of Leicester, widow, taken the 17 of March, 1618, by Sir Henry Hastings, knight, and Samuel Fleming, doctor of divinity, two of his Majesty's Justices of the Peace of the said county of Leicester.

She saith that she told one Cook's wife of Stathern in the said county, labourer, that John Patchett might have had his child alive if he would have sought forth for it in time, and if it were not death-stricken in her [the child's] ways; and that Patchett's wife had an evil thing within her which should make an end of her, and that she knew by her girdle.

She saith further, that Gamaliel Greet of Waltham [-on-the-Wolds] in the said county, shepherd, had a spirit like a white mouse put into him in his swearing; and that if he did look upon anything with an intent to hurt,[15] it should be hurt, and that he had a mark on his left arm which was cut away; and that her own spirit did tell her all this before it went from her.

Further she saith, that Joan Flower, Margaret Flower and she did meet about a week before Joan Flower's apprehension in Blackbarrow Hill, and went from thence home to the said Joan Flower's house, and there she saw two spirits, one like a rat and the other like an owl; and one of them did suck under her right ear, as she thought, and the said Joan told her that her spirits did say that she should neither be hanged nor burned.

Further she saith, that the said Joan Flower did take up some earth and spit upon it, and did work it with her finger and put it up into her purse, and said though she could not hurt the Lord himself, yet she had sped his son, which is dead.

H. Hastings
Samuel Fleming

The examination of Ellen Green of Stathern in the county of Leicester, taken the 17 of March, 1618, by Sir Henry Hastings, knight, and Samuel Fleming, doctor of divinity, two of his Majesty's Justices of the Peace of his said county.

She saith, that one Joan Willimot of Goadby came about six years since to her in the Wolds, and persuaded this examinate to forsake God and betake her to the Devil, and she would give her two spirits, to which she gave her consent; and thereupon the said Joan Willimot called two spirits, one in the likeness of a kitlin [kitten] and the other of a moldiwarp [mole]. The first the said Willimot called 'Puss!', the other 'Hiss, hiss!', and they presently came to her, and she departing left them with this examinate; and they leaped on her shoulder, and the kitlin sucked under her right ear on her neck and the moldiwarp on the left side in the like place.

After they had sucked her, she sent the kitlin to a baker of that town

---

[15] The evil eye (here apparently a *punishment* for sin) occurs rarely in England. Reginald Scot reproduces some 'rational' explanations of it, particularly as it occurs in old women. (*Discovery of Witchcraft*, ed. cit., Bk. XVI, Ch. 8–10.)

whose name she remembers not, who had called her 'Witch' and stricken her, and bade her said spirit go and bewitch him to death. The moldiwarp she then bade go to Anne Daws of the same town and bewitch her to death, because she had called this examinate 'witch, whore, jade', etc.; and within one fortnight after they both died.

And further this examinate saith that she sent both her spirits to Stonesby, to one Willison, a husbandman, and Robert Williman, a husbandman's son, and bade the kitlin go to Willison and bewitch him to death, and the moldiwarp to the other and bewitch him to death, which they did; and within ten days they died. These four were bewitched while this examinate dwelt at Waltham aforesaid.

About three years since, this examinate removed thence to Stathern, where she now dwelt. Upon a difference between the said Willimot and the wife of John Patchett of the said Stathern, yeoman, she the said Willimot called her (this examinate) to go and touch the said John Patchett's wife and her child, which she did, touching the said John Patchett's wife in her bed and the child in the grace-wife's* arms. And then [she] sent her said spirits to bewitch them to death, which they did, and so the woman lay languishing by the space of a month and more, for then she died; the child died the next day after she touched it.

And she further saith, that the said Joan Willimot had a spirit sucking on her under the left flank, in the likeness of a little white dog, which this examinate saith that she saw the same sucking in barley-harvest last, being then at the house of the said Joan Willimot.

And for herself this examinate further saith, that she gave her soul to the Devil to have these spirits at her command, for a confirmation whereof she suffered them to suck her always as aforesaid about the change and full of the moon.

H. Hastings
Samuel Fleming

The examination of Philippa Flower, sister of Margaret Flower, and daughters of Joan Flower, before Sir William Pelham and Mr. Butler, Justices of the Peace, February 4, 1618; which was brought in at the Assizes as evidence against her sister Margaret.

She saith, that her mother and her sister maliced the Earl of Rutland, his Countess and their children, because her sister Margaret was put out of the Lady's service of laundry and exempted from other services about the house; whereupon her said sister, by the commandment of her mother, brought from the Castle the right-hand glove of the

Lord Henry Roos, which she delivered to her mother, who presently rubbed it on the back of her spirit Rutterkin and then put it into hot boiling water. Afterward she pricked it often and buried it in the yard, wishing the Lord Roos might never thrive; and so her sister Margaret continued with her mother, where she often saw the cat Rutterkin leap on her shoulder and suck her neck.

She further confessed, that she heard her mother often curse the Earl and his Lady, and thereupon would boil feathers and blood together, using many devilish speeches and strange gestures.

The examination of Margaret Flower, sister of Philippa Flower, etc., about the 22 of January, 1618.

She saith and confesseth, that about four or five year since her mother sent her for the right-hand glove of Henry, Lord Roos; afterward that her mother bade her go again into the Castle of Belvoir and bring down the glove or some other thing of Henry, Lord Roos, and she asked, 'What to do?' Her mother replied, 'To hurt my Lord Roos,' whereupon she brought down a glove and delivered the same to her mother, who stroked Rutterkin her cat with it, after it was dipped in hot water, and so pricked it often; after which Henry, Lord Roos fell sick within a week and was much tormented with the same.

She further saith, that finding a glove about two or three years since of Francis, Lord Roos, on a dunghill, she delivered it to her mother, who put it into hot water and after took it out and rubbed it on Rutterkin the cat (and bade him go upwards);[16] and after, her mother buried it in the yard and said, 'A mischief light on him! but he will mend again.'

She further saith, that her mother and she and her sister agreed together to bewitch the Earl and his Lady that they might have no more children; and being demanded the cause of this their malice and ill-will, she saith, that about four years since the Countess, growing into some mislike with her, gave her forty shillings, a bolster and a mattress, and bade her lie at home and come no more to dwell at the Castle, which she not only took in ill part but grudged at it exceedingly, swearing in her heart to be revenged.

After this, her mother complained to the Earl against one Peak who had offered her some wrong, wherein she conceived that the Earl took not her part as she expected, which dislike with the rest exasperated her displeasure against him, and so she watched an opportunity to be

---

[16] go upwards, i.e. lie on his back.

revenged. Whereupon she took wool out of the said mattress and a pair of gloves which were given her by Mr. Vavasour, and put them into warm water, mingling them with some blood and stirring it together; then she took the wool and gloves out of the water and rubbed them on the belly of Rutterkin her cat, saying the Lord and the Lady should have more children, but it would be long first.[17]

She further confesseth, that by her mother's commandment she brought to her a piece of a handkercher* of the Lady Katherine, the Earl's daughter, and her mother put it into hot water and then, taking it out, rubbed it on Rutterkin, bidding him 'fly and go'. Whereupon Rutterkin whined and cried 'Mew!', whereupon she said that Rutterkin had no power over the Lady Katherine to hurt her.

The Examination of Philippa Flower, the 25 of February, 1618, before Francis, Earl of Rutland, Francis, Lord Willoughby of Eresby, Sir George Manners, and Sir William Pelham.

She confesseth and saith, that she hath a spirit sucking on her in the form of a white rat, which keepeth her left breast and hath so done for three or four years; and concerning the agreement betwixt her spirit and herself she confesseth and saith, that when it came first unto her she gave her soul to it and it promised to do her good and cause Thomas Simpson to love her, if she would suffer it to suck her, which she agreed unto; and so the last time it sucked was on Tuesday at night, the 23 of February.

The Examination of Margaret Flower at the same time, etc.

She confesseth that she hath two familiar spirits sucking on her, the one white, the other black-spotted; the white sucked under her left breast and the black-spotted within the inward parts of her secrets. When she first entertained them she promised them her soul, and they covenanted to do all things which she commanded them, etc.

She further saith, that about the 30 of January last past, being Saturday, four devils appeared unto her in Lincoln jail at eleven or twelve o'clock at midnight. The one stood at her bed's feet with a black head like an ape and spake unto her, but what, she cannot well

---

[17] The Countess in fact had no more children. The *Gentleman's Magazine*, Vol. LXXIV, pt. ii, p. 909, states that 'In the monument of Francis, sixth earl of Rutland, in Bottesford church, Leicestershire, it is recorded that by his second lady he had "two Sons, both which died in their infancy by wicked practices and sorcery".'

remember, at which she was very angry because he would speak no plainer or let her understand his meaning; the other three were Rutterkin, Little Robin and Spirit, but she never mistrusted them nor suspected herself till then.[18]

There is another Examination of the said Margaret Flower, taken the fourth of February, 1618, tending to this effect.

That being asked what she knoweth concerning the bewitching of the Earl of Rutland, his wife and children, she saith, that it is true that herself, her mother and sister were all displeased with him, especially with the Countess, for turning her out of service; whereupon some four year since her mother commanded her to go up to the Castle and bring her the right-hand glove of the Lord Henry Roos, the Earl's eldest son. Which glove she found on the rushes in the nursery, and delivered the same to her mother, who put it into hot water, pricked it often with her knife, then took it out of the water and rubbed it upon Rutterkin, bidding him 'Hight* and go' and do some hurt to Henry, Lord Roos; whereupon he fell sick and shortly after died, which her mother hearing of, said it was well. But after she had rubbed the glove on the spirit Rutterkin, she threw it into the fire and burned it, etc.[19]

These Examinations and some others were taken and charily* preserved for the contriving of sufficient evidences against them, and when the Judges of Assize came down to Lincoln about the first week of March, being Sir Henry Hobart, Lord Chief Justice of the Common Pleas, and Sir Edward Bromley, one of the Barons of the Exchequer, they were presented unto them; who not only wondered at the wickedness of these persons, but were amazed at their practices and horrible contracts with the Devil to damn their own souls.

And although the right honourable Earl had sufficient grief for the loss of his children, yet no doubt it was the greater to consider the

---

[18] Despite her mother's use of the cat Rutterkin in charms, it sounds as though Margaret had had no conception that a pet animal could be a devil until her examiners suggested it—'she never mistrusted them [the animals she names] nor suspected herself' [for a witch] till she was alone in a dark gaol and seemed to see them as devils.

Doubtless the whole family had engaged in common spells and charms (so, it seems, had half the neighbourhood); thus the tale of pact may be a similar mixture of sheer suggestion by the examiners and distorted memories of actual events re-shaped into the desired pattern.

[19] As with the Lancashire trial, all the evidence recorded comes from confessions, or the confessions of other accused witches.

manner and how it pleased God to inflict on him such a fashion of visitation. Besides, as it amazed the hearers to understand the particulars and the circumstances of this devilish contract, so was it as wonderful to see their desperate impenitency and horrible distraction (according to the rest of that sort) exclaiming against the Devil for deluding them and now breaking promise with them when they stood in most need of his help.

Notwithstanding all these aggravations, such was the unparallelled magnanimity, wisdom and patience of this generous nobleman that he urged nothing against them more than their own confessions, and so quietly left them to judicial trial, desiring of God mercy for their souls, and of men charity to censure them in their condemnation. But God is not mocked and so gave them over to judgment, nor man so reformed but for the Earl's sake they cursed them to that place which they themselves long before had bargained for.

What now remains, gentle reader, but for thee to make use of so wonderful a story and remarkable an accident, out of which (to draw to a conclusion) thou mayest collect these particulars: First, that God is the supreme commander of all things and permitteth wonderful actions in the world for the trial of the godly, the punishment of the wicked, and His own glory, of which man shall never attain to know the reason or occasion. Secondly, that the Devil is the mere servant and agent of God to prosecute whatsoever he shall command rather than give leave unto, limiting him yet thus far in his own nature—that he can go no further than the bounds within which he is hedged.

Thirdly, that this God hath punishments *ad correctionem* (that is to say, chastisements of) the godly, and *ad ruinam* (videlicet, judgments against) the wicked, wherein yet man must disclaim any knowledge and forsake prejudicate opinions. For the very just shall be tried like gold and no man exempted from castigation whom God doth love. Fourthly, that this Devil, though he be God's instrument, yet worketh altogether by deceit; for as he was a liar from the beginning, so let no man trust him, because he aimeth at the confusion of all mankind.

Fifthly, that the wicked (however they may thrive and prosper for a time) yet in the end are sure to be paid home, either with punishment in this life or in the life to come, or both, as a final reward of monstrous impiety. Sixthly, that man in his frailty must not presume of prosperity, but prepare a kind of stooping under the hand of God when it pleaseth Him to strike or punish us.

Seventhly, that there is no murmuring nor repining against God, but quietly to tolerate His inflictings whensoever they chance, of which this worthy Earl is a memorable example to all men and ages. Eighthly, that the punishments of the wicked are so many warnings to all irregular sinners to amend their lives and avoid the judgment to come by penitency and newness of life. Ninthly, that though man could be content to pass over blasphemies and offences against the statutes of princes, yet God will overtake them in their own walks and pull them back by the sleeve into a slaughterhouse, as here you know the evidences against these people took life and power from their own confessions.

Tenthly, and last of all, that private opinion cannot prevail against public censures, for here you see the learned and religious judges cried out with our Saviour, 'Ex ore tuo!'[20] Therefore though it were so that neither witch nor devil could do these things, yet 'Let not a witch live,' saith God and 'Let them die,' saith the law of England, 'that have conversation with spirits, and presume to blaspheme the name of God with spells and incantations.'

Oh then, you sons of men, take warning by these examples, and either divert your steps from the broad way of destruction and inrecoverable gulf of damnation, or with Joshua's counsel to Achan,[21] bless God for the discovery of wickedness and take thy death patiently as the prevention of thy future judgment, and saving innocents from punishment who otherwise may be suspected without a cause.

Utinam tam facile vera invenire possem quam falsa convincere. [If only I could find out the truth as easily as I can show up the lies!][22]

[20] See *Luke* 19: 22; ' "Out of thine own mouth will I judge thee, thou wicked servant." '

[21] *Joshua* 7: 19.

[22] An adaptation of Cicero, *De Finibus Bonorum et Malorum*, ed. and trans. H. Rackham; Loeb Classical Library (London, 1931), Bk. I, pt. 2, sec. 13: 'Verum enim invenire volumus, non tamquam adversarium aliquem convincere.'

Select Bibliography

Exhaustive bibliographies of witchcraft literature may be found in the following books:

K. M. Briggs, *Pale Hecate's Team* (London, 1962)
Rossell Hope Robbins, *The Encyclopaedia of Witchcraft and Demonology* (London, 1959)
Rev. Montague Summers, *The History of Witchcraft* (London, 1926)

The following are indispensable works of reference:
Acts of the Privy Council, New Series (London, 1895)
The Bible: Authorised Version of James I (1611)
Calendar of State Papers, Domestic
G. E. Cokayne, *The Complete Peerage* (revised ed. London, 1910)
Dictionary of National Biography (Oxford, 1921/2)
Encyclopaedia Britannica (ed. of 1968)
C. H. L'Estrange Ewen, *Witch Hunting and Witch Trials* (London, 1929); *Witchcraft and Demonianism* (London, 1933); *Witchcraft in the Star Chamber* (London, 1938)
G. B. Harrison, *The Elizabethan Journals* (Ann Arbor, 1939, 1955); *A Jacobean Journal* (London, 1949); *A Second Jacobean Journal* (Ann Arbor, 1958)
Historical Manuscripts Commission: *Calendars of Manuscripts.*
G. L. Kittredge, *Witchcraft in Old and New England* (Cambridge, Mass., 1929)
H. C. Lea, *Materials towards a History of Witchcraft*, 3 vols. (Philadelphia, 1939; repr. New York, 1957)
John Nichols, *Progresses of Queen Elizabeth*, 3 vols. (London, 1823, repr. New York, 1964)
Wallace Notestein, *A History of Witchcraft in England from 1558 to 1718* (New York 1965, orig. issue 1911)
Oxford English Dictionary, 13 vols. (Oxford, 1933)
P. H. Reaney, *A Dictionary of British Surnames* (London, 1958)
Statutes of the Realm, 11 vols. 1810–21
H. R. Trevor-Roper, 'Witches and Witchcraft', in *Encounter*, May 1967 and June 1967.

The following works are mentioned in the text of this book:

a) Witch pamphlets in chronological order

Francis Coxe., *A short treatise declaringe the detestable wickednesse of magicall sciences, as Necromancie. Conjurations of spirites, Curiouse Astrologie and such lyke.* (London, [1561])

The examination and confession of certaine Wytches at Chensforde in the Countie of Essex, before the Quenes majesties Judges, the xxvi daye of July Anno 1566. (London, 1566)
Repr. H. Beigel, *Philobiblon Society* (London, 1864–5)

The Examination of John Walsh, before Maister Thomas Williams, Commissary to the Reverend father in God William bishop of Excester, upon certayne Interrogatories touchyng Wytchcrafte and Sorcerye, in the presence of divers gentlemen and others. The .xx. of August. 1566. (London, 1566)

The disclosing of a late counterfeyted possession by the devyl in two maydens within the Citie of London. [London, 1574]

A Detection of damnable driftes, practized by three Witches arraigned at Chelmisforde in Essex, at the laste Assises there holden, whiche were executed in Aprill 1579. (London, 1579)

A Rehearsall both straung and true, of hainous and horrible actes committed by Elizabeth Stile, Alias Rockingham, Mother Dutten, Mother Devell, Mother Margaret, Fower notorious Witches, apprehended at winsore in the Countie of Barks. and at Abbington arraigned, condemned, and executed on the 26. daye of Februarie laste Anno 1579. (London, 1579)

W.W., *A true and just Recorde, of the Information, Examination and Confession of all the Witches, taken at S. Oses in the countie of Essex: whereof some were executed, and other some entreated according to the determination of Lawe. Wherein all men may see what a pestilent people Witches are, and how unworthy to lyve in a Christian Commonwealth. Written orderly, as the cases were tryed by evidence, By W.W.* (London, 1582)

The Apprehension and confession of three notorious Witches. Arreigned and by Justice condemned and executed at Chelmes-forde, in the Countye of Essex, the 5. day of Julye, last past. 1589. With the manner of their divelish practices and keeping of their spirits, whose fourmes are heerein truelye proportioned. (London, 1589)

Newes from Scotland, Declaring the Damnable life and death of Doctor Fian, a notable Sorcerer, who was burned at Edenbrough in January last. 1591. Which Doctor was regester to the Divell that sundry times preached at North Barrick Kirke, to a number of notorious Witches. With the true examination of the saide Doctor and Witches, as they uttered them in the presence of the Scottish King. (London, [1591])

G.B., *A Most Wicked worke of a wretched Witch (the like whereof none can *record these manie yeeres in England).* *Wrought on the Person of one Richard Burt, Servant to Maister Edling of Woodhall in the Parrish of Pinner in the Countie of Myddlesex, a myle beyond Harrow. Latelie committed in March last, An. 1592 and newly recognised according to the truth, by G.B. maister of Arts.* [London, 1593]

The most strange and admirable discoverie of the three Witches of Warboys, arraigned, convicted, and executed at the last Assises at Huntington, for the bewitching of the five daughters of Robert Thockmorton Esquire, and divers other persons, with sundrie Divellish and grievous torments: And also for the bewitching to death of the Lady Crumwell, the like hath not been heard of in this age. (London, 1593)

The Brideling, Sadling and Ryding, of a rich Churle in Hampshire, by the subtill practise of one Judeth Philips, a professed cunning woman, or Fortune teller. With a true discourse of her unwomanly using of a Trype wife, a widow, lately dwelling on the back side of S. Nicholas shambles in London, whom she with her conferates, likewise cosened. For which fact, shee was at the Sessions house without New-gate arraigned, where she confessed the same, and had judgement for her offence, to be whipped through the Citie, the 14. of February, 1594. (London, 1595)

The most wonderfull and true storie, of a certaine Witch named Alse Gooderige of Stapenhill, who was arraigned and convicted at Darbie at the Assises there. . . . (London, 1597)

John Darrell, *The Triall of Maist. Dorrell. . . .* (? 1599)

John Darrell, *A True Narration of the strange and grevous Vexation by the Devil, of 7. persons in Lancashire, and William Somers of Nottingham. . . .* (1600)

A Strange Report of Sixe most notorious Witches, who by their divelish practises murdred above the number of foure hundred small Children: besides the great hurtes they committed upon divers other people: Who for the same, and many other like offences, were executed in the princely Cittie of Manchen in high Germanie the .29 of July. 1600. (London, 1601)

Edward Jordan, *A brief discourse of a disease called the Suffocation of the Mother, written upon occasion which hath beene of late taken thereby, to suspect possessions of an evill spirit, or some such like supernaturall power. Wherein is declared that divers strange actions and passions of the body of man, which in the common opinion, are imputed to the devill, have their true naturall causes, and do accompanie this Disease.* (London, 1603)

Stephen Bradwell, *Marie Glovers late woefull case, together with her joyfull deliverance written upon occasion of Doctor Jordens discourse of the Mother. . . .* (Brit. Mus., Sloane MSS. 831)

John Swan, *A True and Briefe Report, of Mary Glovers Vexation, and of her deliverance by the meanes of fastinge and prayer. . . .* (? 1603)

The most cruell and bloody murther committed by an Inkeepers Wife, called

Annis Dell, and her Sonne George Dell. . . . With the severall Witch-crafts, and most damnable practises of one Johane Harrison and her Daughter upon severall persons, men and women at Royston, who were all executed at Hartford the 4 of August last past. 1606. (London, 1606)

Witches Apprehended, Examined and Executed, for notable villanies by them committed both by Land and Water. With a strange and most true triall how to know whether a woman be a Witch or not. (London, 1613)

The Witches of Northamptonshire. . . . Who were all executed at Northampton the 22. of July last. 1612. (London, 1612)

Thomas Potts, *The Wonderfull Discoverie of Witches in the Countie of Lancaster. With the Arraignement and Triall of Nineteene notorious Witches, at the Assizes and generall Gaole deliverie, holden at the Castle of Lancaster, upon Munday, the seventeenth of August last, 1612. Before Sir James Altham, and Sir Edward Bromley, Knights. . . . Published, and set forth by commandement of his Majesties Justices of Assize in the North Parts. By Thomas Potts, Esquier.* (London, 1613), ed. James Crossley, *Chetham Society*, Vol. VI (Manchester, 1845) repr. G. B. Harrison, Bodley Head Quartos (London, 1929)

The Wonderful Discoverie of the Witchcrafts of Margaret and Phillip Flower, daughters of Joan Flower neere Bever Castle: Executed at Lincolne, March 11. 1618. Who were specially arraigned and condemned before Sir Henry Hobart and Sir Edward Bromley, Judges of Assise, for confessing themselves actors in the destruction of Henry Lord Rosse, with their damnable practises against others the Children of the Right Honourable Francis Earle of Rutland. Together with the severall Examinations and Confessions of Anne Baker, Joan Willimot, and Ellen Greene, Witches in Leicestershire. (London, 1619)

Edward Fairfax, *A Discourse of Witchcraft As it was acted in the Family of Mr. Edward Fairfax of Fuystone in the County of York, in the year 1621.* (Brit. Mus. Add. MSS. 32496), ed. R. Monckton Miles, *Philobiblon Society*, Vol. V (London, 1858–1859)

b) Other works

Ady, Thomas. *A Candle in the Dark* (London, 1655)

Aubrey, John. *Aubrey's Brief Lives*, ed. Oliver Lawson Dick (Ann Arbor, 1949)

Batty, Bartholomew. *The Christian Mans Closet*, trans. by William Lowth (London, 1581)

Black, George. *A Calendar of Cases of Witchcraft in Scotland* (New York, 1938); *The Surnames of Scotland* (New York, 1946)

Bodin, Jean. *De la Démonomanie des Sorciers* (Paris, 1580); *De Republica Libri Sex* (enlarged Latin ed., Frankfurt, 1591)

British Medical Journal: 16 November 1966, and 25 February 1967

Butler, E. M. *Ritual Magic* (Cambridge, 1949)

Chettle, Henry. *Kind-Harts Dreame* (London, [1592]); repr. Bodley Head Quartos No. 4 (London 1923)

Cicero, Marcus Tullius. *De Finibus,* ed. and trans. H. Rackham, Loeb Classical Library (London, 1931)

Clébert, Jean-Paul. *The Gypsies* (London, 1963), trans. Charles Duff of *Les Tʒiganes* (1961)

Coke, Sir Edward. *Third Part of the Institutes of the Laws of England* (London, 1797)

Cotta, John. *The Triall of Witchcraft* (London, 1616)

Coxe, Francis. *The unfained retractation of Fraunces Cox, which he uttered at The Pillery in Chepesyde and elsewhere, accordyng to the Counsels commaundment. Anno 1561. The 25 of June; A Prognostication made for 1566*)

Dalton, Michael. *The Countrey Justice* (London, 1618)

Daneau, Lambert. *A Dialogue of Witches,* trans. T. Twyne. (London, 1575)

Early English Text Society. *The Lay Folks' Mass Book,* Vol. 71. (London, 1879); *The Lay Folks' Catechism,* Vol. 118 (London, 1901)

Erra Pater. *The Pronostycacion for ever of Erra Pater . . .* [London, 1535?]

Fairbarn, J. *Fairbarn's Crests* (New York, 1911)

Faust, John. *The historie of the damnable life and deserved death of Doctor John Faustus* (London, 1592)

Filmer, Sir Robert. *An Advertisement to the Jurymen of England, touching witches;* first published 1653, found in *The Free Holders grand inquest* (London, 1679)

Folk Lore. Vol. 71, March 1960

Foxe, John. Actes and Monuments (London, 1562/3)

Fulke, William. *Antiprognosticon,* trans. W. Painter (London, 1560); *A Goodly Gallerye with a most pleasaunt Prospect into the garden of naturall contemplation . . .* (London, 1563)

Gifford, George. *A Discourse of the subtill Practises of Devilles by Witches* (London, 1587); *A Dialogue concerning Witches and Witchcraftes* (London, 1593), repr. Shakespeare Association Facsimiles No. 1 (London, 1931)

Greene, Robert. *A Disputation betweene a Hee Conny-catcher and a Shee Conny-catcher* (London, 1592), repr. Bodley Head Quartos No. 3 (London, 1923)

Halliwell-Phillipps, J. O. *Nursery Rhymes and Nursery Tales of England,* n.d.

Harsnett, Samuel. *A Discovery of the fraudulent practises of John Darrell, Bacheler of Artes. . . .* (London, 1599); *A Declaration of egregious Popish Impostures* (London, 1603, 1604)

Heywood, Thomas. *Plays,* Mermaid Series (London, n.d.)

Hill, Thomas. *Naturall and artificiall Conclusions* (London, 1586)

w—n*

Holinshed, Raphael. *Chronicles of England, Scotlande and Irelande* (London, 1587)

Homer. *Odyssey*, trans. H. B. Cotterrill (London, 1911)

Institoris, Henricus, and James Sprenger. *Malleus Maleficarum* (1486), trans. and ed. Rev. Montague Summers (London, 1928)

James I. *Daemonologie, in forme of a Dialogue* (Edinburgh, 1597), repr. Bodley Head Quartos No. 9 (London, 1924)

Jonson, Ben. *Ben Jonson*, ed. C. H. Herford and P. Simpson, 8 vols. (Oxford 1925–47)

Koestler, Arthur. *Darkness at Noon*, trans. Daphne Hardy (London, 1941)

Lambe, John. *A briefe description of the notorious life of John Lambe, otherwise called Doctor Lambe* (Amsterdam, 1628)

Lavater, Lewes. *Of ghostes and spirites walking by nyght* (London, 1572), ed. J. Dover Wilson and May Yardley (Oxford, 1929)

The Library. C. J. Sisson, *Keep the Widow Waking*, Series IV, Vol. 8, pp. 39–57, 233–59 (June, 1927); G. B. Harrison, *Keep the Widow Waking*, Series IV, Vol. 11. pp. 97–101 (June 1930)

Louthe, John. *Reminiscences of John Louthe*, in *Narratives of the days of the Reformation*, Camden Society Publication No. 77 (London, 1859)

Macfarlane, A. D. J. *Witchcraft in Tudor and Stuart England: a regional study*. (To be published by Routledge and Kegan Paul)

Marlowe, Christopher. *Doctor Faustus*, ed. Irving Ribner (New York, 1963)

Nyndge, A. *A Booke Declaringe the Fearfull Vexasion, of one Alexander Nyndge. Beyinge moste horriblye tormented with an evyll Spirit* (London, [1573/4])

Oat-meale, O. *A Quest of Inquirie.* . . . (London, 1595), printed A. B. Grosart, *Elizabethan England in Gentle and Simple Life*, pp. 143–72, *Occasional Issues*, Vol. XV (London, 1881)

Oesterreich, T. K. *Possession, Demonaical and Other*, trans. D. Ibberson (London 1930, repr. New York, 1966)

Orwell, George. *Nineteen Eighty-Four* (London, 1949)

Paul, Henry N. *The Royal Play of Macbeth* (New York, 1950)

Perkins, William. *A Discourse of the Damned Art of Witchcraft* (Cambridge, 1608)

Pitcairn, Robert. *Criminal Trials* (Edinburgh, 1833)

Raynald, Thomas. *The byrth of mankynde* (London, 1545)

Rituale Romanum. (New York, 1947); rite of exorcism for possessed persons, pp. 326–47.

Scot, Reginald. *The Discoverie of Witchcraft* (London, 1584); ed. Brinsley Nicholson (London, 1886); repr. with introd. Rev. Montague Summers (London, 1930); repr. with introd. Hugh Ross Williamson (London, 1964); repr. of 1886 ed. (Totowa, N.J., 1973).

Shakespeare, William. *Complete Plays and Poems,* ed. W. A. Neilson and
C. H. Hill (Cambridge, Mass., 1942)
Spence, Lewis. *British Fairy Origins* (London, 1946)
Stow, John. *Annales or a General Chronicle of England* (London, 1592 etc.)
Strype, John. *Annals of the Reformation* (London, 1725–1731)
Tilley, M. P. *A Dictionary of Proverbs in England in the Sixteenth and Seventeenth Centuries* (Ann Arbor, 1950)
Vergilius, Publius. *This boke treateth of the lyfe of Virgil* (London, [1562?])
West, John. *The severall Notorious and lewd Cousnages of John West, and Alice West, falsely called the King and Queene of Fayries.* . . . (London, 1613/1614)
West, William. *Symboleography* (London, 1594)

c) Autobiographies of magicians and conjurors
Casaubon, Meric, ed., *A True and Faithful Relation of What passed for many Yeers Between Dr. John Dee . . . and Some Spirits* (London, 1659)
Dee, John. *The Private Diary of Dr. John Dee* (Camden Society, 1842)
Forman, Simon. *The Autobiography and Personal Diary of Simon Forman,* ed. J. O. Halliwell-Phillipps (London, 1849)
Lilly, William. *Mr. William Lilly's History of his Life and Times from the Year 1602 to 1681* (2nd. ed. 1715)

Glossary

The following glossed words are marked in the text with an asterisk.

abuse: misuse, often sexually
accompt: account
accompted: reckoned, considered
admiration: astonishment
aghen-dole: measure of weight, probably 8 lbs.
agues: 'chill' stage of malarial fever
All Hollantide, Allhollon [Scots]: All Hallows
almose: alms
ambassage: mission, errand
angel: gold coin, about 10s.
apprehend: understand
apprehended: arrested, seized
aqua vitae: brandy, strong spirits
assay [n.]: experiment
assay [v.]: put to the test
assotted: infatuated
auxiliant: auxiliary, affording assistance
avaunt: begone
avice: bird (possibly 'mavis' or thrush?)
avoid: depart
ban: curse, chide
barm: yeast, leaven
bewray: betray, reveal
bleach: skin disease (eczema?)
boot: help, remedy
bootless: incurable, useless
brended: brindled, streaked with brown
bruited: rumoured
buck: washing tub or basket
bugs: bugbears, bogies
bulch: swelling, bulge
bun: endearment for squirrel or rabbit

calcar: diviner
canstick: candlestick
cast: vomit
cattle, cattel: cattle
cere-cloth: waxed shroud or winding sheet
cered: sealed up, coffined
chafe: rage
charily: prudently, carefully
charwomen, chairwomen: daily domestic wokers
chattels, cattells: possessions
clap: strike
close [n.]: enclosed field or garden
close: secret
commer [Scots]: friend, companion
conceit: fancy, fantasy
conferates: confederates
conject: conjecture
contemned: despised
conversation: social behaviour, way of life
convince: convict
correspondency: congruity
cozen: cheat, defraud
cruse, crewses: pot, jar
culver: dove, pigeon
cunning body: wise man or woman
cup-shot: drunk
daylight-gate: evening
dere: harm
discrepant: inharmonious
divers: various, sundry, several
doubting: fearing, suspecting
ecstasies: frenzies, trances
eftsoons: again, soon after
excruciation: torment
exotic: uncouth, unnatural

exprobrated, exprobated: reproached
facts: (evil) deeds
farrandly: splendidly
fell: fierce, ruthless
flap: foul, worthless
fleet: skim (milk)
fleeting [Scots dial]:   floating, skimming over
flux, flixe: dysentery
fond: doting
fore-crag [Scots]:   front of throat
fray [v.]:   frighten, make afraid
froward: perverse, ill-disposed
fustian: coarse cloth of cotton and flax
gargette: swelling, inflammation of throat in pigs and cattle
gaster: terrify
gibbets: cudgels, poles
glister: enema
godsgood: a) yeast, b) unowned property
gossips: godparents; baptismal sponsors
gracewife: midwife
gripe: ditch
griping: colic, spasms of pain
groat: coin worth 4d.
grom: grumble, sulk
gub: lump, mass
guerdon: reward
gull, gulle: gouge, wear away
handkercher: handkerchief
haply: perhaps, by chance
hexasticon: hexastichon, six-line poem
hiccock: hiccough, hiccup
hight: probably 'hie it' i.e. hurry
hucklebone: hip-bone
husbandry: domestic management
importunacy: importunity
imposthume, impostume: abscess
induct: introduced into
indurate: hardened
inficious: negative, given to opposition
jurat: municipal officer
kercher: kerchief
kill: kiln, furnace

kirk [Scots]:   church
kit: wooden pail
kitlin, kitling: kitten, young of any animal
lap [n.]:   drink, tipple
lapped: wrapped
let: hinder, prevent
likest: most promising
limbeck: alembic, still
list: wish, desire
loden: laden, burdened
mainprise: suretyship
maleficium, maliface: evil deed of witchcraft
malkin, malking: hare (a witch-animal)
mark: weight of silver worth 13s. 4d.
maslin: mixed grain, bread made of rye and wheat together
measled, a messell: measly, tapeworm disease of swine
meet (with):   be even with
mess: 'made dish', partly liquid
milch: milk-giving
ming: urinate
moldiwarp: mole
mommet, maumet: image, doll
mort [slang]:   girl, woman
mull: grind, crush
murrain: plague (non-specific)
nigromancer: necromancer, magician
occupy: make use of
or: ere, before
ordinary: one having jurisdiction by right
pack: wastrel, drab
pair: pack (of cards)
pattens: high-soled overshoes, often wooden
pick: vomit
pick: pitch, fall upon
pickerel: young pike
pilliwinks: instrument for crushing fingers
pine [trans.]:   torment, exhaust with cold or hunger
pine [intrans.]:   to be tormented or exhausted

pinfold: pound, fold for stray animals

plancher: floor, ceiling of lower room

poke: bag

polled: shorn

potsherd: piece of broken earthenware pot

pox [French]: syphilis

precedency: order of priority

prejudicate: preconceived, settled beforehand

presently: immediately

pretended: professed, intended

privily: secretly, privately

privy: secret, private

privy to: in the secret of

prominence, preminence: prominence or pre-eminence

puissance: power

purloin: steal

quail [trans.]: overpower, overwhelm

quail [intrans.]: lose heart, give way

quondam: former

race, rase: scratch, tear

rack [of meat]: neck, forepart of spine

raddle: mark with red ochre

riddle: sieve

rood: rod, pole or perch; 6–8 yds.

rugged: shaggy

Sabbath, Sabbaoth, sabboth: Sunday

Sabbath, sabbat, of witches: witch service for worship of Devil

safeguard: overskirt, protective outer garment

scalp: skull

seam: 1 packhorse load

seethe: boil

sennight: week

sequestered: unsociable, eccentric

set: place with or at

set: sent

several: separate, distinct

shorter: less adequate

sight [in]: skill in or knowledge of

simoniac: speculator in spiritual benefices or preferments

sodden: boiled, stewed

sorry: worthless, miserable

sort [of]: litter or family

sort: resort

span: thumb-tip to tip of little finger —about 9 in.

spoorn: kind of ghost

spur, sperre: spar, small stick

starve: freeze to death

stint: cease

straitly: narrowly, strictly

stripe: blow with a stick or weapon

successively: in succession, without interruption

sweltered: overheated, sweated to death

Symond's sauce: nothing (hunger)

symptom, symtome: manifestation, phenomenon

tell: reckon

test.: testatur, 'he witnesses'

tewhit (tuit): lapwing

thrave: multitude, a lot

thraw: wrench, twist

threadband: paper for winding thread, thread [rib] band?

thrummed: fringed or tufted with thread-ends

tisick: pthisic or asthmatic affliction

toward: promising, forward

travail: toil, trouble

trening: treen, wooden

trull: trollop

Turkas: pincers

unhappiness: mischief

upright man: high class vagrant

wear: wither, waste

wearied: worried

wether: male sheep

wimpled: veiled, blindfold

wishly: intently

withy: willow

wort: herb

wort: unfermented beer, infusion of malt

wrayed: betrayed, exposed

wring: twist

The following words have been silently emended throughout:

arrant: errand
assoon(e): as soon
bin: been
burthen: burden
charne: churn
chirning(e): churning
cive: sieve
drave: drove
flawed: flayed
gat: got
gent.: gentleman
happily: haply
infeebled: enfeebled
inogh: enough
lenger: longer
M., Mai. Master
moe: more
murther: murder
ne: nor
nevew: nephew
ought: owed
quod: quoth

saieth, sayeth: saith
scritch: screech
shirif, shirriff: sheriff
sith: since
sithens: since
sprite: spirit
stinch: stench
swarve: swerve
telled: told
then: than
thether: thither
thintent: the intent
thone: the one
thorough: through
thother: the other
thresh: thrash
verdit, verdite: verdict
whither: whether
wrinch: wrench
ye, y^e: the
y^t: that

Index of Familiars

Index of Persons

(Names of authors are italicised)

Index of Places